GERMAN
ORDER OF BATTLE
VOLUME TWO

Other titles in the Stackpole Military History Series

THE AMERICAN CIVIL WAR
Cavalry Raids of the Civil War
Pickett's Charge
Witness to Gettysburg

WORLD WAR II
Armor Battles of the Waffen-SS, 1943–45
Army of the West
Australian Commandos
The B-24 in China
Backwater War
The Battle of Sicily
Beyond the Beachhead
The Brandenburger Commandos
The Brigade
Bringing the Thunder
Coast Watching in World War II
Colossal Cracks
D-Day to Berlin
Eagles of the Third Reich
Exit Rommel
Flying American Combat Aircraft
    of World War II
Fist from the Sky
Forging the Thunderbolt
Fortress France
The German Defeat in the East, 1944–45
German Order of Battle, Vols. 1 and 3
Germany's Panzer Arm in World War II
Grenadiers
Infantry Aces
Iron Arm
Luftwaffe Aces
Messerschmitts over Sicily
Michael Wittmann, Vols. 1 and 2
The Nazi Rocketeers
On the Canal
Packs On!
Panzer Aces
Panzer Aces II
The Panzer Legions
Retreat to the Reich

Rommel's Desert War
The Savage Sky
A Soldier in the Cockpit
Stalin's Keys to Victory
Surviving Bataan and Beyond
Tigers in the Mud
The 12th SS, Vols. 1 and 2

THE COLD WAR / VIETNAM
Flying American Combat Aircraft:
    The Cold War
Land with No Sun
Street without Joy

WARS OF THE MIDDLE EAST
Never-Ending Conflict

GENERAL MILITARY HISTORY
Carriers in Combat
Desert Battles

GERMAN
ORDER OF BATTLE
VOLUME TWO

**291st–999th Infantry Divisions,
Named Infantry Divisions,
and Special Divisions in World War II**

Samuel W. Mitcham, Jr.

STACKPOLE
BOOKS

Published by
STACKPOLE BOOKS
5067 Ritter Road
Mechanicsburg, PA 17055
www.stackpolebooks.com

This is a revised and expanded edition of HITLER'S LEGIONS by Samuel W. Mitcham, Jr., originally published in one volume by Stein and Day. Copyright © 1985 by Samuel W. Mitcham, Jr.

Cover design by Tracy Patterson

Cover photo courtesy of HITM Archive, www.hitm-archive.co.uk

Printed in the United States of America

10 9 8 7 6 5 4 3 2 1

ISBN-13: 978-0-8117-3437-0 (Volume Two)
ISBN-10: 0-8117-3437-4 (Volume Two)

Library of Congress Cataloging-in-Publication Data

Mitcham, Samuel W.
  German order of battle / Samuel W. Mitcham, Jr.
    p. cm. — (Stackpole military history series)
  Includes bibliographical references and index.
  ISBN-13: 978-0-8117-3416-5
  ISBN-10: 0-8117-3416-1
  1. Germany. Heer. Infanterie. 2. Germany. Heer—History—World War, 1939–1945. 3. World War, 1939–1945—Regimental histories—Germany. 4. Germany—History, Military—20th century. I. Title.

  D757.3.M57 2007
  940.54'1343—dc22
                                        2007014285

Table of Contents

Introduction

As a young graduate student recently discharged from the U.S. Army, I started writing a book entitled *Hitler's Legions: The Order of Battle of the German Army, World War II* in the mid-1970s and finished it seven years later. Since that time, a huge amount of literature on the order of battle of the German armed forces and their commanders has become available—so much so that *Hitler's Legions* became obsolete. The purpose of this book, and its companion volumes, is to replace the original, to present the order of battle of the German ground forces in World War II, and to trace each division from inception to destruction. I also (insofar as is possible) have listed the divisional commanders and the dates they held command. If they were promoted, killed, or wounded during their tenure, I have included this information as well. I only regret that I was not able to give a short biography of each commander, as I did in *Panzer Legions* and in the endnotes of some of my earlier books.

I would like to thank Chris Evans, the history editor at Stackpole Books, for suggesting this project, and David Reisch at Stackpole for all of his help. I would also like to thank Melinda Matthews, the head of the interlibrary loan department at the University of Louisiana at Monroe, for her usual superb job in tracking down reference material, as well as anyone else who provided useable information for this project. Thanks also go to Paul Moreau and Dr. Donnie Elias for all of their help. Most of all, I would like to thank my long-suffering wife, Donna, and my kids, Lacy and Gavin, for all that they have had to put up with during this process.

Dr. Samuel W. Mitcham, Jr.
Monroe, Louisiana

CHAPTER 1

The 291st–999th Infantry Divisions

291ST INFANTRY DIVISION

Composition: 504th Infantry Regiment, 505th Infantry Regiment, 506th Infantry Regiment, 291st Artillery Regiment, 291st Bicycle Squadron, 291st Tank Destroyer Company, 291st Engineer Battalion, 291st Signal Battalion, 291st Field Replacement Battalion, 291st Divisional Supply Troops

Home Station: Insterburg, Wehrkreis I

Nicknamed the Elk Division, this unit was created on February 10, 1940, from Prussians living in the Masurian Lakes area. Cadres for the new unit came from the 1st, 21st, and 263rd Infantry Divisions. Its bicycle squadron and tank destroyer company were later combined to form the 291st *Schnelle* Battalion. The 291st Division played a minor role in the French campaign before going to Russia in 1941. On June 22–23, the first two days of the invasion, the 291st penetrated forty-four miles in the first thirty-four hours—an astonishing total for a non-motorized infantry division in combat. It soon loosely surrounded Riga and repulsed several desperate attempts by the Soviet garrison to break out of the city. Although casualties were heavy, the division held its line, and contained and eventually helped destroy the Russian garrison. Later that year, it took the major Soviet naval base at Liepaja after a bitter struggle.

Remaining with Army Group North, the 291st fought in the Battle of Volkhov (January–March 1942) before being transferred to the Velikie Luki sector of Army Group Center in late

1

1942. It held a sector of the line here for several months. During the winter of 1942–43, three of its grenadier battalions were disbanded and the remnants were merged together to form a single ski battalion. In October 1943, it joined Army Group South, fought at Kiev, suffered heavy losses in the retreat through the northern Ukraine and, as part of the 1st Panzer Army, again suffered heavy losses in the Kamenetz-Podolsk ("Hube Pocket") battles of 1944. (During these battles, the 1st Panzer Army was surrounded but—brilliantly led by General Hube—it formed a "floating pocket" and broke out, despite the efforts of several Soviet armies to destroy it.)

The 291st was rebuilt as a 1944 type division in February 1944, when each of its grenadier regiments was reduced to two battalions. It also absorbed the 1st Reserve Grenadier Regiment of the 141st Reserve Division. Several months later, on September 10, 1944, it also absorbed the 1135th Grenadier Brigade. Although still greatly reduced in numbers, the 291st took part in the retreat across eastern Poland and fought in the Vistula campaign of late 1944. The veteran infantry division was finally smashed on January 27, 1945, when it tried unsuccessfully to block the Soviet advance into Silesia. The following month, the remnants of the Elk Division were placed under the command of a special staff, directed by Colonel Georg Heinlein (commander of the 504th Grenadier Regiment) and were absorbed by the 6th Infantry Division.

Commanders of the 291st Infantry included Lieutenant Generals Kurt Herzog (February 7, 1940), Major General/Lieutenant General Werner Göritz (June 10, 1942), Colonel/Major General Oskar Eckholt (January 15, 1944), Major General Arthur Finger (July 10, 1944), and Heinlein (January 27, 1945). Colonel Walter Kalkowski served as acting commander in November 1941 while Herzof was on leave.

Notes and Sources*: The 291st spent the period July 1940 to May 1941 back at home in East Prussia. Göritz was promoted to lieutenant general on January 1, 1943. Eckholt was promoted to major general on April 1, 1944. He was seriously wounded on July 12. General Finger was killed in action on January 27, 1945.

---

* For complete bibliography, see Volume Three.

Carell 1966: 20–22, 265, 421; Carell 1971: 510; Chant, Volume 16: 2232; Werner Conze, *Die Geschichte der 291. Infanterie-Division, 1940–1945* (1953); Grossmann: 291; Georg Gundlack, *Wolchow-Kesselschlacht der 291. Infanterie-Division (Bildband)* (1995); Hartmann: 30; Keilig: 78, 90; Nafziger 2000: 278–79; Tessin, Vol. 9: 31–32; OB 42: 102; OB 43: 168; OB 44: 231; OB 45: 228.

292ND INFANTRY DIVISION

Composition: 507th Infantry Regiment, 508th Infantry Regiment, 509th Infantry Regiment, 292nd Artillery Regiment, 292nd Bicycle Squadron, 292nd Tank Destroyer Company, 292nd Engineer Battalion, 292nd Signal Battalion, 292nd Field Replacement Battalion, 292nd Divisional Supply Troops

Home Station: Stargard, Wehrkreis II

Mobilized as part of the 8th Wave on February 6, 1940, this Mecklenburg-Pomeranian division consisted of newly trained young men with battalion-sized cadres from the 5th, 12th, 32nd, 75th, 254th, and 258th Infantry Divisions. It played a secondary role in the French campaign (June 1940), was on occupation and frontier guard duty in Poland (July 1940–June 1941), and spent four years on the Eastern Front (1941–45). After crossing the Bug River with Army Group Center in June 1941, it fought at Brest and Bialystok, in the Battle of the Yelnya Bend, at Vjasma, and in the subsequent drive on Moscow. It helped check the Soviet winter offensive of 1941–42, took part in the defensive actions of 1942 (including Gshatsk and Vjasma), the Rzhev withdrawal (1943), the Battle of Kursk (where it sustained heavy casualties), and Gomel. It took part in the fighting on the Sozh and the Pripjet (Pripyet) marshes, Pinsk, Ostrow, and Narev, and in the retreat into Poland. Down to battle group strength, it retreated through Poland and was destroyed in the Heiligenbeil Pocket in East Prussia in March 1945. Its survivors were absorbed by other divisions on the Hela peninsula that same month.

Commanders of the 292nd Infantry Division included Major General/Lieutenant General Martin Dehmel (February 6, 1940), Major General Willy Seeger (September 29, 1941), Major

General/Lieutenant General Wolfgang von Kluge (August 1942), Colonel/Major General/Lieutenant General Richard John (July 20, 1943), Colonel/Major General Hans Gittner (June 30, 1944), and Colonel/Major General/Lieutenant General Rudolf Reichert (September 1, 1944–end).

Notes and Sources: Dehmel was promoted to lieutenant general on June 1, 1941. Kluge, the brother of the field marshal, was promoted to lieutenant general on April 1, 1943. He was severely wounded on July 20. Richard John was promoted to major general on October 1, 1943, and to lieutenant general on April 1, 1944. Gittner was promoted to major general on August 1, 1944. Reichert was promoted to major general on November 9, 1944, and to lieutenant general on May 1, 1945, according to his personal declaration.

Carell 1966: 9; Carell 1971: 26, 37, 309; Hartmann: 30; Keilig: 17, 174; *Kriegstagebuch des OKW*, Volume IV: 1897; Lexikon; Mehner, Vol. 5: 326; Nafziger 2000: 279–80; Guenther Nitz, *Die 292. Infanterie-Division* (1957); Tessin, Vol. 9: 35–36; RA: 32; OB 42: 168; OB 43: 168; OB 44: 231; OB 45: 228.

293RD INFANTRY DIVISION

Composition: 510th Infantry Regiment, 511th Infantry Regiment, 512th Infantry Regiment, 293rd Artillery Regiment, 293rd Reconnaissance Battalion, 293rd Tank Destroyer Battalion, 293rd Engineer Battalion, 293rd Signal Battalion, 293rd Field Replacement Battalion, 293rd Divisional Supply Troops

Home Station: Berlin, Wehrkreis III

Activated on February 2, 1940, from newly trained young soldiers, and fully organized in April 1940, this unit was known as the Bear Division, because of its ties to the city of Berlin, the symbol of which is a bear. Unit cadres were provided for this unit by the 3rd, 23rd, 25th, 68th, 76th, and 257th Infantry Divisions. The division was sent to Belgium in June 1940, and to the coast of the English Channel of France in July, to take part in the invasion of the United Kingdom which, of course, was never launched. In November, it was posted to to Nantes and was sent to Poland in March 1941. It crossed into Russia on June 22 and fought at Brest-Litovsk, Pinsk, Gomel, Kiev, and Bryansk and against the Soviet winter offensive of 1941/42. It occupied a sector near Mzensk (not far from Orel) from February to September 1942, and a zone in the vicinity of Bolchov (also near Orel) until June 1943. It fought in the Battle of Kursk in July and at Bryansk in August, and suffered heavy losses at Kharkov in September. Remaining in the line at *Kampfgruppe* strength, the 293rd fought at Krementschug and Uman in October and November. The battered division was downgraded to Division Group 293 on November 2, 1943, and was assigned to Corps Detachment A. It was finally destroyed at Jassy, Romania, in August and September 1944.

The commanders of the 293rd Infantry Division were Major General Joseph Russwurm (February 1940), Lieutenant General Justin von Obernitz (June 4, 1940), Colonel/Major General/Lieutenant General Werner Forst (acting commander, December 1941), Obernitz (returned January 1942), Forst (permanent commander, February 19, 1942), and Lieutenant General Karl Arndt (January 10, 1943).

Notes and Sources: Werner Forst was promoted to major general on February 1, 1942, and to lieutenant general on January 1, 1943.

Hartmann: 31; Keilig: 93, 289; Lexikon; Tessin, Vol. 9: 39–40; RA: 46; OB 42: 102; OB 43: 168; OB 44: 232; OB 45: 229.

294TH INFANTRY DIVISION

Composition (1940): 513th Infantry Regiment, 514th Infantry Regiment, 515th Infantry Regiment, 294th Artillery Regiment, 294th Reconnaissance Battalion, 294th Tank Destroyer Battalion, 294th Engineer Battalion, 294th Signal Battalion, 294th Field Replacement Battalion, 294th Divisional Supply Troops

Home Station: Leipzig, later Dresden, Wehrkreis IV

Formed on February 6, 1940, from recently trained Saxon personnel, the 294th took part in the French campaign of 1940 as a follow-up division. It was then stationed on the English Channel (July–August), at Bordeaux (September–December), and on the Demarcation Line with Vichy France (January-February 1941). It was sent to the east in March and took part in the Balkan campaign in April, fighting in Yugoslavia. The

294th crossed into southern Russia that summer and was involved in the drive on Kiev, in the capture of Kharkov and the Donetz, and in the checking of the Soviet winter offensive of 1941–42. Remaining with Army Group South, it was used to stabilize the Romanian 3rd Army in the fall of 1942, and suffered heavy casualties when the Romamans collapsed and set up the Stalingrad debacle.

The bulk of the 8th Luftwaffe Field Division was attached to the 294th in late 1942 during the retreat from the Volga. Remaining in the line, the 294th Infantry fought on the Mius and at Stalino, and was later encircled at Taganrog in August, and again sustained heavy losses in the ensuing breakout. After this, the veteran division was reorganized. It absorbed the remnants of the 333rd Infantry Division and now included the 513rd and 514th Grenadier Regiments (two battalions each), Divisional Group 333 (with the 679th and 680th Regimental Groups), the 333rd Fusilier Battalion, the 333rd Artillery Regiment, the 294th Artillery Regiment, the combined 294th Tank Destroyer/Reconnaissance Battalion, and the usual divisional supply units. The 294th Infantry Division returned to the front and fought in the Nikopol Bridgehead and at Odessa. It was again surrounded and finally destroyed at Kischinev, Romania, west of the lower Dnestr, on August 26, 1944. The few soldiers that escaped the disaster were on leave or in medical facilities. They were attached to the 333rd Infantry Division, which absorbed them when the 294th Infantry Division was officially disbanded on October 9, 1944.

The commanders of the 294th Infantry were Major General/Lieutenant General Otto Gabcke (February 15, 1940), Lieutenant General Ferdinand Neuling (March 23, 1942), Colonel/Major General/Lieutenant General Johannes Block (May 15, 1942), Colonel Kurt Hähling (June 1943), Block (July 1943), Colonel Hermann Frenking (August 12, 1943), Block (returned August 15, 1943), and Colonel/Major General Werner von Eichstädt (December 24, 1943).

Notes and Sources: Gabcke was promoted to lieutenant general on February 1, 1941. Block was promoted to major general to Sep-

A German gun crew prepares to fire. HITM ARCHIVE

tember 1, 1942, and to lieutenant general on January 1, 1943. Werner von Eichstaedt was promoted to major general on March 1, 1944. He was killed in action on August 26, 1944, the day the division was destroyed.

Hartmann: 31; Keilig: 120; *Kriegstagebuch des OKW*, Volume II: 1393; Volume III: 4; Lexikon; Nafziger 2000: 282–83; Tessin, Vol. 9: 43–44; RA: 72; OB 43: OB 44: 232; OB 45: 229.

295TH INFANTRY DIVISION

Composition (1941): 516th Infantry Regiment, 517th Infantry Regiment, 518th Infantry Regiment, 295th Artillery Regiment, 295th Reconnaissance Battalion, 295th Tank Destroyer Battalion, 295th Engineer Battalion, 295th Signal Battalion, 295th Divisional Supply Troops

Home Station: Blankenburg, Wehrkreis XI

The 295th was formed from newly trained soldiers on February 8, 1940. Battalion-sized unit cadres were provided by the 19th, 31st, 36th, 69th, 71st, and 267th Infantry Divisions. The 295th Division was in OKH reserve in May 1940, and was sent to Belgium in June. The following month it was stationed at Lille, France, before being sent to Rouen, where it remained until April 1941. The division was transferred to the 17th Army in southern Poland in May and first saw combat in Russia in 1941, fighting at Vinniza and in the battle of encirclement at Uman. It penetrated the Dnieper and swept across the Ukraine and Donets, only to be turned back by the Russian winter offensive of 1941–42. The next year, the 295th was involved in the Kharkov-Izyum battles, Voronezh, and Kalach, as well as the fighting on the Volga. It was surrounded at Stalingrad in November 1942 and surrendered to the Russians in late January 1943.

A second 295th Infantry Division (this one a static unit) was organized in northern Norway on February 12, 1943, and remained there the rest of the war. Initially it had only one grenadier regiment (three battalions) but was gradually reinforced to three grenadier regiments of three battalions each and an artillery regiment of two battalions. In the summer of 1944, it lost the 518th Grenadier Regiment, which was sent to the Lofoten Islands to form the nucleus of Fortress Brigade

Lofoten. In early 1945, U.S. intelligence reported that the 295th was preparing to leave Norway, but it never did.

The commanders of the 295th Infantry Division were Major General/Lieutenant General Herbert Geitner (February 6, 1940), Colonel/Major General Karl Gümbel (December 8, 1941), Colonel Ulrich Schütze (April 2, 1942), Major General Rolf Wuthmann (May 2, 1942), Colonel/Major General Dr. Otto Korfes (November 16, 1942), Major General/Lieutenant General Georg Dinter (April 1, 1943), Lieutenant General Karl-Ludwig Rhein (July 27, 1944), and Lieutenant General Sigfrid Macholz (January 26, 1945).

Notes and Sources: The second 295th Infantry Division's subordinate units bore the same numbers as the original. Geitner was promoted to lieutenant general on August 1, 1941. He was mortally wounded on December 8, 1941, and died in Berlin on January 22, 1942. Gümbel was promoted to major general on February 1, 1942. Dr. Korfes was promoted to major general on January 1, 1943. He surrendered the original 295th Infantry to the Soviets when Stalingrad fell. Dinter was promoted to lieutenant general on April 1, 1944.

Keilig: 315, 378; Kursietis: 179; Mellenthin 1956: 225; Nafziger 2000: 283–85; Tessin, Vol. 9: 47–48; RA: 172; OB: 43: 169; OB 45: 229–30; Ziemke 1959: 256, 262.

296TH INFANTRY DIVISION

Composition: 519th Infantry Regiment, 520th Infantry Regiment, 521st Infantry Regiment, 296th Artillery Regiment, 296th Reconnaissance (later Fusilier) Battalion, 296th Tank Destroyer Battalion, 296th Engineer Battalion, 296th Signal Battalion, 296th Divisional Supply Troops

Home Station: Nuremberg, Wehrkreis XIII

Organized from cadre battalions provided by the 17th, 46th, 73rd, 260th, and 262nd Infantry Divisions, as well as from newly trained men from northern Bavaria and the western Sudetenland, the 296th was activated on February 5, 1940, and was in Belgium in June, but did not take part in any fighting. From the summer of 1940 until the spring of 1941, it was stationed in the Lille area of northern France before being transferred to Army Group Center for the invasion of Russia. It was heavily engaged at Zhitomir, Kiev, Orel, Tula, and the battles around Moscow in late 1941 and early 1942. It fought in the defensive battles around Orel on the central sector in 1942 and 1943, in the Gomel area in September 1943, and in the Bobruisk sector (1943–44). It was reorganized as a Type 44 (six grenadier battalions) division in the fall of 1943. The 296th Infantry Division was destroyed near Bobruisk in June during the Soviet summer offensive of 1944, and was formally dissolved on August 3, 1944.

Divisional commanders of the 296th Infantry included Major General/Lieutenant General Wilhelm Stemmermann (January 1, 1941), Lieutenant General Friedrich Krischer Elder von Wehregg (January 8, 1942), Major General/Lieutenant General Karl Faulenbach (April 3, 1943), and Major General/Lieutenant General Arthur Kullmer (January 1, 1943).

Notes and Sources: Stemmermann was promoted to lieutenant general on August 1, 1941. Faulenbach was promoted to lieutenant general on January 1, 1943. Kullner was promoted to lieutenant general on September 1, 1943. He gave up command of the division on June 19, 1944—three days before the Soviet offensive struck. He thus escaped the disaster. Who succeeded him as divisional commander is not mentioned in the available records.

Carell 1966: 196; Keilig: 55–56, 188, 193; *Kriegstagebuch des OKW*, Volume IV: 1897; Nafziger 2000: 284–85; RA: 204; OB 42: 103; OB 43: 169–70; OB 44: 233; OB 45: 230.

297TH INFANTRY DIVISION

Composition: 522nd Infantry Regiment, 523rd Infantry Regiment, 524th Infantry Regiment, 297th Artillery Regiment, 297th Reconnaissance Battalion, 297th Tank Destroyer Battalion, 297th Engineer Battalion, 297th Signal Battalion, 297th Field Replacement Battalion, 297th Divisional Supply Troops

Home Station: Engerau, later Olmütz, Wehrkreis XVII

Activated on January 31, 1940, and formed in March and April in the Bruck area, this eighth-wave division was built around battalion-sized cadres provided by the 27th, 44th, 45th, 57th, 78th, and 268th Infantry Divisions. It was part of OKH's reserve in the Western Campaign of 1940, but did not any fighting. It was sent to Poland in July 1940, and remained there until Operation "Barbarossa," the invasion of the Soviet Union, began. The 297th first saw action in Russia with Army Group South in July 1941. It fought at Zhitomir (July), Uman (August), Kiev (September), Kharkov (November), and Rostov (November–December), and opposed the Soviet winter offensive of 1941–42. In 1942, it was with the 6th Army in the Battle of Kharkov, in the clearing of the Izyum Pocket, in the drive across the Don, and in the Battle of Voronezh. It was subsequently encircled at Stalingrad with the 6th Army and destroyed there on January 25, 1943. Its last commander, Major General Moritz von Drebber, surrendered its remnants to the Russians. Most of the survivors later died in Russian prison camps.

A second 297th Infantry Division was created in Bordeaux, France, in the summer of 1943, to replace the division destroyed at Stalingrad. It was officially activated as a three-battalion *Kampfgruppe* (battle group) on March 7 and as a division on April 7. The new 297th Infantry, however, never attained the distinguished record of the first. Its units bore the same number as in the original division, but its grenadier regiments had only two battalions. It was transferred to Serbia in July 1943, and to Albania in September, where it was involved in anti-partisan operations. It remained there until the following autumn, when it withdrew to Montenegro and was heavily engaged against Tito's guerrillas that fall. Later it fought against the Russians and remained on the southern sector of the Eastern Front until the end of the war. It surrendered to the Yugoslavs in the Cilli–Bad Radkersburg area on May 9, 1945, although elements of the division did manage to surrender to the Americans.

Commanders of the second 297th included Lieutenant General Max Pfeffer (April 5, 1940), Drebber (January 16, 1942), Major General/Lieutenant General Friedrich-Wilhelm Deutsch (April 1, 1943), Lietenant General Otto Gullmann (February 17, 1944) and Lieutenant General Albrecht Baier (February 20, 1944–end).

Notes and Sources: Deutsch was promoted to lieutenant general on August 1, 1943. He was injured in an automobile accident in Valona on February 17, 1944, and died on March 2.

Alois Beck, *Die 297. Infanterie-Division* (1983), Carell 1966: 588; Keilig: 19, 69; Lexikon; Nafziger 2000: 286–87; Tessin, Vol. 9: 55–56; RA: 220; OB 42: 103; OB 43: 170; OB 45: 230.

298TH INFANTRY DIVISION

Composition: 525th Infantry Regiment, 526th Infantry Regiment, 527th Infantry Regiment, 298th Artillery Regiment, 298th Reconnaissance Battalion, 298th Tank Destroyer Battalion, 298th Engineer Battalion, 298th Signal Battalion, 298th Divisional Supply Troops

Home Station: Breslau, Wehrkreis VIII

Activated in Troop Maneuver Area Neuhammer on February 6, 1940, and fleshed out in March and April, 1940, the 298th was built around battalion-sized cadres supplied by the 7th, 8th, 28th, 62nd, 252nd and 253rd Infantry Divisions, augmented by newly trained Silesians. The division was sent to France in June 1940 but the French surrendered before it saw any combat. The 298th was sent to Poland in July and first saw action in southern Russia in June 1941. The division fought in the drive to Kiev, in the Battle of Kharhov, and was involved in the subsequent campaigns on the southern sector of the Eastern Front, including the Soviet winter offensive of 1941–42 and the Isjum counteroffensive of 1942. It was attached to the 8th Italian Army when it collapsed during the Stalingrad campaign and escaped only after suffering such heavy casualties that a third of its grenadier battalions had to be disbanded. It suffered further casualties in the retreat from the Volga—so many, in fact, that it had to be disbanded. It officially ceased to exist on March 30, 1943. Its troops were absorbed by the 387th Infantry Division, a "Stalingrad" division then reforming near Prague.

Commanders of the 298th Infantry Division were Major General/Lieutenant General Walter Graessner (February 6, 1940), Colonel/Major General Arnold Szelinski (January 1, 1942) and Colonel Herbert Michaelis (December 27, 1942).

Sources: Graessner was promoted to lieutenant general on October 1, 1941. Szelinski became a major general on February 1, 1942.

Carell 1966: 490, 535; Keilig: 341; *Kriegstagebuch des OKW*, Volume II: 1386, 1394; Nafziger 2000: 287–88; Tessin, Vol. 9: 59-60; RA: 130; OB 42: 104; OB 43: 170; OB 44: 234; OB 44b: D96.

299TH INFANTRY DIVISION

Composition: 528th Infantry Regiment, 529th Infantry Regiment, 530th Infantry Regiment, 299th Artillery Regiment, 299th Reconnaissance Battalion, 299th Tank Destroyer Battalion, 299th Engineer Battalion, 299th Signal Battalion, 299th Field Replacement Battalion, 299th Divisional Supply Troops

Home Station: Siegen, later Buedingen, Wehrkreis IX

The 299th was activated on February 9, 1940. It consisted of cadre battalions from the 9th, 15th, 33rd, 52nd, 86th, and 211th Infantry Divisions and of newly inducted men from the Hesse and Thuringia regions. It served in France in 1940 and was sent to Poland in August. It was involved in the initial invasion of southern Russia in June 1941, and was almost continuously engaged after that, fighting at Zhitomir and Kiev, in the Donets, and at Kursk (1941). It held a sector in the vicinity of Livny (east of Orel) from January 1942 to August 1943. That fall it fought in the Battles of Bryansk and Gomel in 1943, and distinguished itself as a good combat division, although three of its infantry battalions had to be disbanded due to heavy casualties. The survivors of these units were transferred to other grenadier battalions within the division.

On June 22, 1944, the Russians launched their massive summer offensive with 2.5 million men, and their opening attack struck the 299th Infantry; it collapsed within a few hours. Only remnants escaped, but these (along with men returning from leave or convalescent facilities) were used to form a new 299th Infantry Division. This formation, a mere skelton of the original 299th, was the former Corps Detachment G and included the former Division Groups 57, 299, and 337 (now the 528th, 529th, and 530th Grenadier Regiments, respectively), the 299th Artillery Regiment, and assorted divisional troops. It took part in the Polish campaign of 1944 and in the retreat behind the

Vistula, and it continued to fight on the Eastern Front until February 26, 1945, when it was practically destroyed on the Heiligenbeil landfront in northern East Prussia. The remnants of the 299th Infantry Division were officially disbanded on April 4, 1945. Its survivors were used to help form Infantry Division Schlageter (*RAD Division Nr. 1*).

Commanders of the 299th Infantry included Major General/Lieutenant General Willi Moser (April 6, 1940), Major General Viktor Koch (November 1, 1942), Major General Hans Bergen (November 5, 1942), Major General Count Ralph von Oriola (May 3, 1943), Colonel Paul Reichelt (January 15, 1944), Oriola (March 13, 1944), Major General Hans Junck (June 28, 1944), Oriola (returned July 1944), and Colonel Karl Goebel (September 1, 1944).

Notes and Sources: Moser was promoted to lieutenant general on August 1, 1941. Oriola became a lieutenant general on November 1, 1943. Colonel Goebel was mortally wounded on February 16, 1945, the day his division was destroyed. He died on March 2. He was posthumously promoted to major general.

Carell 1971: 26, 583; Hartmann: 32; Keilig: 230; *Kriegstagebuch des OKW*, Volume III: 8; Volume IV: 1887, 1895–1904; Lexikon; Nafziger 2000: 289–90; Tessin, Vol. 9: 62–63; RA: 144; OB 43: 104; OB 44: 234; OB 44b: D96; OB 45: 231.

300TH REPLACEMENT DIVISION

Composition: 237th Field Recruit Regiment, 242nd Field Recruit Regiment

On June 3, 1940, this division was formed to control field recruiter units and replacement battalions in occupied Poland. It was disbanded on August 1, 1940, after the fall of France, because further recruitment efforts seemed unnecessary. Its replacement units were sent back to Germany.

Sources: Lexikon; Nafziger 2000: 575; Tessin, Vol. 9: 67.

SPECIAL ADMINISTRATIVE DIVISION STAFF 300 (DIVISION STAFF z.b.V. 300)

Composition: Estonian 2nd Frontier Guard (Police) Regiment, Estonian 4th Frontier Guard (Police) Regiment, Estonian 5th Frontier Guard (Police) Regiment and Estonian 6th Frontier Guard (Police) Regiment

Home Station: Estonia and Coburg, Wehrkreis XIII

This headquarters was created on May 1, 1944, as a special staff to direct the mobilization of Estonian home guard regiments in the service of Nazi Germany. Its headquarters was the former Staff, 13th Luftwaffe Field Division. It was soon committed to battle on the Lake Ilmen sector and continued to fight in the battles of the Courland Pocket until the end of the war. It surrendered on May 8, 1945. Many of its soldiers were later put to death by the Soviets.

Sources: *Kriegstagebuch des OKW*, Volume IV: 1896; Lexikon; Nafziger 2000: 290; Tessin, Vol. 9: 67; OB 45: 231.

301ST INFANTRY DIVISION

Composition: 3rd Frontier Guard Regiment, 13th Frontier Guard Regiment and 23rd Frontier Guard Regiment

Home Station: Küstrin, Wehrkreis II

Formed in August 1939 from the Brigade Netze, this unit consisted of frontier guard regiments from the 12th Frontier Guard Command (*Grenzschutz-Komandos 12*) in Kuestrin, Pomerania. These units apparently skirmished against the Polish Army in September. The new division was disbanded on October 14, 1939, the week after Poland surrendered.

Sources: Lexikon; Nafziger 2000: 290; Tessin, Vol. 9: 70.

302ND INFANTRY DIVISION

Composition: 570th Infantry Regiment, 571st Infantry Regiment, 572nd Infantry Regiment, 302nd Artillery Regiment, 302nd Reconnaissance Battalion, 302nd Tank Destroyer Battalion, 302nd Engineer Battalion, 302nd Signal Battalion, 302nd Divisional Supply Troops

Home Station: Neustrelitz, Wehrkreis II

This static division was formed on November 12, 1940 from cadre units supplied by the 75th and 292nd Infantry Divisions and troops drafted from eastern Mecklenburg and Pomerania. It spent the next three years on garrison duty in Germany and France. In August 1942, it fought its first battle when the British attempted a major commando-style landing on the continent at Dieppe, France. The 302nd threw them back into the sea and inflicted heavy casualties on the landing force. From then on the 302nd was known as "the Dieppe division."

Sent to southern Russia in January 1943, it was involved in the Donets campaign (where it fought at Voroschilovgrad), on the Mius (April–September 1943), at Saporoshje (October–December), in the Nikopol Bridgehead (January–February 1944), and in the retreat to the Dnieper. It then withdrew into lower Romania. By now its 571st Grenadier Regiment had been disbanded, its other two grenadier regiments had been reduced to two battalions each, and its reconnaissance and tank destroyer battalions had been merged to form the 302nd Mobile Battalion. It had, however, been reinforced with Division Group 125 (the former 125th Infantry Division, with the equivalent of two battalions). It was part of the 6th Army when it was decimated in Romania in August and September 1944. The 302nd Infantry Division was encircled west of the Dnieper on August 25 and was destroyed there. The few members of the division which were not captured were assigned to the 15th and 76th Infantry Divisions.

Commanders of the division included Lieutenant General Konrad Haase (November 1940), Colonel/Major General/Lieutenant General Otto Elfeldt (November 26, 1942), Lieutenant General Dr. Kurt Rüdiger (November 12, 1943), Major General/Lieutenant General Erich von Bogen (January 25, 1944) and Colonel Willi Fischer (July 1944).

Notes and Sources: Haase promoted to lieutenant general on January 1, 1942. Elfeldt was promoted to major general on January 1, 1943 and to lieutenant general on July 1, 1943. Rüdiger was apparently wounded in action on January 25, 1944. Bogen promoted to lieutenant general on July 1, 1944. He was captured by the Russians later that month, whereupon Fischer, the senior regimental commander, assumed command of the division. He had formerly directed the 302nd Artillery Regiment. Fischer was wounded and captured on August 25, 1944.

Keilig: 43; Emil Kilgast, *Rückblick auf die Geschichte der 302. Infanterie-Division* (1976); Lexikon; Nafziger 2000: 511–12; Tessin, Vol. 9: 74–75; RA: 32; OB 42: 104; OB 43: 171; OB 45: 231.

303RD INFANTRY DIVISION

See Infantry Division Döberitz in the next chapter.

304TH INFANTRY DIVISION

Composition: 573rd Infantry Regiment, 574th Infantry Regiment, 575th Infantry Regiment, 304th Artillery Regiment, 304th Reconnaissance Company, 304th Tank Destroyer Battalion, 304th Engineer Battalion, 304th Signal Company, 304th Field Replacement Battalion, 304th Divisional Supply Troops

Home Station: Glauchaus, Wehrkreis IV

Formed on November 15, 1940, this thirteenth-wave static division formed in the area north of Leipzig from new recruits and parts of the 56th and 294th Infantry Divisions, each of which provided the equivalent of a third of a division. Its three artillery battalions were equipped with light howitzers, and its nine infantry battalions each had a mortar company, instead of the usual infantry gun company. It was transferred to Belgium in May 1941, and remained there until the end of 1942. In December 1942, it was rushed to the Eastern Front, where the southern sector was on the verge of collapse. It saw its first action in the Donets, where it behaved badly. The next month, as Army Group Don retreated from Stalingrad, panic again broke out in the ranks of the 304th.

Despite its unreliability, the division continued to serve on the southern sector, defended a sector of the Mius (March–September 1943), and suffered heavy losses at Taganrog and in the withdrawal to the lower Dnieper bend (March 1944). Its performance, however, improved greatly with experience. Meanwhile, each grenadier regiment lost its third battalion, and its 571st Grenadier Regiment was disbanded in October 1943. (It was rebuilt in May 1944, from the 610th Security Regiment of the 403rd Security Division.) It fought at Tiraspol (May–July 1944), in the Ukraine and in southern Poland. It was crushed when the Red Army broke out of the Baranov Bridgehead (west of the Vistula River in Poland) in January 1945. The division was then withdrawn to Prague, where it was reorganized. The 574th Grenadier Regiment absorbed the remnants of the old division, the 573rd Grenadier Regiment absorbed the II and III Battalions of Grenadier Regiment Bohemia-Moravia, the 575th Grenadier Regiment absorbed the 1247th Leadership Training Grenadier Regiment, and the 304th Fusilier Battalion absorbed I/Grenadier Regiment Bohemia-Moravia. The 304th Artillery Regiment absorbed the IV/83rd Artillery Regiment (formerly of the 100th Jaeger Division). Sent back into combat in April, the 304th Infantry Division fought in Upper Silesia and was trapped in the Deutsch-Brod pocket with the 1st Panzer Army, where it surrendered to the Red Army on May 9, 1945.

Its divisional commanders included Major General/Lieutenant General Heinrich Krampft (November 15, 1940), Colonel/Major General/Lieutenant General Ernst Sieler (November 16, 1942), Colonel Alfred Philippi (February 1, 1943), Sieler (returned March 1, 1943), Colonel Norbert Holm (August 30, 1943), Sieler (October 1943), Major General Ulrich Liss (January 10, 1945), Sieler (January 22, 1945), Colonel Robert Bader (April 6, 1945), and Colonel Krüger (April 1945–end).

Notes and Sources: Krampf was promoted to lieutenant general on December 1, 1941. Ernst Sieler was promoted to major general on January 1, 1943, and to lieutenant general on July 1, 1943. General

Liss was severely wounded and captured by the Soviets on or about January 22, 1945.

Carell 1971: 128–29; Keilig: 324; Lexikon; Manstein: 392; Mehner, Vol. 12: 454; Nafziger 2000: 512–13; Tessin, Vol. 9: 83–84; RA: 72; OB 42: 104; OB 43: 171; OB 44: 235; OB 45: 232.

305TH INFANTRY DIVISION

Composition: 576th Infantry Regiment, 577th Infantry Regiment, 578th Infantry Regiment, 305th Artillery Regiment, 305th Reconnaissance Company, 305th Tank Destroyer Battalion, 305th Engineer Battalion, 305th Signal Company, 305th Field Replacement Battalion, 305th Divisional Supply Troops

Home Station: Karlsruhe, later Strasbourg, Wehrkreis V

The original 305th Infantry Division was a 13th Wave static division formed in the Ravensburg area of Wuerttemberg on December 15, 1940, around cadres supplied by the 78th and 296th Infantry Divisions. It was sent to Brittany in May 1941, and to the Russian Front a year later. (Meanwhile, it was made more mobile and moved into the Attack Division category.) It fought in the defense of Kharkov, at Izyum, Voronezh and Kalach, in the push to the Volga, and in the Stalingrad street fighting from August to November 1942. It was encircled at Stalingrad on November 23, 1942, and was forced to surrender at the giant Tractor Works at the end of January 1943. The commanders of the original 305th Infantry Division were Major General/Lieutenant General Kurt Pflugradt (December 15, 1940), Major General Kurt Oppenlaender (April 12, 1942), Colonel/Major General Bernhard Steinmetz (November 1, 1942) and Colonel Albrecht Czimatis (January 1943).

A second 305th was created in Brittany, France on February 17, 1943, from units from all parts of Germany, as well as elements of the 334th and later the 362nd Infantry Division. It was sent to Nice on the Mediterranean, where it helped replace the unreliable Italian 4th Army. The new division's subordinate units bore the same numbers as the old. It entered Italy with Rommel's Army Group B in late summer 1943, occupied the huge Italian naval base at La Spezia in September, and, in November 1943, was sent into battle in southern Italy. It suffered many casualties south of Rome and in January 1944, but also received a considerable number of replacements from the 94th Infantry Division. It was nevertheless reorganized as a Type 44 division (with six grenadier battalions) and its reconnaissance and tank destroyer battalions were combined to form the 305th Mobile Battalion. The division returned to action soon after but that summer was withdrawn to northern Italy to rest and refit. It was back on the front line in autumn and was engaged in the Rimini-Cesena area in October. It was fighting west of Bologna from November 1944 to March 1945 and ended the war on the Italian Front.

Its leaders included Colonel/Major General/Lieutenant General Friedrich Wilhelm Hauck (February 17, 1943), Colonel Friedrich Trompeter (November 14, 1944), and Major General Friedrich von Schellwitz (December 29, 1944–end).

Notes and Sources: Pflugradt was promoted to lieutenant general on April 1, 1942. Steinmetz was promoted to major general on January 1, 1943. Hauck was promoted to major general on June 1, 1943 and to lieutenant general on March 1, 1944.

Blumenson 1969: 315; Fisher: 18, 302; Garland and Smyth: 290–93; Keilig: 129; Lexikon; Nafziger 2000: 513–14; Tessin, Vol. 9: 89–90; RA: 86; OB 42: 104; OB 43: 171; OB 44: 236; OB 45: 233.

306TH INFANTRY DIVISION

Composition: 579th Infantry Regiment, 580th Infantry Regiment, 581st Infantry Regiment, 306th Artillery Regiment, 306th Reconnaissance Company, 306th Tank Destroyer Company, 306th Engineer Battalion, 306th Signal Company, 306th Field Replacement Battalion, 306th Divisional Supply Troops. The 306th Reconnaissance and 306th Tank Destroyer Battalions were loater combined to form the 306th Mobile Battalion.

Home Station: Minden, Wehrkreis VI

Formed on November 15, 1940, the 306th was built around cadres supplied by the 86th and 291st Infantry Divisions (each of which supplied one-third of the division) plus the 129th Field Recruit Regiment and new recruits and draftees from Westphalia and the Rhineland. The new division was sent to

Belgium in May 1941, and was transferred to southern Russia in December 1942. It fought in the Stalingrad relief campaign and on the Don, and opposed the Soviet drive on Rostov. It suffered heavy losses on the Mius and fought at Millerovo (April–September 1943), at Nikopol (early 1944), in the Dnieper bend withdrawal (March 1944), and in the retreat into Bessarabia. It was at battle group strength as early as October 1943. The following month, it absorbed the remnants of the 328th Infantry Division. In August and September 1944, the 306th was destroyed in Romania.

Its commanders included Major General Hans von Sommerfeld (November 15, 1940), Major General Georg Neymann (November 1, 1942), Colonel Gerhard Matthias (November 1942), Lieutenant General Georg Pfeiffer (January 29, 1943), Major General Theobald Lieb (Februrary 21, 1943), Major General/Lieutenant General Karl-Erik Köhler (March 30, 1943), Colonel Karl Baer (January 1, 1944), and Köhler (January 13, 1944).

Notes and Sources: Sommerfeld was promoted to lieutenant general on September 1, 1941. Köhler became a lieutenant general on June 1, 1943. Colonel Baer was killed in action on January 13, 1944. During the Romanian campaign, the division was commanded by its senior colonel. He was killed in action on August 21, 1944.

Keilig: 177, 326; *Kriegstagebuch des OKW*, Volume III: 1158; Kursietis: 182; Lexikon; Manstein: 322; Nafziger 2000: 514–15; Tessin, Vol. 9: 94–95; RA: 102; OB 43: 172; OB 45: 233.

309TH INFANTRY DIVISION

See Infantry Division Berlin in the next chapter.

311TH INFANTRY DIVISION

Composition: 247th Infantry Regiment, 249th Infantry Regiment, 250th Infantry Regiment, 311th Artillery Regiment, 341st Reconnaissance Battalion, 341st Engineer Battalion, 341st Signal Battalion, 341st Divisional Supply Troops

Home Station: Lötzen, Wehrkreis I

A German infantry squad prepares for action. They are spearheaded by a machine-gun crew and supported by a reconnaissance vehicle. HITM ARCHIVE

Created in East Prussia on November 1, 1939, the 311th was made up mostly of older men. Initially it consisted of the 152nd, 161st and 162nd Landwehr Infantry Regiments, which had fought against the Poles in September as Group Brand and Brigade Lötzen. It also included the 161st Landwehr Artillery Regiment, the 311th Reconnaissance Battalion, the 161st Landwehr Engineer Battalion and the 131st Landwehr Signal Battalion. It was reorganized on March 8, 1940, into the composition shown above. Part of OB East, the 311th was one of the units guarding Germany's rear against a possible Soviet attack while Hitler conquered France. The division never left Germany. In June 1940, the 311th was sent to the Grafenwoehr Troop Maneuver Area in Bavaria, where it was disbanded. Most of the older age men were sent home. The artillery staff and the reconnaissance battalion were sent to the 16th Motorized Division; the signal battalion became part of the 11th Panzer Division; the engineer battalion staff was disbanded but its three companies became railroad construction units; and the division headquarters was converted to an administrative command and was sent to Warsaw, where it was still functioning in 1943.

The commanders of the 311th Infantry Division were Lieutenant General Albrecht Brand (November 1, 1939) and Lieutenant General Paul Gerhardt (November 10, 1939).

Sources: Haupt, *Infanterie*, Vol. 2: 119–20; Keilig: 49, 104; *Kriegstagebuch des OKW*, Volume I: 1123; Tessin, Vol. 9: 111–12; OB 42: 105; OB 43: 172; OB 45: 234.

319TH INFANTRY DIVISION

Composition: 582nd Infantry Regiment, 583rd Infantry Regiment, 584th Infantry Regiment, 319th Artillery Regiment, 1265th Fortress Artillery Regiment; 16th Machine Gun Battalion; 319th Reconnaissance Company, 319th Tank Destroyer Battalion, 450th Tank Destroyer Battalion, 319th Mobile Battalion, 319th Engineer Battalion, 319th Signal Company, 319th Divisional Supply Troops.

Home Station: Frankfurt am Main, Wehrkreis IX

On November 15, 1940, this static division was activated. It was formed around cadres supplied by the 87th, 169th, and 299th Infantry Divisions. The new division took over the defense of the English Channel Islands of Guernsey, Jersey, Alderney, Sark, Herm, and Jethou the following summer. It was also responsible for the city of St. Malo on the French mainland and a sector of the French coast in 1941. In 1943 and 1944, Hitler was so convinced that the Allies would have to take the Channel Islands before they could land in France that he reinforced the 319th to the incredible strength of 40,000 men, making it the largest division in the German Army during World War II. (During this period, the division added a machine-gun battalion, a mobile battalion, two tank-destroyer battalions, two Eastern battalions, some coastal artillery and part of the 50th Infantry Division from the Crimea.) Eisenhower bypassed the Channel Islands when he landed on the Normandy coast and isolated the 319th Infantry, which remained isolated until the end of the war. Elements of the division were reportedly transferred back to the continent before the Normandy Front collapsed and fought in the Cotentin peninsula battles of mid-1944. The main body of the division, however, surrendered at 7:14 a.m. on May 9, 1945, seven hours after the official end of the war—having hardly fired a shot in anger during its five years' existence.

The commanders of the Channel Island division included Major General/Lieutenant General Erich Müller (November 19, 1940), Major General/Lieutenant General Count Rudolf von Schmettow (September 1, 1943), and Major General Rudolf Wulf (February 27, 1945).

Notes and Sources: The 643rd Ost Battalion was attached to the 582nd Grenadier Regiment as its fourth battalion. The 823rd Georgian Battalion became the IV/583rd Grenadier Regiment. The division also had the equivalent of a panzer battalion attached to it. Müller was promoted to lieutenant general on June 1, 1942. Count von Schmettow was promoted to lieutenant general on April 1, 1944. Wulf was simultaneously division commander and commandant of Guernsey.

Harrison: 130–31; Hartmann: 32; Keilig: 231; Kursietis: 183; Nafziger 2000: 219–92; Tessin, Vol. 9: 134–35; RA: 144; OB 43: 172; OB 44: 237; OB 45: 234.

320TH INFANTRY
(LATER VOLKSGRENADIER) DIVISION

Composition: 585th Infantry Regiment, 586th Infantry Regiment, 587th Infantry Regiment, 320th Artillery Regiment, 320th Reconnaissance Company, 320th Tank Destroyer Battalion, 320th Engineer Battalion, 320th Signal Company, 320th Divisional Supply Troops

Home Station: Glogau, later Brieg, Wehrkreis VIII

The static 320th Infantry was formed near Luebeck, southern Holstein, on December 2, 1940, with cadres supplied by the 58th and 254th Infantry Divisions. It was sent to Dunkirk, northern France, in May 1941. In June 1942, it was transferred to the Cotentin peninsula of Brittany. In January 1943 it was sent to the southern sector of the Eastern Front and first saw action in the Battle of Isjum (near Kharkov) in February, where it was used to help stabilize the shattered 2nd Hungarian Army. In July, it fought in Operation Citadel, Hitler's last major offensive in the East. Later, the 320th took part in the retreats on the southern zone, including the battles of Kharkov and Krementschug, and was down to battle group strength by October 1943. By now it had been reorganized as a Type 44 division (with six grenadier battalions). In January 1944, it was officially cited for its conduct in the Battle of Kirovograd, and it continued to perform well in the retreats across the Bug and Dnestr. In August, it was encircled in Bessarabia, Romania (west of the lower Dnieper) and was destroyed, along with most of the 6th Army, on September 2. The commanders of the 320th Infantry Division were Lieutenant General Karl Maderholz (December 15, 1940), Major General/Lieutenant General Georg Postel (December 2, 1942), Colonel/Major General Kurt Röpke (May 26, 1943), Postel (August 20, 1943), and Colonel Otto Schell (July 10, 1944).

A second 320th—this one a Volksgrenadier division—was formed in the Gross-Born Troop Maneuver Area on October 27, 1944, when it absorbed the partially formed 588th Volksgrenadier Division and the remnants of other, shattered units.

It had the old division numbers but only two battalions per grenadier regiment. It first saw action near Krakau, Poland, in January 1945, where it was crushed. At *Kampfgruppe* strength, it fought on in Upper Silesia and in the Carpathians. It was trapped in the Deutsch-Brod pocket in Moravia and surrendered to the Red Army.

The commanders of the 320th Volksgrenadier Division included Major General Ludwig Kirschner (November 1, 1944), Colonel Rold Scherenberg (February 11, 1945), and Colonel/ Major General Emmanuel von Kiliani (February 19, 1945).

Notes and Sources: Postel was promoted to lieutenant general on September 1, 1943. Röpke was promoted to major general on August 1, 1943. Colonel Schell was killed in action on September 2, 1944. General Kirschner was killed in action on February 11, 1945. Kiliani was promoted to major general on April 20, 1945.

Carell 1971: 197; Hartmann: 34; Bernhard H. Holst, personal communication, December 30, 2006, *www.forum.axishistory.com*; Keilig: 169, 214; "Frontnachweiser," 15 December 1944; *Kriegstagebuch des OKW*, Volume III: 1156; Nafziger 2000: 292–93; Tessin, Vol. 9: 138–39; RA: 130; OB 43: 172; OB 44: 238; OB 45: 234–35.

321ST INFANTRY DIVISION

Composition: 588th Infantry Regiment, 589th Infantry Regiment, 590th Infantry Regiment, 321st Artillery Regiment, 321st Reconnaissance Company, 321st Tank Destroyer Battalion, 321st Engineer Battalion, 321st Signal Battalion, 321st Field Replacement Battalion, 321st Divisional Supply Troops

Home Station: Hanover, Wehrkreis XI

Activated on December 16, 1940, in the Brunswick area, the 321st included cadres of three battalions each from the 267th and 295th Infantry Divisions. It was posted at Abbeville and Boulogne, northeastern France, in May 1941. In December 1942, it was sent to Russia and was heavily engaged as part of Army Group Center the following spring. It suffered heavy casualties at Bryansk and Rogatschev in September. By October 1943, the division had practically ceased to exist as a separate entity; part of it was attached to the 110th Infantry

Division and part to the 211th Infantry Division. On November 2, 1943, the 321st Infantry was downgraded to Division Group 321 and was assigned to the 110th Infantry Division; some of its men were transferred to France to form the 352nd Infantry Division at St. Lo.

The commanders of the 321st Infantry Division were Major General/Lieutenant General Ludwig Löweneck (December 15, 1940), Major General Wilhelm Thomas (November 16, 1942), Colonel Ulrich Liss (July 28, 1943), Colonel Karl Sievers (August 22, 1943) and Colonel/Major General Georg Zwade (September 23, 1943).

Notes and Sources: The 321st Division Group was destroyed with Army Group Center in June 1944. Löweneck was promoted to lieutenant general on February 1, 1941. Zwade was promoted to major general on October 1, 1943.

Keilig: 208, 324, 384; *Kriegstagebuch des OKW*, Volume III: 1157; Lexikon; Tessin, Vol. 9: 143–44; RA: 172; OB 43: 172; OB 45: 235.

323RD INFANTRY DIVISION

Composition: 591st Infantry Regiment, 592nd Infantry Regiment, 593rd Infantry Regiment, 323nd Artillery Regiment, 323rd Reconnaissance Company, 323rd Tank Destroyer Battalion, 323rd Engineer Battalion, 323rd Signal Company, 323rd Divisional Supply Troops

Home Station: Konstanz, Wehrkreis XIII

The 323rd Infantry Division (Static) was created in northern Bavaria on November 15, 1940, around cadres from the 62nd and 73rd Infantry Divisions, each of which provided three battalions. It spent the May 1941 to April 1942 in northwestern France. By February, it had received enough men, vehicles and weapons to be upgraded to attack division status. In May 1942, it was sent to the southern sector of the Eastern Front and served there for a year, compiling a respectable combat record in heavy defensive fighting around Voronezh, Kastronoje, and Kursk. It suffered heavy casualties in the Russian winter offensive of 1942–43, and was in remnants by April 1943. In July, it was placed under the operational control of the 26th and 88th Infantry Divisions of Army Group Center. Withdrawn, reformed, and sent back to the southern sector in the fall of 1943, it sustained such heavy losses in the retreat from Kiev that it was decided to downgrade it to Division Group 323. It was assigned to the 88th Infantry Division and was eventually destroyed at Cherkassy.

The 323rd Infantry's commanders included Major General/Lieutenant General Max Mühlmann (November 15, 1940), Colonel/Major General Hans Bergen (January 12, 1942), Major General Viktor Koch (November 5, 1942), Colonel Andreas Nebauer (December 25, 1942), and Lieutenant Colonel/Colonel Ronald Koschella (February 2, 1943).

Notes and Sources: Mühlmann was promoted to lieutenant general on September 1, 1941. Bergen became a major general on October 1, 1941. General Koch was killed in action at Voronezh on December 22, 1942. Colonel Nebauer was killed in action at Svary-Oskol on February 2, 1943.

Keilig: 29, 176, 231; *Kriegstagebuch des OKW*, Volume III: 259, 733; Kursietis: 184; Tessin, Vol. 9: 150–51; OB 43: 173; OB 44: 238; OB 45: 235.

324TH INFANTRY DIVISION

See Infantry Division Hamburg in the next chapter.

325TH INFANTRY DIVISION

See Infantry Division Jutland in the next chapter.

325TH SECURITY DIVISION

Composition (1943): 1st Security Regiment, 5th Security Regiment, 6th Security Regiment, 190th Security Regiment, 325th Artillery Regiment, 325th Fusilier Company, 325th Tank Destroyer Company, 325th Engineer Company, 325th Signal Company, 325th Divisional Supply Troops

Home Station: Paris, France

This unit was organized under the Military Governor of France on August 31, 1942, to occupy Paris and control all Army local defense troops and security forces in the French capital. As such, it was the only security division serving on the Western Front in World War II. In August 1944, the division was placed under the 1st Army, Army Group B, for the defense of the city. At that time it had a strength of 25,000 to 30,000 men, but very few of them were combat troops. Although Hitler ordered it to destroy Paris, the 325th did not do so, because the city's commandant, General of Infantry Dietrich von Choltitz, and divisional commander Lieutenant General Baron Wilhelm von Boineburg-Lengsfeld, deliberately withheld the necessary orders. Most of the men of the 325th Security escaped from Paris before it fell. The division, however, had lost its reason for existing. Its soldiers were distributed among other divisions that had suffered heavy losses in the Normandy fighting. The 325th Security was dissolved on December 17, 1944, although it was not officially disbanded until January 8, 1945.

Baron von Boineburg-Lengsfeld commanded it from May 1, 1943, until it was disbanded.

Notes and Sources: The 190th Security Regiment consisted of the 425th, 541st, and 620th Landschützen Battalions.

Blumenson 1960: 592–93; Richard Brett-Smith, *Hitler's Generals* (1976): 181–82 (hereafter cited as "Brett-Smith"); Tessin, Vol. 9: 156–57; OB 45: 236. Also see Pierre Galante, *Operation Valkyrie: The German Generals' Plot Against Hitler* 1981.

326TH INFANTRY (LATER VOLKSGRENADIER) DIVISION

Composition: 751st Grenadier Regiment, 752nd Grenadier Regiment, 753rd Grenadier Regiment, 326th Artillery Regiment, 326th Mobile Battalion, 326th Tank Destroyer Battalion, 326th Engineer Battalion, 326th Signal Battalion, 326th Field Replacement Battalion, 326th Divisional Supply Troops

Home Station: Bielefeld, Wehrkreis VI

Organized and activated on November 9, 1942, the 326th Infantry Division was formed from elements of Wehrkreise VI, XII, and V, and was hurriedly attached to Army Detachment Felber. It took part in the occupation of Vichy France in

November 1942, following the Allied landings in French North Africa earlier that month. After a brief period of occupation duty on the French Mediterranean coast, it was stationed in the Narbonne area from April 1943 until January 1944, and was then sent to northern France. It gave up most of its motorized vehicles in the summer of 1943, and became a static division. Two of its nine grenadier battalions were made up of unreliable Eastern troops.

On July 22, 1944, it relieved the 2nd Panzer Division on the front line in Normandy but because of its inexperience it was overrun by the British at Caumont later that month. In August, it was trapped in the Falaise Pocket, where elements of the division broke out, but the unit as a whole was smashed. In late August, it was collecting its stragglers in the St. Quentin-Somme River area, but was soon sent to a safer region (Galanta, Hungary), where it was rebuilt as a Volksgrenadier division, in part by absorbing the partially formed 579th Volksgrenadier Division. Its 751st, 752nd, and 753rd Grenadier Regiments became the 1195th, 1196th, and 1197th Grenadier Regiments, respectively, and were reduced from three to two battalions each. Its artillery unit became the 1579th Artillery Regiment, and the 326th Mobile Battalion (a bicycle unit) became the 326th Fusilier Company. The 326th reappeared on the Western Front in the Roer River battles in mid-December, where it helped hold the Hellenthaler Wald against the U.S. V Corps. Later it fought in the Ardennes offensive and was defending in the Eifel area south of St. Vith in January 1945. The following month the 326th was smashed in the Schnee Eifel, where the Americans described it as "dazed" and "disorganized." By March, it was in "tiny remnants," retreating along with the German 7th Army. The remnants of the 326th Volksgrenadier ended up in the Ruhr Pocket, where it surrendered to the Americans in April.

The division's commanders included Lieutenant General Max Dennerlein (November 11, 1942), Lieutenant General Karl Böttcher (May 8, 1943), Lieutenant General Viktor von Drabich-Waechter (June 1, 1943), Colonel Kertsch (August 2, 1944), and Colonel/Major General Dr. Erwin Kaschner, Ph.D. (August 15, 1944).

Notes and Sources: General von Drabich-Waechter was killed in action on August 2, 1944. Kaschner was promoted to major general on January 1, 1945. He was not captured until April 28—more than a week after his division was destroyed.

Blumenson 1960: 225, 294–95, 324, 422–42, 582; Chant, Volume 16; 2133; Cole 1965: 87; Keilig: 74; *Kriegstagebuch des OKW*, Volume II: 1398; Kursietis: 185; Lexikon; MacDonald 1963: 599; MacDonald 1973: 87, 89, 204; "Frontnachweiser," 15 December 1944; Tessin, Vol. 9: 159–60; RA: 102; OB 43: 173; OB 44: 239; OB 45: 236.

327TH INFANTRY DIVISION

Composition: 595th Infantry Regiment, 596th Infantry Regiment, 597th Infantry Regiment, 327th Artillery Regiment, 327th Bicycle Battalion, 327th Tank Destroyer Battalion, 327th Engineer Battalion, 327th Signal Company, 327th Field Replacement Battalion, 327th Divisional Supply Troops

Home Station: Znaim, Wehrkreis XVII

The 327th was formed as a static division in Austria on November 15, 1940, around cadres supplied by the 183rd, 198th and 297th Infantry Divisions, each of which provided two battalions. The troops came from Lower Bavaria, Baden and Wuerttemberg. The 327th was sent to eastern France in the spring of 1941. It spent 1942 at LaRochelle in southwestern France and took part in the occupation of Vichy France in November 1942. In the spring of 1943, it was sent to the central sector of the Russian Front, where it received an influx of vehicles and weapons, and was upgraded to attack division status. After the German defeat at Kursk, it was transferred to the southern sector. Fighting in the Ukraine (including the battles of Kiev and Zhitomir, among others), it suffered such heavy losses that it had to be downgraded to Division Group 327 on November 2. It later became the 694th Grenadier Regiment of the 340th Infantry Division and was destroyed in the Brody Pocket.

Divisional commanders of the 327th Infantry included Major General Wilhelm Rupprecht (November 15, 1940), Major General Theodor Fischer (October 1942), Lieutenant General Rudolf Friedrich (October 10, 1942), and Colonel Walter Lang (August 1943).

Sources: Hartmann: 34; Keilig: 96, 289; *Kriegstagebuch des OKW,* Volume III: 733, 1157; Kursietis: 185; Lexikon; Tessin, Vol. 9: 163–64; RA: 220; OB 43: 173; OB 44b: D99; OB 45: 236–37.

328TH INFANTRY DIVISION

Composition: 547th Infantry Regiment, 548th Infantry Regiment, 549th Infantry Regiment, 328th Artillery Regiment, 328th Reconnaissance Company, 328th Tank Destroyer Ballalion, 328th Engineer Battalion, 328th Signal Battalion, 328th Divisional Supply Troops

Home Station: Siegen, Wehrkreis IX; later Guestrow, Viborg and Schwerin, Wehrkreis II

This unit was formed as "Walkere" division on December 19, 1941. Shortly after being activated, it was sent to Army Group Center on the Eastern Front, where it was divided into three parts. Each infantry regiment was assigned to a different corps in the 3rd Panzer and 9th Armies of Army Group Center during the Soviet winter offensive of 1941–42. Its 547th Infantry Regiment and I/328th Artillery Regiment never returned to the division and were eventually absorbed into the 83rd Infantry Division. The bulk of the 328th Infantry Division was not reunited under its own commander until July or August 1942, but after that was again broken up in the defensive battles of 1942–43. It took heavy casualties near Subzow in October 1942. By November, one of its regiments had been returned to the West, where it took part in the occupation of Vichy France. By December 12, half of the division was in the south of France and half in Russia.

On New Year's Day 1943, only one regiment remained in the Soviet Union, and by the spring of 1943, the 328th had again been reunited in Marseilles, on the Mediterranean coast. Here it was rebuilt and added the 569th Grenadier Regiment (three battalions). Its tank destroyer and reconnaissance battalions, meanwhile, were combined into a single mobile battalion (the 328th Schnelle). The division returned to Russia in the late summer of 1943, and was employed on the southern sector this time. It fought at Kursk, Kharkov and Isjum, and was largely destroyed in the retreats to the Dnieper. It was downgraded to division group status on November 2, 1943, and was attached to the 306th Infantry Division, which absorbed it in July 1944, when Division Group 328 was redesignated 549th Grenadier Regiment. This unit was destroyed in Romania the following month.

Commanders of the 328th Infantry Division included Lieutenant General Albert Fett (December 19, 1941), Major General Wilhelm Behrens (December 30, 1941), Colonel/Major General/Lieutenant General Joachim von Treschow (March 3, 1942), Lieutenant General Karl Böttcher (May 8, 1943), and Treschow (returned May 31, 1943).

Notes and Sources: Treschow was promoted to major general on June 1, 1942, and to lieutenant general on March 1, 1943.

Keilig: 348; *Kriegstagebuch des OKW*, Volume II: 1362, 1368, 1381, 1388, 1390, 1395, 1398; Volume III: 6, 8, 732, 1156; Nafziger 2000: 298–99; Tessin, Vol. 9: 167–68; OB 43: 174; OB 44: 240; OB 45: 237.

328TH INFANTRY DIVISION "SEELAND"

See Infantry Division Seeland in the next chapter.

329TH INFANTRY DIVISION

Composition: 551st Infantry Regiment, 552nd Infantry Regiment, 553rd Infantry Regiment, 329th Artillery Regiment, 329th Reconnaissance Company (later Fusilier Battalion), 329th Tank Destroyer Battalion, 329th Engineer Battalion, 329th Signal Company, 329th Field Replacement Battalion, 329th Divisional Supply Troops

Home Station: Aachen, Wehrkreis VI

Known as the "Hammer Division" because of its unit symbol, this formation was created on December 17, 1941, and spent almost its entire combat career with Army Group North (later Courland) in Russia. It was a composite unit, with infantry regiments coming from Wehrkreis VI, X and XI (Westphalia/Rhineland, Schleswig-Holstein and Brunswick/Anhalt/Hanover, respectively). Its division staff had been Staff, 9th Frontier Guard

Command and the 526th Special Purposes Division. Its infantry regiments had only two battalions each. It arrived in Russia in early 1942, and in April it helped reestablish contact with the II Corps, trapped in the Demyansk encirclement. The 329th continued to fight in the desperate battles around Demyansk and Staraja Russa until the II Corps made good its escape in February 1943. Meanwhile, in January 1942, the division's 553rd Infantry Regiment was encircled at Kholm and was not rescued until the following spring. This regiment was disbanded in 1944 (along with III/329th Artillery Regiment) and was replaced by the 42nd Luftwaffe Field Regiment (Jäger-Regiment 42 [L]). The 329th Division continued to serve on the northern sector in the withdrawal to Courland and was officially cited for distinguished conduct in the retreat through eastern Latvia. It was still in the Courland Pocket when the war ended.

Its commanders included Colonel/Major General Helmut Castore (December 1941), Major General Bruno Hippler (March 7, 1942), Colonel/Major General/Lieutenant General Dr. Johannes Mayer (March 23, 1942), Lieutenant General Paul Winter (August 9, 1943), Mayer (returned in September 1943), Colonel of Reserves/Major General of Reserves Werner Schulze (July 18, 1944), Lieutenant General Konrad Menkel (October 20, 1944), Schulze (January 1, 1945) and Menkel (1945–end).

Notes and Sources: Castorf was promoted to major general on February 1, 1942. Hippler was killed in action near Lake Ilmen on March 23, 1942. Mayer was promoted to major general on April 1, 1942, and to lieutenant general on February 1, 1943. Schulze was promoted to major general of reserves on January 1, 1945.

Carell 1966: 427–38; Carell 1971: 288; Keilig: 219, 222; Mehner, Vol. 12: 455; Tessin, Vol. 9: 172–73; RA: 102; OB 43: 174; OB 45: 237.

330TH INFANTRY DIVISION

Composition: 554th Infantry Regiment, 555th Infantry Regiment, 556th Infantry Regiment, 330th Artillery Regiment, 330th Reconnaissance Battalion, 330th Tank Destroyer Battalion, 330th Engineer Battalion, 330th Signal Battalion, 330th Divisional Supply Troops

Home Station: Augsburg, Wehrkreis VII

Organized in Troop Maneuver Area Wandern, Wehrkreis III, on December 19, 1941, the 330th Infantry was a composite unit, with troops from Wehrkreise II, V, VII, VIII, IX, and XII. Its infantry regiments and its artillery regiment had only two battalions each. It was partially equipped with captured Russian guns. The division was in battle shortly after it was formed because of the crisis on the Eastern Front. In January 1942, it held its positions at Demidov, just north of the Moscow-Smolensk Motor Highway, against strong elements of the 4th Soviet Strike Army. The 330th continued to serve in Russia (mostly under 9th Army) in the heavy defensive fighting around Velish (Welish) in 1942 and 1943. The 556th Grenadier Regiment was disbanded in April 1943, and the reconnaissance and tank destroyer battalions were combined. By October 1943, after the Battle of Orscha, the division was at battle group strength and had ceased to function as a separate combat entity. It was downgraded to Division Group 330 (*Divisiongruppe 330*) on November 2, and its grenadier units were attached to the 342nd Infantry Division in the northern Ukraine. Most of the rest of the unit was attached to the 367th Infantry Division in the Balkans. The II/330th Artillery Regiment was assigned to the 35th Infantry Division.

The 330th Infantry Division's commanders included Lieutenant General Karl Graf (December 17, 1941), Major General/ Lieutenant General Count Edwin von Rothkirck und Trach (January 5, 1942), Colonel Georg Zwade (June 22, 1943), Colonel Wilhelm Falley (September 23, 1943), and Major General Hans Sauerbrey (October 5, 1943).

Notes and Sources: Rothkirck und Trach was promoted to lieutenant general on March 1, 1942.

Carell 1966: 385, 390; Keilig: 285; *Kriegstagebuch des OKW*, Volume III: 1157; Lexikon; Tessin, Vol. 9: 176–77; OB 42: 106–7; OB 43: 174; OB 45: 238.

331st INFANTRY DIVISION

Composition: 557th Infantry Regiment, 558th Infantry Regiment, 559th Infantry Regiment, 331st Artillery Regiment, 331st Reconnaissance Company (later Fusilier Battalion), 331st Tank Destroyer Battalion, 331st Engineer Battalion, 331st Signal Battalion, 331st Divisional Supply Troops

Home Station: Amstetten, Wehrkreis XVII

Formed in Troop Maneuver Area Königsbrück, Silesia, on December 15, 1941, this composite 17th Wave division included soldiers from Dresden (Wehrkreis IV), Pilsen (Wehrkreis XIII) and northern Austria (Wehrkreis XVII). The 331st was sent to Army Group Center in January 1942, where it suffered heavy casualties and where it was almost destroyed. Later it was shifted to Army Group North. It fought on the Russian Front for two years, where it suffered further heavy losses in the defensive fighting around Juchnov, Velish, and Nevel in 1942–43. It was reformed in Germany at the Wahn Troop Maneuver Area in March 1944, where it incorporated the partially trained members of Infantry (Shadow) Division Wahn into its ranks. (Shadow divisions were understrength and lacked heavy weapons and division support troops.) Simultaneously, the 557th Grenadier Regiment, which had been disbanded, was reformed, but with only two battalions, as was typical of the Type 1944 divisions. The 558th and 559th Grenadier Regiments were also reduced to two battalions each.

Transferred to Calais, the 331st returned to action in Normandy, was trapped in and broke out of the Falaise Pocket, and participated in the withdrawal through France. On August 28, while defending south of Paris, it was attacked by the U.S. 1st Army, and "just melted away." The survivors of the 331st were regrouped and sent to Holland, where they were transferred to other units. The 331st Infantry Division was declared dissolved on October 7, 1944. The Staff, however, was redesignated Special Administrative Division Staff 331 and continued to operate in the Netherlands, in the rear of Army Group H, until March 23, 1945, when it was finally disbanded.

Commanders of this division included Lieutenant General Fritz Hengen (December 15, 1941), Colonel/Major General/Lieutenant General Dr. Franz Bayer (December 30, 1941), Colonel/Major General/Lieutenant General Karl Rheim (February 22, 1943), Major General Heinz Furbach (January 1, 1944), Rheim (April 25, 1944), Colonel Walter Steinmüller (August 1, 1944), and Lieutenant General Erich Diestel (October 16, 1944).

Notes and Sources: Dr. Bayer was promoted to major general on January 1, 1942 and to lieutenant general on January 1, 1943. Rhein was promoted to major general on May 1, 1943, and to lieutenant general on November 1, 1943.

Blumenson 1960: 575–79; Harrison: 235, Map VI; Keilig: 23; Kursietis: 186; Lexikon; Nafziger 2000: 299–301; Tessin, Vol. 9: 180–81; RA: 220; OB 43: 174–75; OB 44: 241; OB 45: 238.

332ND INFANTRY DIVISION

Composition: 676th Infantry Regiment, 677th Infantry Regiment, 687th Infantry Regiment, 332nd Artillery Regiment, 332nd Bicycle Battalion, 332nd Tank Destroyer Battalion, 332nd Engineer Battalion, 332nd Signal Company, 332nd Field Replacement Battalion, 332nd Divisional Supply Troops

Home Station: Duss/Dieuze, Wehrkreis VIII

This unit was created as a static division in the Guestrow area on November 15, 1940. Cadre battalions were supplied by the 161st, 162nd, and 168th Infantry Divisions (two battalions each) and the 395th Infantry Division (one battalion). The new division was posted in Normandy in June. It remained in France until March 1943, when it was ordered to the southern sector of the Russian Front following the end of resistance in Stalingrad. (Meanwhile, it was issued the standard infantry division allotment of horse-drawn and motorized vehicles.) En route, however, the 332nd was diverted to the 2nd Army on the southern flank of Army Group Center, which had come under heavy attack.

German tank crewmen pause for a break. The panzer on the left is armed with the famous 88mm gun. HTM ARCHIVE

After helping repulse the Soviet winter offensive of 1942–
43, the 332nd Infantry fought in the Kursk offensive and was
smashed on August 3, 1943, in the Third Battle of Kharkov.
Eight days later, the remnants of the division were placed under
the operational control of the 255th Infantry Division. The
remnants of the 332nd Infantry were sent to Poltava (in the
rear of 4th Panzer Army) in September. Here it was reorganized and the 676th Grenadier Regiment was transferred to the
57th Infantry Division. The rest of the division became Division
Group 332, which included Regimental Group 677 (four companies) and Regimental Group 678 (six companies). Assigned
to Corps Detachment B, it was surrounded and destroyed at
Cherkassy in February 1944. About half of the men escaped,
but virtually all of their equipment was lost, including all of its
vehicles and heavy weapons. The 332nd Division Group was
pulled out of the line and dissolved shortly thereafter.

The commanders of the 332nd Infantry Division were Major
General Heinrich Recke (November 14, 1940), Major General/
Lieutenant General Hans Kessel (August 6, 1941), Colonel Walter Melzer (December 7, 1942), Lieutenant General Hans Schae-
fer (January 1, 1943), and Colonel Adolf Trowitz (June 5, 1943).

Notes and Sources: The 332nd Tank Destroyer Battalion became
the 473rd Army Tank Destroyer Battalion on December 8, 1943.
Kessel was promoted to lieutenant general on November 1, 1942.
Carell 1971: 17, 50; Keilig: 167; Manstein: 431; Nafziger 2000:
301–2; Tessin, Vol. 9: 184–85; RA: 130; OB 43: 175; OB 45: 238;
Ziemke 1966: 149.

333RD INFANTRY DIVISION

Composition: 679th Infantry Regiment, 680th Infantry
Regiment, 681st Infantry Regiment, 333rd Artillery Regiment,
333rd Motorcycle Company, 333rd Tank Destroyer Battalion,
333rd Engineer Battalion, 333rd Signal Company, 333rd Divisional Supply Troops

Home Station: Küstrin; later Schwerin/Warthe, Wehrkreis
III

Formed on November 15, 1941, this static division was organized around cadres supplied by the 76th and 293rd Infantry Divisions. About one-third of each division was sent to the 333rd. It was posted to southwestern France in May and then to Brittany in June. It received the standard infantry division's compliment of horse-drawn and motorized vehicles in October 1942. In early 1943, it was transferred to the southern sector of the Russian Front, where it fought in the Donets and Isjum/ Kharkov battles as a part of 1st Panzer Army; however, by November 2, 1943, it had suffered so many casualties that it was downgraded to Division Group 333. It was assigned to the 294th Infantry Division and was destroyed in Romania in August and September 1944.

Its commanders were Major General/Lieutenant General Rudolf Pitz (November 15, 1940), Colonel/Major General Gerhard Grassmann (December 10, 1942), Major General Rudolf von Tschudi (March 22, 1943), Colonel Wilhelm Crisolli (July 1, 1943), and Major General/Lieutenant General Erwin Menny (July 10, 1943).

Notes and Sources: Pitz was promoted to lieutenant general on February 1, 1942. Grassmann became a major general on March 1, 1943. Menny was promoted to lieutenant general on October 1, 1943.

Keilig: 113; *Kriegstagebuch des OKW*, Volume III: 8, 258, 732, 1156; Lexikon; Tessin, Vol. 9: 188–89; RA: 46; OB 42: 106; OB 43: 175; OB 44b: D101; OB 45: 239.

334TH INFANTRY DIVISION

Composition: 754th Grenadier Regiment, 755th Grenadier Regiment, 756th Mountain Grenadier Regiment, 334th Artillery Regiment, 334th Fusilier Battalion, 334th Tank Destroyer Battalion, 334th Engineer Battalion, 334th Signal Battalion, 334th Field Replacement Battalion, 334th Divisional Supply Troops

Home Station: Fürth, Wehrkreis XIII

This division was formed in the Grafenwöhr Troop Maneuver Area on November 25, 1942, as a composite division; its

754th, 755th, and 756th Regiments were raised in the XIII, XVII, and XVIII Military Districts, respectively. It was hurriedly sent to North Africa in December 1942. The 334th Division fought very well in the battles of the Tunisian Bridgehead but was destroyed when Army Group Afrika collapsed in May 1943.

The 334th Infantry Division was remustered in the Bordeaux region of southern France on June 3, 1943, and was formed in July and August 1943, around cadres supplied by the 71st, 76th, 94th, 305th, 371st, and 389th Infantry Divisions. Its headquarters was the former Staff, 80th Infantry Division. Unlike the original 334th, all three of its grenadier regiments came from Wehrkreis XIII. The new division was transferred to Italy in November 1943, where it fought in all the subsequent campaigns of Army Group C. By May 1944, it was down to battle group strength but remained on the front line despite its casualties and shortages in personnel. The 334th suffered heavy losses in the battles of the Gothic Line and, in September 1944, bore the brunt of the Allied push through the Futa Pass. The next month it was still in action, fighting on the Florence-Bologna Road as a part of XIV Panzer Corps. Finally, in December, it was shifted to the relatively inactive Adriatic sector but was not substantially reinforced or rebuilt. In February 1945, the division was back in the center of action in the defense of Bologna; however, it now numbered fewer than 2,600 combat effectives. It was redesignated a Volksgrenadier division on April 3. The 334th was finally destroyed by the U.S. Army on April 23, 1945, along with the rest of the LI Mountain Corps, in the last Allied offensive on the Italian Front.

Commanders of the original 334th included Colonel/Major General Friedrich Weber (November 15, 1942) and Major General Fritz Krause (April 15, 1943). The commanders of the second 334th Infantry Division were Lieutenant General Heinz Ziegler (May 24, 1943), Lieutenant General Walter Scheller (October 20, 1943), Lieutenant General Helmuth Böhlke (February 1, 1944), and Colonel Schenck (April 16, 1945).

Notes and Sources: Weber was promoted to major general on January 1, 1943. Krause was captured in Tunisia on May 9, 1943.

Although the records do not provide his Christian name, Colonel Schenck was probably Heinz-Walter, the former commander of the 94th Mountain Artillery Regiment.

Fisher: 18, 194, 268, 302, 442, 495–96; Hartmann: 35; Keilig: 363; Mehner, Vol. 12: 455; Scheibert: 319; Tessin, Vol. 9: 193–94; RA: 204; OB 43: 173; OB 45: 239.

335TH INFANTRY DIVISION

Composition: 682nd Infantry Regiment, 683rd Infantry Regiment, 684th Infantry Regiment, 335th Artillery Regiment, 335th Bicycle Battalion, 335th Tank Destroyer Battalion, 335th Engineer Battalion, 335th Signal Battalion, 335th Field Replacement Battalion, 335th Divisional Supply Troops

Home Station: Konstanz, Wehrkreis V

The 335th was formed as a *bodenständige* (static) division on November 20, 1940, but was converted into an attack division in October 1942. Its cadres were provided by the 298th Infantry Division (three battalions), the 197th Infantry Division (two battalions) and the 87th Infantry Division (one battalion). Three weeks after it was formed, it had a total strength of 8,308 men. It was sent to central France (on the Demarcation Line with Vichy France) in the summer of 1941. Here it reached its peak strength of 12,362 men. Transferred to Brittany the following January, the 335th took part in the occupation of Vichy France in November 1942, when it seized Marseilles (France's largest port) without opposition. It was sent to southern Russia in February 1943, and was almost continuously in action for the next year and a half. It fought in the Donets, at Woroschilowgrad, at Kursk, in the subsequent retreats through the Donets, at Stalino, in the Dnieper bend battles, in the Zaporoshje Bridgehead (on the Dnieper), at Nikopol, and on the Bug in Bessarabia. By November 1, 1943, it was down to a strength of 2,490 men, although reinforcements and returning wounded increased this figure to 4,357 by January 11, 1944. The 335th was destroyed at Kishinev, Romania, in August 1944.

Its commanders included Lieutenant General Max Dennerlein (November 15, 1940), Major General/Lieutenant General Karl Casper (October 27, 1942), Colonel/Major General/

Lieutenant General Siegfried Rasp (September 7, 1943), and Colonel Dr. Eugen Franz Brechtel (June 30, 1944).

Notes and Sources: The figures for the strength of the division was based on fighting strength (*Gefechtsstärke*), as opposed to ration strength (*Verpflegungsstärke*). Fighting strength was usually 20 to 25 percent below ration strength. See *www.lexikon-der-wehrmacht.de/ Gliederung.htm* for detailed strength reports of this division from December 11, 1940, to February 1, 1944. Casper was promoted to lieutenant general on July 1, 1943, and was wounded in action on September 7, 1943. Rasp became a major general on November 1, 1943, and a lieutenant general on April 1, 1944.

Hartmann: 35; Keilig: 59, 268; Hans Kissel, *Vom Dnjepr zum Dnjestr* (1970); Lexikon; Tessin, Vol. 9: 197–98; RA: 86; OB 43: 176; OB 44: 243; OB 44b: D102; OB 45: 240.

336TH INFANTRY DIVISION

Composition: 685th Infantry Regiment, 686th Infantry Regiment, 687th Infantry Regiment, 336th Artillery Regiment, 336th Fusilier Battalion, 336th Tank Destroyer Battalion, 336th Engineer Battalion, 336th Signal Company, 336th Field Training Battalion, 336th Divisional Supply Troops

Home Station: Naumburg, Wehrkreis IV

This Saxon unit was built around cadres from three battalions of the 61st Infantry Division and three battalions from the 256th Infantry Division on December 15, 1940. It was posted to Belgium in May 1941, to Le Havre in June, and to Brittany in April 1942. Sent to Russia in May 1942, it fought at Kharkov, and was then attached to the 2nd Hungarian Army, under which it fought at Tschir. Later it served with Army Detachment Hollidt in the unsuccessful attempt to relieve Stalingrad. After fighting on the Mius and at Melitopol, the 336th was sent to the Crimea in November 1943, where it faced the Soviet spring offensive of 1944. It bore the brunt of the Russian attack on the Perekop Isthmus that April; most of the division was lost when the XXXXIX Mountain Corps finally gave way. Major General Rolf Hagemann, the divisional commander, was seriously wounded in the fighting and had to be evacuated by airplane. Most of his division was not so lucky: it retreated into Sevastopol, where it was captured when the city fell. Only a few of its soldiers managed to reach the evacuation points and escape by sea before the Russians captured them. They were later incorporated into the 685th Grenadier Regiment of the 294th Infantry Division, and its surviving staff officers were assigned to the 237th Infantry Division. The 336th was never rebuilt.

The commanders of the division included Major General/ Lieutenant General Johann Stever (December 15, 1940), Major General/Lieutenant General Walther Lucht (March 1, 1942), Major General Wilhelm Kunze (July 1, 1943), Colonel Werner von Bülow (acting commander, August 15, 1943), Kunze (September 1, 1943), and Colonel/Major General Wolf Hagemann (December 8, 1943).

Notes and Sources: Stever was promoted to lieutenant general on June 1, 1941. Lucht was promoted to lieutenant general on November 1, 1942. Colonel von Bülow was missing in action near Obrodnoje, west of Taganrog, on August 30, 1943. Hagemann was promoted to major general on March 1, 1944.

Carell 1966: 649; Carell 1971: 538-39; Keilig: 122, 194, 333; Lexikon; Manstein: 319, 388; Tessin, Vol. 9: 201–2; RA: 72; OB 43: 176; OB 44: 243; OB 45: 240.

337TH INFANTRY (LATER VOLKSGRENADIER) DIVISION

Composition (1941): 688th Infantry Regiment, 689th Infantry Regiment, 690th Infantry Regiment, 337th Artillery Regiment, 337th Reconnaissance Company, 337th Tank Destroyer Battalion, 337th Engineer Battalion, 337th Signal Battalion, 337th Field Replacement Battalion, 337th Divisional Supply Troops

Home Station: Kempten, Wehrkreis VII

Created on November 16, 1940, this static division was organized around three battalions supplied by the 57th Infantry Division and two from the 167th Infantry Division—all from Bavaria. The 337th was on garrison duty in central France from June 1941 until late 1942. During this period it gave up the 689th Infantry Regiment to the 246th Infantry Division on the

Eastern Front and received the independent 313th Infantry Regiment from Wehrkreis XII. In late 1942, the division was transferred to the central sector of the Russian Front and remained there until July 1944. By the fall of 1943, the division was down to an infantry strength of six understrength battalions. In November, however, it absorbed the remnants of the 113rd Infantry Division, which now became Division Group 113; at the same time, the 690th Grenadier Regiment was disbanded. Meanwhile, the 337th Infantry Division fought at Rzhev, the Rzhev withdrawal, Yelnja, Smolensk and Orscha, where it was decimated in the Russian summer offensive of 1944. The division's leader, Lieutenant General Otto Schünemann, became commander of the XXXIX Panzer Corps when General Marlinez was killed. Schünemann himself was killed near Mogilev a few days later, and only remnants of his former division escaped.

The remains of the 337th temporarily became Division Group 337 and were attached to Corps Detachment G. They were reformed in East Prussia as a Volksgrenadier unit on September 15, 1944, absorbing the partially trained recruits of the 570th Grenadier Division. The 337th Volksgrenadier fought in Poland, at Warsaw, on the Vistula, and in East Prussia, at a very much reduced strength. It was virtually destroyed near Danzig in February and was dissolved in West Prussia on April 11, 1945. The survivors were mostly assigned to the 391st Security Division.

Commanders of the 337th Infantry Division included Lieutenant General Karl Spang (November 15, 1940), Major General Kurt Pflieger (May 19, 1941), Lieutenant General Erich Marcks (March 15, 1942), Colonel/Major General/Lieutenant General Otto Schünemann (October 1, 1942), Major General/ Lieutenant General Walter Scheller (November 27, 1942) and Schünemann (February 1, 1944). Lieutenant General Eberhard Kinzel commanded the 337th Volksgrenadier Division.

Notes and Sources: The 690th Grenadier Regiment was dissolved in late 1943. The division absorbed Division Group 113 about the same time.

Carell 1971: 309, 596–97; Keilig: 297; *Kriegstagebuch des OKW*, Volume IV: 1886; Nafziger 2000: 520–21; "Frontnachweiser," 15 December 1944; Tessin, Vol. 9: 205–6; RA: 116; OB 43: 176; OB 45: 241.

338TH INFANTRY DIVISION

Composition: 757th Grenadier Regiment, 758th Grenadier Regiment, 759th Grenadier Regiment, 338th Artillery Regiment, 338th Mobile Battalion, 338th Engineer Battalion, 338th Signal Battalion, 338th Field Replacement Battalion, 338th Divisional Supply Troops

Home Station: Schwerin, later Wismer, Wehrkreis II

This static division was formed the Warthelager Troop Maneuver Area on November 9, 1942, as a Wehrkreis II affiliate, with about one-third of the division sent from Wehrkreis I. Its grenadier regiments had only two battalions and its artillery regiment had only three. Probably for this reason, the High Command gave it the 663rd and 665th Ost Battalions in April 1944. The division garrisoned a sector of the Rhone River delta on the French Mediterranean coast west of Marseilles until the Allies landed in August. The 338th lacked enough transportation to evacuate all its men, even after it commandeered all available French vehicles; it thus suffered considerable losses in the retreat to the German frontier, mostly in terms of men captured. Its 758th Grenadier Regiment was mauled, and the 759th Grenadier Regiment was captured. In September (after fighting at Lyon and Belfort), it had only four grenadier battalions remaining. The following month, it was essentially rebuilt as a Type 1944 division from miscellaneous troops (including the 1433rd Fortress Infantry Battalion, the 52nd Fortress Machine Gun Battalion and the 1015th Landesschützen Battalion) and was sent into action in the Vosges Mountains of southern Alsace. The 338th suffered heavy casualties at Mulhouse but remained in action and was even sent to the Roer sector, where it fought in the Battle of the Linnich Bridgehead and other Rhineland battles. The remnants of the veteran division were forced into the Ruhr Pocket in April 1945, and were destroyed there.

Its commanders were Lieutenant General Joseph Folttmann (November 10, 1942), Lieutenant General Rene de l'Homme de Courbiere (January 5, 1944), Major General Hans Oschmann (September 18, 1944), Colonel Hafner (October 1944), Oschmann (returned October 1944), Colonel of Reserves

Rudolf von Oppen (November 14, 1944), Colonel Konrad Barde (December 29, 1944), and Colonel/Major General Wolf Ewert (January 18, 1945).

Notes and Sources: General Oschmann was killed in action at Montbeliard on November 14, 1944. Ewert was promoted to major general on March 1, 1945, and was captured in the Ruhr Pocket on April 15.

Blumenson 1960: 570, 585; Chant, Volume 14: 1914; Harrison: Map VI; Hartmann: 35–38; Keilig: 150, 247; Lexikon; MacDonald 1973: 167, 370; Nafziger 2000: 521–22; Tessin, Vol. 9: 210–11; RA: 32; OB 45: 241.

339TH INFANTRY DIVISION

Composition: 691st Infantry Regiment, 692nd Infantry Regiment, 693rd Infantry Regiment, 339th Artillery Battalion, 339th Bicycle Squadron, 339th Tank Destroyer Battalion, 339th Engineer Battalion, 339th Signal Battalion, 339th Field Replacement Battalion, 339th Divisional Supply Troops

Home Station: Eisenach, Wehrkreis IX

The 339th Infantry Division was mobilized in Thueringen on December 15, 1940, around the battalions of Fortress Infantry Regiment "A," three battalions from the 52nd Infantry Division, and a battalion from the 299th Infantry Division. It was almost immediately sent to central France, where it remained until the fall of 1941. Transferred to Army Group Center on the Russian Front, the 339th took part in several battles from late 1941 until late 1943, including Vitebsk, Rzhev, and Moscow, the subsequent retreats, and the defensive battles of 1942–43, especially around Bryansk. Already greatly reduced by casualties, the 339th was sent to the southern sector in late 1943. It was smashed at Kiev and, on November 2, 1943, was attached to Corps Detachment C as a division group, even though it was below battle group strength. In July 1944, it was surrounded in the Brody Pocket in Byelorussia (White Russia). It broke out but was no longer an effective combat unit. The High Command ordered it disbanded, and its survivors were assigned to the 183rd Infantry Division.

Its commanders included Major General/Lieutenant General Georg Hewelke (December 15, 1940), Lieutenant General Kurt Pflugradt (January 18, 1942), Colonel/Major General Martin Ronicke (December 8, 1942), and Major General Wolfgang Lange (October 1, 1943).

Notes and Sources: Hewelke was promoted to lieutenant general on December 1, 1941. He was killed in action at Bryansk on January 18, 1942. Ronicke was promoted to major general on March 1, 1943. Wolfgang Lange commanded Corps Detachment C.

Keilig: 282; *Kriegstagebuch des OKW*, Volume II: 1361–62; Volume III: 1157; Seaton: 449; Tessin, Vol. 9: 214–15; OB 43: 176; OB 45: 241–42; also see Wolfgang Lange, *Korpsabteilung C* (1961)

340TH INFANTRY (LATER VOLKSGRENADIER) DIVISION

Composition: 694th Infantry Regiment, 695th Infantry Regiment, 696th Infantry Regiment, 340th Artillery Regiment, 340th Reconnaissance Company, 340th Tank Destroyer Battalion, 340th Engineer Battalion, 340th Signal Company, 340th Divisional Supply Troops

Home Station: Königsberg, Wehrkreis I

Activated in Schleswig on November 16, 1940, one-third of this division came from the 68th Infantry Division, two battalions from the 170th Infantry Division, and one battalion from the 290th Infantry Division. Initially a composite, static division, the 340th Infantry Division was stationed in the Hamburg district (Wehrkreis X) until mid-1941, when it was transferred to the Calais area of France. One year later it was moved again, this time to the southern sector of the Russian Front. The 340th fought in a number of bitter engagements near Kiev (1942), Voronezh (August 1942–January 1943) and Kursk (July 1943), and suffered particularly heavy losses in the withdrawal from Kiev in the autumn of 1943. That fall, it absorbed the remnants of the 337th Infantry Division and the 327th Divisional Group to make good its casualties.

In early February 1944, when the 340th Division held the extreme left flank of Army Group South against a Soviet offensive, it still had a strength of only three infantry and two artillery battalions. Four months later it was encircled at Brody (east of Lwow) and was largely destroyed. The remnants that escaped formed the cadre for a reconstituted 340th, which was designated a Volksgrenadier unit on September 9, 1944. Its ranks were filled by the wholesale absorption of recruits from the partially formed 572nd Grenadier Division. This new force first saw action on the Western Front in November. It fought in the battles east of Aachen before being attached to the I SS Panzer Corps in the latter stages of the Battle of the Bulge, where it took heavy casualties from American counterattacks near Bastogne. It also fought in the Eifel and, in March 1945, the division was retreating toward the interior of southern Germany, in "tiny remnants," according to the U.S. Army's Official History. It was dissolved on April 4, 1945, and its few remaining men incorporated into the 4th RAD Division. Its Staff formed the Headquarters, Division Scharnhorst.

The commanders of the 340th Infantry/Volksgrenadier Division included Major General/Lieutenant General Friedrich Wilhelm von Neumann (November 15, 1940), Colonel Otto Butze (March 1, 1942), Colonel/Major General Viktor Koch (August 26, 1942), Butze (November 1, 1942), Colonel/Major General Josef Prinner (February 24, 1943), Colonel/Major General Werner Ehrig (October 25, 1943), Major General Otto Beutler (June 16, 1944), and Colonel/Major General/Lieutenant General Theodor Tolsdorf (September 1, 1944).

Notes and Sources: Neumann was promoted to lieutenant general on February 1, 1942. Koch was promoted to major general on October 1, 1942. Prinner was promoted to major general on March 1, 1943. Ehring became a major general on January 1, 1944. Otto Beutler was killed in action on July 21, 1944. Tolsdorff was promoted to major general on January 30, 1945 and to lieutenant general on March 16, 1945.

Keilig: 176; *Kriegstagebuch des OKW*, Volume I: 1131, 1138; Volume IV: 1147; Kursietis: 189; MacDonald 1963: 559 and Map VII; MacDonald 1973: 34, 201, 204; Mehner, Vol. 6: 542; Nafziger 2000: 522–23; Tessin, Vol. 9: 218–19; OB 42: 108; OB 43: 176–77; OB 45: 242; Ziemke 1966: 247.

342ND INFANTRY DIVISION

Composition: 697th Infantry Regiment, 698th Infantry Regiment, 699th Infantry Regiment, 342nd Artillery Regiment, 342nd Fusilier Battalion, 342nd Tank Destroyer Battalion, 342nd Engineer Battalion, 342nd Signal Company, 342nd Field Replacement Battalion, 342nd Divisional Supply Troops

Home Station: Landstuhl, Wehrkreis XII

Activated on November 19, 1940, in the Koblenz area, a third of the division came from the 79th Infantry Division and about half of the soldiers were transferred from the 72nd Infantry Division. After serving as an occupation force in France (June–September 1941) and Yugoslavia (October 1941–February 1942), the 342nd was sent to Army Group Center, where it fought in the Rzhev salient, at Spass-Demensk, in the Rzhev withdrawal, and in the retreat from Kursk, among other battles. It distinguished itself against the Russians and was twice officially cited for its conduct in the summer of 1944. Meanwhile, three of its grenadier regiments and the Headquarters, 699th Grenadier Regiment were disbanded due to high casualties. In April 1944, the 342nd was briefly sent back to East Prussia, where it reorganized as a "Type 1944" division. It now included the 697th and 698th Grenadier Regiments (two battalions each) and Division Group 330 (Regimental Groups 554 and 555). Sent back to Russia in May, the division fought at Kovel (May–July 1944), in the retreat across eastern Poland, and at the Baranov Bridgehead on the Vistula. When the Red Army broke out of the bridgehead in January 1945, the 342nd Infantry Division was decimated. It nevertheless remained in action on the Eastern Front as a kampfgruppe until the fall of the Third Reich, ending the war in the Halbe Pocket in eastern Germany. Small remnants of the division did manage to escape and surrender to the Americans at Travemünde.

Its commanders included Major General Rudolf Wagner (November 1940), Lieutenant General Dr. Walter Hinghofer (July 2, 1941), Colonel/Major General Paul Hoffmann (November 1, 1941), Colonel Hans Roth (December 1, 1941), Hoffmann (returned January 1942), Major General Baron Albrecht von Digeon von Monteton (May 10, 1942), Hoffmann (July 9, 1942), Major General/Lieutenant General Albrecht Baier (August 1, 1942), and Colonel/Major General/Lieutenant General Heinrich Nickel (September 25, 1943–end).

Notes and Sources: Paul Hoffmann was promoted to major general on June 1, 1942. Baier was promoted to lieutenant general on January 1, 1943. Nickel was promoted to major general on January 1, 1944, and to lieutenant general on July 1, 1944.

Carell 1971: 309; Keilig: 19, 142, 147, 241; *Kriegstagebuch des OKW,* Volume IV: 1875,1896; Lexikon; Nafziger 2000: 306–7; Tessin, Vol. 9: 225–26; RA: 188; OB 42: 108; OB 43: 177; OB 45: 242.

343RD INFANTRY DIVISION

Composition (1944): 851st Fortress Grenadier Regiment, 852nd Fortress Grenadier Regiment, 898th Fortress Grenadier Regiment, 343rd Artillery Regiment, 343rd Fusilier Battalion, 343rd Tank Destroyer Battalion, 343rd Engineer Battalion, 343rd Signal Battalion, 343rd Divisional Supply Troops

Home Station: Neuhaus/Protectorate; later Jermer, Wehrkreis XIII

The 343rd was mustered in at the Grafenwoehr Troop Maneuver Area in southwestern Germany on October 1, 1942. It was a static division, which meant it had very little organic transportation and was short on all forms of equipment. It was made up of troops from Wehrkreise IV, V, IX, and XIII. Initially it included the 851st and 852nd Fortress Grenadier Regiments (two battalions each), the 343rd Artillery Regiment (two battalions), the 343rd Engineer Battalion, and the 343rd Signal Battalion. Early the next spring, it was sent to France, where it guarded a sector of the Atlantic coast near Brest. In the spring of 1944, it was reorganized and reinforced (see Composition). The 851st Regiment still had only two battalions, but the 852nd was reinforced to four battalions (one of *Ostruppen*) and the 898th Fortress Grenadier Regiment was added. It had previously been the 898th Grenadier Regiment of the 266th Infantry Division and it had four battalions (one of Eastern troops). The 343rd Artillery Regiment also added a III Battalion. In mid-August 1944, when the Allies broke through the Normandy front, the 343rd formed part of the German garrison in the siege of Brest. The survivors of the division surrendered when the city fell on September 19, 1944.

The divisional commanders were Lieutenant General Friedrich Zickwolff (September 28, 1942), Major General Hermann Kruse (August 25, 1943), and Lieutenant General Josef Rauch (February 1, 1944), who was taken prisoner when Brest fell on September 19.

Notes and Sources: Zickwolff was wounded (apparently by partisans) on August 25, 1943, and died on September 17.

Blumenson 1960: 639; Harrison: Map VI; Keilig: 269; Lexikon; Tessin, Vol. 9: 230; RA: 204; OB 45: 243.

344TH INFANTRY (LATER VOLKSGRENADIER) DIVISION

Composition: 854th Fortress Grenadier Regiment, 855th Fortress Grenadier Regiment, 344th Artillery Regiment, 344th Fusilier Battalion, 344th Tank Destroyer Battalion, 344th Engineer Battalion, 344th Signal Battalion, 344th Divisional Supply Troops

Home Station: Mutzig, Wehrkreis V

Created on October 1, 1942, with cadres from the 15th, 17th, 327th, 333rd and 335th Infantry Divisions (all then it France), this division included soldiers from Wehrkreise V, VII, XVII and XVIII (southwestern Germany and Austria). It was initially a small division. Its fortress grenadier regiments had only two battalions each and it only had two artillery battalions. The 344th was assigned to occupation duty near Bordeaux in early 1943. In the fall of that year, it was ordered to defend a sector of the Bay of Biscay from Arcachon to Hendaye against a possible Allied invasion. That spring it was reinforced with the 624th and 629th Cossack Battalions, a third artillery battalion and a signal battalion.

In the summer of 1944, the 344th saw its first action and suffered heavy losses in the Battle of Normandy. In late August, it was covering the retreat of the 5th Panzer Army when it was attacked by large elements of the U.S. 1st Army. The 344th "just melted away," to quote the U.S. Army's Official History, but later rallied and was combined with the battered Panzer Lehr Division to form a temporary battle group. Finally taken out of the line that fall, the survivors were lumped together with miscellaneous troops and remnants of the 275th Infantry and 91st Air Landing Divisions to form the 344th Volksgrenadier Division. In November 1944, it was reorganized to include the 1057th Grenadier Regiment (three battalions), the 1058th Grenadier Regiment (three battalions), the 832nd Grenadier Regiment (two Eastern battalions), the 344th Artillery Regiment (four battalions) and assorted divisional troops, including the 344th Tank Destroyer Battalion. It had no organic artillery, but the 405th *Volksartillerie* Corps (a unit of about regimental strength) was attached to it. Later that month, it fought in the Battle of the Hürtgen Forest and again suffered heavy casualties. In January 1945, it was pulled out of the West Wall and sent to the Eastern Front, where it fought at Krakau, Poland, Oppeln, and Upper Silesia. It ended the war at battle group strength fighting the Red Army south of Berlin, and was surrounded and largely annihilated at Spremberg on April 19. Most of the survivors of the 344th surrendered to the Russians, although at least part of it escaped to the west.

Commanders of the division included Colonel/Major General/Lieutenant General Eugen-Felix Schwalbe (September 27, 1942), Luftwaffe Colonel Erich Walther (September 30, 1944), Colonel Rudolf Goltzsch (October 10, 1944), Colonel/Major General Georg Kossmala (October 16, 1944), Colonel Rolf Scherenberg (February 28, 1945), and Major General/Lieutenant General Erwin Jolasse (March 2, 1945).

Notes and Sources: In November 1944, the combined 344th Infantry Division/275th Infantry Division/91st Air Landing Division was briefly designated the 488th Volksgrenadier Division. Schwalbe was promoted to major general on October 1, 1942, and to lieutenant general on October 1, 1943. Walther was a veteran parachute regimental commander. Kossmala was promoted to major general on January 1, 1945. He was missing in action in the Battle of Oberglogau on February 28, 1945. Jolasse was promoted to lieutenant general on April 20, 1945. When the German Wehrmacht surrendered on May 8, he headed across country with twenty-five men and, after infiltrating through Czech forests and mountains, finally reached western Germany. He was thus among those who escaped Soviet captivity.

Blumenson 1960: 576–77, 579; Keilig: 182, 317; Lexikon; MacDonald 1963; 437, 460; Nafziger 2000: 307, 525–26; Tessin, Vol. 9: 233–34; RA: 86; OB 43: 177; OB 45: 243.

346TH INFANTRY DIVISION

Composition (1945): 857th Grenadier Regiment, 858th Grenadier Regiment, 1018th Grenadier Regiment, 346th Artillery Regiment, 346th Fusilier Battalion, 346th Tank Destroyer Battalion, 346th Engineer Battalion, 346th Signal Battalion, 346th Divisional Supply Troops. The 346th Fusilier and 346th Tank Destroyer Battalion were later combined to form the 346th Mobile Battalion.

Home Station: Friedberg, Wehrkreis IX

This two-regiment, static infantry division was formed in Bad Hersfeld, Wehrkreis IX, under OB West on September 21, 1942. Its men came from five units already stationed in France: the 257th, 304th, 319th, 320th, and 332nd Infantry Divisions. It initially included the 857th Fortress Infantry Regiment (two battalions), 858th Fortress Infantry Regiment (three battalions), and the 346th Artillery Regiment (three battalions), but with very few divisional support units. These were added gradually. The division was sent to France in November 1942, where it added the 630th and 857th *Ost* (Eastern) Battalions. It was on duty in the St. Malo sector of Brittany until the spring of 1944, when it was transferred to Le Havre on the north bank of the Seine. It was quickly thrown into the Normandy fighting, where it took part in the Battle of Caen against the British. By June 13, its companies had only thirty-five to sixty men left apiece. On July 15, only six of the division's anti-tank weapons were still operational. The remnants of the 346th Infantry were in the Battle of the Falaise Pocket, where much of Army Group B was encircled and forced to break out with heavy casualties.

The 346th retreated across France and Belgium and was fighting in the Dordrecht area of Holland that fall, and in October and November it was with the LXVII Infantry Corps in the Battle of the Scheldt. Its strength at this time was 2,400 men and thirty-eight 105mm howitzers. The 346th remained in the Netherlands until the end of the war; however, it seems to have been assigned to relatively inactive sectors from November 1944 on, in part because it was considered burned-out after the Battle of the Scheldt. It was reorganized and partially rebuilt in December 1944, when it received the 762nd Grenadier Regiment (two battalions) from the 70th Infantry Division, as well as a battalion each from the 331st and 344th Infantry Divisions and some replacements from the 16th Luftwaffe Field Division, but lost the 1018th Grenadier Regiment and later the 857th Grenadier Regiment as well. It surrendered to the British at Arnhem on May 9, 1945.

Its commanders were Major General/Lieutenant General Erich Diestel (October 1, 1942), Major General Walter Steinmüller (October 16, 1944) and Colonel/Major General Gerhard Lindner (February 1, 1945).

Notes and Sources: Diestel was promoted to lieutenant general on August 1, 1943. Lindner was promoted to major general on April 20, 1945.

Blumenson 1960: 121; Harrison: Map VI; Keilig: 206; *Kriegstagebuch des OKW*, Volume IV: 1900; Kursietis: 191; MacDonald 1963: 216–17, 220; MacDonald 1973: Map XII; Nafziger 2000: 527–28; Ruge: 184, 225; Tessin, Vol. 9: 240–41; RA: 144; OB 45: 242.

347TH INFANTRY DIVISION

Composition (1942): 860th Grenadier Regiment, 861st Grenadier Regiment, 862nd Grenadier Regiment, 347th Artillery Regiment, 347th Fusilier Battalion, 347th Tank Destroyer Battalion, 347th Engineer Battalion, 347th Signal Battalion, 347th Field Replacement Battalion, 347th Divisional Supply Troops

Home Station: Hanover, Wehrkreis XI

A maintenance crew repairs a German half-track. Note the unit emblem on the side of the vehicle. HTM ARCHIVE

Originally a two-regiment static unit, the 347th Infantry was mobilized on October 3, 1942 and sent to Holland soon after. It initially included the 860th and 861st Fortress Infantry Regiments and the 347th Artillery Regiment (two battalions each). In April 1944, it added the 803rd North Caucasus Infantry Battalion and the 787th Turkestan Infantry Battalion to the 860th and 861st Grenadier Regiments, respectively. The 347th occupied a sector of the Dutch coast opposite Amsterdam until the summer of 1944, when it was sent into battle on the Western Front.

The unit arrived in France just as Army Group B was collapsing. It was caught up the retreat from Normandy and suffered heavy losses at Charleville, at Fort Ymuiden in Lille, France, in the subsequent retreats into Belgium, and in the Siegfried Line battles on the German frontier. A *Kampfgruppe* by September, it was rebuilt in October via the incorporation of replacement and training battalions from the west German cities of Mülheim/Ruhr, Bonn, Duesseldorf, Wiesbaden, Koblenz, Idar-Oberstein, and Detmold into its ranks. These units formerly belonged to the 526th Replacement Division. The 880th Grenadier Regiment was also assigned to the 347th Infantry Division. Each grenadier regiment, however, had only two battalions. In September 1944, the 347th was back in action on the Siegfried Line, where it fought at Schleiden in the Eifel (the German Ardennes). It was later transferred to the Saar sector and was fighting near Saarlautern by January 1945. The division remained on the Western Front until the end of the war. The 347th surrendered in Thueringen on May 8, 1945. Curiously, it was redesignated the 347th Volksgrenadier Division on May 7, 1945—one day before the end of hostilities.

Its commanders were Lieutenant General Friedrich Bayer (September 27, 1942), Lieutenant General Karl Böttcher (October 12, 1943), Lieutenant General Wolf Trierenberg (December 8, 1943), Lieutenant General Maximilian Siry (March 1945), and Trierenberg (April 1945–end).

Notes and Sources: The 347th Artillery Regiment had four battalions by 1944. General Siry was captured on April 10, 1945.

Air University File (SRGG 1192 [c]): Cole 1950: 506; Harrison: Map VI; Hartmann; 38; *Kriegstagebuch des OKW*, Volume II: 1390; MacDonald 1963: 83; Ruge: 184,225; Speidel: 41; Tessin, Vol. 9: 244–45; RA: 32; OB 43: 178; OB 45: 244.

348TH INFANTRY DIVISION

Composition (1942): 863rd Grenadier Regiment, 864th Grenadier Regiment, 348th Artillery Regiment, 348th Fusilier Battalion, 348th Tank Destroyer Battalion, 348th Engineer Battalion, 348th Signal Battalion, 348th Field Replacement Battalion, 348th Divisional Supply Troops

Home Station: St. Avoid, later Saargemuend, Wehrkreis XII

Another two-regiment static division, the 348th Infantry was formed on October 3, 1942, given to 15th Army, and sent to the Dieppe area of France in November. Its cadres came from the 106th, 167th, 304th, 306th, and 321st Infantry Divisions of OB West. Initially it included the 863rd and 864th Fortress Infantry Regiments (later Grenadier Regiments) (three battalions each). In the fall of 1943, the III/863rd Fortress Grenadier Regiment was sent to the Eastern Front. The following spring it was replaced by the 813rd Armenian Infantry Battalion. Meanwhile, the 348th continued to guard the Channel coast until the autumn of 1944, when the Allied armies broke through the Normandy Front, crossed the Seine, and attacked the German 15th Army in the rear. The 348th Infantry was sent to Normandy in August, just in time to be overrun. It suffered such heavy losses in the subsequent fighting retreat that it had to be disbanded. It officially ceased to exist on September 29.

Commanders of the division included Major General/ Lieutenant General Karl Gumbel (September 27, 1942), Colonel Heinrich Satorius (November 1942), Gümbel (returned, November 1942), and Lieutenant General Paul Seyffardt (February 5, 1944).

Notes and Sources: The 346th Tank Destroyer Battalion was used to form the 190th Tank Destroyer Battalion in 1945. Guembel was promoted to lieutenant general on January 1, 1943. Seyffardt was captured at Marbaix during the retreat toward Germany in September 1944.

Blumenson 1960: 597–98; Harrison: Map VI; Keilig: 117; Lexikon; Nafziger 2000: 529; Tessin, Vol. 9: 248; RA: 188; OB 45: 244.

349TH INFANTRY (LATER VOLKSGRENADIER) DIVISION

Composition: 911th Grenadier Regiment, 912th Grenadier Regiment, 913th Grenadier Regiment, 349th Artillery Regiment, 349th Fusilier Company, 349th Tank Destroyer Battalion, 349th Engineer Battalion, 349th Signal Battalion, 349th Field Replacement Battalion, 349th Divisional Supply Troops

Home Station: Lomscha, Wehrkreis I

This unit was formed on October 25, 1943, and was initially assigned to the Calais area of France. On December 14, it absorbed the 217th Infantry Division and reorganized as a Type 44 division. In April 1944, however, it was transferred to the Russian Front, where it arrived just in time to be overrun by the massive Soviet summer offensive. The 349th was encircled at Brody in Belorussia (Byelorussia) in July, along with the rest of General Hauffe's XIII Corps. Divisional commander Lieutenant General Otto Lasch led it in a successful breakout attempt but with heavy losses. Sent to the rear, the 349th was reformed as a Volksgrenadier division in August and September 1944, by absorbing the 567th Volksgrenadier Division. In the process, its grenadier regiments were reduced to only two battalions and its fusiilier battalion was reduced to a company. It was then sent back to the Eastern Front. It was fighting in East Prussia in early 1945, and continued in action there until the end of the war. It was isolated in the Heiligenbeil Pocket in March, when its Staff (250 men) was ordered back to the Reich. It turned its combat elements over to the 21st Infantry Division and proceeded to Jueterbog, where it was ordered to build a field training unit for the recently activated 12th Army. It had just begun this task when the Soviets overran the area and the 349th ceased to exist.

The commanders of the division were Lasch (November 20, 1943) and Colonel/Major General Karl Kötz (September 11, 1944).

Notes and Sources: Koetz was promoted to major general on December 1, 1944.

Keilig: 179; Lexikon; Nafziger 2000: 308; "Frontnachweiser," 15 December 1944; Seaton: 446–49; Tessin, Vol. 9: 251–52; RA: 20; OB 45: 245.

351st INFANTRY DIVISION

Composition: 641st Infantry Regiment, 642nd Infantry Regiment, 643rd Infantry Regiment, 351st Artillery Battery, 351st Reconnaissance Squadron, 351st Divisional Supply Troops

Home Station: Linz (?), Wehrkreis XVII

This static, Landesschützen division was formed in eastern Austria on March 10, 1940, and was dissolved on August 21 of the same year, after the fall of France. Three companies of the division were sent to OB East in Poland in June and the rest of its men were returned to the civilian sector of the economy or were assigned to 16th Army (and later the Military Governor of Belgium and Northern France). The 351st never saw combat.

Its commander was Major General Paul Göldner.

Sources: Keilig: 109; Lexikon; Nafziger 2000: 308; Tessin, Vol. 9: 257; RA: 220; OB 45: 245.

352nd INFANTRY (LATER VOLKSGRENADIER) DIVISION

Composition: 914th Grenadier Regiment, 915th Grenadier Regiment, 916th Grenadier Regiment, 352nd Artillery Regiment, 352nd Fusilier Battalion, 352nd Tank Destroyer Battalion, 352nd Engineer Battalion, 352nd Signal Battalion, 352nd Field Replacement Battalion, 352nd Divisional Supply Troops

Home Station: Northeim, Wehrkreis XI

Formed originally from elements of the 321st Infantry Division (an Eastern Front unit), as well as parts of the 223rd,

275th, and 389th Infantry Divisions, on November 5, 1943, this non-static division was assigned a sector of the eastern Cotentin peninsula in late 1943. On June 6 it was struck by the Allied invasion. Pounded by fierce aerial bombardments and the big guns of the Allied navies, it was attacked by three British and Canadian infantry divisions and two armored brigades, as well as by strong American units at Omaha Beach. By June 7, it was down to battle group strength; however, the 352nd was directly responsible for denying the vital city of Caen to Field Marshal Montgomery on D-Day and thus delayed the collapse of the entire Western Front for several weeks. It also decimated and nearly repulsed the American forces landing on Omaha Beach and significantly delayed the U.S. 1st Army. The survivors of June 6 remained in the line, and by June 24, it had lost 5,407 men. By July 11, it had repulsed several more American attacks, but had lost another 2,479.men. On July 30, 7th Army listed it as no longer fit for combat. In early August, the division's commander was killed and the 352nd had so few men left that it was temporarily absorbed by the 2nd Panzer Division.

It was reconstituted as a separate division later that month, was withdrawn from the Normandy sector, and was rebuilt as a Volksgrenadier unit (with six grenadier battalions) in the Flemsburg area of Schleswig-Holstein area of northern Germany in September. Part of the 352nd was rebuilt at Worms. During this process, it absorbed the 581st Volksgrenadier Division and several *Volkssturm* (Home Guard) battalions. Returned to action on the Western Front, the 352nd fought in the Eifel battles, in the Ardennes offensive, at Trier and Mosel, and in the Rhineland operations south of Remagen. By March 1945, its 914th and 916th Grenadier Regiments had been disbanded. The division was at Darmstadt on April 14, where it absorbed the 805th Replacement Division of the Home Army, and the 914th and 916th Regiments were resurrected. The 352nd Volksgrenadier Division was finally trapped and surrendered to the Americans on April 29, 1945.

The divisional commanders of the 352nd included Lieutenant General Dietrich Kraiss (November 6, 1943), Major General Eberhard von Schuckmann (August 2, 1944), Colonel

Erich-Otto Schmidt (October 6, 1944), Major General Richard Bazing (December 23, 1944), and Major General of Reserves Rudolf von Oppen (February 21, 1945).

Notes and Sources: Kraiss was in command on D-Day. He was mortally wounded near St. Lo on August 2 and died on August 6, 1944.

Blumenson 1960: 247, 442, 570; Chant, Volume 14: 1850; Volume 16: 2133; Cole 1965; 214; Harrison: 334, Map VI; Keilig: 183; Kursietis: 192; Lexikon; Nafziger 2000: 309–10; "Frontnachweiser," 15 December 1944; MacDonald 1973: 286; Hermann Riedel, *Aasen/Schicksal einer Division (352. Volks-Grenadier Division)* (1969); Tessin, Vol. 9: 260-61; *spearhead1944.com/toe1.htm*, accessed November 19, 2006; RA: 172; OB 45: 245. For a detailed description of the 352nd on D-Day, see Paul Carell, *Invasion: They're Coming* (1973) (hereafter cited as "Carell 1973").

353RD INFANTRY (LATER VOLKSGRENADIER) DIVISION

Composition: 941st Grenadier Regiment, 942nd Grenadier Regiment, 943rd Grenadier Regiment, 353rd Artillery Regiment, 353rd Fusilier Battalion, 353rd Tank Destroyer Battalion, 353rd Engineer Battalion, 353rd Signal Battalion, 353rd Field Replacement Battalion, 353rd Divisional Supply Troops

Home Station: Schwerin, Wehrkreis II

Cadres from and the Staff of the veteran 328th Infantry Division (which had been smashed on the Eastern Front) were used to form this division on November 5, 1943. The 306th Infantry Division also contributed two grenadier battalions. The 353rd was organized in Brittany under Headquarters, 7th Army, and was engaged in the Normandy fighting in June 1944. In late July, elements of the much-reduced 353rd attempted to halt the decisive American breakthrough but without success. The 353rd was almost constantly in action for several weeks; in August it was surrounded near Falaise and broke out of the huge pocket with the II Parachute Corps. Perhaps half of the survivors of the division escaped capture. Because of Allied pressure, the 353rd was allowed only a brief respite. It was back at the front in September, controlling a miscellaneous assortment of five local security battalions, an infantry replacement-training regiment, and a Luftwaffe Field unit of battalion strength. It was redesignated a Volksgrenadier division in October. With this composite force, it fought in the battles of the Siegfried Line campaign, including Maastricht, Trier, and Dueren. The 353rd fought in the Roer River battles and was with the LVIII Panzer Corps in the Battle of Cologne in March. By the time it escaped, it was again a burned-out shell. Its survivors finally surrendered to the Americans at the end of the Battle of the Ruhr Pocket.

The 353rd Infantry's commanders included Major General/Lieutenant General Paul Mahlmann (November 20, 1943), Lieutenant General Erich Müller (July 1944), Colonel Thieme (August 1944), Mahlmann (returned August 1944), and Colonel Kurt Hummel (February 15, 1945).

Notes and Sources: Mahlmann was promoted to lieutenant general on June 1, 1944. Colonel Thieme was the commander of the 943rd Grenadier Regiment and senior regimental commander in the division.

Blumenson 1960: 247; 547; Keilig: 215; MacDonald 1963: 70, 330, 583, Map IV; MacDonald 1973: 161, 191; Nafziger 2000: 312; Speidel: 42; Tessin, Vol. 9: 265–66; RA: 32; OB 45: 246.

355TH INFANTRY DIVISION

Composition: 866th Grenadier Regiment, 867th Grenadier Regiment, 868th Grenadier Regiment, 355th Artillery Regiment, 355th Fusilier Battalion, 355th Tank Destroyer Battalion, 355th Engineer Battalion, 355th Signal Battalion, 355th Field Replacement Battalion, 355th Divisional Supply Troops

Home Station: Konstanz, Wehrkreis V

Formed in southern France on May 1, 1943, from the 157th, 165th and 182nd Reserve Divisions (each of which supplied a two-battalion grenadier regiment), this division was sent to the Crimea in July and August. Each grenadier regiment received a III Battalion that summer. The division first saw combat near Kharkov in southern Russia in September of that year. By February 11, 1944, it had suffered such heavy losses during the retreats following the battles of Saporoshje and Krivoy Rog that it had to be downgraded to division group (i.e., regimental) status. It was assigned to (and later absorbed by) the 161st Infantry Division and eventually became the 866th Grenadier Regiment, which continued to serve on the Eastern Front. Its commander for its entire existence as a division was Lieutenant General Dietrich Kraiss.

Sources: Lexikon; Mehner, Vol. 6: 542; Nafziger 2000: 312–13; Tessin, Vol. 9: 271–72; RA: 86; OB 45: 246.

356TH INFANTRY DIVISION

Composition: 869th Grenadier Regiment, 870th Grenadier Regiment, 871st Grenadier Regiment, 356th Artillery Regiment, 356th Fusilier Battalion, 356th Tank Destroyer Battalion, 356th Engineer Battalion, 356th Signal Battalion, 356th Field Replacement Battalion, 356th Divisional Supply Troops

Home Station: Siegen, later Fulda, Wehrkreis IX

This division was created in Toulon, France on May 1, 1943, from reserve formations. Its 869th Grenadier Regiment was the former 252nd (B) Reserve Grenadier Regiment of the 148th Reserve Division; the 870th Grenadier Regiment was the former 214th (B) Reserve Grenadier Regiment of the 159th Reserve Division; and the 871st Grenadier Regiment was the former 15th (B) Reserve Grenadier Regiment of the 189th Reserve Division, which also contributed an artillery battalion. The 356th Engineer Battalion was the former 9th Engineer Replacement Battalion of Wehrkreis IX. Each grenadier regiment had three battalions, but this was reduced to two in late 1943.

The 356th Infantry Division functioned as a training unit until November 1943, when it was transferred to the Italian Front. Not considered a first-rate fighting unit, the division performed coastal defense duties and conducted anti-partisan operations in the Genoa area and along the Italian Riviera until May 1944. At this time the crisis at Anzio forced Field Marshal Kesselring to commit the division to the front line. The 356th Infantry spent the next six months at the front, fighting at Orvieto, Rimini and Triest, before being sent to Hungary in January 1945. By this time, the 869th Grenadier Regiment had been disbanded and the Linz Grenadier Regiment had been attached to the division. The 356th Infantry Division was crushed at Stuhlweisenburg in February and, by April, was in remnants, but it was still in combat as part of the 6th SS Panzer Army in the Battle of Vienna and in the Austrian campaign. The survivors of the division surrendered to the Americans at Wiener-Neustadt in May 1945.

Commanders of the unit included Major General Egon von Neindorff (May 1, 1943), Lieutenant General Faulenbach (May 15, 1943), Colonel Kleinhenz (December 10, 1944), and Colonel Sylvester von Saldern (February 1945).

Notes and Sources: Colonel von Saldern was commander of the 869th Grenadier Regiment in 1944 and, as senior regimental commander, was acting divisional commander in 1945.

Fisher: 19, 302, 419; Harrison: 38–39; Lexikon; Nafziger 2000: 313–14; Scheibert: 312; Tessin, Vol. 9: 275–76; RA: 144; OB 45: 246–47.

357TH INFANTRY DIVISION

Composition: 944th Grenadier Regiment, 945th Grenadier Regiment, 946th Grenadier Regiment, 357th Artillery Regiment, 357th Fusilier Battalion, 357th Tank Destroyer Battalion, 357th Engineer Battalion, 357th Signal Battalion, 357th Divisional Supply Troops

Home Station: Brünn, Wehrkreis XVII

The 357th Infantry Division was activated in the Radom Troop Maneuver Area in Poland on November 11, 1943. Its Staff and several of its battalions were provided by the 327th Infantry Division, with other elements supplied by the 39th, 106th and 52nd Infantry Divisions. It was organized as a Type 44 division (i.e., with six grenadier regiments) and was attached to the 4th Panzer Army on the Eastern Front in April 1944. It was heavily engaged at Kovel, Tarnopol and in the retreat across the northern Ukraine and southern Poland. To replace its losses, it absorbed Infantry Division "Breslau," a shadow division, on August 28, 1944. In September 1944, it was shifted to Slovakia and then the Carpathian sector, where it suffered heavy casualties in October and November. In December, it was sent to the Hungarian sector north of Budapest, where it was again subjected to heavy Soviet attacks. Later, it joined Panzer Corps Feldherrnhalle and ended the war fighting the Russians in the Protectorate. It surrendered at Deutsch-Brod in May 1945.

Its commanders included Lieutenant General Wolfgang von Kluge (December 1, 1943), Major General Curt Eberding (April 1, 1944), Colonel/Major General Norbert Holm (May 10, 1944), Major General/Lieutenant General Joseph Rintelen (September 12, 1944), Colonel Walter Krüger (March 1945), and Rintelen (April 1945–end).

Notes and Sources: Holm was promoted to major general on August 1, 1944. Rintelen became a lieutenant general on March 16, 1945.

Keilig: 87; *Kriegstagebuch des OKW*, Volume I: 1145; Lexikon; Manstein: 526; Mehner, Vol. 12: 455; Nafziger 2000: 314; Seaton: 498; Tessin, Vol. 9: 279–80; OB 45: 247.

358TH INFANTRY DIVISION

Composition: 644th Infantry Regiment, 645th Infantry Regiment, 646th Infantry Regiment, 358th Artillery Battalion, 358th Reconnaissance Squadron, 358th Signal Company, 358th Divisional Supply Troops

Home Station: Görlitz, Wehrkreis VIII

A Landesschuetzen division consisting of older men, this unit was activated in Krakau, Poland, on March 3, 1940, from the Staff, *Oberfeldkommandantur* 540 (Higher Field Administrative Command or OFK 540), a territorial command. It was sent to Flanders just after Belgium and northern France were conquered. It was disbanded on August 8, 1940, after the French surrender in June 1940, and was never involved in combat. Its units became the 654th, 655th, 656th, 657th, 658th, and 658th Landesschuetzen Battalions and were used to guard prisoner of war camps.

Its commander was Colonel/Major General Rudolf Pitz.

A motorized communications vehicle, typical of the kind found in German armored and motorized units. The man with his back to the camera is wearing the black uniform of the panzer troops. Panzer troops and Waffen SS were often mistaken by the Allies because their black uniforms were similar. HITM ARCHIVE

Notes and Sources: Normally, each Landesschützen battalion guarded one POW camp. Pitz was promoted to major general on February 1, 1940.

Keilig: 257; *Kriegstagebuch des OKW*, Volume I: 1124; Nafziger 2000: 315; Tessin, Vol. 9: 283; RA: 130; OB 42: 108; OB 43: 178; OB 45: 247.

359TH INFANTRY DIVISION

Composition: 947th Grenadier Regiment, 948th Grenadier Regiment, 949th Grenadier Regiment, 359th Artillery Regiment, 359th Fusilier Battalion, 359th Tank Destroyer Battalion, 359th Engineer Battalion, 359th Signal Battalion, 359th Field Replacement Battalion, 359th Divisional Supply Troops

Home Station: Landsberg/Wartha, Wehrkreis III

On November 11, 1943, this 21st Wave division was mobilized in Troop Maneuver Area Radom in Poland. Its Staff and many of its soldiers came from the 293rd Infantry Division, which had been decimated on the Eastern Front. Smaller elements came from the 159th Reserve and the 340th Infantry Divisions. A Type 44 division, its grenadier regiments had only two battalions each. The new division was sent to the 4th Panzer Army in southern Russia in early 1944. It defend positions west of Tarnopol against heavy Soviet attacks in April and May and later fought in southern Poland and Upper Silesia. Even though it absorbed the 1134th Grenadier Brigade on September 14, 1944, it was at battle group strength by February 1945. The 359th remained on the Eastern Front until the end of the Third Reich, surrendering to the Soviets at Eulengebirge, in present-day Czechoslovakia, in May 1945.

Its commander throughout its existence was Lieutenant General Karl Arndt.

Notes and Sources: The 359th Infantry Division absorbed the 1134th Grenadier Brigade on September 14, 1944.

Keilig: 13; *Kriegstagebuch des OKW*, Volume I: 1146; Volume IV: 1896; Lexikon; Manstein: 526; Nafziger 2000: 315; Tessin, Vol. 9: 286–87; OB 45: 247.

361ST INFANTRY (LATER VOLKSGRENADIER) DIVISION

Composition: 951st Grenadier Regiment, 952nd Grenadier Regiment, 953rd Grenadier Regiment, 361st Artillery Regiment, 361st Fusilier Battalion, 361st Tank Destroyer Company, 361st Engineer Battalion, 361st Signal Battalion, 361st Field Replacement Battalion, 361st Divisional Supply Troops

Home Station: Herford, later Muenster, Wehrkreis VI

Organized in Denmark in October and November 1943, and activated on November 26, the Staff and many of the soldiers of this division came from the defunct 86th Infantry Division, which had been destroyed on the Eastern Front. The 94th Infantry, 141st Reserve and 137th Infantry Divisions also contributed a battalion each. The 361st Infantry Division had only six grenadier battalions. It was sent to the Russian Front in March 1944, and fought in the Battle of Tarnapol in April. It was badly damaged in the summer of 1944, when it was smashed, along with the rest of Army Group Center. The division was encircled at Brody in White Russia with Hauffe's XIII Corps. Elements of the 361st managed to break out, but most of the division—including its commander, Major General Gerhardt Lindemann—was captured. After retreating into Poland, the remnants of the 361st were withdrawn from the line and sent to Germany to rebuild. The unit incorporated the 569th Volksgrenadier Division and other (smaller) formations into its ranks and by the fall of 1944 had completed its training. The newly designated Volksgrenadier division (as of September 21) fought in the Arnhem battles on the Western Front before being transferred to the Saar sector. After fighting in eastern France, the 361st was posted to the Vosges Mountains, where it absorbed elements of the 553rd Infantry Division before being absorbed itself by the 559th Volksgrenadier Division on March 10, 1945.

Its commanders included Lieutenant General Baron Siegmund von Schleinitz (November 20, 1943), Colonel/Major

General Lindemann (May 30, 1944), and Colonel/Major General Alfred Philippi (September 1, 1944).

Notes and Sources: Lindemann was erroneously reported as killed in action by the German press. He was, however, both wounded and captured. He had been promoted to major general on July 1, 1944. Philippi was promoted to major general on January 1, 1945.

Cole 1950: 311–12; Harrison: 235; *Kriegstagebuch des OKW*, Volume IV: 1891; Kursietis: 194; Lexikon; Nafziger 2000: 315–16; Seaton: 446–49; Tessin, Vol. 9: 292–93; RA: 102; OB 45: 248.

362ND INFANTRY DIVISION

Composition: 954th Grenadier Regiment, 955th Grenadier Regiment, 956th Grenadier Regiment, 362nd Artillery Regiment, 362nd Fusilier Battalion, 362nd Tank Destroyer Battalion, 362nd Engineer Battalion, 362nd Signal Battalion, 362nd Field Replacement Battalion, 326th Divisional Supply Troops

Home Station: Füssen, Wehrkreis VII

This division was formed in the Rimini area of northern Italy in October and November and was activated on November 15, 1943. Its Staff and many of its soldiers came from the recently disbanded 268th Infantry Division, which had fought on the Eastern Front. The 44th, 52nd, 76th, and 305th Infantry Divisions also contributed a battalion or more each. The new Type 44 division was sent to Italy and remained there throughout its career, fighting in all the major campaigns on that front. It first saw action in the Anzio sector in January 1944, and was overrun four months later, when the Allies broke out of the bridgehead. Virtually destroyed at Cisterna near Rome in June, the division was rebuilt that summer, when it absorbed the 1059th and 1060th Grenadier Regiments of the defunct 92nd Infantry Division into its table of organization, and the decimated 954th and 955th Grenadier Regiments were officially disbanded. The 362nd returned to action in the Gothic Line near Florence and was engaged at Bologna in December 1944. The division was finally shattered in the last Allied offensive in Italy. On April 23, 1945, it was encircled near the Po and forced to surrender to the U.S. Army.

Its commanders included Lieutenant General Heinz Greiner (November 1944), Colonel/Major General Max Reinwald (January 1, 1945), Major General Alois Weber (February 1945), and Reinwald (April 17, 1945).

Notes and Sources: The 556th Eastern Battalion became the III/955th Grenadier Regiment in late March 1944, and was destroyed at Anzio. Reinwald was promoted to major general on April 1, 1945.

Blumenson 1969: 361; Fisher: 166, 302, 494, Map III; Heinz Greiner, *Kampf um Roma—Inferno am Po: Der Weg der 362. Infanterie-Division, 1944/45* (1968); Keilig: 272, 363; Mehner, Vol. 12: 455; Tessin, Vol. 9: 297–98; RA: 116; OB 45: 248.

363RD INFANTRY (LATER VOLKSGRENADIER) DIVISION

Composition: 957th Grenadier Regiment, 958th Grenadier Regiment, 959th Grenadier Regiment, 363rd Artillery Regiment, 363rd Fusilier Company (later Battalion), 363rd Tank Destroyer Battalion, 363rd Engineer Battalion, 363rd Signal Battalion, 363rd Divisional Supply Troops

Home Station: Kassel, Wehrkreis IX

Organized in Poland in October and November 1943, from the Staff and surviving elements of the defunct 339rd Infantry Division, as well as a battalion from the 147th Reserve Division and a few other units, the 363rd was officially activated on December 28, 1943. It had six grenadier battalions. It trained in Poland before being sent to the Jutland peninsula of Denmark in March and April 1944. From there it was again transferred in June, this time to Rouen, northern France. The next month it first appeared in combat in Normandy, where it was surrounded at Falaise in August. Only 2,500 of its men escaped in the subsequent breakout. These were sent to St. Quentin on the Somme River for a rest, before being sent on to the Wildflecken Troop Maneuver Area in Germany to reform. Here it merged with the 566th Volksgrenadier Division on September 17 to form the 363rd Volksgrenadier Division. In late September 1944, the 363rd was back in combat, fighting the U.S. 101st Airborne Division near Nijmegen and later the

British in the Arnhem area of Holland. In late November, the division was shifted to the Roer River area and opposed the U.S. 9th Army in the Roer River-Siegfried Line battles. In March 1945, the remnants of the 363rd were part of the 5th Panzer Army, still resisting in the vicinity of Dueren and Cologne. It was destroyed in the Ruhr Pocket in April and surrendered to the Americans.

Lieutenant General Augustus Dettling was the commander of the 363rd throughout its existence.

Notes and Sources: General Dettling was wounded in the Battle of the Falaise Pocket in August 1944, but nevertheless continued to command his division. The 363rd absorbed the 566th Grenadier Division in the fall of 1944.

Blumenson 1960: 296, 552, 582; Keilig: 69; Lexikon; MacDonald 1963: 201–2, 572–73; MacDonald 1973: 155, 190; Nafziger 2000: 317; "Frontnachweiser," 15 December 1944; Tessin, Vol. 9: 300–301; RA: 144; OB 45: 249.

364TH INFANTRY DIVISION

Composition: 971st Grenadier Regiment, 972nd Grenadier Regiment, 973rd Grenadier Regiment, 364th Artillery Regiment, 364th Fusilier Battalion, 364th Tank Destroyer Battalion, 364th Engineer Battalion, 364th Signal Battalion, 364th Field Replacement Battalion, 364th Divisional Supply Troops

Home Station: Wehrkreis V

Formed in Poland in November 1943, this division consisted mainly of the survivors of the 355th Infantry Division, which had been destroyed in Russia. On January 22, 1944, the 364th was itself disbanded. It Staff and most of its personnel were transferred to the 77th Infantry Division, which was then forming in the Muensingen Troop Maneuver Area. Later it was destroyed on the Western Front.

Lieutenant General Walter Poppe commanded the 364th throughout its existence.

Sources: Keilig: 260; Lexikon; Tessin, Vol. 9: 304; RA: 86; OB 45: 249.

365TH INFANTRY DIVISION

Composition: 647th Infantry Regiment, 648th Infantry Regiment, 649th Infantry Regiment, 365th Cannon Battery, 365th Bicycle Squadron, 365th Signal Company, 365th Divisional Supply Troops

Home Station: Esslingen, Wehrkreis V

This division was made up of Landesschuetzen personnel-trained reserve soldiers in the thirty-five to forty-five year old age group. Its Staff was the former Higher Field Area Command Tarnow (OFK Tarnow). It was organized on March 10, 1940, was sent to Poland as a part of OB East later that month, and was disbanded on August 1, 1940, after the fall of France. The Headquarters was not dissolved but was sent to Lemberg (Lwow), Poland, as Higher Field Area Command 365 (*Oberfeldkommandatur 365*, or OFK 365) in late 1940.

Its commander was Major General Konrad Haase.

Notes and Sources: Lemberg, or Lwow (Lvov), is now Lviv, Ukraine. The 365th Artillery Regiment (two battalions) was created on June 24, 1940.

Keilig: 120; Tessin, Vol. 9, 307; RA: 86; OB 42: 30, 102; OB 45: 249; *www.diedeutschewehrmacht.de.*

367TH INFANTRY DIVISION

Composition: 974th Grenadier Regiment, 975th Grenadier Regiment, 976th Grenadier Regiment, 367th Artillery Regiment, 367th Fusilier Battalion, 367th Tank Destroyer Battalion, 367th Engineer Battalion, 367th Signal Battalion, 367th Field Replacement Battalion, 367th Divisional Supply Troops

Home Station: Augsburg, Wehrkreis VII

Formed in the Balkans in October and November 1943, from elements of the disbanded 330th Infantry Division and parts of the 71st and 297th Infantry Divisions, this division had six grenadier battalions. It was sent to Croatia in December and on to the Russian Front in the spring of 1944. Meanwhile, it absorbed a few remnants of the 113th, 137th and 342nd

Infantry Divisions. It was with the II SS Panzer Corps in March and helped rescue the 1st Panzer Army, which had been surrounded in Galicia. The 367th later fought at Brody, Bialystok, Poland, and East Prussia, and was destroyed at the end of the Battle of Köenigsberg on April 8, 1945.

Its commanders were Major General Georg Zwade (November 15, 1943), Colonel/Major General Adolf Fischer (May 10, 1944) and Major General/Lieutenant General Hermann Hähnle (August 1, 1944).

Notes and Sources: Hähnle was promoted to lieutenant general on March 1, 1945.

Carell 1971: 523; Keilig: 122; Lexikon; *Kriegstagebuch des OKW*, Volume IV: 1876, 1897; Nafziger 2000: 318–19; Tessin, Vol. 9: 307; RA: 116; OB 45: 250; Ziemke 1966: 280.

369TH INFANTRY DIVISION (*KROATISCH*)

Composition: 369th Croatian Infantry Regiment, 370th Croatian Infantry Regiment, 369th Croatian Artillery Regiment, 369th Croatian Fusilier Battalion, 369th Croatian Tank Destroyer Battalion, 369th Croatian Engineer Battalion, 369th Croatian Signal Battalion, 369th Croatian Field Replacement Battalion, 369th Divisional Supply Troops

Home Station: Stockerau, Wehrkreis XVII

The 369th, nicknamed the "Devil's Division," consisted mainly of Croatians. Its forerunner, the 369th Croatian (*kroatisch*) Infantry Regiment, had been attached to the 100th Jäger Division and had been destroyed with it at Stalingrad. The new division—staffed by German officers and NCOs—was formed in Troop Maneuver Area Doellersheim on August 21, 1942. It served mainly in Croatia, protecting the Axis lines of communications and constantly fighting Tito's guerrillas and later fighting against the Russians. It also suffered heavy desertion rates. The 369th was down to battle group strength by late 1944, when it absorbed the 1001st and 1012th Fortress Infantry Battalions. It was still operating on the Balkans sector of the Eastern Front when the war ended but managed to surrender to the British in May 1945. Unlike its predecessor, the 369th Croatian Infantry

Regiment, the 369th Division was an unstable and relatively poor combat unit.

The commanders of the 369th Infantry Division (*kroatisch*) were Colonel/Major General/Lieutenant General Fritz Neidholdt (August 21, 1942) and Colonel/Major General/Lieutenant General Georg Reinicke (October 5, 1944-end).

Notes and Sources: Neidholdt was promoted to major general on October 1, 1942, and to lieutenant general on October 1, 1943. Georg Reinicke became a major general on January 1, 1945, and to lieutenant general on May 1, 1945.

Hartmann: 39; Keilig: 239, 272; *Kriegstagebuch des OKW*, Volume IV: 1903; Lexikon; Nafziger 2000: 319–20; Franz Schraml, *Kriegsschauplatz Kroatien: Die deutsch-kroatischen Legionärs-Divisionen-369. 373. 392. Infanterie-Division (kroat.)* (1962); Tessin, Vol. 9: 318; RA: 220; OB 43: 178; OB 45: 250.

370TH INFANTRY DIVISION

Composition: 666th Infantry Regiment, 667th Infantry Regiment, 668th Infantry Regiment, 370th Artillery Regiment, 370th Fusilier Battalion, 370th Tank Destroyer Battalion, 370th Engineer Battalion, 370th Signal Company, 370th Field Replacement Battalion, 370th Divisional Supply Troops

Home Station: Diedenhofen, later Neutitschein, Wehrkreis VIII

The 370th was formed in the Reims area of France on February 17, 1942. Its 666th, 667th, and 668th Infantry Regiments were provided by the 320th, 304th, and 302nd Infantry Divisions, respectively. All were from the 15th Army. The new infantry division was sent to the Russian Front almost as soon as its organization was completed. It fought on the Mius, at Rostov, in the Caucasus campaign, and in the Kuban Bridgehead, before being sent to the lower Dnieper in autumn 1943. The following May it suffered heavy losses in the Dnieper withdrawal, took part in the retreat through the Ukraine, and in August and September 1944, was encircled and destroyed at Kishinev, Romania, with the IV Corps of the 6th Army. The few surviving members of the division were not present at Kishinev. They were absorbed by the 76th and 15th Infantry Divisions.

The commanders of the 370th were Major General Dr. Ernst Klepp (April 1, 1942), Major General/Lieutenant General Fritz Becker (September 15, 1942), Colonel Erich von Bogen (December 15, 1942), Becker (January 20, 1943), Colonel Hermann Böhme (August 2, 1943), Becker (September 7, 1943), and Major General/Lieutenant General Count Botho von Hülsen (June 1, 1944).

Notes and Sources: Becker was promoted to lieutenant general on April 20, 1943. Count von Hülsen was promoted to lieutenant general on July 1, 1944, and was captured at Kishinev.

Keilig: 25, 41; Seaton: 481–84; Tessin, Vol. 9: 321–22; RA: 130; OB 43: 178; OB 45: 250–51.

371st INFANTRY DIVISION

Composition: 669th Infantry Regiment, 670th Infantry Regiment, 671st Infantry Regiment, 371st Artillery Regiment, 371st Reconnaissance Company, 371st Tank Destroyer Battalion, 371st Engineer Battalion, 371st Signal Company, 371st Field Replacement Battalion, 371st Divisional Supply Troops

Home Station: Düsseldorf, later Paderborn, Wehrkreis VI

The 371st Infantry Division was formed in Troop Maneuver Area Beverloo, Belgium, on February 17, 1942, under the supervision of the 15th Army, with cadres from the 306th, 321st, 711th, 716th, and 719th Infantry Divisions. The new division had a full compliment of nine infantry battalions. It completed its training in France in May 1942 and joined the 6th Army on the Eastern Front that summer. With this army it penetrated across the Don and to the Volga in heavy fighting. Involved in the street fighting in Stalingrad, it was encircled with 6th Army in November 1942 and was destroyed when the city fell in January 1943.

A second 371st Infantry was formed in Brittany under 7th Army on March 1, 1943, to replace the division destroyed at Stalingrad. It completed its organization in June 1943, and was sent to Italy and Slovenia in November, and to Croatia in December. A month later, it was transferred to the Russian Front and remained there until the end of the war, fighting at Zhitomir in the Ukraine, in the Hube Pocket, at Brody, in southern Poland, and in Silesia (southeastern Germany). It ended the war in the Deutsch-Brod Pocket east of Prague.

Its commanders were Major General/Lieutenant General Richard Stempel (April 1, 1942), Colonel/Major General/Lieutenant General Hermann Johannes Niehoff (April 1, 1943), Colonel Hans-Joachim Baurmeister (June 10, 1944), Niehoff (returned July 10, 1944), and Colonel/Major General Rold Scherenberg (March 2, 1945).

Notes and Sources: Stempel was promoted to lieutenant general on December 1, 1942. He was wounded and captured at Stalingrad on January 26, 1943, and died in Soviet captivity later that day. Niehoff was promoted to major general on June 1, 1943, and to lieutenant general on April 1, 1944. Scherenberg was promoted to major general on April 20, 1945.

Keilig: 242, 332; *Kriegstagebuch des OKW*, Volume I: 1146; Volume IV: 1875, 1896; Mellenthin 1956: 225; Tessin, Vol. 10: 1–2; RA: 102; OB 43: 179; OB 45: 251.

372ND INFANTRY DIVISION

Composition: 650th Infantry Regiment, 651st Infantry Regiment, 652nd Infantry Regiment, 372nd Field Cannon Battery, 372nd Bicycle Squadron, 372nd Tank Destroyer Company, 372nd Signal Company, 372nd Divisional Supply Troops

Home Station: Weissenfels, Wehrkreis IV

The 372nd Infantry Division was organized in the Radom Troop Maneuver Area, Poland, from Landwehr (older) personnel and from several Landesschützen battalions on March 20, 1940. The 372nd spent its entire existence in Poland. It was dissolved on August 20, 1940, after the fall of France. Its Staff became Higher Field Area Command 372 and was sent to Kielce, Poland, where it came under the supervision of the General Gouvernement. Its infantry components became the 984th, 985th, 986th, 987th, 988th, and 989th Landesschützen Battalions.

Sources: Lexikon; Nafziger 2000: 321; Tessin, Vol. 10: 5; RA: 72; OB 42: 30, 108; OB 45: 251.

373RD INFANTRY DIVISION (*KROATISCH*)

Composition: 383rd Grenadier Regiment, 384th Grenadier Regiment, 373rd Artillery Regiment, 373rd Reconnaissance (later Bicycle) Battalion, 373rd Tank Destroyer Battalion, 373rd Engineer Battalion, 373rd Signal Battalion, 373rd Field Replacement Battalion, 373rd Divisional Supply Troops

Home Station: Stockerau, Wehrkreis XVII

A Croatian (*kroatisch*) division led by German cadres, this force was organized on January 6, 1943 and spent most of its career fighting Tito's guerrillas in Yugoslavia. It was a fourth-rate combat unit that suffered excessive rates of desertion throughout its existence. The 373rd (which had six grenadier battalions) saw action against the Russians in the last few months of the war. Most of its men ended up in Yugoslav captivity and were subsequently murdered.

Its commanders included Major General/Lieutenant General Emil Zellner (December 1, 1942), Lieutenant General Eduard Aldrian (August 5, 1943), and Colonel/Major General Hans Gravenstein (October 20, 1944).

Notes and Sources: The 373rd was built around the Croatian 7th Mountain Brigade (four battalions). Zellner was promoted to major general on April 1, 1943. Gravenstein was promoted to major general on January 1, 1945. He was hanged by the Yugoslavs in 1947.

Hartmann: 39; Keilig: 114, 380; *Kriegstagebuch des OKW*, Volume I: 1145; Kursietis: 196; Lexikon; Nafziger 2000: 322; Tessin, Vol. 10: 8; RA.220; OB 45: 251–52.

376TH INFANTRY DIVISION

Composition: 672nd Infantry Regiment, 673rd Infantry Regiment, 767th Infantry Regiment, 376th Artillery Regiment, 376th Reconnaissance Battalion, 376th Tank Destroyer Battalion, 376th Engineer Battalion, 376th Signal Battalion, 376th Field Replacement Battalion, 376th Divisional Supply Troops

Home Station: Kempten, Wehrkreis VII

Formed on March 21, 1942, near Angouleme in southwestern France, its 672nd Infantry Regiment was formed from men from the 337th Infantry Division, the men of the 673rd Infantry Regiment came from the 335th Infantry Division, and the soldiers of the 767th were veterans of the 327th Infantry Division. Each division also supplied at least one artillery battalion. The new division first saw action in the drive on Stalingrad, fighting near Kharkov, in the clearing of the Don Bend, in the drive to the Volga and in the subsequent street fighting, which the Germans called "the war of the rats." Surrounded in the city, its commander—Lieutenant General Alexander Edler von Daniels—surrendered it to the Russians without 6th Army's approval in late January 1943. Almost all of its men died in the Battle of Stalingrad or later in Siberian prison camps.

The second 376th Infantry Division was created in Holland on February 17, 1943. It took several months to bring it up to strength. Its artillery regiment had only three battalions, and they were equipped with captured Russian guns. Finally ready in November 1943, it was sent to Russia, where it fought in the Battle of Kirovograd and in the Dnieper and Dnestr campaigns. By January 1944, its 767th Grenadier Regiment had suffered so many casualties that it had to be disbanded, and its other two grenadier regiments had been reduced to two battalions. Meanwhile, however, it had been given Division Group 167 (the former 167th Infantry Division), with the 315th and 331st Regimental Groups. The 376th was encircled during the Romanian withdrawal and destroyed at Jassy, along with the rest of IV Corps and most of the rebuilt 6th Army. The remnants of the division—men returning from hospitals or from leave—were transferred to the 76th or 15th Infantry Divisions.

The commanders of this division included von Daniels (March 1942–January 1943), Colonel Hans Kissel (February 17, 1943), Lieutenant General Arnold Szelinski (April 1, 1943), and Colonel/Major General/Lieutenant General Otto Schwarz (December 11, 1943).

Notes and Sources: Division Group 167 was redesignated the 694th Grenadier Regiment on July 20, 1944. Daniels was the only commander the original 376th Infantry Division ever had. General Szelinski was killed in the Battle of Krementschug on December 9, 1943. The division was led by its senior regimental commander until

December 11, when Otto Schwarz arrived. He was promoted to major general on February 1, 1944, and to lieutenant general on August 1, 1944. He was captured in Romania and was a Soviet prisoner until 1955.

Keilig: 318, 341; Hartmann: 39; Lexikon; Mehner, Vol. 6: 542; Nafziger 2000: 323–24; Seaton: 481–84; Tessin, Vol. 10: 15–16; OB 43: 179; OB 45: 252.

377TH INFANTRY DIVISION

Composition: 768th Infantry Regiment, 769th Infantry Regiment, 770th Infantry Regiment, 377th Artillery Regiment, 377th Mobile Battalion, 377th Engineer Battalion, 377th Signal Battalion, 377th Divisional Supply Troops

Home Station: Aschaffenburg, Wehrkreis IX

Created at Le Mans, France on March 31, 1942, under the direction of the 7th Army, this division included one regiment (the 768th) from the 332nd Infantry Division, another (the 769th) from the 333rd, and one infantry battalion each from the 708th, 709th, and 715th Infantry Divisions. The new division was sent to the southern—and later the central—sector of the Russian Front that summer. It fought at Kursk and Voronezh in 1942, and suffered heavy casualties in the Stalingrad campaign and the subsequent retreats and defensive battles that five of its nine grenadier battalions had been destroyed or absorbed by other elements of the 377th Infantry Division. By the end of February 1943, the remnants of the 377th were under the operational control of the 340th Infantry Division. Remaining in action, it was largely destroyed by the Soviets during the retreat across central Russia in the spring of 1944. Its survivors were absorbed by the 340th Infantry Division.

Its commanders were Major General Erich Baessler (April 1, 1942), Lieutenant General Adolf Lechner (December 14, 1942), and Lieutenant General Adolf Sinzenger (January 29 to February 25, 1943).

Notes and Sources: General Lechner was reported as missing in action near Voronezh on January 29, 1943. He has not been heard from since.

A motorized 20mm light anti-aircraft gun, mounted on a half-track. Most anti-aircraft units belonged to the Luftwaffe, although the army had a number of Fla and Flak units. They were mainly used to provide protection for panzer and panzer grenadier units. HITM ARCHIVE

Keilig: 199, 325; *Kriegstagebuch des OKW*: Volume III: 733; Kursietis: 197; Nafziger 2000: 324–25; Tessin, Vol. 10: 19–20; RA: 144; OB 43: 179; OB 45: 252.

379TH INFANTRY DIVISION

Composition: 653rd Infantry Regiment, 654th Infantry Regiment, 655th Infantry Regiment, 379th Artillery Battery, 379th Bicycle Squadron, 379th Signal Company, 379th Divisional Supply Troops

Home Station: Frankfurt/Main (?), Wehrkreis IX

Created from Landesschützen personnel on March 15, 1940, this unit was a line-of-communications division, made up of older reservists. It was formed in Lublin, Poland, from the Special Purposes Administrative Staff 424. A sizable number of the men of this division were sent back to Hesse and discharged. On August 15, 1940, the division was formally dissolved, and its headquarters became Higher Field Area Command 379 (OFK 379). It remained in Lublin. Its infantry battalions became the 617th, 619th, 620th, 621st, 622nd, 623rd, 624th, 636th, 637th, and 638th Landesschützen Battalions.

The commanders of the 379th Infantry Division were Major General Ludwig Müller (March 1940) and Major General Wilhelm von Altrock (May 28, 1940).

Sources: Keilig: 10; Kursietis: 197; Nafziger 2000: 325–26; Tessin, Vol. 10: 23; RA: 144; OB 42: 30,108; OB 45: 253.

381ST FIELD TRAINING DIVISION

Composition: 381st Motorized Infantry Field Training Regiment, 614th Infantry Field Training Regiment, 615th Infantry Field Training Regiment, 616th Infantry Field Training Regiment

Home Station: Salzburg, Wehrkreis XVIII

The 381st was formed in southern Russia, behind the front of Army Group A, on September 8, 1942, and was considered to be solely the property of Army Group A. Field training divisions—unlike other divisions—were not transferred between army groups except in extremely rare cases; instead, they remained under a single army group headquarters throughout their existence. They generally did not have artillery units or much in the way of divisional support troops. Its Staff was supplied by Wehrkreis XVIII, with units provided by Wehrkreise V, VI, VII, VIII, and XIII, and the Reich Labor Service (RAD). The 381st was engaged in training personnel in the rear areas of southern Russia until February 26, 1943, when it was disbanded, and its men were disturbed among the units of the 17th Army. The men of the 381st Motorized Training Regiment were sent to the 13th Panzer and 101st Jäger Divisions; the soldiers of the 615th Regiment went to the 336th and 98th Infantry Divisions; and the veterans of the 616th Regiment were transferred to the 9th Infantry and 97th Jäger Divisions. The 614th Training Regiment had already been dissolved. The Staff of the 381st Division was sent to the Crimea, where it was disbanded on August 10, 1943.

Major General Helmuth Eisenstuck commanded it throughout its existence.

Sources: Keilig: 81; *Kriegstagebuch des OKW*, Volume II: 1385; Lexikon; Nafziger 2000: 575; Tessin, Vol. 10: 27; OB 45: 254.

382ND FIELD TRAINING DIVISION

Composition: 617th Infantry Field Training Regiment, 618th Infantry Field Training Regiment, 619th Infantry Field Training Regiment, 620th Infantry Field Training Regiment

Home Station: Eschwege, Wehrkreis IX

Formed in the rear area of Army Group B the Eastern Front on September 9, 1942, the 382nd was the property of Army Group B during the Stalingrad campaign. Its Staff came from Wehrkreis IX, with troops provided by Wehrkreise III, IV, IX, XII, and XVII, and the RAD. It conducted training of soldiers en route to other units in Russia and possibly took part in some anti-partisan operations. Meanwhile, the destruction of the German 6th Army at Stalingrad, coupled with massive

Soviet attacks, brought the Eastern Front to the verge of collapse. Every German reserve—including the training units—were thrown into the fray. The 620th Field Training Regiment was sent to Army Detachment Fretter-Pico as a grenadier (i.e., combat) unit on January 24, 1943. The 618th Regiment was sent to the 2nd Army shortly thereafter, while the rest of the division was committed to the zone of the Italian 8th Army. After a few weeks in combat, the 382nd Field Training Division was declared dissolved on February 25, 1943. Its extant units were absorbed by the 213th Security Division, except for the 620th Regiment, which remained with Fretter-Pico.

Major General Paul Hoffmann commanded the 382nd throughout its existence.

Notes and Sources: In January 1943, part of the 620th Field Training Regiment became Army Battalion Fretter-Pico. The following month, the rest of the regiment was absorbed by the 304th Infantry Division. The headquarters became Staff, 620th Security Regiment.

Keilig: 147; *Kriegstagebuch des OKW*, Volume II: 1385; Volume III: 5; Lexikon; Nafziger 2000: 575; Tessin, Vol. 10: 29; Seaton: 347; OB 45: 254.

383RD INFANTRY DIVISION

Composition: 531st Infantry Regiment, 532nd Infantry Regiment, 533rd Infantry Regiment, 383rd Artillery Regiment, 383rd Fusilier Battalion, 383rd Tank Destroyer Battalion, 383rd Engineer Battalion, 383rd Signal Battalion, 383rd Field Replacement Battalion, 383rd Divisional Supply Troops

Home Station: Königsberg, Wehrkreis I

The 383rd Infantry was a composite unit, organized at Troop Maneuver Area Arys on January 26, 1942. Its infantry regiments (in numerical order) came from Königsberg (Wehrkreis I), Stettin (Wehrkreis II), and Berlin (Wehrkreis III). The 383rd was a *Rheingold* (Rhine Gold) division, hastily assembled to help alleviate the crisis on the Eastern Front. It was sent to Russia in several trains from April to June 1942. Initially with Army Group South, then B, and finally Center, the division was continuously and often heavily engaged throughout its existence. It fought at Voronezh in the early stages of the Stalingrad advance and against the massive but unsuccessful attacks the Soviets hurled at the 2nd Panzer Army in early 1943. Later it fought at Bryansk, Mogilev, and Bobruisk (1943–44). It was reorganized as a Type 44 division on September 30, 1943, when each of its grenadier regiments lost a battalion; in addition, with reconnaissance and tank destroyer battalions were combined to form the 383rd Mobile Battalion, which had two tank destroyer companies and a bicycle company. The 383rd Infantry Division was destroyed, along with most of the rest of Army Group Center, in the Russian summer offensive of 1944, being overwhelmed at Bobruisk on June 28.

Its commanders included Lieutenant General Johann Haarde (January 26, 1942), Colonel/Major General Eberhard Fabrice (February 20, 1942), Colonel/Major General/Lieutenant General Richard John (September 27, 1942), Colonel/Major General/Lieutenant General Edmund Hoffmeister (July 1, 1943), and Lieutenant General Adolf Hamann (June 20, 1944).

Notes and Sources: Fabrice was promoted to major general on March 1, 1942. John was promoted to major general on November 1, 1942 and to lieutenant general on May 1, 1943. Hoffmeister was promoted to major general on September 1, 1943 and to lieutenant general on March 1,1944. Hamann was simultaneously division commander and commandant of Fortified Place Bobruisk. Captured on June 28, he was hanged by the Soviets on December 30, 1945.

Keilig: 159; *Kriegstagebuch des OKW*, Volume II: 1379, 1387; Volume III: 259; Mehner, Vol. 4: 381; Nafziger 2000: 326; Tessin, Vol. 10: 31; OB 45: 254. See Seaton for the story of the Russian attacks on 2nd Army in early 1943.

384TH INFANTRY DIVISION

Composition: 534th Infantry Regiment, 535th Infantry Regiment, 536th Infantry Regiment, 384th Artillery Regiment, 384th Reconnaissance Battalion, 384th Tank Destroyer Battalion, 384th Engineer Battalion, 384th Signal Battalion, 384th Field Replacement Battalion, 384th Divisional Supply Troops

Home Station: Döbeln, Wehrkreis IV

Formed on January 10, 1942, the 384th was another "Rhein-gold" or composite division. It was formed in the Troop Maneuver Area Koenigsbrueck. The 534th Infantry Regiment was from Dresden (Wehrkreis IV), the 535th was from Breslau (Wehrkreis VIII), and the 536th Regiment was from Vienna (Wehrkreis XVII). Each of these three Wehrkreise contributed an artillery battalion. The 384th sent to the southern sector of the Russian Front in April 1942. It fought in the Battles of Kharkov and Isjum as part of the III Panzer Corps, 1st Panzer Army, before departing for the Stalingrad area. Here its combat units were surrounded in the Russian offensive of November 1942, but the headquarters of the 384th were located to the west of the main Soviet thrust and thus escaped encirclement. Within the pocket, half of the division's combat troops were attached to the 44th Infantry Division and the other half to the 376th Infantry Division, both of which were destroyed, along with the rest of the 6th Army, in late January 1943. Meanwhile, the divisional HQ controlled miscellaneous formations and combat groups under the 4th Panzer Army and later Group Meith (later IV Corps) of Army Detachment Hollidt.

After Stalingrad fell the divisional headquarters was sent to northern France, where it began forming a new division with its old regimental numbers but with only two grenadier battalions per grenadier regiment. In late 1943 the 384th Infantry returned to southern Russia and was involved in the Dnieper bend battles, the Battle of Krivoy Rog (October 1943), in the Nikopol Bridgehead (November 1943–February 1944), at Uman (March 1944) and in the retreat to the Bug. It was encircled at Kishinev, Romania, west of the lower Dnestr, and was destroyed there in autumn 1944. The remnants of the division were absorbed by the 76th and 15th Infantry Divisions in Hungary.

Its commanders were Colonel/Major General Kurt Hoffmann (January 10, 1942), Lieutenant General Baron Eccard von Gablenz (February 13, 1942), Colonel Hans Doerr (January 16, 1943), and Colonel/Major General/Lieutenant General Hans de Salengre-Drabbe (February 24, 1943).

Notes and Sources: Hoffmann was promoted to major general on February 1, 1942. Salengre-Drabbe was promoted to major general on May 1, 1943, and to lieutenant general on January 1, 1944. He was killed in action east of the Pruth on August 25, 1944.

Carell 1966: 490; Hartmann: 14, Keilig: 290; *Kriegstagebuch des OKW*, Volume II: 1393; Volume III: 4; Lexikon; Tessin, Vol. 10: 34; OB 43: 180; OB 45: 254.

385TH INFANTRY DIVISION

Composition: 537th Infantry Regiment, 538th Infantry Regiment, 539th Infantry Regiment, 385th Artillery Regiment, 385th Cavalry Squadron, 385th Tank Destroyer Battalion, 385th Engineer Battalion, 385th Signal Battalion, 385th Divisional Supply Troops (including the 6th Supply Troops Replacement Battalion)

Home Station: Namur, Wehrkreis VI

Activated in the Bergen Troop Maneuver Area (Wehrkreis XI) on January 10, 1942, the 385th Infantry Division was a composite (Rhine Gold) unit. Its 537th Infantry Regiment was from Muenster (Wehrkreis VI), the 538th was from Hanover (Wehrkreis XI), and the 539th Infantry Regiment was from Hamburg (Wehrkreis X). Each of the three Wehrkreise contributed an artillery battalion to the 385th Artillery Regiment. The division was sent to Russia in early spring 1942. It never fought as a united division. One-third of it was sent to Army Group North, and the rest went to the southern flank of Army Group Center. The units on the northern sector of the Eastern Front were under the direct control of L Corps but were eventually attached to the 24th Infantry Division. The southern elements fought at Jucknov, Kursk and Voronezh, and then were sent to the aid of the 8th Italian Army when it collapsed during the encirclement of Stalingrad. These elements suffered heavy losses in the Don Bend (Donbogen) battles, and in the retreat from the Volga and Don. The Army High Command decided to disband the division on February 17, 1943, as a result of these casualties. The process was finished by the end of March. Its remnants were absorbed by the 387th Infantry Division.

The commanders of the division were Colonel/Major General Karl Eibl (January 7, 1942) and Colonel/Major General Eberhard von Schuckmann (December 18, 1942).

Notes and Sources: Eibl was promoted to major general on April 1, 1942.

Keilig: 314; *Kriegstagebuch des OKW,* Volume II: 1358, 1367, 1370, 1389; Volume III: 5, 258; Lexikon; Tessin, Vol. 10: 38–39; RA: 102; OB 43: 180; OB 45: 254.

386TH INFANTRY DIVISION

Composition (1940): 659th Infantry Regiment, 660th Infantry Regiment, 661st Infantry Regiment, 386th Artillery Battery, 386th Reconnaissance Squadron, 386th Signal Company, 386th Divisional Supply Troops

Home Station: Cottbus, Wehrkreis III

The 386th Infantry made up of older reservists. It was formed in Poland on April 1, 1940, under Headquarters, OB East. Its Staff was the former Headquarters, OFK 530 in Warsaw. It was transferred to Germany while the first-line Wehrmacht divisions overran France and was disbanded on August 8, 1940. Its infantry battalions eventually became the 343rd, 344th, 345th, 346th, 347th, 348th, and 349th Landesschützen Battalions.

See also 386th Motorized Division (Volume Three).

Sources: Lexikon, Nafziger 2000: 328; Tessin, Vol. 10: 42; RA: 102; OB 42: 109; OB 43: 180; OB 44b: D-109; OB 45: 254.

387TH INFANTRY DIVISION

Composition (1942): 541st Infantry Regiment, 542nd Infantry Regiment, 543rd Infantry Regiment, 387th Artillery Regiment, 387th Fusilier Battalion, 387th Tank Destroyer Battalion, 387th Engineer Battalion, 387th Signal Battalion, 387th Divisional Supply Troops (including the 7th Motorcycle Replacement Battalion)

Home Station: Munich, Wehrkreis VII

Nicknamed the "Rheingold Division," this force was created on February 1, 1942, in Troop Maneuver Area Doellersheim in Austria. Typical of the early 1942 composite divisions of Wave 18, which were hurriedly raised due to the crisis on the Eastern Front, its units did not come from one region. The 541st Infantry Regiment was a Württemberger unit raised in Stuttgart, Wehrkreis V; the Bavarian 542nd Infantry Regiment was formed in Munich, Wehrkreis VII; the Austria 543rd Infantry Regiment originated from Salzburg, Wehrkreis XVIII; and the 387th Artillery Regiment had battalions from all three Wehrkreise.

The 387th Infantry Division was sent to the southern sector of the Russian Front shortly after it was formed. It was continuously and frequently heavily engaged in fighting on the Eastern Front from the summer of 1942 until May 1944. The 387th Infantry took part in the fighting around Kursk (April–June 1942), in the Battle of Voronezh (July–August) and the drive to the Volga. It was attached to the 2nd Hungarian Army and then the 8th Italian Army in the Don Bend battles (December 1942–January 1943), where it suffered heavy casualties, was reduced to *Kampfgruppe* strength, and temporarily ceased to exist as a separate division. Pulled out of the line in March, it was rebuilt at Krementschug and was back in action in May, opposing the Soviet drive through the Donets. It also fought at Isjum (August–September), Krivoy Rog (October–December) and in the Nikopol Bridgehead (January–February 1944). Considered burned out, the 387th was withdrawn from the line in the February 1944, and was downgraded to Division Group 387 in March. Assigned to the 258th Infantry Division until August 1944, it was destroyed in Romania. Meanwhile, on June 15, the division headquarters became Staff, 98th Infantry Division.

Commanders of the division included Lieutenant General Arno Jahr (February 1, 1942), Colonel Kurt Gerok (January 21, 1943), Colonel/Major General Eberhard von Schuckmann (February 15, 1943), Major General Erwin Menny (May 6, 1943), Schuckmann (returned July 10, 1943), Colonel Werner Eichstädt (October 13, 1943), and Schuckmann (December 24, 1943–end).

Notes and Sources: Schuckmann was promoted to major general on August 1, 1943.

Keilig: 314; *Kriegstagebuch des OKW:* Volume II: 1394; Kursietis: 198–99; Lexikon; Mehner, Vol. 4: 381; Vol. 6: 543–45; Nafziger 2000: 329; Tessin, Vol. 10: 46–47; RA: 116; OB 43: 181; OB 45: 255.

388TH FIELD TRAINING DIVISION

Composition: 639th Field Training Regiment, 640th Field Training Regiment, 388th Supply Office

Home Station: Schröttersburg, later Marienburg, Wehrkreis I

Formed in the rear area (communications zone) of Army Group North on the northern sector of the Russian Front on September 9, 1942, the 388th engaged in training men for Army Group North (16th and 18th armies). By late December 1943, it controlled six grenadier training regiments but had no artillery or divisional support troops. It retreated into the Courland Pocket after the Soviets broke the Siege of Leningrad and was still there at the end of the war. The division was redesignated Field Training Division "Nord" on May 19, 1944, and Field Training Division "Kurland" on February 2, 1945, when Army Group's North name was changed to Army Group Courland. It was gradually reduced to three battalions, as it provided two grenadier battalions to the 61st Infantry Division and one to the 126th Infantry Division. It was upgraded to infantry division status in April 1945, and its regiments became grenadier regiments, but it had apparently not been committed to the front lines when the war ended.

Its commander throughout its existence was Lieutenant General Johannes Pflugbeil.

Sources: The 639th Regiment was from Breslau, Silesia (Wehrkreis VIII); the 640th came from Stettin, Wehrkreis II. Marienburg is now Malbork, Poland. Breslau is now Wroclaw, Poland.

Keilig: 256; *Kreigstagebuch des OKW*, Volume II: 1389; Volume III: 1158; Volume IV: 1877, 1897, Lexikon; Tessin, Vol. 10: 50; Vol. 14: 133, 175; OB 45: 255.

389TH INFANTRY DIVISION

Composition: 544th Infantry Regiment, 545th Infantry Regiment, 546th Infantry Regiment, 389th Artillery Regiment, 389th Reconnaissance Battalion, 389th Tank Destroyer Battalion, 389th Engineer Battalion, 389th Signal Battalion, 389th Field Replacement Battalion, 389th Divisional Supply Troops

Home Station: Commercy, Wehrkreis XII

This division was organized as a composite "Rheingold" (Rhine gold) division during the crisis on the Eastern Front in the winter of 1941–42. Activated on January 27, 1942, at Troop Maneuver Area Milowitz (near Prague), the grenadier regiments of the 389th Division came from Kassel, Wiesbaden, and Nuremberg (Wehrkreise IX, XII, and XIII, respectively). The 389th Artillery Regiment consisted of battalions provided by all three Wehrkreise. The 389th was sent to Russia in April 1942 (after the crisis had passed) and fought on the southern sector of the Russian Front at Kharkov, during the drive across the Don and the Volga, and during the street fighting in the siege of Stalingrad. It was encircled in Stalingrad when the Soviets turned the tables on 6th Army in November 1942, and surrendered to the Russians in late January 1943.

A second 389th Infantry Division was formed in France in the summer of 1943. (It was officially activated on April 1, but was not fully organized and equipped until September 1.) The new division bore the same unit numbers as its predecessor, but its grenadier regiments had only two battalions each. Like its predecessor, this division was sent to the southern sector of the Russian Front. It first saw action on the Dnieper (October–December 1943) and, in February 1944, was surrounded at Cherkassy, where only 200 of its men managed to escape. These survivors were temporarily assigned to the 57th Infantry Division; however, the 389th was resurrected in western Hungary shortly thereafter. It absorbed Shadow Division Milowitz and, with two grenadier regiments of three battalions each, was transferred to Army Group North in May 1944, and took part in the retreat through the Baltic States. It was isolated in the Courland Pocket in the fall of 1944. The 389th Infantry, however, was brought back to Germany by sea in February 1945, where it participated in the largely unsuccessful attempt to defend East Prussia. It was cut off on the Hela peninsula near Danzig in the final campaign. The divisional headquarters was placed in OKH reserve and was apparently in the process of disbanding when the war ended. The remnants of the division surrendered to the Russians in May 1945.

Its divisional commanders included Lieutenant General Erwin Jaenicke (February 1, 1942), Major General Erich Magnus (November 1, 1942), Colonel/Major General Erwin Gerlach (April 1, 1943), Colonel Kurt Kruse (June 1, 1943), Gerlach (returned July 1943), Major General Paul Herbert Forster (November 30, 1943), Lieutenant General Walter Hahm (April 1, 1944), and Lieutenant General Fritz Becker (September 30, 1944).

Notes and Sources: General Magnus was captured on February 1, 1943, the day before the last resistance in Stalingrad ended. Gerlach was promoted to major general on July 1, 1943.

Carell 1966: 490, 615–16; Hartmann: 42; Keilig: 105, 214; Kursietis: 199; Lexikon; Mitcham 1983: 31, 136, 174; Plocher 1943: 323; Tessin, Vol. 10: 53–54; RA: 188; OB 43: 181; OB 45: 255; Ziemke 1966: 234.

390TH FIELD TRAINING (LATER SECURITY) DIVISION

Composition (1942): 635th Infantry Field Training Regiment, 636th Infantry Field Training Regiment, 637th Infantry Field Training Regiment. The 390th Artillery Field Training Battalion was added in January 1944, and the 390th Field Replacement Battalion was created in February 1944.

Home Station: Hanover, Wehrkreis XI

This unit was created in the rear area of Army Group Center in Russia on September 4, 1942. It lost its 635th Regiment to the 52nd Field Training Division when it was created in December 1943, but it added the Staff, 566th Grenadier Regiment in February 1944, when the 390th was reorganized as a combat division. This was no real gain, however, because the 566th had no battalions; the 636th and 637th Regiments each transferred a battalion to it, so all three regiments now had two battalions. On April 1, 1944, the division effectively ceased to exist, as its subordinate units were transferred to combat divisions. The 566th Grenadier Regiment went to the 129th Infantry Division, the 636th Grenadier Regiment went to the 134th

Infantry Division, and the 637th Grenadier Regiment went to the 45th Infantry Division. The 390th Artillery Battalion became I Lehr Battalion of the NCO School of Army Group Center. The Headquarters of the 390th was converted into a static, special purposes security division under Army Group Center in White Russia on July 19, 1944. It controlled Regimental Security Group 603, the 390th Divisional War School (four companies), the 390th Engineer Company and the 390th Signal Company, as well as the 497th Grenadier Replacement Battlaion. The 390th Security Division was in combat on the northern wing of Army Group Center by August and was pushed into the Courland Pocket in October. It was absorbed by the 79th Volksgrenadier Division on November 10, 1944.

The commanders of the division were Major General Walter Hartmann (September 10, 1942), Colonel August Wittmann (February 1, 1943), and Major General/Lieutenant General Hans Bergen (May 3, 1943).

Notes and Sources: Bergen was promoted to lieutenant general on October 1, 1943.

Keilig: 29; *Kriegstagebuch des OKW*, Volume II: 1387; Volume IV: 1876; Tessin, Vol. 10: 58–60; RA: 172; OB 45: 256.

391ST FIELD TRAINING (LATER SECURITY) DIVISION

Composition: 718th Infantry Field Training Regiment, 719th Infantry Field Training Regiment, 720th Infantry Field Training Regiment

Home Station: Bautzen, Wehrkreis IV

The 391st Field Training Division was created on August 31, 1942, under the headquarters of Army Group Center. The 718th Regiment was from Koenigsberg, Wehrkreis I, the 719th was from Wiesbaden, Wehrkreis XII and the 720th was from Hamburg, Wehrkreis X. Later, the division lost the 720th Field Training Regiment to the newly formed 52nd Field Training Division, but gained the Staff, 567th Grenadier Field Training Regiment. By early 1944, each of its three grenadier regiments had two battalions. The division also controlled the 391st Grenadier Field Training Battalion. In the spring of 1944, the

Two Germans attempt to free a motorcycle from the mud. This photograph was probably taken in Russia, where virtually all of the roads were unimproved and were famous for turning into rivers of mud. The motorcycle, with or without a sidecar, was a very effective vehicle in all theaters of operation except North Africa, where the desert sand caused such severe maintenance problems that the Afrika Korps' motorcycle units were converted into motorized infantry battalions. HITM ARCHIVE

division was essentially dissolved. The 567th Grenadier Regiment was absorbed by the 78th Sturm Division; the 718th Grenadier Regiment was absorbed by the 263rd Infantry Division; and the 719th Grenadier Regiment became part of the 87th Infantry Division. The divisional headquarters became Staff, 391st Special Purposes Security Division, on March 23, 1944. It was given command over the 93rd Grenadier Regiment (four Alarm battalions), the 1233rd Fahnenjunker (officer-candidate) Regiment, the 391st Artillery Regiment Staff (which apparently controlled only one artillery battalion), the 391st Supply Regiment and the 171st Grenadier Replacement Battalion. It was sent into combat in the spring of 1945. As part of the 9th Army, part of the 391st was cut off east of Berlin and destroyed in the Halbe Pocket on or about April 29, 1945. The rest of the division was destroyed in the city itself.

Its commanders were Major General/Lieutenant General Baron Albrecht Digeon von Monteton (September 10, 1942), Major General Rudolf Sieckenius (September 5, 1944), Lieutenant General Alexander Goeschen (February 1945), and Sieckenius (March 1945–end).

Notes and Sources: Baron von Digeon was promoted to lieutenant general on June 1, 1943. Sieckenius was killed in action leading a suicide attack at the Görlitzer Station in Berlin on April 28, 1945.

Keilig: 70; *Kriegstagebuch des OKW*, Volume IV: 1898; Lexikon; Tessin, Vol. 10: 61–63; RA: 188; OB 45: 256.

392ND INFANTRY DIVISION (*KROATISCH*)

Composition: 846th Grenadier Regiment (*kroat.*), 847th Grenadier Regiment (*kroat.*), 392nd Artillery Regiment (*kroat.*), 392nd Fusilier Battalion (kroat.), 392nd Tank Destroyer Battalion (*kroat.*), 392nd Engineer Battalion (*kroat.*), 392nd Signal Battalion (*kroat.*), 392nd Field Replacement Battalion (*kroat.*), 392nd Divisional Supply Troops (*kroat.*)

Home Station: Stockerau, Wehrkreis XVII

This division consisted of Croatian soldiers led by German cadres. It was formed in the Döllersheim Troop Maneuver

Area (Austria) on August 17, 1943, and was sent to Croatia in 1944. It behaved better than the other German-Croatian divisions and was even cited for distinguished action against the partisans in Yugoslavia. Later it fought the Soviets when they overran the Balkans. The 392nd ended the war north of Fiume (Rijeka), on the Adriatic Sea in Croatia, on the southern sector of the Eastern Front. It surrendered to the Yugoslavs.

Its commander for most of its existence was Lieutenant General Johann Mickl, who was mortally wounded on April 9. He was succeeded by Colonel Reindl, the commander of the 392nd Artillery Regiment.

Notes and Sources: Mickl was shot by a sniper and died in a military hospital on April 10.

Hartmann: 39; Keilig: 227; Tessin, Vol. 10: 64; RA: 220; OB 45: 256.

393RD INFANTRY DIVISION

Composition: 662nd Infantry Regiment, 663rd Infantry Regiment, 664th Infantry Regiment, 393rd Cannon Battery, 393rd Reconnaissance Squadron, 393rd Signal Company, 393rd Divisional Supply Troops

Home Station: Bromberg, Wehrkreis VI

This line-of-communications division was made up of older (*Landesschützen*) troops. It was activated on March 10, 1940, was sent to Warsaw, Poland, under OB East. It guarded the German rear in case Stalin launched an attack while the main field divisions were fighting France and Britain. This never happened and the 393rd was disbanded as a combat division on August 1, 1940, after Paris surrendered. Its headquarters was converted into Field Area Command 393 and was sent to Warsaw. Later it was posted to Kiev and was disbanded in 1944. Its infantry battalions became the 494th, 495th, 496th, 497th, 498th, 499th, 972nd, 973rd, and 947th Landesschützen Battalions. The commanders of the 393rd Infantry Division were Major General Baron Theodor von Wrede (March 1940) and Major General Karl von Oven (May 16, 1940–end).

Notes and Sources: Bromberg is now Bydgoszcz, Poland.
Keilig: 250, 377; Lexikon; Nafziger 2000: 332; Tessin, Vol. 10: 67;
RA: 102; OB 42: 30, 110; OB 45: 257.

394TH FIELD TRAINING DIVISION

Composition: 562nd Grenadier Field Training Regiment,
563rd Grenadier Field Training Regiment, 564th Grenadier
Field Training Regiment

Home Station: Wehrkreis III

This division began forming in January 1944, under Army
Group North Ukraine, from elements of the 143rd and 153rd
Reserve Divisions. The process had only just begun, however,
when the decision to create the division was reversed. The men
already assembled were transferred to Field Training Regiment
North Ukraine.

Sources: Nafziger 2000: 579; Tessin, Vol. 10: 69.

395TH INFANTRY DIVISION

Composition: 665th Infantry Regiment, 674th Infantry
Regiment, 675th Infantry Regiment, 395th Artillery Regiment
(two battalions), 395th Bicycle Squadron, 395th Signal Company, 395th Divisional Supply Troops

Home Station: Alt-Bunzlau, later Schröttersberg, Wehrkreis I

An East Prussian *Landwehr* division, this unit was organized
at Tilsit on March 16, 1940, when it absorbed the 521st Infantry Division. It was provisioned with captured Polish equipment. It was disbanded after the fall of France. Its former units
were reorganized as seven Home Guard battalions, which were
used to guard prisoner-of-war camps. It never left East Prussia
and never saw combat. The divisional headquarters was converted into FK 395 (Field Area Headquarters 395) and was
later sent to Salonika, Greece.

Major General Stengal was the last commander of the 395th
Infantry Division.

Notes and Sources: Tilsit is now Sovetsk, Russia.
Keilig: 332; *Kriegstagebuch des OKW*, Volume I: 1123, 1125; Kursietis: 200–01; Lexikon; Nafziger 2000: 332; Tessin, Vol. 10: 71; OB 43: 180; OB 44b: D110; OB 45: 257.

399TH INFANTRY DIVISION

Composition: 662nd Infantry Regiment, 663rd Infantry Regiment, 664th Infantry Regiment, 399th Artillery Battery, 399th Reconnaissance Squadron, 399th Signal Company, 399th Divisional Supply Troops

Home Station: Lissa, Wehrkreis XXI

Like the 395th Infantry Division, the 399th was created on March 15, 1940, from older reservists. Its Headquarters came from Staff, 421st Special Purposes Infantry Division (*Inf. Div. z.b.V. 421*). It never left southern East Prussia and its reason for existence was mainly to guard against a surprise Russian invasion of eastern Germany and Poland, while the main German armies were busy in France. The Russians, of course, did not invade, and the reason for the 399th's existence expired with the surrender of France on June 21. The 399th's regiments were dissolved on August 8, 1940, and its battalions became seven Home Guard (*Heimat Wach*) battalions. Five of these were disbanded shortly thereafter. The divisional headquarters was sent to eastern Poland as Field Area Command 399 (FK 399). It was stationed in France in 1942 and White Russia in 1943. It was disbanded in September 1944. The commander of the 399th Infantry Division throughout its existence was Major General Helmuth von Kropff.

Sources: Keilig: 188; *Kriegstagebuch des OKW*, Volume I: 1123, 1125; Lexikon; Nafziger 2000: 332; Tessin, Vol. 10: 79–80; OB 43: 191; OB 45: 257.

400TH REPLACEMENT DIVISION

Composition: 264th Field Recruit Infantry Regiment, 265th Field Recruit Infantry Regiment

Home Station: Dresden, Wehrkreis IV

The staff of this division was formed in Saxony on June 3, 1940. It took over seven infantry replacement battalions in order to provide garrison (occupation) troops for parts of Poland (including Krakau) and to serve as field recruiter units in the Generalgouvernement. France surrendered less than three weeks later and regular army units became available for these purposes; consequently, the 400th was disbanded on August 1.

Sources: Nafziger 2000: 579; Tessin, Vol. 10: 81; OB 45: 257.

401ST REPLACEMENT DIVISION

Composition: 161st Grenadier Replacement Regiment (four battalions), 228th Grenadier Infantry Replacement Regiment (five battalions), 1st Artillery Replacement and Training Regiment, 1st Reconnaissance (Cavalry) Replacement Battalion, 31st Fla Replacement and Training Battalion, 1st Engineer Replacement Battalion

Home Station: Tilsit, Wehrkreis I

This division began its career as the 401st *Landesschützen* or Special Purposes Division at Koenigsberg on January 16, 1940. Its Headquarters was the former Staff, 422nd Infantry Division z.b.V. As such, it controlled a dozen local defense battalions in East Prussia until the fall of 1942. At that time, the 141st and 151st Replacement Divisions were upgraded to reserve divisions and sent to Russia. The 404th was in turn upgraded to a replacement division on September 25 and took over the replacement battalions of the departing units. It conducted some training but was primarily responsible for implementing the German draft. (The 1st Artillery Replacement and Training Regiment, for example, controlled seven battalions, including the 37th Artillery Replacement and Training Battalion and the 1st Forward Observer Replacement and Training Battalion. Its other five battalions were replacement units only.) In early 1945, as the Russians pushed deep into East Prussia, the 401st Replacement was disbanded on or about February 22. Its troops were sent to Wehrkreis X (Schleswig-Holstein).

Its divisional commanders included Lieutenant General Oskar von Beneckendorf und von Hindenburg (March 1, 1940), Lieutenant General Hubert Gercke (January 10, 1941), Major General Max von Diringshofen (January 10, 1942), Colonel/Major General Siegfried Ruff (June 1942), Diringshofen (returned July 1942), Ruff (September 25, 1942), Lieutenant General Paul Stöwer (April 1, 1944), Lieutenant General Fritz Kühlwein (December 29, 1944), and Lieutenant General Karl Faulenbach (January 1, 1945).

Notes and Sources: Hindenburg was the son of the World War I field marshal. Ruff was promoted to major general on December 1, 1942.

Keilig: 287; Kursietis: 201; Mehner, Vol. 4: 328; Nafziger 2000: 333; Tessin, Vol. 10: 84; 23; OB 43: 131; OB 44b: D123; OB 45: 258.

402ND LANDESSCHÜTZEN (LATER REPLACEMENT) DIVISION

Composition: 258th Grenadier Replacement Regiment, 522nd Grenadier Replacement Regiment, 2nd Artillery Replacement and Training Regiment, 5th Cavalry Replacement Battalion, 2nd Mobile Replacement and Training Battalion, 2nd Motorcycle Replacement and Training Battalion, 2nd Engineer Replacement and Training Battalion, 2nd Construction Engineer Replacement and Training Battalion, 2nd Signal Replacement and Training Battalion, 272nd Army Anti-Aircraft Replacement and Training Battalion

Home Station: Stettin, Wehrkreis II

Organized on October 25, 1939, the 402nd was originally a special administrative division staff used to control twenty-four Landesschützen battalions in the II Military District. In the fall of 1942, it was upgraded to a replacement division when Wehrkreis II lost the 152nd and 192nd Replacement Divisions. The 402nd continued to provide training and replacement services until early 1945, when Pomerania was invaded by the Russians. The 402nd was pressed into front line fighting and took part in the siege of Kolberg (now Kolobrzeg, Poland) in

February and March 1945. It fought very well, but when the city fell on March 18, Division 402 was crushed and many of the soldiers of the division were killed. The remnants of the division were withdrawn to Schwerin and then Usedom and Swinemünde, where they were used to form the 402nd Training Division. In April 1945, this unit included the 522nd Grenadier Training Regiment (four battalions), the 2nd Artillery Training Regiment (three battalions), the Staff, 85th Hungarian Infantry Regiment, the 27/172nd Fusilier Training Battalion, the 100th Cavalry Training Battalion, the 22nd Fla Training Battalion, and the Hungarian Infantry School Varpalota. Like the rest of the 3rd Panzer Army, this division surrendered to the British at the end of the war.

The division's commanders included General of Infantry Hans Petri (September 25, 1939), Colonel/Major General Hans Windeck (February 1, 1940), Major General Erich von Keiser (May 1, 1940), Major General/Lieutenant General Hubert Stenzel (September 25, 1942), Colonel Werner von Boltenstern (November 1, 1943), Stenzel (December 17, 1943), Lieutenant General Baron Siegmund von Schleinitz (October 1, 1944), and Major General Ernst von Bauer (March 1945–end).

Notes and Sources: Windeck was promoted to major general on April 1, 1940. Stenzel became a lieutenant general on April 1, 1944. Schleinitz was captured at Kolberg and remained a Russian POW until 1955.

Chant, Volume 16: 2235; Keilig: 45; Tessin, Vol. 10: 87–88; RA: 34–35; OB 42:18; OB 43: 26; OB 45: 258.

403RD SECURITY DIVISION

Composition: 177th Landesschützen Regiment, 406th Reinforced Infantry Regiment, II/8th Police Regiment, 705th Guard Battalion, 403rd Eastern (Ost) Battalion, 403rd Tank Destroyer Company, 403rd Engineer Company, 826th Signal Battalion, 466th Divisional Supply Troops. The III/213th Artillery Regiment was added in the spring of 1942.

Home Station: Berlin/Spandau, Wehrkreis III

Originally created as 403rd Landesschützen Division on October 25, 1939, this unit spent the first year of the war supervising ten Landesschützen (local defense) battalions in the III Military District. In August 1940, it was sent to the 6th Army in Brittany, France, and on March 15, 1941, was reorganized as a security division. It was sent to the 9th Army on the central sector of the Russian Front in June and July 1941. Later employed behind Army Group South, the 403rd was disbanded on May 31, 1943, after providing the staff for the 265th Infantry Division. Its 177th Regiment (now a security unit) was transferred to the 213rd Security Division, and the 406th Security (now Grenadier) Regiment was transferred to the 201st Security Division and was destroyed at Bobruisk in June 1944. The 403rd Security Division was never committed to the main battle area as a combat unit, but elements were periodically assigned to front-line corps and sent into the fighting.

The division's commanders were Colonel/Major General/Lieutenant General Wolfgang von Ditfurth (October 25, 1939) and Lieutenant General Wilhelm Russwurm (May 15, 1942).

Notes and Sources: Ditfurth was promoted to major general on September 1, 1940, and to lieutenant general on October 1, 1941. He was hanged at Riga by the Soviets on February 3, 1946.

Keilig: 71; *Kriegstagebuch des OKW*, Volume II: 1367, 1369, 1374; Lexikon; Tessin, Vol. 10: 90–92; OB 42: 19; OB 43: 215; OB 44b: D117; OB 45: 258.

404TH REPLACEMENT DIVISION

Composition: 524th Grenadier Replacement Regiment, 544th Grenadier Replacement Regiment, 554th Infantry Replacement Regiment, 4th Artillery Replacement and Training Regiment, 10th Bicycle Replacement Battalion, 24th Engineer Replacement Battalion, Technical Replacement and Training Battalion

Home Station: Dresden, Wehrkreis IV

This division was formed as the 404th Landesschützen Division in Dresden on October 24, 1939. It controlled 17 battalions of older age troops until September 24, 1942; then it became a replacement division when the 154th and 174th Replacement Divisions of Wehrkreis IV were upgraded to reserve divisions and sent to Poland. In the latter part of 1944, after the 154th and 174th were fully committed to battle on the Eastern Front, the 404th expanded some of its existing replacement units into replacement and training units. The division was redesignated the 404th Grenadier Training Division and committed to combat when the Soviets overran the IV Military District in the spring of 1945. After Hitler killed himself, the replacement elements of the division managed to surrender to the Americans but most of the training units (which were at the front) fell into Russian hands.

The commanders of the 404th were Lieutenant General Arthur Schubert (October 24, 1939), Major General Karl Maderholz (October 26, 1939), Schubert (returned November 27, 1939), Lieutenant General Fritz Brodowski (September 25, 1942), Lieutenant General Baron Eccard von Gablenz (March 15, 1943), Lieutenant General Hermann Meyer-Rabingen (July 1, 1944), Major General Gerhard Sturt (February 1, 1945), and Meyer-Rabingen (returned March 27, 1945).

Sources: Keilig: 214; *Kriegstagebuch des OKW*, Volume I: 1147; Lexikkon; Tessin, Vol. 10: 93–94; RA: 72–81; OB 43: 28, 182; OB 45: 259.

405TH LANDESSCHÜTZEN (LATER REPLACEMENT) DIVISION

Composition (late 1942): 5th Infantry Replacement Regiment, 35th Infantry Replacement Regiment, 78th Infantry Replacement Regiment, 403rd Landesschützen Battalion, 406th *Landesschuetzen* Battalion, 427th Landesschützen Battalion, 506th Landesschützen Battalion, 25th Artillery Replacement Regiment, 35th Engineer Replacement Battalion, 5th Driver Replacement Battalion, 5th Construction Engineer Replacement Battalion, 5th Bridge Construction Battalion, 5th Landesschützen Replacement Battalion

Home Station: Heilbronn, Wehrkreis V

Created in Stuttgart to control eight local defense battalions, this unit functioned as a Landesschützen division from October 23, 1939 until May 10, 1942. Reorganized as a replacement division, it was transferred to Strasbourg, where it controlled replacement units in Alsace until the German defenses in Normandy collapsed. In September 1944, the unit was in charge of fortification work in the Vosges. Later it retreated to Oberkirch, where it worked on the Rhine defenses in addition to carrying out its regular duties. It was committed to combat as part of the 19th Army in February 1945, and fought in western Germany in the last campaign of the war.

Its commanders included Major General Otto Schellert (October 1939), Lieutenant General Adolf Hüttmann (April 10, 1940), Lieutenant General Otto Tscherning (April 10, 1942), Lieutenant General Willy Seeger (May 1, 1943), and Lieutenant General Karl Faulenbach (February 22, 1945).

Notes and Sources: Seeger was promoted to lieutenant general on September 1, 1943.

Keilig: 360; *Kriegstagebuch des OKW*, Volume I: 1147; Lexikon; Mehner, Vol. 4: 384; Tessin, Vol. 10: 97–98; RA: 88–89; OB 42: 20; OB 43: 182; OB 45: 259.

406TH LANDESSCHÜTZEN DIVISION

Composition (1939): 33rd Landesschützen Regiment, 172nd Landesschützen Regiment, 183rd Landesschützen Regiment, 6th Replacement (later Replacement and Training) Battalion

Home Station: Muester, Wehrkreis VI

This Westphalian division was activated on October 12, 1939, and spent most of the war directing older age soldiers in the VI Military District. Initially it controlled 24 battalions, although this number decreased as the war wore on. In September 1944, it was sent to Geldern, western Germany, where it apparently engaged in training attached local defense battalions. The crisis on the Western Front forced a premature end to the training process and, in October 1944, the 406th was sent to Arnhem, where it held a section of the West Wall. A month later it was smashed near Gross-Beck. The division was returned to Germany, rebuilt, and was back on the front lines again in December 1944, still directing three Landesschützen training formations of marginal value. It did, however, control the Wehrkreis VI Non-Commissioned Officers' School (1,774 men) and the Army NCO Schools of Düren and Jülich (866 and 575 men, respectively), as well as the VI Sharpshooters' Training Company (106 men), which increased the division's combat value considerably. Its total strength at one point was 8,143 men, which was perhaps a little above average for a German infantry division in the fifth year of the war. It only had two batteries of artillery, however. The 406th was trapped and largely destroyed in the Wesel Pocket west of the Rhine in March 1945. It was disbanded on March 13.

Its commander for most of its career was Colonel/Major General/Lieutenant General Gerd Scherbening, who assumed command on October 1, 1939, before the division was formally activated. He was killed in action on December 18, 1944. He was succeeded by his deputy division commander, Colonel Kurt Kühme, who was killed near Hellschlag in the Eifel on December 25.

Notes and Sources: Scherbening was promoted to major general on September 1, 1941, and to lieutenant general on September 1, 1943. Kühme as an *Obergruppenführer* in the SA (General of Storm Troopers) and a *Pour le Merite* holder from the First World War. He was posthumously promoted to major general on January 25, 1945, to date from December 1, 1944. Who succeeded him as divisional commander is not revealed by the available records.

Keilig: 298; MacDonald 1973: Maps VII and VIII; OB 43: 30; Nafziger 2000: 334; OB 45: 259; Dieter Zinke, personal communication, *www.forum.axishistory.com*, January 4, 2007.

407TH REPLACEMENT DIVISION

Composition (1943): 307th Grenadier Replacement Regiment, 527th Grenadier Replacement Regiment, 27th Artillery Replacement Regiment, 27th Engineer Replacement Battalion

Home Station: Munich (later Augsburg), Wehrkreis VII

Initially created as a Landesschützen division, this unit directed older age troops in Bavaria until October 1, 1942, when it became a full-fledged replacement division. The next year, as the German reserve and field training divisions were sent into combat, the 407th assumed a training mission as well. It was disbanded on September 15, 1944, and its men incorporated into the 467th Replacement Division.

A second 407th Replacement Division was created from Training Division Bavaria and the 467th Replacement Division on March 26, 1945. It included the 407th and 467th Grenadier Regiments (five battalions total), the 407th Artillery Battalion, the 407th *Werfer* (Rocket Launcher) Battalion, the 407th Engineer Battalion, the 7th Engineer Training Battalion, and the troops of the Engineer Officers Training School II and the Army NCO School for Engineers. Initially it was engaged in constructing defensive positions in southern Germany and, in April, was ordered to hold Augsburg at all costs. The divisional commander, Major General Franz Fehn, refused to blow up the city's bridges or engage in futile house-to-house fighting. He evacuated all military hospitals and gave several hundred tons of stockpiled rations to the civilian population shortly before the Americans arrived. Fehn surrendered his command to the U.S. 3rd Infantry Division.

Previous divisional commanders included Major General Ritter Otto von Saur (October 25, 1939), Major General/Lieutenant General Friedrich Dümlein (October 15, 1940), Colonel/Major General Walter Hartmann (May 1, 1942), Colonel Alexander Ratcliffe (August 29, 1942), and Lieutenant General Oskar Blümm (November 1, 1942–September 15, 1944).

Notes and Sources: As of November 1940, the 407th Landesschützen Division controlled the 71st Landesschützen Regiment (three battalions), the 74th Landesschützen Regiment (two battalions) and the 7th Landesschützen Battalion.

Keilig: 75; MacDonald 1973: 435–36; Mehner, Vol. 4: 382; Vol. 5: 335; Nafziger 2000: 334; Tessin, Vol. 10: 104–5; RA: 118; OB 43: 182; OB 45: 260.

408TH REPLACEMENT DIVISION

Composition (1943): 332nd Grenadier Replacement Regiment, 518th Grenadier Replacement Regiment, 8th Reconnaissance Replacement Battalion, 8th Motorcycle Replacement Battalion, 18th Artillery Replacement Battalion, 300th Assault Gun Replacement and Training Battalion, 28th Engineer Replacement and Training Battalion, 213th Engineer Replacement Battalion, 518th Construction Engineer Battalion, 273rd Army Anti-Aircraft Artillery Replacement and Training Battalion, 48th Fla Replacement and Training Battalion

Home Station: Breslau, Wehrkreis VIII

Originally formed as a Landesschützen division under Wehrkreis VIII, the 408th controlled the 86th and 87th Landesschützen Regiments (fifteen battalions) in October 1940. It was converted to a replacement division in the fall of 1942, when the training and replacement functions of the Home Army were directed. In the summer of 1944 the division began training operations as well. The 408th itself was sent into the battle zone in early 1945 when the Russians invaded Germany and besieged Breslau. The 408th Replacement was given to 17th Army and fought in the battles to defend its home province of Silesia. Its survivors went into Soviet captivity when the Third Reich fell.

Its commanders included Major General/Lieutenant General Wolfgang Otterstedt (October 25, 1939), Lieutenant General Alfred von Puttkamer (October 1, 1942), Lieutenant General Friedrich Bayer (November 20, 1943), and Lieutenant General Heinrich Wosch (June 15, 1944).

Notes and Sources: Otterstedt was promoted to lieutenant general on July 1, 1941.

Keilig: 249; Kursietis: 203; Lexikon; Nafziger 2000: 335; Tessin, Vol. 10: 107; RA: 132; OB 43: 182; OB 45: 260.

409TH REPLACEMENT DIVISION

Composition (1943): 519th Grenadier Replacement Regiment, 529th Grenadier Replacement Regiment, 15th Motorized Artillery Replacement and Training Regiment, 3rd Reconnaissance Replacement Battalion, 9th Motorized Replacement and

Training Battalion, 9th Driver Replacement and Training Battalion, 15th Driver Replacement and Training Battalion, 9th Engineer Replacement Battalion, 29th Engineer Replacement and Training Battalion, 9th Construction Engineer Replacement and Training Battalion, 3rd Railroad Engineer Replacement and Training Battalion, Engineer Lehr Battalion z.b.V., and the 9th or 40th Signal Replacement and Training Battalion

Home Station: Kassel, Wehrkreis IX

On October 25, 1939, this divisional staff was formed as the 409th Landesschuetzen Division to control older age local defense troops in Hesse and part of Thuringia (Wehrkreis IX). As of March 1940, it controlled the 93rd Landesschützen Regiment (ten battalions) and the 9th Landesschützen Replacement Battalion. In the fall of 1942, it received the replacement elements of the 159th and 189th Reserve Divisions when they went to France. It was redesignated 409th Replacement Division on October 1. After these reserve divisions were committed to battle on the Western Front, the 409th assumed their training duties as well. Elements of the 409th were sent to the front in the last days of the war, but they did not see heavy fighting.

The division's commanders included Colonel/Major General Hans Ehrenberg (October 25, 1939) and Lieutenant General Albert Zehler (April 1, 1943–end).

Notes and Sources: Ehrenberg was promoted to major general on August 1, 1941.

Keilig: 78; Lexikon; Mehner, Vol 5: 335; Vol. 6: 549; Nafziger 2000: 335; Tessin, Vol. 10: 110–11; RA: 146–47; OB 43: 33; OB 45: 260.

410TH LANDESSCHÜTZEN DIVISION (DIVISION z.b.V. 410)

Composition (1940): 105th Landesschützen Regiment, 106th Landesschützen Regiment, 10th Landesschützen Replacement Battalion

Home Station: Hamburg, Wehrkreis X

Created on October 23, 1939, the 410th controlled seven battalions of older-age men in the Hamburg area until March

1944. At that time, for reasons not made clear by the records, it was dissolved.

The division's commanders included Major General Kurt Woytasch (October 25, 1939), Colonel/Major General Baron Willibald von Langerman und Erlenkamp (December 1, 1939), Major General/Lieutenant General Adolf Pötter (May 7, 1940), Lieutenant General Karl Maderholz (January 20, 1943), Lieutenant General Rene l'Homme de Courbiere (November 20, 1943) and Lieutenant General Karl Bornemann (January 5, 1944).

Notes and Sources: Langerman was promoted to major general on March 1, 1940. Poetter became a lieutenant general on February 1, 1941.

Keilig: 150; Kursietis: 203–04; Lexikon; Tessin, Vol. 10: 113; OB 43: 34; OB 45: 261.

411TH LANDESSCHÜTZEN DIVISION

Composition (December 1943): 111th Landesschützen Regiment (10 battalions); 701st Landesschützen Battalion, 704th Landesschützen Battalion, 708th Landesschützen Battalion, 711th Landesschützen Battalion, 11th Landesschützen Replacement Battalion

Home Station: Hanover, Wehrkreis XI

The 411th was formed on October 25, 1939, to control its older age (Landesschützen) local defense and POW camp guard troops. (Generally speaking, one battalion of Landesschützen men guarded each prisoner-of-war camp.) It was officially disbanded on September 24, 1944, and its missions were taken over by the Staff, 31st Landesschützen Regiment.

Its commanders were Major General/Lieutenant General Heinrich Kannengiesser (October 22, 1939) and Colonel/Major General Gero von Gersdorff (December 31, 1942–end).

Notes and Sources: Kannengiesser was promoted to lieutenant general on April 1, 1941. Gersdorff was promoted to major general on January 1, 1943.

Keilig: 105, 163; Lexikon; Tessin, Vol. 10: 115; OB 43: 35; OB 45: 261.

412TH LANDESSCHÜTZEN DIVISION

Composition: 765th Landesschützen Battalion, part of the 759th Landesschützen Battalion, 12th Landesschützen Replacement Battalion

Home Station: Wiesbaden, Wehrkreis XII

The 412th was formed in Wiesbaden on January 12, 1940, from the Staff, Division z.b.V. 445, to control Landesschützen(older age) units in Wehrkreis XII and to build defensive works (*Verteidigung*) against possible French attacks. The division was disbanded on October 23, 1940, and its staff was used to form the 4th Mountain Division. Its commander throughout its existence was Colonel/Major General Friedrich Genthe.

Notes and Sources: Genthe was promoted to major general on September 1, 1940.
Keilig: 104; Schmitz et al., Vol. 1; 277; Tessin, Vol. 10: 117; OB 42: 26; OB 43: 36; OB 45:261.

413TH LANDESSCHÜTZEN DIVISION

Composition (1942): 131st Landesschützen Regiment (seven battalions), 805th Landesschützen Battalion, 806th Landesschützen Battalion, 820th Landesschützen Battalion, 13th Landesschützen Replacement Battalion

Home Station: Fuerth, Wehrkreis XIII

Activated in Nuremberg on October 25, 1939, the 413th was initially a Landesschützen division, controlling one regiment (the 131st) and seven independent battalions. Its men were used for various purposes, including POW guards. It was disbanded on June 10, 1942.

The commanders of the 413th Landesschützen Division were Colonel/Major General/Lieutenant General Karl Leistner (October 25, 1939), Major General Wilhelm Behrens (May 1, 1942), and Major General Heinrich Thoma (June 1–10, 1942).

Notes and Sources: Leistner was promoted to major general on September 1, 1940, and to lieutenant general on December 1, 1941.
Keilig: 200; *Kriegstagebuch des OKW*, Vol. I: 1147; Vol. II: 1462; Tessin, Vol. 10: 120.

413TH REPLACEMENT DIVISION

Composition: 113th Grenadier Replacement Regiment (six battalions), 17th Artillery Replacement and Training Regiment (three battalions), 17th Reconnaissance Replacement Battalion, 13th Driver Replacement and Training Battalion, 46th Engineer Replacement Battalion, 13th Construction Engineer Replacement and Training Battalion, 47th Anti-Aircraft Replacement and Training Battalion, 13th Driver Replacement and Training Battalion

Home Station: Nuremberg, Wehrkreis XIII

The 413th Replacement Division was activated on July 11, 1943, when the 173rd Replacement Division was upgraded to reserve division status and sent to Croatia. In 1944 the 413th expanded its subordinate elements into replacement-training units and operated in this role until the Allies approached Nuremberg. The 413th was then thrown into battle and was still resisting when the war ended.

Commanders of the division included Major General Johann Meyerhoffer (August 1, 1943), Lieutenant General Baron Sigmund von Schacky und Schonfeld (July 27, 1944), Major General Hellmuth Hiepe (April 1, 1945), Major General Eugen Theilacker (April 3, 1945), and Hiepe (April 1945).

Notes and Sources: In early April 1945, General Theilacker simultaneously 413th, 445th, and 464th Divisions.

Keilig: 141; *Kriegstagebuch des OKW*, Volume I: 1147; Volume II: 1462; Mehner, Vol. 12: 461; Tessin, Vol. 10: 120–21; RA: 206; OB 43: 37; OB 45: 261.

416TH INFANTRY DIVISION

Composition (1944): 712th Grenadier Regiment, 713th Grenadier Regiment, 714th Grenadier Regiment, 416th Artillery Regiment, 416th Fusilier Company, 416th Tank Destroyer Battalion, 416th Engineer Battalion, 416th Signal Battalion, 416th Divisional Supply Troops

Home Station: Röskilde, later Schleswig and then Oldenburg, Wehrkreis X

The 416th began its career in Brunswick on December 20, 1941. At that time, it controlled the 416th, 441st and 443rd Infantry Regiments and the 416th Artillery Battalion. That winter, it was sent to the Aalborg area of Denmark, where it remained until September 1944. In 1943, its infantry regiments were sent to Army Group Center on the Eastern Front, and it took charge of the 712th and 713th Fortress (later Grenadier) Regiments. The 416th consisted mainly of older soldiers, with an average age of thirty-eight, and was nicknamed the "Whipped Cream Division" because of the special diets many of its men required.

In early September 1944, it was earmarked for the seizure and occupation of the Aland Islands in the Baltic Sea, south of the Gulf of Bothnia, between Finland and Sweden; however, the orders were cancelled by Hitler, who decided that the 416th could not be spared. The following month it was committed to battle on the Saar sector of the Western Front. At that time it had 8,500 men but very little artillery. In November it withdrew across eastern France, under heavy pressure from the U.S. Army Air Force. The 416th fought in the Merzig area of the Saar, in the so-called Saar-Moselle triangle, in the West Wall battles, and was continuously engaged from November 1944 to February 1945. (Meanwhile, it added the 774th Grenadier Regiment in late December 1944.) Its men took part in the retreat across Germany and surrendered to the Americans near Traunstein, southeastern (Upper) Bavaria, at the end of the war.

The 416th's commanders included Lieutenant General Hans Barbänder (December 1941), Lieutenant General Werner Heuhner (June 1943) and Lieutenant General Kurt Pflieger (July 1, 1943).

Sources: Cole 1950: 384, 387–88; Keilig: 49; MacDonald 1973: 118; Tessin, Vol. 10: 128–29; RA: 160; OB 43: 183; OB 44b: D110; OB 45: 262; Ziemke 1966: 268, 391.

417TH LANDESSCHÜTZEN DIVISION

Composition: 172nd Infantry Replacement and Training Regiment, 174th Infantry Replacement and Training Regiment, (417th) Guard Battalion Vienna

Home Station: Vienna, Wehrkreis XVII

The 417th was formed on October 25, 1939, to control thirteen older age battalions under XVII Military District. It supervised the operation of local defense and POW guard troops in the Wehrkreis until March or April 1945, when it was disbanded. Its soldiers were incorporated into units of the 6th SS Panzer Army for the defense of Vienna in April 1945.

Its commanders included Major General/Lieutenant General Ferdinand Pichler (October 23, 1939), Lieutenant General Rudolf Wanger (May 1, 1942), and Lieutenant General Adalbert Mikulicz (January 1, 1944).

Sources: Hoffmann: 466; Keilig: 228, 257; Kursietis: 205; Lexikon; Tessin, Vol. 10: 131; OB 43: 38; OB 45: 262.

418TH REPLACEMENT DIVISION

Probable Composition (1944): 137th Mountain Infantry Replacement Regiment, 138th Mountain Infantry Replacement Regiment, 112th Mountain Artillery Replacement and Training Regiment, 48th Tank Destroyer Replacement Battalion, 2nd Reconnaissance Replacement Battalion, 48th Tank Destroyer Replacement and Training Battalion, 82nd Mountain Engineer Replacement and Training Battalion, 18th Mobile Replacement and Training Battalion, 18th Motorcycle Replacement and Training Battalion, 700th Mountain Fla Replacement and Training Battalion

Home Station: Salzburg, Wehrkreis XVIII

This unit was activated in Klagenfurt, northern Austria, on May 15, 1943, when the 188th Reserve Division was sent to northern Italy. By late 1944, its subordinate units expanded replacement units to units with combined replacement and training missions. The 418th was still in Salzburg when the war ended.

Its commanders were Major General Jais (May 10, 1943), Lieutenant General Ernst Schlemmer (May 15, 1943), Jais (November 1, 1943), and Lieutenant General Otto Schörherr (March 20, 1944).

Notes and Sources: As the only replacement division in Wehrkreis XVIII, the 418th probably controlled all the Wehrkreis XVIII replacement training units (see "Probable Composition"), although a few of these may have come directly under Wehrkreis control.

Keilig: 157, 301, 310; Mehner, Vol. 12: 466; Tessin, Vol. 10: 133; OB 43: 183; OB 45: 262.

421ST LANDESSCHÜTZEN DIVISION

Composition: Various attached recruiting and mobilization units from the former Guard Sector North

Home Station: Allenstein (?), Wehrkreis I

Originally formed as a z.b.V. ("for special purposes") divisional staff in East Prussia on November 8, 1939, the 421st was involved in recruiting, drafting and training various attached units until March 15, 1940, when it was absorbed by the 399th Infantry (Landesschützen) Division.

Its commander was Major General Helmuth von Kropff.

See also 399th Infantry Division earlier in this chapter.

Sources: Keilig: 188; Kursietis: 205; Tessin, Vol. 10: 139; RA: 20–23; OB 43: 24, 183.

422ND LANDESSCHÜTZEN DIVISION

The 422nd was formed in the area of Guard Sector North (Wehrkreis I) on October 24, 1939, to control and support headquarters and local defense troops in West Prussia. Much of this area had been taken from Poland in September 1939, and contained many Polish nationals. The 429th was absorbed by the 401st Replacement Division on January 16, 1940.

Its commander was Major General Oskar von Beneckendorf und von Hindenburg, the son of Field Marshal Paul von Hindenburg.

See 401st Replacement Division earlier in this chapter.

Sources: Keilig: 27; Tessin, Vol. 10: 141; OB 42: 28; OB 43: 184; OB 45: 263.

423RD LANDESSCHÜTZEN DIVISION

The 423rd was formed in the Saxon industrial city of Chemnitz (Wehrkreis IV) to control older age local defense and prison guard troops. It was redesignated 393rd Infantry (Landesschützen) Division on August 1, 1940. Its commander was Major General Baron Theodor von Wrede.

See 393rd Infantry Division earlier in this chapter.

Sources: Keilig: 377; Lexikon; Tessin, Vol. 10: 143.

424TH LANDESSCHÜTZEN DIVISION

Formed in Karlsbad, Wehrkreis XIII, on October 24, 1939, to control northern Bavarian Landesschützen units in the East, the 424th was redesignated 379th Infantry Division on February 1, 1940.

Major General Ludwig Mueller was its commander throughout its existence.

Sources: Müller remained in charge of the 379th Infantry Division. Keilig: 233; Lexikon; Tessin, Vol. 10: 145.

425TH LANDESSCHÜTZEN DIVISION

Composition: 210th Field Recruit Infantry Regiment, 214th Field Recruit Infantry Regiment, 95th Artillery Battalion, 95th Engineer Battalion

Home Station: Berlin (?)

Formed in Krasnik, Poland, on October 24, 1939, this division controlled a number of field recruit (training and replacement) battalions in Poland. It was redesignated Staff, 100th Replacement Command (*Kdr. der Ersatztruppen 100*) on June 1, 1940.

Sources: Lexikon; Tessin, Vol. 10: 148.

426TH LANDESSCHÜTZEN DIVISION

The 426th was formed in the East on October 23, 1939. It was an Upper Rhine unit affiliated with the XII Military District and controlled various older age units. It was redesignated 556th Infantry Division on February 1, 1940, and was sent to a quiet sector on the Western Front.

Lieutenant General Georg Poten was the 426th Landesschützen only commander.

Sources: Keilig: 261; Lexikon; Tessin, Vol. 10: 150.

427TH LANDESSCHÜTZEN DIVISION

This north Bavarian (Wehrkreis XIII) unit was established in Poland on October 24, 1939. On February 16, 1940, it was redesignated 557th Infantry Division and was sent to the Western Front (Upper Rhine) as a positional division.

Its commander was Major General Maximilian Zwern.

See 557th Infantry Division later in this chapter.

Sources: Keilig: 383; Lexikon; Tessin, Vol. 10: 152.

428TH LANDESSCHÜTZEN DIVISION

Composition (1939): 1st Landesschützen Regiment, 2nd Landesschützen Regiment, 3rd Landesschützen Regiment

Home Station: Stettin, Wehrkreis II

Formed under the staff of Wehrkreis XX on October 25, 1939, this unit controlled Pomeranian Landesschützen units. In the fall of 1940, it was reorganized to control the 23rd Infantry Regiment (265th, 363rd, and 717th Landesschützen Battalions), with the 259th, 354th, 713th, 714th, 397th, and 985th Landesschützen Battalions coming directly under divisional control. The division was dissolved on December 20, 1942.

Its commanders were Colonel/Major General Kurt Wolff (October 25, 1939) and Major General/Lieutenant General Adolf Janssen (February 7, 1940).

Notes and Sources: Stettin is now Szczecin, Poland. Wolff was promoted to major general on November 1, 1939. Keilig: 376; Lexikon; Tessin, Vol. 10: 154.

429TH LANDESSCHÜTZEN DIVISION

Composition: 33rd Landesschützen Regiment, 103rd Landesschützen Regiment, 312th Landesschützen Battalion, 356th Landesschützen Battalion, 475th Landesschützen Battalion

Home Station: Kassel, Wehrkreis IX

This divisional staff was formed on October 21, 1939, to control Landesschützen units in what was formerly western and southern Poland, under the command of Wehrkreis XXI. It also engaged in occupation duties. By October 1940, the division controlled only the 312th, 356th and 475th Landesschützen Battalions (without any regimental headquarters), and its men were employed in guarding French and Belgian prisoners-of-war. The 429th was dissolved on March 26, 1943.

Its commanders included Lieutenant General Baron Heinrich von Hadeln (September 25, 1939), Major General Wilhelm Mittermaier (January 6, 1941), and Major General/Lieutenant General Werner Schartow (February 19, 1942).

Notes and Sources: General Hadeln died suddenly in Posen on December 28, 1940. The senior regimental commander directed the division under General Mittermaier arrived. Schartow was promoted to lieutenant general on March 1, 1943.
Keilig: 294; Tessin, Vol. 10: 156; OB 42: 28; OB 43: 40; OB 45: 263.

430TH INFANTRY DIVISION (z.b.V.)

Composition: 301st Landesschützen Battalion, 310th Landesschützen Battalion, 369th Landesschützen and 723rd Landesschützen Battalion

Home Station: Cottbus, Wehrkreis III

The 430th was formed in western Poland on October 24, 1939, to control Landesschützen units between Brody and the Ukraine (Galicia). It was sent to Holland in May 1940 and was

there when the French surrendered. The division was disbanded on July 25, 1940, and its Staff was used to form Corps Command XXXVII (later LXXXII Corps). Its battalions were given
to the 429th and 431st Landesschützen Divisions. Its commanders were Major General Kurt Schreiber (September 1939) and
Major General Maximilian Renz (December 1, 1939).

Sources: Keilig: 273; Nafziger 2000: 339; Tessin, Vol. 10: 158; OB
42: 28; OB 45: 263.

431ST LANDESSCHÜTZEN DIVISION

Composition: 53rd Landesschützen Regiment, 103rd Landesschützen Regiment

Home Station: Leipzig, Wehrkreis IV

The 431st Landesschützen Division (*Div z.b.V. 431*) was
formed in Saxony on October 20, 1939, to control six Landesschützen battalions. In October 1940, it was transferred to Litz-
mannstadt, Generalgouvernment (formerly Lodz, Poland), to
guard POW camps in that area. It was dissolved on March 26,
1943.

Its commanders included Colonel/Major General Hermann Meyer-Rabingen (October 25, 1939), Lieutenant General Emil Zimmermann (December 1, 1939), Major General/
Lieutenant General Manfred von Schwerin (October 1, 1941)
and Major General Johann von Stein (early 1943).

Sources: Meyer-Rabingen was promoted to major general on
November 1, 1939. Manfred von Schwerin was promoted to lieutenant general on July 1, 1941.
Keilig: 226, 319; Kursietis: 207; Lexikon; Tessin, Vol. 10: 160; OB
42: 28; OB 43: 40; OB 45: 263.

432ND LANDESSCHÜTZEN DIVISION

Composition: 41st Landesschützen Regiment, 84th Landesschützen Regiment

Home Station: Cosel, Wehrkreis VIII

Originally organized in Oppeln, Silesia (now Oppolie,
Poland) on October 24, 1939, the 432nd was reorganized as a

replacement division on October 1, 1942, when the Home Army divided the replacement and training missions of Wehrkreis VIII. By the end of 1943, it included the 370th Grenadier Replacement Regiment (six battalions), the 528th Grenadier Replacement Regiment (five battalions), the 16th Artillery Training Regiment (four battalions), the 8th Engineer Replacement Battalion, the 8th Driver Replacement Battalion and the 8th Driver Training Battalion. It took charge of replacement units in Silesia and, in 1944, expanded them into replacement and training units when the 148th and 158th Reserve Divisions gave up their training functions. The 432nd was still engaged in these operations in early 1945, when the Soviets invaded Silesia. In September 1944, elements of the divisional staff were involved in collecting infantrymen from disorganized units at Königshutte, Upper Silesia, and the division headquarters was located at Gleiwitz at the end of 1944. The 432nd was incorporated into the field army in the spring of 1945. The exact date this occurred is not clear, but it was probably on March 16, 1945, the day the "March of the Goths" began in the East (i.e., the day most of the Home Army was sent to the front).

Its divisional commanders were Lieutenant General Fritz von der Lippe (October 25, 1939), Major General/Lieutenant General Ivo von Trotha (January 10, 1940), Major General/ Lieutenant General Heinrich Thoma (August 3, 1942), Lieutenant General Rene de l'Homme de Courbiere (September 8, 1943), and Thoma (October 20, 1943–end).

Notes and Sources: Trotha was promoted to lieutenant general on April 1, 1941. Thoma was promoted to lieutenant general on September 1, 1943. He died in a Soviet prison in 1948.

Keilig: 206, 349; *Kriegstagebuch des OKW*, Volume II: 1462; Kursietis: 207; Lexikon; Mehner, Vol. 12: 461; Tessin, Vol. 10: 162; RA: 132; OB 43: 184; OB 45: 264.

433RD REPLACEMENT DIVISION (MOTORIZED)

Composition: 533rd Grenadier Replacement Regiment (five battalions), 543rd Grenadier Replacement Regiment (six battalions), 168th Artillery Replacement Regiment, 9th Reconnaissance Replacement Battalion, 68th Engineer Replacement

A Landser observes the enemy through a set of heavy binoculars. This man is a member of a mountain unit. He wears the Edelweiss—the emblem of the mountain troops—on the left side of his cap. HITM ARCHIVE

Battalion, 1st Railroad Engineer Replacement and Training Battalion, 3rd Construction Engineer Replacement and Training Battalion, 3rd Driver Replacement and Training Battalion, 23rd Motorcycle Replacement and Training Battalion

Home Station: Frankfurt-on-the-Oder, Wehrkreis III

The 433rd was established in Küstrin on June 1, 1943, when the 233rd Motorized Replacement Division was upgraded to a reserve panzer division and was sent to Denmark. The 433rd took over the replacement units formerly belonging to the 233rd. The new division directed a variety of replacement and replacement-training units until January 1945, when the Russians threatened the German capital. The 433rd was then sent into battle on the Eastern Front, along with all the other miscellaneous formations Hitler could muster. It was smashed by January 31, 1945. It remnants were incorporated into the ad hoc Division Raegener on February 4. The survivors of the 433rd were still serving in eastern Germany when Berlin fell. The division's commander throughout its existence was Lieutenant General Max Dennerlein (1945).

Sources: Keilig: 68; Lexikon; Mehner, Vol. 12: 461; Tessin, Vol. 10: 164; OB 45: 264.

438TH REPLACEMENT DIVISION (LATER SPECIAL PURPOSE DIVISIONAL [z.b.V.] COMMAND)

Composition: 18th Landesschützen Regiment, 184th Landesschützen Regiment, Frontier Guard Sector XVIII

Home Station: Klagenfurt, Wehrkreis XVIII

Created on November 1, 1943, the 438th was almost immediately made responsible for guarding the former German (Austrian)–Yugoslav frontier in the southeastern part of the XVIII Military District and probably for guarding POW camps as well. Apparently the Home Army intended to make it a replacement unit but, with these missions, the plan was aborted. The division was redesignated the 438th Special Purposes Divisional Command (*Division Kommandos z.b.V. 438*) in late 1943. It continued to perform these duties until the end of the war.

Lieutenant General Ferdinand Noeldechen commanded the 438th throughout its existence.

Sources: Keilig: 244; Mehner, Vol. 12: 461; Tessin, Vol. 10: 184; OB 45: 264.

440TH ASSAULT DIVISION (ASSAULT DIVISION RHODES)

Composition: Panzer Battalion Rhodes, Storm Regiment Rhodes, IV/999th Artillery Regiment, 999th Panzer Reconnaissance Battalion, 999th Engineer Company, Signal Company Rhodes, Fla Company Rhodes, Field Replacement Battalion Rhodes, 999th Divisional Supply Troops

Home Station: Zittau, Wehrkreis IV

This division was formed on the island of Rhodes (in the Aegean Sea, off the coast of Greece) in June 1943 from Assault Brigade Rhodes. Its infantry components were from the 440th Grenadier Regiment of the 164th Light Afrika Division (or at least those elements that had escaped the German collapse in North Africa) and the remnants of the 999th Light Afrika Division (Penal), which had been destroyed in Tunisia in May 1943. (A sizable minority of the 999th had not yet been sent to Tunisia when Army Group Afrika collapsed.) The division remained in Rhodes until September 1944, when it evacuated the island during the general withdrawal from the Aegean Sea and the southern Balkans. The division was sent to Belgrade, where it was absorbed by Panzer Grenadier Division Brandenburg on October 17, 1944. Its men went on to fight on the Russian Front.

Its commanders were Lieutenant General Ulrich Werner Kleeman (June 1943) and Major General Ludwig Fricke (September 1, 1944).

Sources: Keilig: 91, 171, 244; *Kriegstagebuch des OKW*, Volume IV: 1882; Kursietis: 208; Mehner, Vol. 12: 461; Tessin, Vol. 14: 207-8; OB

45: 285; also see Paul Carell, *Foxes of the Desert* (1960) (hereafter cited as "Carell 1960").

441ST LANDESSCHÜTZEN DIVISION

Composition: 148th Machine Gun Regiment and various Landesschützen battalions

Home Station: Wehrkreis VI

Formed in Westphalia and the Rhineland on October 18, 1939, this unit guarded a sector of the Western Front during the "Phoney War" period until February 15, 1940, when it was reorganized and redesignated 554th Infantry Division (a positional unit). Its commander was Lieutenant General Baron Anton von Hirschberg.

See 554th Infantry Division later in this chapter.

Sources: Keilig: 244; Mehner, Vol. 12: 461; Tessin, Vol. 10: 174; OB 45: 265.

442ND LANDESSCHÜTZEN DIVISION

The 442nd was formed on October 18, 1939, to control Landesschützen battalions in the rear area of the 5th Army on the Lower Rhine sector of the Western Front. It was sent to the Eastern Front in 1943, where it served as a line-of-communications division for Army Group Center. It was disbanded on August 24, 1944, after the army group had been crushed in Operation "Bagration." Its men were sent to various decimated divisions.

Its commanders included Lieutenant General Karl Bornemann (January 10, 1940), Major General Count Erwin von Rothkirch und Trach (April 25, 1940), Bornemann (October 11, 1940), Major General Count Bogislav von Schwerin (January 1, 1944), and Lieutenant General Friedrich Fuerst (February 20, 1944).

Notes and Sources: The 442nd was associated with Wehrkreis VI. Keilig: 46, 319; Lexikon; Tessin, Vol. 10, 182; RA: 130; OB 42: 115; OB 43: 213; OB 45: 265.

443RD LANDESSCHÜTZEN DIVISION

This Hanover-Brunswick-Anhalt division was formed on October 18, 1939, to control older-age (Landesschützen) battalions near the Western Front. It was reorganized and redesignated 555th Infantry Division on February 10, 1940.

Its commander was Colonel Dr. Waldemar Henrici.

See also 555th Infantry Division later in this chapter.

Notes and Sources: The 443rd was associated with Wehrkreis XI. Keilig: 136; Lexikon; Tessin, Vol. 10: 184.

444TH SECURITY DIVISION

Composition: 45th Security Regiment, 602nd Security Regiment, 444th Reconnaissance Company, 444th Tank Destroyer Company, 444th Engineer Company, 444th Signal Company, 360th Divisional Supply Troops

Home Station: Darmstadt, Wehrkreis XII

Formed on October 24, 1939, as a special purpose division staff (*Divisionsstab z.b.V. 444*) in the rear of the 1st Army on the Western Front, the 444th consisted of the 33rd Infantry Replacement Regiment and some GHQ units, but with no artillery. Stationed in France and placed under 9th Army in the second half of 1940, the 444th was redesignated a security division on March 15, 1941, and was sent to Russia, where it served in the communications zone of the southern and central sectors until 1944. By February 1942, it controlled the 360th Reinforced Infantry Regiment (formerly of the 221st Infantry Division), the 708th Wach (Guard) Battalion, the 445th Panzer Company, the II/221st Artillery Regiment (three batteries), and the 46th Landesschützen (later Security) Regiment. (A reinforced infantry regiment normally had its own organic artillery battalion.) Later it added the 828th Signal Battalion, the 444th Cossack Cavalry Unit, the 445th Panzer Company (equipped with captured tanks) and the 811th Turk Battalion. The division was reorganized again in the spring of 1944, and lost most of its depleted combat units. This was probably a result of the casualties it suffered in the anti-partisan fighting of 1943–44. The Staff, however, continued to operate under the Wehrmacht Commander Ukraine and later Korueck 558 (the rear area command of 8th Army) until May 11, 1944, when it was disbanded.

Its commanders included Major General Ritter Josef Alois von Molo (October 25, 1939), Lieutenant General Wilhelm Russwurm (April 1, 1941), Lieutenant General Helge Auleb (February 3, 1942), and Major General/Lieutenant General Adalbert Mikuliscz (March 4, 1942).

Notes and Sources: Mikuliscz was promoted to lieutenant general on February 1, 1943.

Keilig: 229; *Kriegstagebuch des OKW*, Volume I: 1127; Nafziger 2000: 506; RA: 188; OB 43: 215; OB 45: 265.

445TH SPECIAL ADMINISTRATIVE DIVISION STAFF (*DIVISIONSSTAB z.b.V. 445*)

This special purposes divisional staff was from in Koblenz, Wehrkreis XII, on October 14, 1939, to control Landwehr troops behind the West Wall. It was absorbed by the 412th Landesschützen Division on October 12, 1940. Colonel Friedrich Genthe commanded the 445th during the winter of 1939–40.

Sources: Bradley et al., Vol. 4: 229–30; Keilig: 104; Nafziger 2000: 340; Tessin, Vol. 10: 189

454TH SECURITY DIVISION

Composition: 57th Security (formerly Landesschützen) Regiment, 375th Security (formerly Reinforced Infantry) Regiment, III/221st Artillery Regiment (later 454th Artillery Battalion), 454th Ost (Eastern) Cavalry Battalion (later Regiment), 454th Ost Engineer Battalion, 829th Signal Battalion, 375th Divisional Supply Troops

Home Station: Dresden, Wehrkreis IV; 1941: Breslau, Wehrkreis VIII

This division was formed on June 1, 1940, as a special administrative division staff to control replacements on route to the Western Front. It was sent to the Netherlands that summer and was involved in preparations for Operation "Sea Lion," the invasion of the United Kingdom. It was upgraded to security division status on March 19, 1941, and served in the rear area of Army Group South in Russia in 1941. As such it guarded key installations and conducted anti-partisan operations in the Ukraine and nearby regions from 1941 until the end of 1943. Elements of the 454th Security fought on the front line in the Kharkov-Isjum battles of May and June 1942. In early 1944, the division was attached to the 4th Panzer Army and was given the responsibility of defending Rovno, an important railroad junction west of Kiev. The 454th Division held the city from January 6 to February 2, 1944, against regular Soviet forces, but was finally forced to retreat. In July 1944, it was again in the front line, opposing the Russian summer offensive. It was encircled and largely destroyed with XIII Corps at Brody in Belorussia. After this battle, the surviving remnants of the 454th Security were withdrawn from the line and disbanded.

Commanders of the 454th Security Division included Major General/Lieutenant General Rudolf Krantz (June 1, 1940), Major General/Lieutenant General Hermann Wilck (September 29, 1941), Major General/Lieutenant General Hellmuth Koch (December 9, 1941), Colonel Joachim Wagner (April 25, 1944), and Major General Johannes Nedtwig (May 1, 1944).

Notes and Sources: Krantz was promoted to lieutenant general on February 1, 1941. He gave up command of the division due to illness and died in Dresden on October 22, 1941. Wilck was promoted to lieutenant general on October 1, 1941. Koch was promoted to lieutenant general on November 1, 1942. Nedtwig was wounded and captured at Brody.

Keilig: 184; *Kriegstagebuch des OKW*, Volume I: 1127, Seaton: 446–49; Tessin, Vol. 10: 207–9; OB 43: 215; OB 45: 265; Ziemke 1966: 246.

460TH LANDESSCHÜTZEN DIVISION

Composition: 105th Landesschützen Regiment, 106th Landesschützen Regiment, 1–3./460th Landesschützen Artillery Regiment

Home Station: Lübeck, Wehrkreis X

Formed by Army Group B behind the Western Front, the 460th was created on April 24, 1940, to direct older age troops. A month later it was sent to Denmark, and was dissolved on October 25, 1940, in the partial demobilization after the fall of France.

Its commander was Lieutenant General Baron Guenther von Hammerstein-Equord.

Notes and Sources: The 104th Landesschützen Regiment may have been part of the division, but this is not certain. The 105th and 106th Regiments controlled two battalions each. Guenther von Hammerstein's younger brother Kurt was the former commander-in-chief of the German Army.

Keilig: 124; Kursietis: 209, Lexikon; Tessin, Vol. 10: 221.

461ST REPLACEMENT DIVISION

Composition: 11th Grenadier Replacement and Training Regiment, 491st Grenadier Replacement and Training Regiment, 521st Grenadier Replacement Regiment, 1st Transportation Replacement and Training Battalion, 311th Engineer Replacement and Training Battalion, 2nd Construction Engineer Replacement and Training Battalion, 1st Driver Replacement and Training Battalion

Home Station: Bialystok, Wehrkreis I

On August 1, 1941, this division's headquarters was organized as Special Purpose Division Command Bialystok. It controlled Landesschützen battalions and miscellaneous formations in what was formerly eastern Poland until September 24, 1942, at which time it became the 461st Replacement Division and took over several replacement battalions and some replacement and training units in the I Military District. It also had the mission of establishing raiding detachments for special missions, mainly on the Russian Front. In the latter part of 1944, as the Soviets overran Poland, the 461st was transferred from the southeastern part of the Wehrkreis to Osterode, on the western edge. It was disbanded in March 1945, and its units were transferred to combat divisions. Its subordinate units had been transferred to combat divisions some weeks before.

The 461st's commanders included Lieutenant General Hans Erich Nolte (August 1, 1941), Major General Richard zu und von Wenk (September 25, 1942), and Lieutenant General Wolf Schede (April 1, 1944).

Sources: Keilig: 295; Kursietis: 209; Mehner, Vol. 10; Tessin, Vol. 10: 223; RA: 22-23; OB 43: 184; OB 45: 266.

462ND VOLKSGRENADIER DIVISION

Composition: 1215th Grenadier Regiment, 1216th Grenadier Regiment, 1217th Grenadier Regiment, 1462nd Artillery Regiment, 462nd Fusilier Company, 1462nd Tank Destroyer Battalion, 1462nd Engineer Battalion, 1462nd Signal Company, 1462nd Field Replacement Battalion, 1462nd Divisional Supply Regiment

Home Station: Metz, Wehrkreis XII

The 462nd was created in the city of Nancy in the Lorraine province of France as a replacement unit. Activated on October 10, 1942, it assumed command of the replacement units formerly belonging to the 182nd Reserve Division, then on its way to the English Channel. It was filled out from miscellaneous school and fortress units and, by December 1943, included the 246th Grenadier Replacement Regiment (three battalions) in Luxembourg, the 552nd Grenadier Replacement Regiment (six battalions) in the Metz area, the 572nd Grenadier Replacement Regiment (seven battalions) around Saarburg, the 25th Artillery Replacement Regiment (three battalions) in the Metz sector, the 14th Machine Gun Battalion in Metz, and the 3rd Bridge Construction Replacement and Training Battalion, also in the garrison city of Metz.

After D-Day, the division was reorganized for combat and was sent into battle in August 1944, following the collapse of the German front in Normandy. The following month, it was upgraded to full combat division status and was redesignated a Volksgrenadier unit. The 462nd Volksgrenadier Division included the 1215th Grenadier Regiment (also known as Regiment Stoessel), the 1216th Grenadier Regiment (also known as

Regiment Wagner), and the 1217th Grenadier Regiment (the former 1010th Security Regiment). It also included the 1462nd Artillery Regiment (four battalions), the 462nd Fusilier Company, the 1462nd Engineer Battalion and the 1462nd Field Replacement Battalion. On November 1, the 1216th Grenadier Regiment was transferred to the nearby 19th Volksgrenadier Division and to fill the gap the 1010th Security Regiment was extracted from the 1217th Grenadier Regiment and reorganized. (This did not increase the number of men available to the division, however.)

From early November until November 28, 1944, the 462nd defended Metz, its old home station, against vastly superior elements of Patton's U.S. 3rd Army. The division had only 7,000 men when the battle began and lacked heavy weapons; however, its student units included some of the best young soldiers in Nazi Germany. The ranks of the 1215th Regiment at Metz, for example, were made up almost entirely of second lieutenants who had won battlefield commissions, mainly on the Eastern Front. During the siege the divisional commander, Lieutenant General Vollrath Luebbe, suffered a stroke and had to be relieved on November 8. He was replaced by Major General Heinrich Kittel, a tough veteran who had successfully defended fortresses on the Russian Front. Two weeks later, he was seriously wounded in front-line fighting. Finally, after a heroic defense, the 462nd was overwhelmed and the fortress fell on November 28. General Kittel was captured in a field hospital and only about 1,100 men from the 462nd Volksgrenadier escaped the fall of fortress Metz; almost all of these were wounded men who had been evacuated earlier. The division was officially disbanded shortly afterward.

Commanders of the 462nd Division included Major General Otto Schilling (October 5, 1942), Lieutenant General Ernst Güntzel (December 5, 1942), Lieutenant General Hans von Sommerfeld (December 17, 1942), Lieutenant General Walter Krause (July 15, 1944), Lübbe (October 15, 1944), Kittel (November 8, 1944), and Colonel Joachim Wagner (November 22, 1944).

Notes and Sources: Lothringen was the German name for Lorraine. General Güntzel died suddenly on December 17, 1942. Kittel was unconscious and in field hospital when he was captured. He had been wounded in the foot and doctors had just operated on him. Colonel Joachim Wagner, former commander of the NCO School of Wehrkreis XII, which had been converted into the 1216th Grenadier Regiment, commanded the division during the final stages of the Battle of Metz.

Chant, Volume 15: 2095; Cole 1950; 48, 125, 430, 446–47; Keilig: 170, 299; Anthony Kemp, *The Unknown Battle: Metz, 1944* (1981); Lexikon; Tessin, Vol. 10: 225–26; RA: 188, 190–91; OB 45: 266.

463RD REPLACEMENT DIVISION

Composition: 293rd Infantry Replacement Regiment, 523rd Infantry Replacement Regiment, 23rd Artillery Replacement Regiment (Motorized), 3rd Engineer Replacement Battalion, 23rd Engineer Replacement and Training Battalion, 208th Panzer Engineer Replacement Battalion, 4th Railroad Engineer Replacement and Training Battalion, 3rd Driver Replacement and Training Battalion

Home Station: Potsdam, Wehrkreis III

In the reorganization of the Replacement Army in the fall of 1942, the 143rd and 153rd Replacement Divisions were sent to Russia as field training and reserve divisions, respectively. The 463rd was created on October 1, 1942, to control the replacement units (and some replacement-training units) they left behind. In 1944, it was expanded to include more replacement and training units. In January 1945, the 463rd was assigned to the 4th Panzer Army on the Oder and was involved in front line fighting during the last campaign on the Eastern Front, which ended in the fall of Berlin.

Its commanders included Major General/Lieutenant General Eugen Demoll (September 25, 1942), Major General/Lieutenant General Rudolf Habenicht (May 1, 1943), and Lieutenant General Hans Schitting (March 28, 1945).

Notes and Sources: The Hungarian 13th Artillery Battalion and the I/87th (Hungarian) Infantry Regiment were attached to the division on March 23, 1945. Demoll was promoted to lieutenant general on November 1, 1942. Habenicht reached the same rank on June 1, 1943. As the U.S. Army pushed into the rear of the German armies in the East, they captured General Habenicht on March 28, 1945.

Keilig: 66, 121, 300; Mehner, Vol. 12: 461; Nafziger 2000: 585; Tessin, Vol. 10: 229–30; OB 45: 267.

464TH REPLACEMENT (LATER TRAINING) DIVISION

Composition: 14th Grenadier Replacement and Training Regiment, 534th Grenadier Replacement Regiment, 24th Artillery Replacement Regiment, 4th Transportation Replacement and Training Battalion, 14th Engineer Replacement Battalion, 4th Construction Engineer Replacement and Training Battalion, 4th Driver Replacement and Training Battalion

Home Station: Chemnitz, Wehrkreis IV

This Saxon division was created by IV Military District on September 23, 1942, when the 154th and 174th Replacement Divisions were upgraded to reserve division status. The 464th took over the replacement units that they left behind and some replacement and training units as well. In late 1944, the division expanded its subordinate elements into replacement-training units. On March 25, 1945, it was redesignated a training division. The next day, *Ostgotenbewegung* ("Eastern March of the Goths") began. In this operation, the Home Army was basically dissolved and sent to the front. (The Western March of the Goths—the transfer of Home Army units to the Western Front —began on March 28.) The 464th Training Division was sent into action on the Eastern Front, fighting as infantry and defending east Saxony as part of the 4th Panzer Army. The remnants of the 545th Volksgrenadier Division were attached to the 464th for this last battle. Most of the 464th surrendered to the Americans on May 9, 1945.

The commanders of this division included Colonel/Major General Wolfgang Hauser (September 23, 1942), Lieutenant General Rudolf von Tschudi (July 27, 1944), Lieutenant General Rudolf Pilz (August 27, 1944), Major General Eugen Theilacker (April 1945), and Lieutenant General Otto Heidkämper (April 27, 1945).

Sources: The 1st Rocket Launcher Training Regiment (four battalions) was attached to the division on March 26, 1945. Wolfgang Hauser was promoted to major general on August 25, 1942.

Keilig: 130; *Kriegstagebuch des OKW*, Volume I: 1147; Nafziger 2000: 585; Tessin, Vol. 10: 233; RA: 72–74; OB 45: 267.

465TH REPLACEMENT DIVISION

Composition: 515th Grenadier Replacement, 525th Grenadier Replacement Regiment, 25th Artillery Replacement Regiment, 18th Reconnaissance Replacement Battalion, 5th Panzer Engineer Replacement and Training Battalion, 5th Construction Engineer Replacement and Training Battalion, 55th Army Fla Replacement and Training Battalion, 5th Heavy Mortar (Rocket Launcher) Replacement and Training Battalion

Home Station: Ludwigsburg, Wehrkreis V

Created on September 29, 1942, in the Epinal area, the new division assumed command of the replacement units the 165th Reserve Division left behind when it went to France. In late 1942, the 465th was transferred to the Epinal area of eastern France but returned to Ludwigsburg the next year. In autumn 1944, it was expanded to include replacement and training units. It was still conducting these functions in 1945, when the Western Allies overran Württemberg and Baden. The 465th Replacement Division, meanwhile, joined the field army and continued to operate until the end of the war.

Its commanders were Colonel/Major General Gottfried von Erdmannsdorff (October 1942) and Lieutenant General Kurt Hoffmann (March 1944).

Notes and Sources: Gottfried von Erdmannsdorff was promoted to major general on December 1, 1942.

Keilig: 83; Lexikon; Mehner, Vol. 12: 461; Tessin, Vol. 10: 233; RA: 72–74, 88, 90; OB 45: 267.

466TH REPLACEMENT DIVISION

Composition: 416th Grenadier Replacement Regiment, 426th Grenadier Replacement Regiment, 15th Bicycle (*Radfahr*) Replacement Battalion, 26th Engineer Replacement Battalion,

A machine-gun unit advancing across the steppe. Early in the war, most German infantry battalions had three rifle companies and a machine-gun company. Some, however, had a heavy-weapons or mortar company instead of the MG company. HTM ARCHIVE

6th Engineer Replacement and Training Battalion, 2nd Engineer Bridge Replacement Battalion, 6th Motorized Replacement and Training Battalion, 46th Fla Replacement and Training Battalion, 276th Army Anti-Aircraft Replacement and Training Battalion, 6th Forward Observer Replacement and Training Battalion, 6th Driver Replacement and Training Battalion

Home Station: Bielefeld, Wehrkreis VI

This division was created on November 23, 1944, when the 176th Replacement Division was converted into an infantry division and sent to the front. It took control of the units the 176th left behind. It lost almost all of its subordinate regiments and battalions to the front-line combat divisions when the "Western March of the Goths" began on March 28, 1945. The division staff, however, was withdrawn to Driburg, where it took charge of the 571st Grenadier Replacement and Training Regiment. It was on the Western Front when the war ended and surrendered to the British on May 11, 1945.

Lieutenant General Friedrich Karst commanded the 466th throughout its existence.

Sources: Keilig: 163; Lexikon; Mehner, Vol. 12: 461; Tessin, Vol. 10: 236.

467TH REPLACEMENT DIVISION

Composition: 387th Grenadier Replacement Regiment, 517th Grenadier Replacement Regiment, 537th Mountain Jaeger Replacement Regiment, 79th Mountain Artillery Replacement Regiment, 7th Forward Observer Replacement and Train-ing Battalion, 7th Reconnaissance Replacement Battalion, 7th Engineer Replacement Battalion, 54th Engineer Replacement and Training Battalion, 3rd Engineer Lehr (Demonstration) Battalion, 7th Motorized Replacement and Training Battalion, 7th Driver Replacement and Training Battalion, 2nd Administrative Troops Replacement and Training Battalion

Home Station: Munich, Wehrkreis VII

This unit was formed on October 1, 1942, when the replacement and training functions of the 157th Reserve Division were divided. It took over the subordinate units of the 407th Replacement Division when it was disbanded in September 1944, and the subordinate units of the 467th became replacement and training units again. It was still conducting these missions in the Bavaria- Palatinate-Swabia region when the Western Allies overran southern Germany in the early spring of 1945. The 467th, meanwhile, sent its subordinate units to combat divisions in late March 1945 (during the March of the Goths), but it was simultaneously redesignated Training Division Bavaria and took charge of the 407th and 467th Grenadier Training Regiments.

The divisional commanders of the 467th were Lieutenant General Karl Graf (October 1, 1942), Lieutenant General Karl Maderholz (November 2, 1943), and Lieutenant General Rudolf Sintzenich (January 13, 1944–end).

Sources: Keilig: 113, 214; Lexikon; Tessin, Vol. 10: 239; RA: 118; OB 43: 184; OB 45: 267

469TH SPECIAL ADMINISTRATIVE DIVISION STAFF

Formed in Eisenach, Thuringia (central Germany) on September 24, 1944, under the IX Military District, this division remained in Hessen-Thuringia until April 25, 1945, when it was sent to join the 4th Panzer Army in Saxony. It was still there when the war ended. The staff apparently managed to surrender to the Americans.

Lieutenant General Horst von Uckermann commanded the 469th.

Sources: Keilig: 351; Lexikon; Tessin, Vol. 10: 244.

471ST REPLACEMENT DIVISION

Composition: 551st Grenadier Replacement Regiment, 561st Grenadier Replacement Regiment, 571st Grenadier Replacement Regiment, 13th Artillery Replacement Regiment, 14th Reconnaissance Replacement Battalion, 4th Panzer Engineer Replacement Battalion, 4th Engineer Replacement Battalion, 11th Construction Engineer Replacement and Training Battalion, 11th Motorized Replacement and Training Battalion, 11th Driver Replacement and Training Battalion

Home Station: Hanover, Wehrkreis XI .

The 471st was organized on September 28, 1942, to take over the replacement functions of the 171st and 191st Reserve Divisions, which had been sent to the English Channel area. When these units were committed to the fighting on the Western Front, the 471st assumed their training missions as well, and its subordinate units became replacement-training units. The 471st ceased operations when Hanover was overrun in the spring of 1945. During the "March of the Goths," when the units of the Home Army were sent to the fronts (March 26–29, 1945), the 561st Grenadier Training Regiment, the 13th Artillery Training Regiment, the 4th Engineer Training Battalion and the 11th Construction Engineer Training Battalion were sent to the 3rd Panzer Army on the Eastern Front. The rest of the division—the 551st and 571st Grenadier Training Regiment, the 19th Artillery Training Battalion, the 13th Signal Training Battalion, the 19th Panzer Engineer Training Battalion, the 11th Landesschützen Training Battalion, as well as the Officers' Training Unit of the 31st Artillery Training Battalion and the Army NCO Schools for Rocket Launcher and Infantry troops—were sent to the 1st Parachute Army on the Western Front.

The division's commanders were Lieutenant General Erich Denecke (September 28, 1942) and Lieutenant General Ernst Häckel (February 1945).

Sources: Keilig: 67; Kursietis: 211; Lexikon; Tessin, Vol. 10: 248–49; RA: 174–78; OB 45: 268.

476TH REPLACEMENT DIVISION

Composition: 211th Grenadier Replacement Regiment, 253rd Grenadier Replacement Regiment, 536th Grenadier Replacement Regiment, 16th Artillery Replacement Regiment

Home Station: Wuppertal, Wehrkreis VI

This division's formation was authorized in October 1944, but it was not organized until January 7, 1945, from part of the

526th Replacement Division. It was sent to the Western Front on March 28, 1945. It joined the 15th Army on the lower Rhine and was quickly destroyed by the U.S. Army on March 29, 1945, as it maneuvered to encircle Army Group B in the Ruhr Pocket.

Lieutenant General Hans Bergen commanded the 476th Replacement Division.

Notes and Sources: Bergen was captured on March 29, when the division was overrun.

Bradley, Vol. 1; Keilig: 29; Lexikon; Tessin, Vol. 10: 259.

480TH REPLACEMENT DIVISION

Composition: 22nd Grenadier Replacement and Training Regiment, 269th Grenadier Replacement and Training Regiment, 22nd Artillery Replacement and Training Regiment, 20th Cavalry Replacement Battalion, 30th Engineer Replacement and Training Battalion, 34th Engineer Replacement and Training Battalion, 52nd Fla Replacement and Training Battalion

Home Station: Verden, Wehrkreis X

The 480th Replacement Division was activated on November 1, 1944, from part of the 180th Replacement Division, most of which had gone to the Netherlands. The 480th continued to function as a replacement/training division until March 28, 1945, when the Home Army was basically dissolved and its units sent to the front. Part of the "Western Goths," the 480th was sent to the Weser River on the Western Front with a strength of 7,491 men, making it was one of the stronger divisions in OB West. It was still on the northern sector of the Western Front when the war ended.

Its commander was Lieutenant General Martin Gilbert. Colonel Martin was acting commander on April 30, 1945, the day Hitler committed suicide.

Notes and Sources: The division added the 2nd Rocket Launcher Training Regiment in late March 1945.

Keilig: 107; Lexikon; Mehner, Vol. 12: 461; Nafziger 2000: 588; Tessin, Vol. 10: 268.

487TH REPLACEMENT DIVISION

Composition (late 1942): 557th Grenadier Replacement Regiment, 587th Grenadier Replacement Regiment, 96th Artillery Replacement Battalion, 86th Engineer Replacement Battalion, 17th Motorized Replacement and Training Battalion. The 277th Army Anti-Aircraft Replacement and Training Battalion was added later.

Home Station: Linz, Wehrkreis XVII

Created during the "People's Mobilization" of October 1, 1942, this unit supplied replacements from northern Austria until its facilities were overrun by the Russians in the spring of 1945. It was expanded to include training functions in 1944, and was mobilized for front-line duty on March 25, 1945.

Its commanders were Major General Rudolf-Eduard Licht (October 1, 1942) and Major General Paul Wagner (June 15, 1943).

Sources: Keilig: 360; Kursietis: 262; Lexikon; Tessin, Vol. 10: 283; RA: 222–23; OB 45: 268.

490TH REPLACEMENT DIVISION

Composition (January 1945): 30th Grenadier Replacement and Training Regiment, 520th Grenadier Replacement and Training Regiment, 225th Artillery Replacement and Training Regiment, 20th Engineer Replacement and Training Battalion, 10th Fusilier Replacement and Training Battalion, 10th Motorized Replacement and Training Battalion, 10th Driver Replacement and Training Battalion

Home Station: Neumuenster, Werhkreis X

This division was activated on November 1, 1944, and included elements of the 190th Replacement Division, which was now in the Netherlands. The 490th provided replacement and training services for the divisions affiliated with the X Military District until March 27, 1945, when it was ordered to the Weser sector of the Western Front. It was with the 1st Parachute Army of OB Northwest when the war ended. It surrendered to the British on May 8, 1945.

Its commanders were Major General Ernst Wisselinck (November 1944) and Colonel/Major General Heinrich Behrend (April 1945–end).

Notes and Sources: Behrend was promoted to major general on April 17, 1945. When the 490th Replacement Division went to the front, it absorbed the 10th Army NCO School for Infantry and another small training school from Lübeck—a total of 2,159 men.

Keilig: 26, 373; Lexikon; Mehner, Vol. 12: 461; Tessin, Vol. 10: 289.

521ST INFANTRY DIVISION

Composition: 51st Frontier Guard Regiment, 61st Frontier Guard Regiment

Home Station: Allenstein, Wehrkreis I

The 521st Infantry was formed from the 15th Frontier Guard Sector Command in East Prussia on November 1, 1939. On March 18, 1940, it was reorganized into the 395th Infantry Division. It never saw combat.

The commanders of the 521st Infantry were Major Generals Wolf Schele (November 1939) and Hans Stengel (January 10, 1940).

526TH FRONTIER GUARD (LATER REPLACEMENT) DIVISION

Composition: 211th Infantry Replacement Regiment, 253rd Infantry Replacement Regiment, 536th Infantry Replacement Regiment, 26th Artillery Replacement Regiment, 6th Motorized Replacement Battalion, 6th (later 16th) Motorized Training Battalion, 26th Motorized Replacement Battalion, 26th Motorized Training Battalion, 16th Engineer Training Battalion, 253rd Engineer Training Battalion, 109th Fla Replacement Battalion

Home Station: Aachen, Wehrkreis VI

Formed in Cologne from Frontier Guard Sector Command 9 on October 15, 1940, this division initially controlled the 6th and 16th Frontier Guard Regiments (six battalions total) on the

German western border and later in Belgium until October 1940, when it took charge of the 33rd and 76th Landesschuetzen Regiment.s and seven independent Landesschuetzen battalions in the Aachen-Cologne area. The division was dissolved on December 15, 1941, and its soldiers were transferred to the 406th Replacement Division. The division headquarters became Staff, 329th Infantry Division.

Five days after the original 526th was disbanded, elements of the old division were used to form "*Div. Stab 'Aachen' (526. Div.).*" By September 1942, this headquarters controlled the units listed above (see Composition). In 1944 it began conducting training operations as well and most of its units became replacement and training formations. In September 1944, as the Americans reached the West Wall and the British paratroopers landed at Arnhem, the 526th (which had 12,711 men) was hurriedly sent to the Western Front, where it fought in the Battle of Aachen. It was redesignated 526th Reserve Division in late September. It now included the 253rd Reserve Grenadier Regiment, the 416th Reserve Grenadier Regiment, the 536th Reserve Grenadier Regiment, the I/76th Reserve Artillery Regiment, the 253rd Reserve Engineer Battalion, and the 526th Reserve Signal Company. After Aachen, the 526th's combat units fought in the West Wall battles and in the Eifel, before being shifted south to the Rhineland. The unit was still operating in western Germany at the end of the war.

Its commanders included Major General Hans von Sommerfeld (October 25, 1939), Lieutenant General Baron Guenther von Hammerstein-Equord (November 15, 1940), Lieutenant General Fritz Kühne (March 7, 1941), Lieutenant General Kurt Schmidt (March 15, 1944), Lieutenant General Hans Bergen (December 12, 1944), Schmidt (March 2, 1945), and Colonel of Reserves Neumann (March 3, 1945).

Notes and Sources: General Schmidt was killed in action on March 3, 1945.

Bradley et al., Vol. I: 323–25; Cole 1950: 587; Keilig: 29, 305; Lexikon; Tessin, Vol. 10: 75–76; Mehner, Vol. 12: 461; RA: 103; OB 43: 30, 185; OB 45: 268.

537TH FRONTIER GUARD DIVISION

Composition: 191st Frontier Guard Sector, 192nd Frontier Guard Sector

Home Station: Innsbruck, Wehrkreis XVIII

Created on December 9, 1939, to control miscellaneous units on the southern (Austrian) frontier of the Third Reich, the 537th guarded the German-Austrian-Swiss border area until December 9, 1940, when it was disbanded.

Its commander was Major General Heinrich Doehla.

Notes and Sources: Doehla held the honorary rank of lieutenant general.

Keilig: 72; Kursietis: 212; Lexikon; Tessin, Vol. 11: 102; OB 43: 185; OB 45: 268.

538TH FRONTIER GUARD DIVISION

Composition: 193rd Frontier Guard Sector, 194th Frontier Guard Sector, 195th Frontier Guard Sector

Home Station: Sectors headquartered at Spittal, Klagenfurt and Graz, Wehrkreis XVIII, respectively

Along with the 537th Frontier Guard Division, the 538th patrolled the southern border of what was formerly Austria (i.e., the German-Italian and German-Yugoslavian borders) from December 9, 1939 until April 18, 1941, when it was disbanded after the Wehrmacht overran Yugoslavia.

Its commander was Lieutenant General Emmerich von Nagy.

Sources: Keilig: 237; Lexikon; Nafziger 2000: 343; Tessin, Vol. 11: 104; OB 43: 185; OB 45: 269.

539TH LANDESSCHÜTZEN DIVISION

Composition (October 1943): 72nd Landesschützen Regiment, 49th Landesschützen Regiment, 539th Artillery Battalion, 539th Signal Company

Home Station: Frankenburg, later Tabor, Wehrkreis IV

The 539th was formed in the Czech capital on October 15, 1939, to control older age guard and local defense units in northern Bohemia. In October 1942, it took over the few replacement and training battalions in Wehrkreis Bohemia and Moravia. It was still in operation in 1945, when the Russians entered Slovakia. It was then downgraded to a special division command (*Division-Kommandos z.b.V.*) and most of its combat troops were sent to the 48th Infantry Division in Slovakia and to the 168th Infantry Division in Silesia. Part of it, however, continued to fight under divisional command on the Eastern Front. The 539th Special Purposes Division Command surrendered to the Americans on May 9, 1945.

Its commanders included Major General/Lieutenant General Dr. Richard Speich (September 1939) and Lieutenant General Wilhelm Thomas (April 1, 1944). Sources conflict as to who commanded the division next. Some list Major General/Lieutenant General Clemens Betzel (September 1, 1944) and Lieutenant General Helmuth Beukemann (September 4, 1944). According to Bradley et al., Beukemann surrendered the command to the Americans on May 9, 1945.

Sources: Speich was promoted to lieutenant general on February 1, 1941. Betzel was promoted to lieutenant general on January 1, 1945. He was killed in action on the Eastern Front on March 27, 1945.

Bradley et al., Vol. 1: 369–70, 372–73; Hoffmann: 463; Keilig: 32; Kursietis: 213; Mehner, Vol. 12: 461; Tessin, Vol. 11: 104; RA: 262; OB 43: 185; OB 45: 269.

540TH LANDESSCHÜTZEN DIVISION

Composition: Staff, 182nd Landesschützen Regiment, 655th Landesschützen Battalion, 905th Landesschützen Battalion, 911th Landesschützen Battalion and 912th Landesschützen Battalion, 540th Division Battery, 540th Signal Company

Home Station: Bruenn, Wehrkreis Bohemia and Moravia

Formed on October 15, 1939, from the 11th Landesschützen Command, the 540th controlled older age local defense troops in the Moravia area of the Protectorate (formerly Czechoslovakia) until 1943. At that time, it was redesignated a special purposes divisional command and directed local defense and General Headquarters troops until Moravia was overrun by the Soviets in the spring of 1945. It was on the front lines of the Eastern Front with 4th Panzer Army at the end of the war.

Its divisional commanders included Lieutenant General Karl Tarbuk Elder von Sensenhorst (November 15, 1939). Colonel/Major General Gustav Wagner (November 31, 1942), Lieutenant General Benignus Dippold (October 15, 1943), Lieutenant General Hans Windeck (March 1, 1944), and Major General Friedrich-Carl Gottschalk (April 1945).

Notes and Sources: Wagner was promoted to major general on October 1, 1943. General Gottschalk was captured by the Russians, who handed him over to the Czechs, who sentenced him to death in 1950. Later he managed to have his sentence reduced to twenty years imprisonment. He was released in the late 1950s and died in 1960.

Keilig: 112; Kursietis: 213; Mehner, Vol. 12: 443, 461; Nafziger 2000: 343; Tessin, Vol. 11: 106; OB 43: 185; OB 45: 269.

541ST GRENADIER (LATER VOLKSGRENADIER) DIVISION

Composition: 1073rd Grenadier Regiment, 1074th Grenadier Regiment, 1075th Grenadier Regiment, 1541st Artillery Regiment, 1541st Fusilier Battalion, 1541st Tank Destroyer Battalion, 1541st Engineer Battalion, 1541st Signal Battalion, 1541st Field Replacement Battalion

Home Station: Blankenburg, Wehrkreis XI

This unit was organized as a *Sperr* (blocking) division on July 7, 1944, and was trained as a grenadier division in the summer of 1944. It absorbed the 1043rd through 1048th March Battalions. Each of its grenadier regiments had two battalions. In August 1944, it was sent to the central sector of the Russian Front, where the battered Army Group Center had retreated after the 4th and 9th armies had been smashed by the Soviet summer offensive. The 541st, which was redesignated a Volksgrenadier division on October 9, 1944, fought at Narev, in Poland and was forced into the East Prussian Pocket in early

1945. It remained in action there against repeated Russian attacks for the rest of the war. It was down to battle group strength by February 1945.

Its commanders were Major General/Lieutenant General Wolf Hagemann (July 1944) and Colonel Kuhnert (January 26, 1945).

Notes and Sources: Hagemann was promoted to lieutenant general on September 1, 1944. Colonel Kuhnert was probably Alfred Kuhnert, who led the 38th Motorcycle Battalion (1941–42).

Keilig: 122; *Kriegstagebuch des OKW*, Volume IV: 1897; Lexikon; Mehner, Vol. 12: 457; Nafziger 2000: 343–44; Tessin, Vol. 11: 109; RA: 172; OB 45: 269.

542ND GRENADIER (LATER VOLKSGRENADIER) DIVISION

Composition: 1076th Grenadier Regiment, 1077th Grenadier Regiment, 1078th Grenadier Regiment, 1542nd Artillery Battalion, 1542nd Fusilier Company, 1542nd Tank Destroyer Company, 1542nd Engineer Battalion, 1542nd Signal Battalion, 542nd Divisional Supply Troops

Home Station: Prussian Eylau, Wehrkreis I

Originally formed in East Prussia as a grenadier unit on July 8, 1944, the 542nd was upgraded to infantry division status on August 12, and was sent to Army Group Center the same month. It became a Volksgrenadier division on October 9; meanwhile, it fought on the Narev (Narew), in Poland, and in its home area of East Prussia. It was disbanded on April 8, 1945, and its troops were assigned to other units on the Hela peninsula.

Its commander was Lieutenant General Karl Loewrich.

Notes and Sources: Prussian Eylan is now Bagrationovsk, Russia. General Loewrick was reportedly mortally wounded at Pillau on March 28, 1945. He died on April 8 and was not replaced. Apparently his Ia, Major Schmidt, took charge of the headquarters during its last days.

Keilig: 209; Lexikon; Mehner, Vol. 12: 457; Nafziger 2000: 344–45; Tessin, Vol. 11: 113; RA: 20; OB 45: 270.

543RD GRENADIER DIVISION

Composition: 1079th Grenadier Regiment, 1080th Grenadier Regiment, 1081st Grenadier Regiment, 1543rd Artillery Regiment, 543rd Fusilier Company, 1543rd Tank Destroyer Battalion, 1543rd Engineer Battalion, 1543rd Signal Battalion, 1543rd Divisional Supply Troops

Home Station: Konstanz, Wehrkreis V

On July 10, 1944, this division was formed in the Münsingen Troop Maneuver Area with men from the Wuerttemberg-Baden-Alsace region. It was part of the German Army's 29th mobilization wave. (Its men had formerly been part of the Infantry [Shadow] Division Münsingen.) On July 18, it was disbanded, and its men were used to rebuild the 78th Sturm Division.

Sources: Tessin, Vol. 11: 117; OB 45: 270.

544TH GRENADIER (LATER VOLKSGRENADIER) DIVISION

Composition: 1082nd Grenadier Regiment, 1083rd Grenadier Regiment, 1084th Grenadier Regiment, 1544th Artillery Regiment, 1544th Fusilier Company, 1544th Tank Destroyer Battalion, 1544th Engineer Battalion, 1544th Signal Battalion, 1544th Field Replacement Battalion, 1544th Divisional Supply Troops

Home Station: Wehrkreis IV

Activated on July 10, 1944, in the Grafenwoehr Troop Maneuver Area in northern Bavaria, this Saxon grenadier unit was the former Infantry (Shadow) Division Grafenwöhr. It was upgraded to the 544th Volksgrenadier Division on October 9, 1944, and sent to the reeling Army Group Center on the Eastern Front. It suffered heavy casualties in Poland and Upper Silesia in 1944-45, and was down to battle group strength by March 1, 1945. The 544th was still fighting in Moravia when the war ended. It surrendered to the Russians.

Its commander was Major General/Lieutenant General Werner Ehrig.

Notes and Sources: Ehrig was promoted to lieutenant general on November 9, 1944.

Keilig: 79; *Kriegstagebuch des OKW*, Volume IV: 1897; Lexikon; Mehner, Vol. 12: 457; Tessin, Vol. 11: 120; OB 45: 270.

545TH GRENADIER (LATER VOLKSGRENADIER) DIVISION

Composition: 1085th Grenadier Regiment, 1086th Grenadier Regiment, 1087th Grenadier Regiment, 1545th Artillery Regiment, 545th Fusilier Battalion, 1545th Tank Destroyer Battalion, 1545th Engineer Battalion, 1545th Signal Battalion, 1545th Divisional Supply Troops

Home Station: Wiesbaden, Wehrkreis XII

One of the several 29th wave divisions, the 545th was formed as a *Sperr* (blocking) division on July 10, 1944, in the Hessian capital of Wiesbaden. Later (on October 9) it was upgraded to a Volksgrenadier division, and its fusilier, tank destroyer, engineer and signal companies were brought to battalion strength. It was sent to Army Group Center on the Eastern Front in August and fought in the Battle of the Baranov Bridgehead, where it was crushed in January 15. The remnants of the division were temporarily placed under the command of Headquarters, 78th Sturm Division. The 545th Volksgrenadier, however, was reorganized in Silesia in April, and the 2nd *Ostland* Security Regiment became the 1087th Grenadier Regiment. It surrendered to the Russians near Guben on May 12, 1945.

Its commanders included Colonel/Major General Otto Obenaus (October 1, 1944), Colonel Emmaneul von Kiliani (November 1944), and Colonel/Major General Hans-Ernst Kohlsdorfer (February 1945).

Notes and Sources: Obenaus was promoted to major general on October 1, 1944. He was missing in action near Jaslo on January 15, 1945. Kohlsdorfer was promoted to major general on April 20, 1945.

Keilig: 168, 180, 244–45; *Kriegstagebuch des OKW*, Volume I: 1146; Lexikon; Nafziger 2000: 346–47; Tessin, Vol. 11: 123–24; OB 45: 271

An infantry NCO looks through a pair of binoculars. This man wears the Iron Cross, 1st Class; the Infantry Assault Badge; and the ribbon of the Iron Cross, 2nd Class. HITM ARCHIVE

546TH GRENADIER DIVISION

Composition: 1088th Grenadier Regiment, 1089th Grenadier Regiment, 1090th Grenadier Regiment, 1546th Artillery Regiment, 546th Fusilier Company, 1546th Tank Destroyer Battalion, 1546th Engineer Battalion, 1546th Signal Company, 1546th Divisional Supply Troops

Home Station: Wehrkreis XVII

Mobilized on July 7, 1944, this unit ceased to exist 12 days later. It was merged with the 45th Grenadier Division to form a new 45th Infantry Division, which was sent to Army Group Center on the Eastern Front. The commander of 546th Grenadier Division was Colonel Richard Daniel.

See also 45th Infantry (later Volksgrenadier) Division (Volume One).

Sources: Keilig: 64; Lexikon; Tessin, Vol. 11: 126; OB 45: 271.

547TH GRENADIER (LATER VOLKSGRENADIER) DIVISION

Composition: 1091st Grenadier Regiment, 1092nd Grenadier Regiment, 1093rd Grenadier Regiment, 1547th Artillery Regiment, 547th Fusilier Company, 1547th Tank Destroyer Battalion, 1547th Engineer Battalion, 1547th Signal Battalion, 1547th Divisional Supply Troops

Home Station: Luxembourg, Wehrkreis XII

Originally a grenadier unit, the 547th was formed at Stuttgart on July 11, 1944, as a blocking division. It was soon in action on the central sector of the Eastern Front, which had recently collapsed. It took part in the retreat through Poland, and in the battles of East Prussia, and was pushed back to the Danzig area with the 2nd Army. Meanwhile, it had been redesignated a Volksgrenadier division on October 9, 1944, and had absorbed the remnants of the grenadier units of the 170th Infantry Division in February. It was evacuated by sea in March and was assigned to the 3rd Panzer Army on the Oder front; meanwhile, it absorbed the two grenadier regiments of Shadow

Division Hanover on March 10. The 1547th Artillery Regiment, however, was so depleted by losses that it was downgraded to battalion status. After the fall of Berlin, the 547th Volksgrenadier Division managed to surrender to the Americans near Schwerin on May 4, 1945.

Its commanders included Colonel/Major General of Reserves Dr. Ernst Meiners (July 1944) and Major General Erich Fronhöfer (April 1, 1945).

Notes and Sources: Meiners was promoted to major general on October 1, 1944. He was wounded in action on February 8, 1945, and was captured by the Russians. He was not released until 1955. Who commanded the division between February 8 and March 31, 1945 is not absolutely clear, but it was apparently Fronhöfer.

Keilig: 98, 220-21; *Kriegstagebuch des OKW*, Volume IV: 1898; Kursietis: 214; Lexikon; Mehner, Vol. 12: 457; Nafziger 2000: 347; Tessin, Vol. 11: 128–29; OB 45: 271. Also, see Seaton: 524.

548TH GRENADIER (LATER VOLKSGRENADIER) DIVISION

Composition: 1094th Grenadier Regiment, 1095th Grenadier Regiment, 1096th Grenadier Regiment, 1548th Artillery Regiment, 548th Fusilier Company, 1548th Tank Destroyer Battalion, 1548th Engineer Battalion, 1548th Signal Battalion, 1548th Divisional Supply Troops

Home Station: Dresden, Wehrkreis IV

The 548th was formed, like the other divisions of its series, as a grenadier division on July 11, 1944. It was redesignated a Volksgrenadier unit and sent to the central sector of the Eastern Front, where it fought in Lithuanian, at Tilsit, in Poland, in East Prussia and at Pillau before being destroyed by the Russian Army at Koenigsberg on April 9, 1945.

The division's commander, Colonel/Major General Erich Sudau, was killed in action that same day.

Notes and Sources: Sudau was promoted to major general on October 1, 1944.

Keilig: 340; Lexikon; Tessin, Vol. 11: 131; OB 45: 272.

549TH GRENADIER (LATER VOLKSGRENADIER) DIVISION

Composition: 1098th Grenadier Regiment, 1099th Grenadier Regiment, 1549th Artillery Regiment, 549th Fusilier Company, 1549th Tank Destroyer Battalion, 1549th Engineer Battalion, 1549th Signal Battalion, 1549th Divisional Supply Troops

Home Station: Schwerin, Wehrkreis II

The 549th was formed in the Mecklenburg-Pomerania region of northeastern Germany on July 11, 1944. It was upgraded to Volksgrenadier status on October 9; meanwhile, it was transferred to Army Group Center on the Eastern Front. It fought in Poland, East Prussia, West Prussia and on the Oder (at Stettin) from autumn 1944 until the end of the war. It was in remnants by April 1945, having suffered heavy losses at Pasewalk, but managed to surrender to the Americans in Mecklenburg on May 8, 1945.

Its commander was Colonel/Major General/Lieutenant General Karl Jank. Colonel Kraus was acting commander in April 1945.

Sources: Jank was promoted to major general on October 1, 1944, and to lieutenant general on April 19, 1945.

Keilig: 157; *Kriegstagebuch des OKW*, Volume IV: 1898; Lexikon; Mehner, Vol. 12: 457; Tessin, Vol. 11: 134; RA: 32; OB 45: 272.

550TH GRENADIER DIVISION

Composition: 1110th Grenadier Regiment, 1111th Grenadier Regiment, 1112th Grenadier Regiment, 1550th Artillery Regiment, 550th Fusilier Company, 1550th Tank Destroyer Battalion, 1550th Engineer Battalion, 1550th Signal Battalion, 1550th Divisional Supply Troops

Home Station: Brunswick, Wehrkreis XI

Organized on July 11, 1944, the 550th Grenadier was a blocking division. It was merged with the 31st Grenadier (formerly Infantry) Division on July 22, 1944. Its men ended up on the Eastern Front.

See also 31st Infantry (later Volksgrenadier) Division (Volume One).

Sources: Lexikon; Tessin, Vol. 11: 137; OB 45: 272.

551ST GRENADIER (LATER VOLKSGRENADIER) DIVISION

Composition: 1113rd Grenadier Regiment, 1114th Grenadier Regiment, 1115th Grenadier Regiment, 1551st Artillery Regiment, 551st Fusilier Company, 1551st Tank Destroyer Battalion, 1551st Engineer Battalion, 1551st Signal Battalion, 1551st Divisional Supply Troops

Home Station: Belgrad, Wehrkreis II

Formed at the Thorn Maneuver Area in Wehrkreis XX on July 11, 1944, the 551st was another Wave 29 blocking division. It was redesignated a Volksgrenadier division on October 9; meanwhile, it was sent to Army Group Center in August 1944. It fought in Lithuania, Poland and East Prussia (including the Battle of Tilsit) and was later cut off in the Samland-Danzig area by the rapid Soviet drive into northeastern Germany. In remnants by January 1945, it ended the war in the East Prussian Pocket and surrendered to the Red Army in May 1945.

Its commander was Colonel/Major General/Lieutenant General Siegfried Verhein.

Notes and Sources: Verhein was promoted to major general on October 1, 1944, and to lieutenant general on April 1, 1945. He was a Soviet POW until 1955.

Keilig: 354; *Kriegstagebuch des OKW*, Volume IV: 1897; Nafziger 2000: 348–49; Tessin, Vol. 11: 140; RA: 32; OB 45: 273.

552ND GRENADIER DIVISION

Composition: 1116th Grenadier Regiment, 1117th Grenadier Regiment, 1118th Grenadier Regiment, 1552nd Artillery Regiment, 552nd Fusilier Company, 1552nd Tank Destroyer Battalion, 1552nd Engineer Battalion, 1552nd Signal Battalion, 1552nd Divisional Supply Troops

Home Station: Bielefeld, Wehrkreis V

This division was created in the 29th wave as a blocking division on July 11, 1944, and was basically absorbed by the 6th Grenadier (formerly Infantry) Division on July 25. The new unit was redesignated 6th Volksgrenadier Division shortly thereafter. The 552nd Grenadier was commanded by Colonel Otto-Hermann Bruecker.

See also 6th Infantry (later Volksgrenadier) Division (Volume One).

Sources: Keilig: 52; Tessin, Vol. 11: 144; OB 45: 273; also see *Kriegstagebuch des OKW*, Volume IV.

553RD GRENADIER (LATER VOLKSGRENADIER) DIVISION

Composition (1944): 1119th Grenadier Regiment, 1120th Grenadier Regiment, 1121st Grenadier Regiment, 1553rd Artillery Regiment, 553rd Fusilier Company, 553rd Tank Destroyer Battalion, 553rd Engineer Battalion, 553rd Signal Battalion, 1553rd Divisional Supply Troops

Home Station: Strassburg, Wehrkreis V

Mustered in as a grenadier division at the Muensingen Maneuver Area, Wehrkreis V, on July 11, 1944, the 553rd was a 29th Wave blocking division. It was upgraded to Volksgrenadier status on October 9. It was sent to the Western Front, where it was smashed near Nancy, in the Lorraine province of France, in early September 1944. Briefly withdrawn in October, it absorbed the 1416th Fortress Infantry, 51st and 56th Machine Gun, and 110th and 960th Grenadier Replacement and Training Battalions. In mid-November, it defended the Saverne Gap in the Vosges Mountains against the U.S. 7th Army and held it up for several days. Eventually, however, the 553rd was overwhelmed. Its commander, Major General Johannes Bruhn, was captured by French troops on November 22, and the road to Strasbourg was opened for the Allies.

The remnants of the division were temporarily absorbed by the 361st Infantry Division. Meanwhile, the headquarters of the 553rd was sent to the Karlsruhe area and given charge of miscellaneous combat units. Here the division was rebuilt, but with only the 1119th and 1120th Grenadier Regiments (two battalions each) and the usual compliment of other troops. In early January 1945, it took part in Himmler's Operation "Northwind," aimed at retaking Strasbourg. The rebuilt division did well and even succeeded in reaching the outskirts of the city before being turned back. Taken out of the line, the 553rd Volksgrenadier was the only division in Army Group G's reserve in March 1945. It ended the war on the southern sector of the Western Front, surrendering to the Americans in Wuerttemberg in May 1945.

The division's commanders included Colonel Erich Loehr (July 1944), Bruhn (September 23, 1944), Major General Gerhard Huether (November 23, 1944), and Colonel Utz (January 1945–end).

Notes and Sources: Colonel Loehr was relieved of his command by General von Knobelsdorff, the commander of the 1st Army, on September 23, 1944. He was reportedly court-martialled in 1945. Brunn was promoted to major general on November 1, 1944.

Chant, Volume 16: 2111, 2274; Volume 17: 2277; Cole 1950: 49, 114, 288; Keilig: 53; Mehner, Vol. 12: 457; Nafziger 2000: 349; Tessin, Vol. 11: 147–48; RA: 172; OB 45: 273.

554TH INFANTRY DIVISION

Composition: 621st Infantry Regiment, 622nd Infantry Regiment, 623rd Infantry Regiment, 554th Artillery Regiment, 554th Forward Observer Battalion, 554th Signal Battalion, 554th Divisional Supply Troops

Home Station: Wehrkreis V

The 554th was formed on Feburary 15, 1940, as a positional (*Stellungs*) division. As part of the 7th Army, it faced the French across the Maginot Line on a quiet sector of the front. It was disbanded on August 31, 1940, in the partial demobilization following the fall of France. Its men who remained in the army were used to form the 439th through 445th Landesschuetzen Battalions.

Its commander was Lieutenant General Baron Anton von Hirschberg.

Sources: Keilig: 143; *Kriegstagebuch des OKW*, Volume I: 1123; Nafziger 2000: 350; Tessin, Vol. 11: 151; RA: 86; OB 43: 185; OB 45: 274.

555TH INFANTRY DIVISION

Composition: 624th Infantry Regiment, 625th Infantry Regiment, 626th Infantry Regiment, 627th Infantry Regiment, 555th Artillery Regiment, 555th Forward Observer Battalion, 555th Signal Company, 555th Divisional Supply Troops

Home Station: Graudenz, Wehrkreis VI

Formed as a *Stellungs* (positional) division on February 10, 1940, the 555th was part of 7th Army on the Siegfried Line. It was disbanded on September 25, 1940, shortly after the fall of France. The 555th was unusual because it had four infantry regiments and a forward observer battalion.

Its commander was Major General Dr. Waldemar Henrici. Its men who remained in the service were incorporated into home defense (*Heimat Wach*) battalions.

Sources: Keilig: 136; *Kriegstagebuch des OKW*, Volume I: 1123; Tessin, Vol. 11: 154; OB 43: 185; OB 45: 274.

556TH INFANTRY DIVISION

Composition: 628th Infantry Regiment, 629th Infantry Regiment, 630th Infantry Regiment, 556th Artillery Regiment, 556th Forward Observer Battalion, 556th Reconnaissance Company, 556th Tank Destroyer Company, 556th Engineer Company, 556th Signal Battalion, 556th Divisional Supply Troops

Home Station: Mannheim, Wehrkreis XII

Like most of Hitler's other positional divisions, the 556th was created on February 11, 1940. It was disbanded on July 26 of that same year. It served on the Siegfried Line (called the West Wall by the Germans) in 1940. Many of its personnel were

from older men (thirty-five and over) and returned to the civilian labor force inside the Reich. The rest were used to form
Landesschuetzen battalions numbered 784 through 789.

Major General/Lieutenant General Kurt von Berg commanded the 556th.

Notes and Sources: Berg was promoted to lieutenant general on
March 1, 1940.

Keilig: 29; *Kriegstagebuch des OKW*, Volume I: 1123; Nafziger 2000:
350; Tessin, Vol. 11: 157; RA: 188; OB 43: 186; OB 45: 274.

557TH INFANTRY DIVISION

Composition: 632nd Infantry Regiment, 633rd Infantry
Regiment, 634rd Infantry Regiment, 557th Artillery Regiment,
557th Forward Observer Battalion, 557th Reconnaissance
Company, 557th Tank Destroyer Company, 557th Engineer
Company; 557th Signal Battalion, 557th Divisional Supply
Troops

Home Station: Komotau, Wehrkreis IV

The 557th was created in the Saxony-Thuringia region as a
positional division on February 15, 1940. It served as part of the
7th Army, Army Group C, opposite the French Maginot Line. It
was dissolved on Hitler's orders on August 31, 1940, after the
French surrendered in June 1940. Its men were used to form
the 975th through 983rd Landesschützen Battalions.

The commander of the 557th Infantry Division was Major
General Hermann Kuprion.

Sources: Kuprion retired after giving up command of the 557th.
He received an honorary promotion to lieutenant general.

Keilig: 194; Nafziger 2000: 350; Tessin, Vol. 11: 160; OB 43: 186;
OB 44b: 0111, OB 45: 274.

558TH GRENADIER (LATER VOLKSGRENADIER) DIVISION

Composition: 1122nd Grenadier Regiment, 1123rd Grenadier Regiment, 1124th Grenadier Regiment, 1558th Artillery
Regiment, 558th Fusilier Company, 1558th Tank Destroyer

Battalion, 1558th Engineer Battalion, 558th Signal Battalion, 1558th Divisional Supply Troops

Home Station: Augsburg, Wehrkreis VII

This division was organized as a grenadier (blocking) division on July 11, 1944. On October 9, 1944, it was redesignated a Volksgrenadier unit; meanwhile, it was sent to the central sector of the Eastern Front, where it fought in the Polish campaign of 1944–45. It fought at Pillau and suffered heavy casualties before the town fell on April 25, 1945. Trapped as a result, the remnants of the division surrendered on April 28, 1945.

Its commanders were Lieutenant General Arthur Kullmer (August 1944) and Lieutenant General Werner von Bercken (April 5, 1945).

Notes and Sources: Pillau is now Baltisk, Russia.

Keilig: 28, 193; *Kriegstagebuch des OKW*, Volume IV: 1897; Tessin, Vol. 11: 163; Thorwald: 96; OB 45: 274.

559TH GRENADIER (LATER VOLKSGRENADIER) DIVISION

Composition (December 1944): 1125th Grenadier Regiment, 1126th Grenadier Regiment, 1127th Grenadier Regiment, 1559th Artillery Regiment, 559th Fusilier Company, 1159th Tank Destroyer Battalion, 1559th Engineer Battalion, 1559th Signal Battalion, III/103rd Anti-Aircraft Regiment, 805th Anti-Aircraft Battalion, 1559th Divisional Supply Troops

Home Station: Wehrkreis IX

Formed in Troop Maneuver Area Baumholder on July 11, 1944, the 559th was originally a 29th Wave blocking (grenadier) division; however, unlike most of the 1944 grenadier units, this one had a high proportion of young veterans. Upgraded to Volksgrenadier status on October 9, it was fighting the Americans in the Nancy area of eastern France in September. The 559th was heavily engaged in the Saar area and in northern Alsace in late 1944, and was pretty well burned-out by New Year's Day 1945. In January, however, it absorbed the remnants of the 361st Infantry Division and continued to fight in the West Wall battles. It fought in the Saar (January), at Saarbrücken (February) and Mosel (March). In late March 1945, the division was holding part of the southern sector of the German line on the Western Front, when it was cut off and largely destroyed on the western bank of the Rhine. The remnants of the division surrendered to the Americans near Muensingen in May 1945.

Its commander was Major General/Lieutenant General Baron Kurt von Mühlen.

Notes and Sources: Baron von Mühlen was promoted to lieutenant general on April 20, 1945.

Cole 1950: 245, 249, 473; Keilig: 231; MacDonald 1973: 243, 286; Nafziger 2000: 351; Tessin, Vol. 11: 166; RA: 144; OB 45: 275.

560TH GRENADIER (LATER VOLKSGRENADIER) DIVISION

Composition: 1128th Grenadier Regiment, 1129th Grenadier Regiment, 1130th Grenadier Regiment, 1560th Artillery Regiment, 560th Fusilier Battalion, 1560th Tank Destroyer Battalion, 1560th Engineer Battalion, 1560th Signal Battalion, 1560th Divisional Supply Troops

Home Station: Lüneburg, Wehrkreis X

Originally a grenadier unit, the 560th was formed from miscellaneous units and Luftwaffe personnel stationed in Norway and Denmark on August 1, 1944. Initially headquartered in the Moss area of southern Norway, the 560th was upgraded by the High Command and earmarked for the Eastern Front; however, Hitler countermanded that order and transferred it to Denmark instead. The division first saw combat in the Battle of the Bulge in December 1944, where it formed part of the 5th Panzer Army. The following January, it was with the II SS Panzer Corps and fought in the Eifel area, near St. Vith. The next month it was part of Army Group B's reserve but was committed to the Battle of Echternach against the U.S. 3rd Army after the collapse of the 212th Volksgrenadier Division. It was finally destroyed in the Ruhr Pocket on April 16.

Its commanders were Lieutenant General Erich Hofmann (July 27, 1944), Colonel/Major General Rudolf Bader (November 10, 1944), and Colonel Rudolf Langhauser (March 31, 1945).

Notes and Sources: Bader was promoted to major general on January 1, 1945.

Chant, Volume 16: 2133; Cole 1965: 195–96; Keilig: 148; MacDonald 1973: 26, 105; Tessin, Vol. 11: 169; RA: 160; OB 45: 275; 9th U.S. Air Force Interrogation Report, 30 Jan 45, Air University Files.

561ST GRENADIER (LATER VOLKSGRENADIER) DIVISION

Composition: 1141st Grenadier Regiment, 1142nd Grenadier Regiment, 1143rd Grenadier Regiment, 1561st Artillery Regiment, 561st Fusilier Company, 1561st Tank Destroyer Battalion, 1561st Engineer Battalion, 1561st Signal Battalion, 1561st Divisional Supply Troops

Home Station: Sensburg, Wehrkreis I

Organized in the Preussisch Eylau area of East Prussia (now Bagrationovsk, Russia) on July 24, 1944, it was originally designated the 1st East Prussian Grenadier Division (*Grenadier-Division Ostpreussen 1*). Three days later, it became the 561st Grenadier Division. It was almost immediately sent to Army Group Center on the Eastern Front and was fighting in Lithuania in August. It was redesignated the 561st Volksgrenadier Division on October 9, 1944. It fought in the Vistula, in the Battle of Tilsit, and in the East Prussian campaigns, and was largely destroyed at Königsberg in March and April 1945. Its remnants were still resisting near Pillau at the end of the war.

The 561st Volksgrenadier Division was commanded by Colonel/Major General Walter Gorn (July 21, 1944) and Colonel Felix Becker (March 1, 1945–end).

Notes and Sources: Colonel Walter Gorn was promoted to major general on October 1, 1944. He fell ill in February 1945.

Hoffmann: 434; Keilig: 111; *Kriegstagebuch des OKW*, Volume IV: 1897; Tessin, Vol. 11: 172; OB 45: 275.

A member of Panzer Group Afrika stops to take a photograph of a sign, Libya, 1941. General Archibald Wavell was the British C-in-C, Middle East, in 1941. He destroyed the Italian 10th Army and captured most of Libya for the British Empire. To prevent this, Hitler sent the 15th and 21st Panzer Divisions to North Africa under the command of Erwin Rommel, the "Desert Fox," who defeated Wavell—hence the alteration of the sign from "Wavell Way" to "Rommel Weg." HITM ARCHIVE

562ND GRENADIER (LATER VOLKSGRENADIER) DIVISION

Composition: 1144th Grenadier Regiment, 1145th Grenadier Regiment, 1146th Grenadier Regiment, 1562nd Artillery Regiment, 562nd Fusilier Company, 1562nd Tank Destroyer Battalion, 1562nd Engineer Battalion, 1562nd Signal Battalion, 1562nd Divisional Supply Troops

Home Station: Heiligenbeil, Wehrkreis I

Created in the Stablack Troop Maneuver Area as the 2nd East Prussian Grenadier Division on July 24, 1944, this unit had only four grenadier battalions. It was renamed the 562nd Grenadier Division on July 27, and was upgraded to Volksgrenadier status on October 9. It had already been sent to the 4th Army, Army Group Center, on the Eastern Front in August. It fought at Augustowo, Narew, and in the battles for East Prussia. It was crushed in the Battle of the Heiligenbeil Pocket. Only remnants of the division escaped by sea to the Hela peninsula of East Prussia with the 4th Army. It was dissolved on April 16, 1945, and its survivors surrendered to the Soviets early the following month.

Its commanders were Colonel/Major General Johannes-Oskar Brauer (July 20, 1944) and Colonel Helmuth Hufenbach (January 22, 1945).

Notes and Sources: Brauer was promoted to major general on October 1, 1944. Hufenbach was killed in action near Kahlholz, East Prussia, on March 27, 1945. Apparently he was never officially replaced, since the division was in remnants.

Keilig: 50, 154; *Kreigstagebuch des OKW*, Volume IV: 1897; Kursietis: 217; Nafziger 2000: 352; Tessin, Vol. 11: 176; OB 45: 276.

563RD GRENADIER (LATER VOLKSGRENADIER) DIVISION

Composition: 1147th Grenadier Regiment, 1148th Grenadier Regiment, 1149th Grenadier Regiment, 1563rd Artillery Regiment, 563rd Fusilier Company, 1563rd Tank Destroyer

Battalion, 1563rd Engineer Battalion, 1563rd Signal Battalion, 1563rd Divisional Supply Troops

Home Station: Spandau, Wehrkreis III

The 563rd was formed in Troop Maneuver Area Doeberitz on August 17, 1944, and was almost immediately sent to Army Group North. It fought at Dorpat (Tartu), Estonia (August–October 1944), and suffered heavy casualties that its 1147th Grenadier Regiment had to be disbanded. The survivors were transferred to the Fusilier unit, which was upgraded to a battalion. By November 1944, the division was isolated in western Latvia, where it fought in the six battles of the Courland Pocket and suffered such heavy losses that it was down to kampfgruppen strenght by the end of November 1944. It nevertheless remained in the line until May 8, 1945, when it surrendered to the Red Army.

Its commanders were Colonel/Major General Ferdinand Bruehl (August 3, 1944) and Colonel/Major General Werner Neumann (February 25, 1945).

Notes and Sources: Breukl was promoted to major general on November 9, 1944. Neumann was promoted to major general on April 20, 1945. He was held in Soviet prisons until 1955.

Keilig: 240; Lexikon; Tessin, Vol. 11: 180; OB 45: 276.

564TH GRENADIER (LATER VOLKSGRENADIER) DIVISION

Composition: 1150th Grenadier Regiment, 1151st Grenadier Regiment, 1152nd Grenadier Regiment, 1564th Artillery Regiment, 564th Fusilier Battalion, 1564th Tank Destroyer Battalion, 1564th Engineer Battalion, 1564th Signal Battalion, 1564th Divisional Supply Troops

Home Station: Wehrkreis XVII

This unit was organized in Troop Maneuver Area Doellersheim, Austria, on August 26, 1944, when it absorbed the Shadow Division Doellersheim. It was renamed the 564th Volksgrenadier Division at the end of August, and combined with the 183rd Infantry Division to form the 183rd Volksgrenadier Division on September 16. Its 1150th, 1151st, and 1152nd Grenadier Regiments became the 330th, 343rd and 351st Grenadier Regiments, respectively, and its 1564th Artillery Regiment became the 219th Artillery Regiment. Most of its men ended up in the Ruhr Pocket on April 15, 1945.

Lieutenant General Wolfgang Lange was the commander of the 564th Volksgrenadier Division.

Sources: Keilig: 197; Tessin, Vol. 11: 183; RA: 220; OB 45: 276.

565TH GRENADIER DIVISION

Composition: 1153rd Grenadier Regiment, 1154th Grenadier Regiment, 1155th Grenadier Regiment, 1565th Artillery Regiment, 565th Fusilier Battalion, 1565th Tank Destroyer Battalion, 1565th Engineer Battalion, 1565th Signal Battalion, 1565th Divisional Supply Troops

Home Station: Wehrkreis XIII

The division was activated in Troop Maneuver Area Milowitz, Bohemia, on August 26, 1944, by absorbing Shadow Division Moravia and some of the remnants of the 78th Sturm Division. It was disbanded on September 15, and its men were absorbed by the 246th Volksgrenadier Division. Its 1153rd, 1154th, and 1155th Grenadier Regiments became the 352nd, 404th, and 689th Grenadier Regiments, respectively, and its artillery regiment, divisional support units and divisional supply troops took the number 246. The men of the former 565th Volksgrenadier Division fought on the Western Front until the end of the war.

Sources: Nafziger 2000: 353; Tessin, Vol. 11: 185; RA: 204; OB 45: 277.

566TH GRENADIER DIVISION

Composition: 1156th Grenadier Regiment, 1157th Grenadier Regiment, 1158th Grenadier Regiment,1566th Artillery Regiment, 566th Fusilier Battalion, 1566th Tank Destroyer Battalion, 1566th Engineer Battalion, 1566th Signal Battalion, 1566th Divisional Supply Troops

Home Station: Wehrkreis IX

The 566th was created in Troop Maneuver Area Wildflecken in the thirty-first mobilization wave on August 26, 1944. It absorbed Division Roehn (which had been formed on August 3) and was itself absorbed by the 363rd Volksgrenadier Division on September 17. Its soldiers were sent to the Western Front at the end of the month. Its 1156th, 1157th, and 1158th Grenadier Regiments were merged with survivors of the 363rd and became the 957th, 958th and 959th Grenadier Regiments, respectively. The other divisional units adopted the number 363. The 363rd Volksgrenadier was later destroyed in the Ruhr Pocket by the U.S. Army in April 1945.

See also 363rd Infantry (later Volksgrenadier) Division.

Sources: Lexikon; Nafziger 2000: 354; Tessin, Vol. 11: 187; OB 45: 277.

567TH VOLKSGRENADIER DIVISION

Composition: 1159th Grenadier Regiment, 1160th Grenadier Regiment, 1161st Grenadier Regiment, 1567th Artillery Regiment, 567th Fusilier Battalion, 1567th Tank Destroyer Battalion, 1567th Engineer Battalion, 1567th Signal Battalion, 1567th Divisional Supply Troops

Home Station: Wehrkreis XIII

Created in the Grafenwoehr Troop Maneuver Area on August 25, 1944, this unit's men were merged with the 349th Infantry Division to form the 349th Volksgrenadier Division of the 32nd wave. The 567th Volksgrenadier Division was dissolved on September 2, 1944, only a week after it was formed. Its men were sent to the Eastern Front.

Notes and Sources: The 567th Volksgrenadier Division was a thirty-first-wave unit.

Lexikon; Nafziger 2000: 354; "Frontnachweiser," 15 December 1944; Tessin, Vol. 11: 189; OB 45: 277.

568TH VOLKSGRENADIER DIVISION

Composition: 1162nd Grenadier Regiment, 1163rd Grenadier Regiment, 1164th Grenadier Regiment, 1568th Artillery Regiment, 568th Fusilier Battalion, 1568th Tank Destroyer Battalion, 1568th Engineer Battalion, 1568th Signal Battalion, 1568th Divisional Supply Troops

Home Station: Wehrkreis IV

Activated on August 25, 1944, in the Koenigsbrueck Troop Maneuver Area in Saxony, the 568th was only briefly extant. It ceased to exist on September 25, when it was merged with the 256th Infantry Division, which had been badly damaged in the Battle of the Scheldt, to form the 256th Volksgrenadier Division. The new division was sent to the Western Front.

Sources: Nafziger 2000: 354; Tessin, Vol. 11: 191; RA: 72; OB 45: 277.

569TH VOLKSGRENADIER DIVISION

Composition: 1165th Grenadier Regiment, 1166th Grenadier Regiment, 1167th Grenadier Regiment, 1569th Artillery Regiment, 569th Fusilier Battalion, 1569th Tank Destroyer Battalion, 1569th Engineer Battalion, 1569th Signal Battalion, 1569th Divisional Supply Troops

Home Station: Wehrkreis VI

Formed on August 25, 1944 in Troop Maneuver Area Wahn, a few miles south of Cologne, the 569th was part of the thirty-second-wave. It merged with the 361st Infantry Division on September 17 to form the 361st Volksgrenadier Division. Its men subsequently served on the Western Front.

Sources: Lexikon; Tessin, Vol. 11: 193; RA: 102; OB 45: 278.

570TH GRENADIER DIVISION

Composition: 1168th Grenadier Regiment, 1169th Grenadier Regiment, 1170th Grenadier Regiment, 1570th Artillery

Regiment, 570th Fusilier Battalion, 1570th Tank Destroyer Battalion, 1570th Engineer Battalion, 1570th Signal Company, 1570th Divisional Supply Troops

Home Station: Wehrkreis II

Organized on August 26, 1944, in the Gross-Born Troop Maneuver Area, the 570th Grenadier absorbed Shadow Division Gross-Born a few days later. The 570th ceased to exist on September 17, 1944, when it was merged with the remnants of the 337th Infantry Division to form the 337th Volksgrenadier Division. The new division was sent to the Eastern Front.

Sources: *Kriegstagebuch des OKW,* Volume IV: 1883; Nafziger 2000: 355; "Frontnachweiser," 15 December 1944: Tessin, Vol. 11: 195; OB 45: 278.

571ST VOLKSGRENADIER DIVISION

Composition: 1171st Grenadier Regiment, 1172nd Grenadier Regiment, 1173rd Grenadier Regiment, 1571st Artillery Regiment, 1571st Reconnaissance Company, 1571st Tank Destroyer Battalion, 1571st Engineer Battalion, 1571st Signal Company, 1571st Divisional Supply Troops

Home Station: Wehrkreis V

The 571st was mobilized on August 25, 1944, in Troop Maneuver Area Oskbüll (near Esbjerg on the western coast of the Jutland peninsula of Denmark). It was merged with the 18th Infantry Division on September 2 to form the 18th Volksgrenadier Division, which was sent to the Western Front.

See also 18th Infantry (later Volksgrenadier) Division (Volume One).

Notes and Sources: The 571st was apparently initially formed directly under the Headquarters, Replacement Army. It presumably came under Wehrkreis V when it was decided that it would be absorbed by the 18th Volksgrenadier.

Kriegstagebuch des OKW, Volume IV: 1883; Lexikon; Nafziger 2000: 355; "Frontnachweiser," 15 December 1944; Tessin, Vol. 11: 198; OB 45: 278.

572ND VOLKSGRENADIER DIVISION

Composition: 1174th Grenadier Regiment, 1175th Grenadier Regiment, 1176th Grenadier Regiment, 1572nd Artillery Regiment, 1572nd Reconnaissance Company, 1572nd Tank Destroyer Battalion, 1572nd Engineer Battalion, 1572nd Signal Company, 1572nd Divisional Supply Troops

Home Station: Wehrkreis II

Organized in Thorn, Wehrkreis XX, on August 25, 1944, this division's troops were merged with the 340th Infantry Division (which had been smashed at the Battle of Lwow, Poland, on the Eastern Front), in order to form the 340th Volksgrenadier Division. The 572nd Volksgrenadier Division ceased to exist on September 15, 1944. The new 340th was sent to the Aachen sector of the Western Front.

See also 340th Infantry (later Volksgrenadier) Division earlier in this chapter.

Sources: Lexikon; Nafziger 2000: 355; "Frontnachweiser," 15 December 1944; Tessin, Vol. 11: 201; OB 45: 242, 278.

573RD VOLKSGRENADIER DIVISION

Composition: 1177th Grenadier Regiment, 1178th Grenadier Regiment, 1179th Grenadier Regiment, 1573rd Artillery Regiment, 1573rd Reconnaissance Company, 1573rd Tank Destroyer Battalion, 1573rd Engineer Battalion, 1573rd Signal Company, 1573rd Divisional Supply Troops

Home Station: Wehrkreis VIII

Another of the partially formed thirty-second-wave divisions, this unit was activated in Slovakia on August 25, 1944. It was merged with the remnants of the 708th Infantry Division, which had been smashed in Normandy, to form the 708th Volksgrenadier Division on September 4, 1944. The 573rd never saw action as a unit. It men were sent to the Western Front.

See also 708th Infantry (later Volksgrenadier) Division later in this chapter.

Sources: *Kriegstagebuch des OKW,* Volume IV: 1883; Nafziger 2000: 356; "Frontnachweiser," 15 December 1944; Tessin, Vol. 11: 201. Also see OB 45 and RA.

574TH VOLKSGRENADIER DIVISION

Composition: 1180th Grenadier Regiment, 1181st Grenadier Regiment, 1182nd Grenadier Regiment, 1574th Artillery Regiment, 1574th Tank Destroyer Battalion, 1574th Engineer Battalion, 1574th Signal Company, 1574th Divisional Supply Troops

Home Station: Wehrkreis XVII

The 574th Volksgrenadier was formed in Hungary on August 25, 1944. On September 4, it was merged with the 277th Infantry Division, which had been decimated in Normandy, to form the 277th Volksgrenadier Division. The 574th never saw combat under the designations mentioned above. The 277th Volksgrenadier Division was sent to the Western Front.

See also 277th Infantry (later Volksgrenadier) Division (Volume One).

Sources: *Kriegstagebuch des OKW,* Volume IV: 1883; Lexikon; Nafziger 2000: 356; "Frontnachweiser," 15 December 1944; Tessin, Vol. 11: 205; RA; OB: 45.

575TH GRENADIER DIVISION

Composition: 1183rd Grenadier Regiment, 1184th Grenadier Regiment, 1185th Grenadier Regiment, 1575th Artillery Regiment, 1575th Reconnaissance Company, 1575th Tank Destroyer Battalion, 1575th Engineer Battalion, 1575th Signal Company, 1575th Divisional Supply Troops

Home Station: Wehrkreis XI

This division—like a dozen others—was partially formed when it was activated on August 25, 1944. This took place in the Doeberitz Troop Maneuver Area near Berlin. The Replacement Army discontinued this process and merged the 575th with the 272nd Infantry Division (which had been crushed in

Normandy) to form the 272nd Volksgrenadier Division on September 17, 1944.

See also 272nd Infantry (later Volksgrenadier) Division (Volume One).

Sources: *Kreigstagebuch des OKW,* Volume IV: 1883; Nafziger 2000: 356; "Frontnachweiser," 15 December 1944; Tessin, Vol. 11: 209; RA; OB 45.

576TH VOLKSGRENADIER DIVISION

Composition: 1186th Grenadier Regiment, 1187th Grenadier Regiment, 1188th Grenadier Regiment, 1576th Artillery Regiment, 1576th Reconnaissance Company, 1576th Tank Destroyer Battalion, 1576th Engineer Battalion, 1576th Signal Company, 1576th Divisional Supply Troops

Home Station: Wehrkreis XIII

Formed on August 25, 1944, in Tyrnau, Slovakia, the 576th Grenadier was merged with the 271st Infantry Division on September 17, to form the 271st Volksgrenadier Division. The new division was sent to the Hungarian sector of the Eastern Front.

See also 271st Infantry (later Volksgrenadier) Division (Volume One).

Sources: *Kreigstagebuch des OKW,* Volume IV: 1883; Lexikon; "Frontnachweiser," 15 December 1944; Tessin, Vol. 11: 209.

577TH VOLKSGRENADIER DIVISION

Composition: 1189th Grenadier Regiment, 1190th Grenadier Regiment, 1191st Grenadier Regiment, 1577th Artillery Regiment, 1577th Reconnaissance Company, 1577th Tank Destroyer Battalion, 1577th Engineer Battalion, 1577th Signal Company, 1577th Divisional Supply Troops

Home Station: Wehrkreis IX

This division began forming in Aarhus, Denmark on August 25, 1944. On September 17, 1944, prior to the completion of this process, its draftees were transferred to the 47th Infantry Division, which was rebuilding as a Volksgrenadier division.

A German howitzer crew at work in the Western Desert. Panzer Group (later Army) Afrika was well supported by the 104th Artillery Command (Arko 104), which was not organic to any division; its batteries were attached to the divisions on an "as needed" basis. Because of the hard soil and the lack of cover in the desert, artillery fire inflicted more casualties in North Africa than rifle fire, tank fire, bombing, or any other type of action. HITM ARCHIVE

The headquarters of the 577th Volksgrenadier was disbanded. The last members of the former 577th apparently left Aarhus on November 10. They later fought on the Western Front.

See also 47th Infantry (later Volksgrenadier) Division (Volume One).

Sources: *Kriegstagebuch des OKW,* Volume IV: 1883; "Frontnachweiser," 15 December 1944; Tessin, Vol. 11: 211. Also see RA and OB 45.

578TH VOLKSGRENADIER DIVISION

Composition: 1192nd Grenadier Regiment, 1193rd Grenadier Regiment, 1194th Grenadier Regiment, 1578th Artillery Regiment, 1578th Reconnaissance Company, 1578th Tank Destroyer Battalion, 1578th Engineer Battalion, 1578th Signal Company, 1578th Divisional Supply Troops

Home Station: Munich (?), Wehrkreis VII

This division was in the process of organizing on August 22, 1944. Instead of allowing it to complete its training, however, the Home Army merged it with the 212th Infantry Division on September 17 to form the 212th Volksgrenadier Division, where its men were used as replacements. The original 212th had been smashed on the Eastern Front. The new 212th was sent to the Western Front.

See also 212th Infantry (later Volksgrenadier) Division (Volume One).

Sources: *Kriegstagebuch des OKW,* Volume IV: 1883; Lexikon; "Frontnachweiser," 15 December 1944; Tessin, Vol. 11: 213.

579TH VOLKSGRENADIER DIVISION

Composition: 1195th Grenadier Regiment, 1196th Grenadier Regiment, 1197th Grenadier Regiment, 1579th Artillery Regiment, 1579th Reconnaissance Company, 1579th Tank Destroyer Battalion, 1579th Engineer Battalion, 1579th Signal Company, 1579th Divisional Supply Troops

Home Station: Wehrkreis VI

The 579th Volksgrenadier Division began forming on August 25, 1944 in Kaposvar, Hungary. It was only partially formed on September 17, 1944, when it was merged with the remnants of the 326th Infantry Division to form the 326th Volksgrenadier Division. The new division was sent to the Western Front.

See also 326th Infantry (later Volksgrenadier) Division earlier in this chapter.

Notes and Sources: The original 326th Infantry Division had been largely destroyed in Normandy.

Kriegstagebuch des OKW, Volume IV: 1883; Lexikon; "Frontnachweiser," 15 December 1944; Tessin, Vol. 11: 215; also see RA and OB45.

580TH VOLKSGRENADIER DIVISION

Composition: 1198th Grenadier Regiment, 1199th Grenadier Regiment, 1200th Grenadier Regiment, 1580th Artillery Regiment, 1580th Reconnaissance Company, 1580th Tank Destroyer Battalion, 1580th Engineer Battalion, 1580th Signal Company, 1580th Divisional Supply Troops

Home Station: Göttingen, Wehrkreis XI

Formed in Troop Maneuver Area Gruppe in West Prussia on August 26, 1944, it was soon disbanded and—like the other 32nd Wave divisions—was used to fill out the ranks of previously decimated units. On September 4, it was merged with the 276th Infantry Division to create the 276th Volksgrenadier Division, which was sent to the Western Front in November.

See also 276th Infantry (later Volksgrenadier) Division (Volume One).

Sources: *Kriegstagebuch des OKW*, Volume IV: 1883; "Frontnachweiser," 15 December 1944; Tessin, Vol. 11: 217; RA; OB 45.

581ST VOLKSGRENADIER DIVISION

Composition: 1203rd Grenadier Regiment, 1204th Grenadier Regiment, 1205th Grenadier Regiment, 1581st Artillery Regiment, 1581st Reconnaissance Company, 1581st Tank

Destroyer Battalion, 1581st Engineer Battalion, 1581st Signal Company, 1581st Divisional Supply Troops

Home Station: Northeim, Wehrkreis XI

Created on August 26, 1944, in the Flensburg area of Schleswig, this 32nd mobilization wave division was not permitted to complete its training. Its regiments were sent to France and, on September 21, were merged with the 352nd Infantry Division (which had been crushed on D-Day) to form the 352nd Volksgrenadier Division. The new division was in combat on the Western Front by November.

See also 352nd Infantry (later Volksgrenadier) Division earlier in this chapter.

Sources: *Kriegstagebuch des OKW*, Volume IV: 1883; Lexikon; Nafziger 2000: 358; "Frontnachweiser," 15 December 1944; Tessin, Vol. 11: 220; also see RA: OB 45.

582ND VOLKSGRENADIER DIVISION

Composition: 1206th Grenadier Regiment, 1207th Grenadier Regiment, 1208th Grenadier Regiment, 1582nd Artillery Regiment, 1582nd Reconnaissance Company, 1582nd Tank Destroyer Battalion, 1582nd Engineer Battalion, 1582nd Signal Company

Home Station: Wehrkreis VI

This unit, like its sister divisions, never got out of the organizational stages. It was formed in the Warthelager area near Posen (Wehrkreis XX) on August 25, 1944, and, on September 17, was merged with the decimated 26th Infantry Division to form the 26th Volksgrenadier Division. The new division was sent to the Western Front, while the 582nd Volksgrenadier Division ceased to exist.

See also 26th Infantry (later Volksgrenadier) Division (Volume One).

Sources: *Kriegstagebuch des OKW*, Volume IV: 1883; Lexikon; "Frontnachweiser," 15 December 1944; Tessin, Vol. 11: 223; RA; OB 45.

583RD VOLKSGRENADIER DIVISION

Probable Composition: Grenadier Regiment Neuhammer 1, Genadier Regiment Neuhammer 2, Grenadier Regiment Neuhammer 3, Artillery Regiment Neuhammer

Home Station: Wehrkreis VIII

Shortly after its activation process began in the Neuhammer Troop Maneuver Area of Silesia in September 1944, the 583rd was disbanded on September 22. Its soldiers were to used as replacements for the 62nd Volksgrenadier (formerly Infantry) Division, which had been decimated on the Eastern Front. The new division was sent to the Western Front.

See also 62nd Infantry (later Volksgrenadier) Division (Volume One).

Sources: *Kriegstagebuch des OKW,* Volume IV: 1883; Lexikon; "Frontnachweiser," 15 December 1944; Tessin, Vol. 11: 226.

584TH VOLKSGRENADIER DIVISION

Composition: Grenadier Regiment Dennewitz 1, Grenadier Regiment Dennewitz 2, Grenadier Regiment Dennewitz 3, Artillery Regiment Dennewitz

Home Station: Wehrkreis IX

Authorized in September 1944, the 584th was in the early organizational stages in the Esbjerg area of Denmark, when the Replacement Army decided to use it to rebuild decimated 9th Infantry Division, which had been almost completely destroyed by the Soviets in Rumania. The two divisions were merged to form the 9th Volksgrenadier Division, which was sent to the Western Front. The 584th's divisional headquarters was disbanded on or about October 13.

See also 9th Infantry (later Volksgrenadier) Division (Volume One).

Sources: *Kriegstagebuch des OKW,* Volume IV: 1883; Lexikon; "Frontnachweiser," 15 December 1944; Tessin, Vol. 11: 230.

585TH VOLKSGRENADIER DIVISION

Composition: Grenadier Regiment Niedergoersdorf 1, Grenadier Regiment Niedergörsdorf 2, Grenadier Regiment Niedergörsdorf 3, Artillery Regiment Niedergoersdorf

Home Station: Wehrkreis XVII

The 585th was partially formed in the Doellersheim Troop Maneuver Area on September 2, 1944, from the remnants of the 17th Luftwaffe Field Division. It also absorbed Shadow Division Niedergoersdorf. In October, however, the Home Army merged it with the 167th Infantry Division to form the 167th Volksgrenadier Division in Slovakia. The new 167th was sent to the Western Front in January 1945.

See also 167th Infantry (later Volksgrenadier) Division (Volume One).

Sources: *Kriegstagebuch des OKW*, Volume IV: 1883; Lexikon; "Frontnachweiser," 15 December 1944; Tessin, Vol. 11: 230.

586TH VOLKSGRENADIER DIVISION

Composition: Grenadier Regiment Katzbach 1, Grenadier Regiment Katzbach 2, Grenadier Regiment Katzbach 3, Artillery Regiment Katzbach

Home Station: Wehrkreis XX

This "peoples' grenadier" division existed for only a short time in the fall of 1944. It was formed in West Prussia in September 1944, where it absorbed Shadow Division "Katzbach" on September 28. On October 27, it merged with the remnants of the 79th Infantry Division (which had been virtually annihilated in Romania) to form the 79th Volksgrenadier Division, which was then forming in the Thorn area of Poland (Wehrkreis XX). The new division was sent to the Rhine in December.

See also 79th Infantry (later Volksgrenadier) Division (Volume One).

Sources: *Kriegstagebuch des OKW*, Volume IV: 1883; Lexikon; "Frontnachweiser," 15 December 1944; Tessin, Vol. 11: 232; OB 45: 166.

587TH VOLKSGRENADIER DIVISION

Composition: Grenadier Regiment Gross-Goerschen 1, Grenadier Regiment Gross-Goerschen 2, Grenadier Regiment Gross-Goerschen 3, Artillery Regiment Gross-Goerschen

Home Station: Wehrkreis III

The 587th began forming in the Wandern Troop Maneuver Area (Wehrkreis III) in September 1944. It absorbed Shadow Division "Gross-Görschen" on September 28. On October 13, it was merged with the remnants of the 257th Infantry Division (which was then rebuilding in Poland) to form the 257th Volksgrenadier Division. The new 257th was sent to the Western Front in December.

See also 257th Infantry (later Volksgrenadier) Division (Volume One).

Sources: *Kriegstagebuch des OKW*, Volume IV: 1883; Lexikon; "Frontnachweiser," 15 December 1944; Tessin, Vol. 11: 234; OB 45: 216–17.

588TH VOLKSGRENADIER DIVISION

Composition: Grenadier Regiment Möckern 1, Grenadier Regiment Möckern 2, Grenadier Regiment Möckern 3; Artillery Regiment Moeckern

Home Station: Wehrkreis II

This unit was created in Troop Maneuver Area Gross-Born (Pomerania) in early September 1944, and absorbed Shadow Division "Möckern" on September 28. It was sent to Poland, where it merged with the remnants of the 320th Infantry Division to form the 320th Volksgrenadier Division on October 27. The new unit was sent to the Eastern Front.

See also 320th Volksgrenadier Division earlier in this chapter.

Sources: *Kriegstagebuch des OKW*, Volume IV: 1883; Nafziger 2000: 360; "Frontnachweiser," 15 December 1944; Tessin, Vol 11: 236; OB: 234–35.

600TH INFANTRY DIVISION (*RUSSISCH*)

Composition: 1601st Grenadier Regiment, 1602nd Grenadier Regiment, 1603rd Grenadier Regiment, 1600th Artillery Regiment, 1600th Reconnaissance Battalion, 1600th Engineer Battalion, 1600th Tank Destroyer Battalion, 1600th Signal Battalion, 1600th Field Replacement Battalion, 1600th Divisional Supply Troops

Formed under the auspices of the General of Volunteer Formations at OKH, this division was organized at Troop Maneuver Area Münsingen, Wehrkreis V on December 1, 1944. Its men were former Soviet prisoners-of-war who preferred enlisting in the German Army to starving to death in a Nazi prison camp. The division trained in Münsingen until April 1945; meanwhile, it became part of General Vlassov's anti-Communist Russian Army, the *Russkaja Oswobodennaja Armija* or ROA. A very unreliable formation, OKH did not commit it to action until the Soviets were at the gates of the capital of the Reich. It was destroyed between the Oder and Berlin. Most of its men were subsequently executed on Stalin's orders.

Major General Sergei Buniachenfo was the division's commander.

Notes and Sources: The 600th Division's grenadier regiments had only two battalions each. Andrei Vlassov was a former Soviet general captured by the Germans in 1942. He subsequently led anti-Communist Russian troops under the banner of Nazi Germany. Like General Buniachenfo, he was executed by the Reds after the war.

Kursietis: 220; Lexikon; Tessin, Vol. 11: 260.

601ST LANDESSCHÜTZEN DIVISION (601ST SPECIAL PURPOSES DIVISION)

Composition: 11th Fortress Regiment Staff z.b.V., 1017th Security Battalion, Frontier Guard Battalion Gruenwald, Police Guard Battalion Krakau, 209th Police Battalion

Home Station: Nnaim, Wehrkreis XVII

Formed under Army Group A in Krakow (Krakau), Poland, on October 14, 1944, this headquarters was used to control miscellaneous older-age units on the southern sector of the Eastern Front. It fought in Poland and Upper Silesia and ended the war in the Deutsch-Brod pocket east of Prague.

Its commanders were Lieutenant General Max Hartlieb gen. Walsporn (October 14, 1944) and Major General Hermann Kruse (April 1945).

Notes and Sources: The Staff of the 601st came from OFK 225 (Warsaw). General Kruse remained a Polish prisoner until 1950.

Keilig: 126; *Kriegstagebuch des OKW*, Volume IV: 1896; Lexikon; Tessin, Vol. 11: 263; OB 45: 278.

602ND LANDESSCHÜTZEN DIVISION (602ND SPECIAL PURPOSES DIVISION)

Composition: 65th Landesschuetzen Regiment, II/25th SS Police Regiment, 207/XII Luftwaffe Construction Battalion, 207/XVII Luftwaffe Construction Battalion

Home Station: Kolberg, Wehrkreis II

Like its sister divisions, the 601st and 603rd, this headquarters was formed in Krakow (Krakau), Poland, to controlled miscellaneous units of older men on the southern sector of the Eastern Front. Formed on October 14, 1944, it served on the Eastern Front until the end of the war, fighting in Poland and Upper Silesia. It was trapped in the Deutsch-Brod Pocket with most of Army Group Center and surrendered to the Red Army in May 1945.

Its commander was Lieutenant General Werner Schartow.

Notes and Sources: The headquarters of the 602nd was the former Staff, OFK 226 (Krakow).

Kriegstagebuch des OKW, Volume IV: 1896; Lexikon; Tessin, Vol. 11: 267; OB 45: 278.

603RD LANDESSCHÜTZEN DIVISION (603RD SPECIAL PURPOSES DIVISION)

Composition: 62nd Fortress Machine Gun Battalion, 1st SS Motorized Gerdarne [Police] Battalion, Frontier Guard Battalion Mehl, 115/XIII Luftwaffe Construction Battalion

Home Station: Osnabrueck, Wehrkreis VI

Organized by Army Group A on October 14, 1944, from the Higher Field Area Command 603 staff in Kielce, Poland, the 603rd controlled older-age GHQ units on the southern sector of the Russian Front, fighting in Poland and Silesia. It ended the war at Glatz and, along with the rest of the 17th Army, surrendered to the Russians in May 1945.

Its commander was Lieutenant General Erich Mueller.

Sources: *Kriegstagebuch des OKW*, Volume IV: 1896; Lexikon; Nafziger 2000: 360; Tessin, Vol. 11: 271; OB 45: 279.

604TH SPECIAL PURPOSES DIVISION

Composition: Miscellaneous units from the Netherlands

Home Station: Wehrkreis XI

Also known as Division von Tettau, this headquarters was formed under OB West on November 4, 1944, from units which had fought in Operation Market Garden. It was commanded by Lieutenant General Hans von Tettau, the director of operations and training of the Armed Forces Netherlands, and consisted of miscellaneous German Alarm (emergency) battalions. They had been sent into battle at Arnhem against the British 1st Airborne Division, on the western flank of the II SS Panzer Corps' battle line, and fought well; the British parachute division suffered more than 50 percent casualties against Division von Tettau and the SS. The 604th later fought in the Utrecht vicinity, and was sent to Pomerania on the Eastern Front in early 1945. It had been dissolved by March 1945, however.

Sources: Lexikon; MacDonald 1963; Map V; Tessin, Vol. 11: 275; OB 45: 279. Also see Ellis, Volume II: 29–55.

605TH LANDESSCHÜTZEN DIVISION (DIV. z.b.V. 605)

This division was formed on November 7, 1944, at Loetzen, East Prussia (now Gizycko, in the northeast corner of present-day Poland). It consisted of older-age men assigned to the Fortress Commander Loetzen and some miscellaneous army troops from Army Group Center. The former fortress staff became the staff of the division. It fought in the retreat from Loetzen to the Heiligenbeil pocket, where it was destroyed. It was officially dissolved in March 1945.

Sources: Lexikon; Tessin, Vol. 11: 278.

606TH SPECIAL PURPOSES DIVISION

Composition: 3rd Panzer Replacement and Training Battalion, Alarm Battalion Potsdam, Alarm Battalion Spandau, Alarm Battalion Brandenburg, Police Battalion Bremen, 1606th Tank Destroyer Company, 606th Engineer Battalion, 606th Signal Battalion (later Company), 1606th Supply Regiment

Home Station: Wehrkreis V

This division was formed in the Netherlands on November 7, 1944. It included the Staff, signal battalion and division service troops of the 344th Infantry Division, as well as the service support troops of the 180th Infantry Division. In February 1945, the division was sent to the Oder sector, near Küstrin, where it received the 3rd Panzer Placement and Training Battalion and the four Alarm and Police battalions shown above. It received the rest of its divisional troops in April. The 606th was, in fact, an infantry division by now and some sources refer to it as such; however, it apparently never officially received this designation, at least according to the War Diary of the Operations Branch of the High Command of the Armed Forces. Meanwhile, the 606th fought on the Vistula as part of the 9th Army and ended the war with the 21st Army in central Germany. It surrendered to the Americans.

Its commanders were Major General Rudolf Raessler (November 7, 1944), Colonel/Major General Rudolf Goltzsch (December 1, 1944), and Colonel/Major General Dr. Maximilian Rosskopf (March 5, 1945).

Notes and Sources: Goltzsch was promoted to major general on December 1, 1944. Rosskopf reached the same rank on April 20, 1945.

Keilig: 111, 284; Kursietis: 221; Lexikon; Mehner, Vol. 12: 442, 462; Tessin, Vol. 11: 282; OB 45: 279.

German infantry in a foxhole near a well-camouflaged tank.

607TH SPECIAL PURPOSES DIVISION

Composition: Weapons School, Army Group North; 1607th Signal Company

Home Station: Breslau, Wehrkreis VIII

The 607th was created by Army Group Center (later North) on November 13, 1944. It fought in Lithuania and, in February 1945, became Fortress Command Pillau under Army Detachment Samland in East Prussia. It was destroyed on April 25, 1945, when the old Baltic Sea port of Pillau fell to the Russians. Pillau is now Baltijsk, Poland.

Sources: *Kriegstagebuch des OKW*, Volume IV: 1897; Lexikon; Tessin, Vol. 11: 285.

608TH SPECIAL PURPOSES DIVISION

Composition (February 1945): Brigade Staff 100 (Grenadier Regiment Staffs Hellback and Peter); 83rd Grenadier (Alarm) Regiment, 92nd Grenadier (Alarm) Regiment, 95th Grenadier (Alarm) Regiment, 1st Police Regiment, Police Regiment Krause, 6th SS Gendarme Regiment, six Volkssturm battalions, three Alarm battalions, 608th Signal Company

This staff was initially formed by Army Group A on November 22, 1944, from the Staff, 82nd Infantry Division, to control GHQ units and/or to collect stragglers. It served directly under army group headquarters at first. By March 1945, however, it was being used as a combat division on the Oder with 4th Panzer Army on the Eastern Front. The 35th SS Police Division was under the operational control of the 608th in the last campaign. An infantry division in everything but name, the 608th was destroyed east of Dresden during the last Soviet offensive. Its commander was Major General Franz Becker.

Notes and Sources: General Becker was wounded on April 12 and captured in the hospital by the British on April 19.
Keilig: 25; *Kriegstagebuch des OKW*, Volume IV: 1896; Lexikon; Tessin, Vol. 11: 288.

609TH INFANTRY DIVISION

Composition: Regiment Reinkober, Regiment Kersten, Regiment Schulz, Regiment Seybold, 609th Signal Company, 1609th Signal Company, 1609th Field Military Police Troop

Home Station: Dresden, Wehrkreis IV

This unit was formed in Dresden on January 26, 1945, from stragglers, Volkssturm, men on leave, and rear-area SS men. Part of the division headquarters was used to from Staff, Fortress Command Breslau. Sent to Breslau in February, it was soon surrounded in the Silesian capital. Despite its hopeless position, the 609th defended Breslau in bitter house-to-house fighting in a most creditable manner. It was still fighting in the ruins of the city, even after the fall of Berlin. It surrendered to the Soviets in May 1945.

Its commander was Major General/Lieutenant General Siegfried Ruff.

Notes and Sources: Ruff was promoted to lieutenant general on March 1, 1945. Captured when Breslau fell, he was sent back to the Soviet Union and hanged on February 3, 1946.

Chant: 192; Keilig: 287; Lexikon; Tessin, Vol. 11: 291.

610TH SPECIAL PURPOSES DIVISION

Composition: Miscellaneous units, Alarm battalions and the 1610th Signal Company

Home Station: Wehrkreis IX

This unit was organized in the rear area of Army Group Vistula on January 25, 1945, and controlled General Headquarters units, Alarm (emergency) battalions, and miscellaneous ad hoc formations. It fought near Stettin and on the Oder during the Berlin campaign—the last of the war. As part of 3rd Panzer Army, part of it managed to surrender to the Anglo-Americans in May 1945.

The commanders of this division were Lieutenant General Hubert Lendle (January 28, 1945), Colonel/Major General Fritz Fullriede (April 18, 1945), and Lendle (April 27, 1945–end).

Notes and Sources: Fullriede was promoted to major general on April 20, 1945.

Bradley et al., Vol. 4: 151-53; *Kriegstagebuch des OKW*, Volume IV: 1898; Lexikon; Mehner, Vol. 12: 462; Tessin, Vol. 11: 294.

611TH SPECIAL PURPOSES DIVISION (DIV. z.b.V. 611)

Composition: Miscellaneous GHQ units, Alarm battalions, 1611th Signal Company

Home Station: Wehrkreis II

This division began forming on January 26, 1945. Three days later, on January 29, its headquarters became Staff, Infantry Division Döberitz (also dubbed the 303rd Infantry Division) and its men were transferred to the 615th Special Purposes Division.

Sources: Lexikon; Tessin, Vol. 11: 297.

612TH SPECIAL PURPOSES DIVISION

Composition: Alarm battalions; 1612th Signal Company

Home Station: Tingleff, Wehrkreis X

Activated under Army Group Vistula on January 26, 1945, the 612th was never fully formed. Its staff was used to form Headquarters, *Oderkorps* (Corps Oder) in February 1945. Its commander was Lieutenant General Wolf Hagemann (January 26–February 28, 1945).

Sources: Keilig: 122; Lexikon; Tessin, Vol. 11: 300.

613TH SPECIAL PURPOSES DIVISION

Composition: 193rd Grenadier Brigade (two battalions); 503rd Grenadier Brigade (three battalions)

Home Station: Narvik (?), Norway

Organized on January 30, 1945, after the German evacuation of Finland and much of Lapland, this unit controlled two GHQ brigades in Petsamo, Norway, as part of 20th Mountain

Army's reserve. It never saw combat and surrendered to the British on May 8, 1945. Its commander was Major General Baron Adrian van der Hoop.

Sources: Keilig: 150; *Kriegstagebuch des OKW*, Volume IV: 1899, Lexikon; Mehner, Vol. 12: 462; Tessin, Vol. 11: 303.

614TH SPECIAL PURPOSES DIVISION (INFANTRY DIVISION "JUTLAND")

Composition: Miscellaneous occupation units

Home Station: Luebeck, Wehrkreis X

The 614th Special Division Staff was organized on January 30, 1945, to direct miscellaneous combat and territorial German forces in western Jutland (i.e., the Danish peninsula). It was redesignated the 325th Infantry Division (also called Infantry Division "Jutland") on March 9, 1945.

Its commander was Lieutenant General Heinrich von Behr.

See also Infantry Division "Jutland" later in this chapter.

Sources: *Kriegstagebuch des OKW*, Volume IV: 1899; Lexikon; Tessin, Vol. 11: 306.

615TH SPECIAL PURPOSES DIVISION

Composition: Miscellaneous combat units

Home Station: Potsdam, Wehrkreis III

This headquarters was organized in Silesia on February 4, 1945, to control miscellaneous GHQ and ad hoc Alarm units in the zone of the 4th Panzer Army of Army Group Center. It fought in Silesia, at Görlitz, and in the vicinity of Erzgebirge (a mountainous district in the extreme southeastern part of present-day Germany) on the Eastern Front. It was still resisting in the Dresden area when the war ended. Its men wound up in Soviet captivity.

Its commander was Colonel/Major General of Reserves Gerd-Paul von Below.

Notes and Sources: General von Below died in a Soviet prison in late 1953. *Kriegstagebuch des OKW,* Volume I: 1146; Volume IV: 1896; Tessin, Vol. 11: 309.

616TH SPECIAL PURPOSES DIVISION

Formed near Landau, in the southern Rhineland-Palatinate region of Germany just north of the Swiss border, this division consisted of units and troops combed from the rear area of Army Group G. Its headquarters was the former staff of the ad hoc Division Rässler, which had been created in February 1945, and which was redesignated 616th Special Purposes Division in April. The division was sent to the Western Front and held a sector of the middle Rhine under the 1st Army. It was overrun in late April, as the Allies overran western Germany.

Its commander was Major General Rudolf Rässler.

Sources: Keilig: 267; Kursietis: 221; Lexikon; Mehner, Vol. 12: 462; Tessin, Vol. 11: 312.

617TH SPECIAL PURPOSES DIVISION

The Division z.b.V. 617 was formed on the Dutch coast in April 1945, to control General Headquarters troops in the 25th Army's zone of operations. It surrendered to the British on May 8, 1945.

Its commander (according to Mehner) was Lieutenant General von Schwerin.

Sources: Lexikon; Mehner, Vol. 12: 462; Tessin, Vol. 11: 315.

618TH SPECIAL PURPOSES DIVISION

Composition: 558th Grenadier Regiment, 559th Grenadier Regiment, 324th Artillery Regiment, 324th Fusilier Battalion, 324th Engineer Battalion, 324th Signal Battalion, 342th Divisional Supply Troops

This unit was formed near Essen in the Ruhr Pocket in April 1945, after the U.S. Army had surrounded the industrial district. It was created from the Staff, Infantry Division Hamburg, and included virtually all of that division. It only existed for a few days and surrendered to the Americans on or about April 15, 1945.

Its commander was Lieutenant General Walter Steinmüller.

Sources: Keilig: 331; Lexikon; Mehner, Vol. 12: 462; Tessin, Vol. 11: 318.

619TH SPECIAL PURPOSES DIVISION

This division was formed in Samland around the former Staff, 286th Infantry Division. What components Army Detachment Samland (the former XXVIII Corps) intended to assign to it is not known. The area was overrun by the Red Army before the 619th was fully organized.

Sources: Lexikon; Mehner, Vol. 12: 434; Tessin, Vol. 11: 320.

650TH INFANTRY DIVISION (*RUSSISCH*)

Composition: 1651st Grenadier Regiment, 1652nd Grenadier Regiment, 1653rd Grenadier Regiment, 1650th Artillery Regiment, 1650th Engineer Battalion, 1650th Signal Battalion, 1650th Field Replacement Battalion, 1650th Divisional Supply Regiment

Home Station: Wehrkreis V

The 650th Infantry Division was formed in Troop Maneuver Area Heuberg (in the Black Forest) in March 1945. It was scheduled to become part of General Vlassov's anti-Communist Russian Army, the Russian Liberation Army (the ROA), which was fighting for the Third Reich. The 650th Infantry Division, however, never completed its training and was at the Muensingen Troop Maneuver Area in Swabia at the end of the war. Most of its men were later turned over to the Soviets, who murdered them.

Its commander was Major General G. A. Zverev.

Notes and Sources: The grenadier regiments of the 650th had only two battalions each. General Zverev resisted being handed over to the Russians. The Allies killed his aide and wounded and captured the general, who was hanged in 1946.

Lexikon; Mehner, Vol. 12: 455; Tessin, Vol. 12: 39. For an excellent article on the Vlassov Army, see Lieutenant General Wladyslaw Anders and Antonio Munoz, "Russian Volunteers in the German Wehrmacht in World War II" at *www.feldgrau.com/rvol.html.*

702ND INFANTRY DIVISION

Composition: 722nd Infantry Regiment, 742nd Infantry Regiment, 662nd Artillery Battalion, 702nd Engineer Company, 702nd Signal Company, 702nd Divisional Supply Troops

Home Station: Schwerin, later Wismar, Wehrkreis II

Formed in Stettin from older personnel on April 16, 1941, the 702nd was sent to southern Norway the following month. By the end of June, it was in northern Norway, and it remained in the Drontheim area for the rest of the war. A static division, the 702nd performed garrison and coastal watch duty until the end. It added a tank destroyer battalion in April 1945, at the same time its engineer and signal companies became battalions.

Its commanders included Colonel/Major General Herbert Lemke (April 17, 1941), Major General/Lieutenant General Kurt Schmidt (September 4, 1941), Lieutenant General Karl Edelmann (September 1, 1943), and Lieutenant General Dr. Ernst Klepp (February 11, 1945). For at least part of 1942, its 742nd Infantry Regiment was attached to the 181st Infantry Division.

Notes and Sources: Lemke was promoted to major general on August 1, 1941. Schmidt became a lieutenant general on October 1, 1942.

Keilig: 201; Kursietis: 223-24; Lexikon; Tessin, Vol. 12: 44; RA: 32; OB 42: 110; OB 43: 187; OB 45: 279.

703RD INFANTRY DIVISION

Composition: 219th Grenadier Regiment, 495th Grenadier Regiment, 579th Grenadier Regiment, 703rd Fusilier Battalion, 973rd Tank Destroyer Battalion, 1973rd Divisional Supply Troops

The Staff, 703rd Infantry Division was formed on March 22, 1945, from the staff of the Fortress Commandant Ijmuiden in the Netherlands. Its men were former sailors and Eastern troops, and its units were well below their authorized strengths. Its 219th Grenadier Regiment was the former 10th Ships Cadre Battalion (*10. Schiffs-Stamm-Abt.*), the 495th Grenadier Regiment was the former 787th Turk Battalion, and the 579th was the former 24th Ships Cadre Battalion. The new division was assigned to the 25th Army of OB Northwest and surrendered to the British at the end of the conflict. Its commander was Major General Hans Hüttner.

Sources: Keilig: 154; Kursietis: 224; Lexikon; Tessin, Vol. 12: 147.

704TH INFANTRY DIVISION

See 104th Jäger Division in chapter 3.

707TH INFANTRY DIVISION

Composition: 727th Infantry Regiment, 747th Infantry Regiment, 657th Artillery Battalion, 707th Engineer Company, 707th Signal Company, 707th Divisional Supply Troops

Home Station: Lindau, Wehrkreis VII

On March 2, 1941, this division was mustered in. Like all the 700-series units, its was both static and considerably smaller than the normal German infantry division and was well under-strength in artillery and support troops. Its infantry regiments, for example, had no anti-tank, machine-gun, mortar, or heavy-weapons companies. The 707th was sent to the Eastern Front and was performing line-of-communications duties for Army Group Center in August. In the winter of 1942–43 and summer of 1943, it was fighting on the front line near Bryansk and Orel. In June 1944, it was one of only two divisions in 9th Army's reserve when the massive Soviet summer offensive hit Army Group Center. Quickly committed, the 707th was soon smashed. Major General Gihr, the divisional commander, was taken prisoner near Bobruisk, along with most of his men. The remnants of the little division were officially disbanded soon after.

Commanders of the 707th included Colonel/Major General Baron Gustav von Mauchenheim gennant Bechtolsheim (May 3, 1941), Colonel Baron Hans von Falkenstein (February 22, 1943), Lieutenant General Wilhelm Russwurm (April 25, 1943), Major General/Lieutenant General Rudolf Busich (June 1, 1943), Colonel Alexander Conrady (December 3, 1943), Busich (returned January 12, 1944), and Gihr (May 15, 1944).

Notes and Sources: Baron von Mauchenheim was promoted to major general on August 1, 1941. Busich was promoted to lieutenant general on December 1, 1943. Gihr was in Soviet prisons until 1955.

Keilig: 107; *Kriegstagebuch des OKW*, Volume III: 1157; Lexikon; Tessin, Vol. 12: 156–57; OB 42: 110–11; OB 43: 187; OB 45: 280.

708TH INFANTRY (LATER VOLKSGRENADIER) DIVISION

Composition (1945): 728th Grenadier Regiment, 748th Grenadier Regiment, 1708th Artillery Regiment, 708th Fusilier Battalion, 708th Tank Destroyer Battalion, 708th Engineer Battalion, 708th Signal Battalion, 708th Divisional Supply Troops

Home Station: Moerchingen, later Bielitz (Upper Silesia), Wehrkreis VIII

Formed in the Strasbourg area from Landesschützen personnel on May 2, 1941, the 708th originally consisted of only two infantry regiments, an artillery battalion and the 708th Engineer and Signal Companies. In November 1941, this static division was posted to central and southwestern France and later served in Brittany. In early 1944, it was reorganized; its artillery battalion became a regiment, its engineer and signal companies became battalions, and it added the 360th (Cossack) Grenadier Regiment. The other two grenadier regiments, however, lost their third battalions, so the quality of the division actually declined. That summer, the 708th was transferred from the Garonne River estuary north of Bordeaux to Normandy. Rated as a poor-quality fighting unit, it was largely destroyed by the French 2nd Armored Division, which overran it near Falaise on August 9. The remnants were sent to Slovakia, where the 708th was hastily rebuilt as a Volksgrenadier division with normal supporting units. The 708th absorbed the 573rd Grenadier Division in the fall of 1944. Returned to the Western Front in November, it suffered heavy losses in Alsace south of Strasbourg and was destroyed in the Colmar Bridgehead on February 3, 1945.

Its commanders included Colonel/Major General Walter Drobenig (May 3, 1941), Lieutenant General Hermann Wilck (March 1, 1942), Major General Edgar Arndt (July 30, 1943), and Colonel Wilhelm Bleckwenn (November 20, 1944). Colonel Bruno Gerloch was acting commander from August 9 to 19, 1944.

Notes and Sources: Drobenig was promoted to major general on July 1, 1941. General Arndt was killed in action on near Groghy, France, on August 24, 1944.

Blumenson 1960: 422, 498, 566; Bradley, Vol. 1: 86–87, Vol. 4: 248–49. Chant, Volume 14: 1855, 1864; Harrison: Map VI; Keilig: 36, 370; Kursietis: 224; Lexikon; "Frontnachweiser," 15 December 1944; Tessin, Vol. 12: 159–60; RA: 130; OB 43: 187; OB 45: 280.

709TH INFANTRY DIVISION

Composition (1943): 729th Infantry Regiment, 739th Infantry Regiment, 709th Artillery Battalion, 709th Engineer Battalion, 709th Signal Company, 709th Divisional Supply Troops

Home Station: Butzbach, later Fulda, Wehrkreis IX

This understrength static division was formed from older men on May 2, 1941, and was sent to Brittany, France, on garrison duty in June. In the spring of 1943, it was transferred to Cherbourg and served as the city garrison. While there, it received the 919th Grenadier Regiment from the 242nd Infantry Division and was reorganized, but its personnel remained overage. The average soldier in the 709th was 36 years old in 1944. By early 1944, the 709th Infantry Division included the 729th Fortress Grenadier Regiment (four battalions, one of them Eastern troops); the 919th Grenadier Regiment (three battalions, all German); the 1709th Artillery Regiment (three battalions); and assorted divisional troops. Despite the advanced age of its men, the German battalions of the 709th nevertheless fought credibly from D-Day until the fall of Cherbourg on June 30, 1944, where its remnants were destroyed. It was officially dissolved on July 25.

The division's commanders were Major General Arnold von Bessel (May 3, 1941), Major General Albin Nake (July 15, 1942), Lieutenant General Curt Jahn (March 15, 1943), Major General Eckkard von Geyso (July 1, 1943), and Major General/Lieutenant General Karl-Wilhelm von Schlieben (December 12, 1943). Schlieben surrendered the city of Cherbourg to the U.S. Army on June 30, 1944.

Notes and Sources: The I/739th Grenadier Regiment was an Eastern (Georgian) Battalion. Schlieben was promoted to lieutenant general on May 1, 1944.

Harrison: Map VI, 147; Keilig: 302; Lexikon; Nafziger 2000: 367–69; Tessin, Vol. 12: 163; RA: 144; OB 42: 111; OB 43: 186; OB 45: 281. For the story of the fall of Cherbourg, see Carell 1973.

710TH INFANTRY DIVISION

Composition: 730th Infantry Regiment, 740th Infantry Regiment, 650th Artillery Battalion, 710th Engineer Company, 710th Tank Destroyer Company, 710th Signal Company, 710th Divisional Supply Troops

Home Station: Heide, later Oldenburg, Wehrkreis X

Formed on May 2, 1941, as an undersized static division from Landesschuetzen (older) personnel, the 710th was posted to Oslo, Norway, where it replaced the younger, full-strength and better-equipped 163rd Infantry Division. (The 163rd was sent to northern Finland, where it fought on the Far North sector of the Eastern Front.) The 710th Infantry Division, meanwhile, performed occupation duties at Oslo and later Kristiansand, Norway, and in Denmark. In December 1944, it was sent to the Adriatic sector of the Italian Front to free more experienced units for service in the East. It was withdrawn north of Venice in January 1945, and was sent to the I SS

Panzer Corps of the 6th SS Panzer Army in Hungary, where it fought against the Russians in the battles and retreats through western Hungary and in the Battle of Vienna. It was still resisting in Austria when the war ended. The division managed to disengage from the Russians and reach Steyr, where it surrendered to the Americans on May 8, 1945.

Commanders of the 710th included Major General/Lieutenant Generals Theodor Petsch (May 3, 1941), Lieutenant General Rudolf-Eduard Licht (November 1, 1944), and Major General Walter Gorn (April 15, 1945).

Notes and Sources: The 710th Division's infantry regiments had three battalions each in 1942. Its artillery battalion was redesignated a regiment in May 1941, but did not receive a second battalion until July 1944. The 650th Artillery Regiment added a III and IV Battalion in 1945. Its engineer company was expanded into a battalion in 1943. The division added the 710th Tank Destroyer Company in February 1945. This unit became the 710th Tank Destroyer Battalion in March, when it added a second tank destroyer company and a Fla (light anti-aircraft) company. Petsch was promoted to lieutenant general on November 1, 1942.

Fisher: 420; Keilig: 254; Nafziger 2000: 369–70; Tessin, Vol. 12: 166; RA: 160; OB 42: 111; OB 43: 187; OB 45: 281; Ziemke 1959: 139.

711TH INFANTRY DIVISION

Composition (1943): 731st Infantry Regiment, 744th Infantry Regiment, 651st Artillery Battalion, 711th Engineer Company, 711th Signal Company, 711th Divisional Supply Troops

Home Station: Brunswick, Wehrkreis XI

The 711th Infantry was formed from older troops on May 1, 1941, and was sent to northeastern France in June. In December 1941, the static unit was posted to Rouen, and in the spring of 1944, moved to the Deauville area, in the 15th Army's zone south of the Seine, where it headquartered at Pont L'Eveque. It fought in Normandy, where it suffered heavy casualties and was withdrawn to Holland to rebuild. Reconstituted south of Rotterdam, the 763rd Grenadier Regiment was added to the division, and its strength was brought up to three battalions of German and two battalions of Eastern troops. In October and November, the 716th fought in the Battle of the Scheldt, and it was defending a sector near Gorinchem in December, when it was transferred to the Eastern Front. It fought in Hungary, in the Battle of Lake Balaton (Plattensee) and Gran, and, at only battle group strength, was surrounded in the Deutsch-Brod Pocket (east of Prague) and surrendered to the Russians on May 9, 1945.

The commanders of the 711th included Colonel/Major General Dietrich von Reinersdorff-Paczensky und Tenczin (May 1, 1941), Major General Wilhelm Haverkamp (April 1, 1942), Major General Friedrich-Wilhelm Deutsch (July 15, 1942), and Major General/Lieutenant General Josef Reichert (March 15, 1943).

Notes and Sources: Reinersdorff-Paczensky was promoted to major general on June 1, 1941. Reichert was promoted to lieutenant general on September 1, 1943. He was severely injured in an automobile accident on April 14, 1945. Apparently OKW was not aware of this. Its operational war diary lists him as the commander of the division at the end of the war, but he was not. Who surrendered the 711th Infantry to the Soviets is not clear, although it may have been Lieutenant Colonel Gerber, the Ia. Reichert was captured by the Americans.

Keilig: 270–71; Harrison: Map VI; Hartmann: 42; MacDonald 1963: 216–17, 220; Mehner, Vol. 12: 460; Nafziger 2000: 370–71; Tessin, Vol. 12: 169–70; OB 43: 187-88; OB 45: 281–82.

712TH INFANTRY DIVISION

Composition: 732nd Infantry Regiment, 745th Infantry Regiment, 652nd Artillery Battalion, 712th Engineer Company, 712th Signal Company, 712th Divisional Supply Troops

Home Station: Luxembourg, later Saargemünd, Wehrkreis XII

Organized as a static division on May 5, 1941, the 712th was sent to northeastern France in July and to the Demarcation line between occupied France and Vichy France in October. In the spring of 1942, it was posted to a sector of the Belgian-Dutch coast near Zeebrugge and remained there until autumn 1944, when the British and Americans arrived. It fought against Operation Market-Garden in September and attacked and delayed British relief columns heading for Arnhem. It later opposed the British 32nd Guards (Tank) Brigade in the Battle of Oss, took part in the withdrawal across the Maas in October, and fought in the Heusden area that winter. In January 1945, the remnants of the 712th were sent to the Eastern Front, where they fought on the Oder. Most of the division's combat elements were absorbed by Panzer Division Kurmark in February. The remnants of the division returned to the line, however, and were destroyed by the Russians in the Halbe Pocket (also called the Buchholz-Halbe Pocket) southeast of Berlin in late April.

Its commanders included Colonel/Major General Georg von Döhren (May 3, 1941), Lieutenant General Friedrich-Wilhelm Neumann (April 16, 1942), and Major General Joachim von Siegroth (February 1, 1945).

Notes and Sources: Doehren was promoted to major general on July 1, 1941. Siegroth was reported as missing in action on April 2, 1945. No replacement for him had been named when the division surrendered.

Chant, Volume 17: 2376, Keilig: 72; Kursietis: 226; MacDonald 1963: Map V; Tessin, Vol. 12: 172–73; OB 43: 188; OB 45: 282.

713TH INFANTRY DIVISION

Composition: 733rd Infantry Regiment, 746th Regiment, 713th Artillery Battalion, 713th Engineer Company, 713th Signal Company, 713th Divisional Supply Troops

Home Station: Karlsbad, Wehrkreis XIII

This static division—made up of Landesschützen personnel—was created in the 15th Wave on May 2, 1941. By autumn, part of the division was in southern Greece and the rest in Crete, where they remained until January 15, 1942, when the 713th was disbanded. Its staff was used to form Fortress Brigade Crete.

Its commander was Colonel/Major General Franz Fehn.

A German formation in Oslo, Norway, circa 1941. The German Army had many more bicycles and bicycle units than most people realize.

Notes and Sources: Fehn was promoted to major general on June 1, 1941. Keilig: 86; Lexikon; Tessin, Vol. 12: 175; RA: 204; OB 43: 188; OB 45: 282.

714TH INFANTRY DIVISION

See 114th Jäger Division in chapter 3.

715TH INFANTRY DIVISION

Composition (1942): 715th Infantry Regiment, 735th Infantry Regiment, 671st Artillery Battalion, 715th Reconnaissance Company, 715th Engineer Battalion, 715th Signal Company, 715th Divisional Supply Troops

Home Station: Baden-Baden, Wehrkreis V

The 715th (Static) Infantry Division was activated on May 8, 1941, and sent to southwestern France that fall. In late summer 1943, it took over the Cannes-Nice sector on the Mediterranean coast when elements of the Italian 4th Army returned home. In January 1944, the 715th was sent to Italy following the Anzio landings and fought there until June, suffering heavy losses when the Allies broke out of the beachhead and took Rome. Sent to the rear, the 715th was rebuilt, largely from troops of the reinforced 1028th Grenadier Regiment and Shadow Division Wildflechen, which it absorbed. The division fought in the Gothic Line battles in September and was transferred to the Adriatic sector soon after. Rebuilt again in February 1945, it now included the 725th, 735th, and 774th Grenadier Regiments (two battalions each), the 671st Artillery Regiment (three battalions), the 715th Fusilier Battalion, the 715th Engineer Battalion, the 715th Tank Destroyer Battalion, the 715th Signal Company and the 715th Field Replacement Battalion. In early 1945, it was sent to the 1st Panzer Army on the Eastern Front, fought in Upper Silesia and surrendered in the Tabor-Pisek area of Czechoslovakia on May 2.

Its commanders included Colonel/Major General Ernst Wening (May 3, 1941), Major General/Lieutenant General Kurt Hoffmann (June 1, 1942), Major General/Lieutenant General Hans-Georg Hildebrandt (January 5, 1944), Colonel/Major

General Hans von Rohr (July 1, 1944), Colonel Hans-Joachim Ehlert (September 18, 1944), and von Rohr (September 30, 1944–end).

Notes and Sources: Ernst Wening was promoted to major general on June 1, 1941. Kurt Hoffmann became a lieutenant general on July 1, 1943. Hildebrandt reached the same rank on June 1, 1944. Rohr was promoted to major general on December 1, 1944.

Blumenson 1969: 361, 419–21; Fisher: Map III; Garland and Smyth: 294; Hartmann: 42–43; Keilig: 147; Kursietis: 226; Tessin, Vol. 12: 179; RA: 86; OB 42: 112; OB 43: 188; OB 45: 283.

716TH INFANTRY DIVISION

Composition: 726th Infantry Regiment, 736th Infantry Regiment, 656th Artillery Battalion (later 1716th Artillery Regiment), 716th Reconnaissance Company, 716th Engineer Battalion, 716th Signal Company, 716th Divisional Supply Troops

Home Station: Bielefeld, later Aachen, Wehrkreis VI

Formed from older personnel, the 716th was mustered in on May 2, 1941, and was sent to Rouen in June and to the Caen area of Normandy in July. It remained in the area until D-Day, when it was smashed by the British 2nd Army. It did, however, help prevent Montgomery from taking Caen on June 6 and thus allowed Field Marshal Rommel time to bottle up the Allies in hedgerow country for weeks. The 716th was withdrawn to Perpignan on the Mediterranean coast for refitting but was caught up in the battle for southern France instead. After suffering heavy losses at Chalon-sur-Saone, the 716th was withdrawn to Alsace and reformed again from miscellaneous troops. At the start of 1945, however, it had only 4,546 men. The 716th Infantry was virtually destroyed in the Colmar bridgehead on January 18. Remnants of the division managed to escape and were still fighting in the Swabian area of southern Germany in April. They surrendered to the Americans near Kempten on May 8.

The division's commanders included Colonel/Major General/Lieutenant General Otto Matterstock (May 3, 1941), Major General/Lieutenant General Wilhelm Richter (April 1, 1943),

Colonel Ludwig Krug (June 8, 1944), Richter (June 10, 1944), Colonel Otto Schiel (August 14, 1944), Richter (September 1, 1944), Colonel/Major General Ernst von Bauer (September 7, 1944), Colonel Wolf Ewert (December 30, 1944), and Colonel Hafner (April 1945).

Notes and Sources: The 726th Infantry Regiment was transferred from the 166th Replacement Division. The 736th came from the 156th Replacement Division. The division added the 706th Grenadier Regiment in late 1944, when the other regiments were reduced to two battalions. Its artillery battalion was expanded to four-battalion regiment on November 1, 1944. Matterstock was promoted to major general on September 1, 1941, and to lieutenant general on November 1, 1942. Richter became a lieutenant general on April 1, 1944. Bauer was promoted to major general on October 1, 1944. Colonel Hafner was commander of the 736th Grenadier Regiment and was the senior regimental commander of the division.

Chant, Volume 14: 1914; Volume 17: 2274; Harrison: Map VI; Keilig: 28; *Kriegstagebuch des OKW*, Volume I: 1147; Tessin, Vol. 12: 186; RA: 102; OB 42: 112; OB 43: 189; OB 45: 283.

717TH INFANTRY DIVISION

See 117th Jäger Division in chapter 3.

718TH INFANTRY DIVISION

See 118th Jäger Division in chapter 3.

719TH INFANTRY DIVISION

Composition: 723rd Infantry Regiment, 743rd Infantry Regiment, 719th Artillery Battalion, 719th Engineer Company, 719th Signal Company, 719th Divisional Supply Troops

Home Station: Potsdam, later Berlin-Spandau, Wehrkreis III

This over-age, static unit was created on May 3, 1941, and was sent to the Dordrecht area of Holland in June 1941, as an occupation force. It remained there until being sent into action against the British on the Dutch-Belgian frontier in the summer of 1944. Despite the age of its troops, the 719th fought very well at Tilburg and in the Battle of the Scheidt, where it was badly cut up. Reformed at Dordrecht, the division was sent to Saarbrucken in the 1st Army's zone, where the staff referred to its artillery as "the Artillery Museum of Europe," so old and diverse were its guns. The rebuilt 719th (which now had an artillery regiment and a fusilier battalion) was committed to the battles in the Saar and ended the war in southwestern Germany as part of the 19th Army. It surrendered to the U.S. Army near Muensingen in May 1945.

Its commanders included Colonel/Major General/Lieutenant General Erich Hocker (May 3, 1941), Lieutenant General Max Horn (January 10, 1944), Major General Carl Wahle (February 15, 1944), Major General Karl Sievers (July 30, 1944), Lieutenant General Felix Schwalbe (September 30, 1944), Colonel Rudolf Goltzsch (October 3, 1944), Schwalbe (October 10, 1944), and Major General Heinrich Gaede (December 22, 1944).

Notes and Sources: Erich Hocker was promoted to major general on June 1, 1941, and to lieutenant general on November 1, 1942. General Gaede was captured on March 30, 1945.

Bradley et al., Vol. 4: 166–67; Cole 1950: 553; Harrison: Map VI; Keilig: 144; MacDonald 1963: 123, 219; Speidel: 41; Tessin, Vol. 12: 190; OB 43: 189; OB 45: 284.

805TH REPLACEMENT DIVISION (DIVISION NR. 805)

Composition: 3rd Volunteer *Stamm* (Cadre) Regiment, 5th "Upper Rhine" Regiment (three Volkssturm battalions), 1212th Grenadier Regiment, 1089th Artillery Regiment, 1089th Engineer Battalion, 6/V Engineer Company, 805th Signal Company, 805th (?) Divisional Supply Troops

Home Station: Wehrkreis V

Formed on January 7, 1945, from elements of the 465th Replacement Division and other miscellaneous formations in

Wuerttemberg, the 805th was a very ad hoc formation. It was sent to the 19th Army on the Upper Rhine in February and was absorbed by the 352nd Volksgrenadier Division on April 14.

Its commander was Major General of Reserve Rudolf von Oppen.

Sources: Keilig: 247; Lexikon; Tessin, Vol. 13: 7.

DIVISION NR. 905

Composition: 2nd Police Grenadier Regiment, 3rd Upper Hesse Grenadier Regiment, 905th Light Artillery Battalion, 95th SS Light Tank Destroyer Company, 905th Engineer Company, 500th Signal Company, 905th Military Police Company

Home Station: Wehrkreis V

This "division" was formed on January 7, 1945, from the ad hoc Division von Witzleben. Its actual strength was less than a regiment. It was nevertheless sent to the 1st Army in the Saar sector in February and was destroyed on the Western Front the following month. Its commander was Major General Hermann von Witzleben.

Sources: Keilig: 357; Kursietis: 225; Lexikon; Tessin, Vol. 13: 110.

999TH INFANTRY DIVISION (PENAL)

See 999th Light Afrika Division in chapter 3.

CHAPTER 2

The Named Infantry Divisions

FIELD REPLACEMENT DIVISION A*

Composition: A/1 Field Replacement Regiment, A/2 Field Replacement Regiment, A/3 Field Replacement Regiment, A/4 Field Replacement Regiment, A/5 Field Replacement Regiment

Home Station: Wehrkreis IV

Formed in August 1941, this division was created to ferry troops from Germany to the field armies deep in Russia. After this mission was completed, the division was disbanded on January 15, 1942.

Its commanders were Lieutenant General Heinrich Curtze and Lieutenant General Adolf von Kleist.

Sources: Keilig: 63, 192; Kursietis: 229; Tessin, Vol. 14: 13–16.

FIELD REPLACEMENT DIVISION B

Composition: B/1 Field Replacement Regiment, B/2 Field Replacement Regiment, B/3 Field Replacement Regiment, B/4 Field Replacement Regiment

This division was formed in August 1941, to move troops from Germany to Russia. It completed this mission and was disbanded in January 1942. Major General Wolf Boysen commanded this division.

---

*Named infantry divisions are arranged alphabetically as follows: Field Replacement Division A is under A, Division Bärwalde is under B, Field Division Crete is under C, and so on.

A second Field Replacement Division B was created in early 1942. It had the same mission as the first, but only three regiments (B/1, B/2 and B/3). It was created in January 1942, and was dissolved on September 25, 1942.

Its commanders were Lieutenant Generals Wolf Boysen (August 15, 1941) and Fritz von Brodowski (early 1942).

Sources: Keilig: 48; Kursietis: 229; Lexikon; Tessin, Vol. 14: 32.

DIVISION BÄRWALDE

Composition: 1st Regiment Division Bärwalde, 2nd Regiment Division Bärwalde, 3rd Regiment Division Bärwalde, 4th Regiment Division Bärwalde, 5th Regiment Division Bärwalde, Artillery Regiment Division Bärwalde, Engineer Battalion Division Bärwalde, Signal Battalion Division Bärwalde

Home Station: Gross-Born

This division was formed in Pomerania on January 20, 1945, and consisted of Alarm and Volkssturm battalions, as well as Artillery School 1 at Gross-Born, which provided the divisional staff. It was sent to the Eastern Front (which was already in Pomerania) in February. As part of the 3rd Panzer Army, it fought in the Battle of the Dievenow Bridgehead and was crushed on March 12, 1945. The remnants of the division were disbanded after that.

It was commanded by Lieutenant General Wilhelm Raithel.

Sources: Keilig: 267; *Kriegstagebuch des OKW*, Vol. IV: 1898; Kursietis: 229; Lexikon; Tessin, Vol. 14: 31.

TRAINING DIVISION BAVARIA

Composition: 407th Grenadier Regiment, 467th Grenadier Regiment

Created in early April during the "Western March of the Goths" (*Westgoten*), when the subordinate elements of the Home Army were sent to the Eastern and Western Fronts, this division was formed in Bavaria from the elements the 407th and 467th

Divisions left behind. The 407th Grenadier Regiment consisted of two grenadier battalions, an artillery battalion and a rocket launcher battalion. The 467th Grenadier Regiment had three grenadier battalions. The new division was sent to the Western Front shortly after it was created, where it was placed under the control of the 212th Infantry Division. It surrendered to the Americans at the end of the war.

Sources: Lexikon; Tessin, Vol. 14: 30

INFANTRY DIVISION BERLIN

Composition: Grossdeutschland Watch Regiment, 652nd Grenadier Regiment, 653rd Grenadier Regiment, 309th Artillery Regiment, 309th Fusilier Battalion, 309th Tank Destroyer Battalion, 309th Engineer Battalion, 309th Signal Battalion, 309th Field Replacement Battalion, 309th Supply Regiment

Home Station: Berlin, Wehrkreis III

This unit was formed at the infantry base of Döberitz on February 1, 1945, as an Alarm (emergency) unit. Originally designated 309th Infantry Division, it was redesignated Infantry Division Berlin on February 7. It was sent to the 9th Army east of Berlin, fought at Kuestrin in March, and was destroyed in the Halbe Pocket on or about April 29, 1945.

Its only commander was Colonel/Major General Heinrich Voigtsberger.

Notes and Sources: The 309th Tank Destroyer Battalion was the former 200th Tank Destroyer Battalion of the 21st Panzer Division. Voigtsberger was promoted to major general on April 1, 1945.
Keilig: 357; *Kriegstagebuch des OKW*, Volume IV: 1898; Lexikon; Tessin, Vol. 9: 105.

INFANTRY DIVISION BOHEMIA

Composition: 1st Grenadier Regiment Bohemia, 2nd Grenadier Regiment Bohemia, Artillery Battalion Bohemia, Engineer Battalion Bohemia

Home Station: Troop Maneuver Area Milowitz, Wehrkreis XIII

This division was formed as a shadow division in the 26th Wave on April 17, 1944. It was sent to southern France and absorbed by the 198th Infantry Division on June 12.

Sources: Lexikon; Tessin, Vol. 14: 29.

INFANTRY DIVISION BRESLAU

Formed in the Neuhammer Troop Maneuver Area on August 3, 1944, this shadow division (*Schatten-Division*) of the 31st Wave was absorbed by the 357th Infantry Division on August 28. This unit was soon sent to the Eastern Front.

Sources: Lexikon; Tessin, Vol. 14: 29.

DIVISION VON BROICH

See Division von Manteuffel later in this chapter.

FIELD REPLACEMENT DIVISION C

Composition: C/1 Field Replacement Regiment, C/2 Field Replacement Regiment, C/3 Field Replacement Regiment, C/4 Field Replacement Regiment, C/5 Field Replacement Regiment

This division was formed in August 1941 to move troops from Germany to Russia. It completed this mission and was disbanded in January 1942.

A second Field Replacement Division C was formed shortly thereafter with the same mission and composition. It continued to operate until 1943.

Both divisions were commanded by Major General Rudolf Habenicht.

Sources: Keilig: 121; Lexikon; Tessin, Vol. 14: 32.

FORTRESS DIVISION CRETE

Composition: 382nd Infantry Regiment, 433rd Infantry Regiment, 440th Infantry Regiment, 220th Artillery Regiment.

Apparently it also included the 220th Reconnaissance Battalion, 220th Tank Destroyer Battalion, 220th Engineer Battalion, 220th Signal Battalion and 220th Divisional Supply Troops

This division was formed on January 10, 1942, from the 164th Infantry Division. Its mission was to guard the strategic island of Crete against an Allied invasion. When Rommel's drive on Cairo stalled, however, it was decided to reinforce him. The Staff, Fortress Division Crete formed the headquarters of the 164th Light Afrika Division, effective September 9, 1942. The 382nd and 433rd Infantry Regiments were converted into panzer grenadier regiments and were sent to Egypt, along with most of the division's supporting troops. The 440th Infantry Regiment, however, remained behind to form the Fortress Brigade Crete. The I and IV Battalions of the 220th Artillery Regiment also remained on the island.

Lieutenant General Joseph Folttmann was the commander of Fortress Division Crete.

Sources: Keilig: 93; Lexikon; Tessin, Vol. 14: 134–35.

FIELD REPLACEMENT DIVISION D

Composition: D/1 Field Replacement Regiment, D/2 Field Replacement Regiment, D/3 Field Replacement Regiment, D/4 Field Replacement Regiment

This division was formed in August 1941, to move troops from Germany to units deep in Russia. It completed this mission and was disbanded in January 1942.

It was commanded by Major General Franz Seuffert.

Sources: Keilig: 42; Lexikon; Tessin, Vol. 14: 54.

FORTRESS DIVISION DANZIG

Composition: Six grenadier and Alarm battalions, Kamfgruppe Freytag and sixteen companies of miscellaneous local defense (fortress) troops.

Home Station: Danzig, Wehrkreis I

Formed on January 31, 1945, this division held Danzig against repeated attacks from the Red Army. It was destroyed when the Soviets finally overran the city on March 28.

It was commanded by Major General Walter Freytag.

Sources: Keilig: 96; Lexikon; Tessin, Vol. 14: 54.

INFANTRY DIVISION DEMBA

Formed on January 27, 1944, in Troop Maneuver Area Demba in the General Gouvernement (formerly Poland), this unit was a shadow division. It was disbanded on February 2, 1944. Its men were assigned to the 141st Reserve and 68th Infantry Divisions. Its staff was used to form the 64th Infantry Division.

Sources: Lexikon; Tessin, Vol. 14: 52–53.

INFANTRY DIVISION "DÖBERITZ"
(303RD INFANTRY DIVISION)

Composition: 300th Grenadier Regiment, 301st Grenadier Regiment, 302nd Grenadier Regiment, 303rd Artillery Regiment, 303rd Tank Destroyer Battalion, 303rd Fusilier Battalion, 303rd Engineer Battalion, 303rd Signal Battalion, 303rd Field Replacement Battalion, 303rd Divisional Supply Troops

Home Station: Wehrkreis III

This division was formed in Troop Maneuver Area Döberitz as an alarm unit. Its staff was the former Staff, 611th Special Purposes Division (Div. z.b.V. 611). It was initially sent to the fortress of Küstrin. As part of the 9th Army, it opposed the Red Army's drive on Berlin. It was surrounded in the Halbe Pocket and was destroyed there in late April 1945.

Its commanders were Major General/Lieutenant General Dr. Rudolf Hübner (January 31, 1945) and Colonel Scheunemann (March 9, 1945).

Notes and Sources: Huebner, a dentist, was promoted to lieutenant general on March 1, 1945.

Keilig: 152; Lexikon; Mehner, Vol. 12: 456; Nafziger 2000: 387–88; Tessin, Vol. 9: 79.

INFANTRY DIVISION DÖLLERSHEIM

Composition: 1st Grenadier Regiment Döllersheim, 2nd Grenadier Regiment Doellersheim, Artillery Battalion Döllersheim, Engineer Battalion Doellersheim, Tank Destroyer Battalion Döllersheim

Home Station: Döllersheim Troop Maneuver Area, Wehrkreis XVII

Formed as a shadow division (*Schatten-Division*) on August 3, 1944, this Austrian division was absorbed into the 564th Volksgrenadier Division later that month. Most of the men of the division ended up on the Western Front.

Sources: Lexikon; Tessin, Vol. 14: 53.

INFANTRY DIVISION DONAU (DANUBE)

Composition: 1st Grenadier Regiment Danube, 2nd Grenadier Regiment Danube, Artillery Battalion Danube; Engineer Company Danube.

Infantry Division Donau (Danube) was formed as a shadow division on March 18, 1945. Its troops came from Bavaria and Austria. Its grenadier regiments contained two battalions each. Its was absorbed by the 26th Volksgrenadier Division in Franconia on April 12 and spent the last days of the war on the Western Front. Its surviving men surrendered to the Americans in May 1945.

Sources: Lexikon; Tessin, Vol. 14: 53.

INFANTRY DIVISION DRESDEN

Formed on March 7, 1945, as a shadow division in the 34th mobilization wave, it had two regiments of two battalions each, as well as an artillery battalion and an engineer company. It was absorbed by the 6th Volksgrenadier Division on March 10 and was sent to Silesia on the Eastern Front.

Sources: Lexikon; Tessin, Vol. 14: 53.

FIELD REPLACEMENT DIVISION E

Composition: E/1 Field Replacement Regiment, E/2 Field Replacement Regiment, E/3 Field Replacement Regiment, E/4 Field Replacement Regiment

This division was formed in August 1941, to move troops from Germany to Russia. It completed this mission was disbanded in January 1942.

A second division with the same name, mission and composition was formed in January 1942. It was disbanded in March.

Commanders of Field Replacement Division E were: Major General Wilhelm Mittermaier (August 1941), Colonel Kurt Wuthenow (January 22, 1942), and Major General Friedrich-Karl Wachter (February 20, 1942).

Sources: Keilig: 228, 359, 378; Lexikon; Tessin, Vol. 14: 66.

INFANTRY DIVISION EAST PRUSSIA

Composition: Grenadier Regiment East Prussia 1, Grenadier Regiment East Prussia 2, Artillery Battalion East Prussia, Engineer Battalion East Prussia

Home Station: Zegrze, Wehrkreis I

Formed on April 17, 1944, in Troop Maneuver Area Mielau, East Prussia, this shadow division was part of the 26th Mobilization Wave. It was sent to Army Group C in Italy in June and, on July 3, 1944, was absorbed by the 65th Infantry Division, which was then fighting against the Allied Anzio (Neuttuno) bridgehead.

Source: Tessin, Vol. 14: 189.

FIELD REPLACEMENT DIVISION F

Composition: F/1 Field Replacement Regiment, F/2 Field Replacement Regiment, F/3 Field Replacement Regiment

Home Station: Wehrkreis VI

This division was formed in the Westphalia-Rhineland region in January 1942, to transport replacement units to Russia. It was disbanded in 1942 after it completed its mission.

It was commanded by Major General Franz Seuffert.

Sources: Keilig: 322; Lexikon; Tessin, Vol. 14: 79.

INFANTRY DIVISION FERDINAND VON SCHILL

Composition: 1st Grenadier Regiment Schill, 2nd Grenadier Regiment Schill, 3rd Artillery Regiment Schill, Sturm Brigade Schill, 394th Assault Gun Brigade, Fusilier Battalion Schill, Engineer Company Schill, Signal Battalion Schill

Home Station: Burg, Wehrkreise XI

Formed from Kampfgruppe Burg on April 20, 1945, this division fought with 12th Army on the Elbe and participated in the Battle of Potsdam. It surrendered to the Americans at the end of the war, but its men were handed over to the Soviets between May 8 and 10, 1945. Its commander was Lieutenant Colonel Alfred Müller.

Sources: Lexikon; Tessin, Vol. 14: 79; Klaus Voss and Paul Kehlenbeck, *Letzte Divisionen—Die Panzerdivision Clausewitz und die Infanteriedivision Schill* (2000).

FORTRESS DIVISION FRANKFURT/ODER

Composition: 1st Fortress Grenadier Regiment, 2nd Fortress Grenadier Regiment, 3rd Fortress Grenadier Regiment, 4th Fortress Grenadier Regiment, 1449th Fortress Infantry Battalion, 84th Fortress Machine Gun Battalion, 59th Artillery Replacement and Training Battalion, 1325th Fortress Artillery Battalion, 1326th Fortress Artillery Battalion, 3157th Fortress Artillery Battalion, XXVI Fortress Anti-Tank Unit, 952nd Engineer Blocking Battalion

Formed in Frankfurt/Oder to defend the key city in Army Group Vistula's Oder River line, this division was organized in January 1945. It held its positions despite repeated Russian assaults in April 1945. The Red Army was forced to bypass it on its way to Berlin. The division was commanded by Lieutenant General Hermann Meyer-Rabingen.

Sources: Keilig: 226; Kursietis: 232; Lexikon; Tessin, Vol. 14: 79. Also see Ryan, *Last Battle.*

INFANTRY DIVISION FRIEDRICH LUDWIG JAHN (2ND RAD DIVISION)

Composition: Grenadier Regiment Friedrich Ludwig Jahn, Artillery Regiment Friedrich Ludwig Jahn, Fusilier Battalion Friedrich Ludwig Jahn, Engineer Battalion Friedrich Ludwig Jahn

This division was formed on March 31, 1945, from *Reichsarbeitsdienst* (Reich Labor Service, or RAD, troops) in Troop Maneuver Area Jueterbog, south of Berlin. It had 7,500 men and its headquarters was the former Staff, 251st Infantry Division, whose combat units had been destroyed in Poland and East Prussia. It fought the Soviets south of Berlin but retreated west of the Elbe and surrendered to the U.S. Army in May 1945. The Americans, however, turned them over to the Russians.

Its commanders included Lieutenant General Friedrich-Wilhelm von Löper (March 1945), Colonel Ludwig Zöller (April 1945), Colonel Klein (April 1945) and Colonel Franz Weller (April 24, 1945–end).

Notes and Sources: Colonel Klein was reported as missing in action on April 24, 1945.
Keilig: 208; Lexikon; Mehner, Vol. 12: 456; Tessin, Vol. 14: 78–79.

FÜHRER BEGLEIT DIVISION

Composition: 102nd Panzer Regiment, 100th Panzer Grenadier Regiment, 100th Panzer Artillery Regiment, 673rd Tank Destroyer Battalion, 120th Panzer Engineer Battalion, 120th Signal Battalion, 120th Field Replacement Battalion, 120th Divisional Supply Troops

Home Station: Berlin, Wehrkreis III

Unlike most of the German divisions created in 1945, this was a good combat formation. Its cadre unit, the Führer Begleit (escort) Brigade had been created in Rastenburg in November 1944, had fought well in the Battle of the Bulge, and had played a major role in the German victory at St. Vith. The division was officially established on January 26, 1945, in the Cottbus area. It fought on the Vistula, at Lauban, Ratibor and Spremberg, where it was surrounded and largely destroyed on April 19. The survivors of the division ended the war in the Deutsch-Brod Pocket east of Prague.

Its commander was Colonel/Major General Otto-Ernst Remer (1945).

Notes and Sources: Remer was promoted to major general on January 31, 1945.

Keilig: 273; *Kriegstagebuch des OKW*, Volume IV: 1896; James Lucas, *Germany's Elite Panzer Force: Grossdeutschland* (1978): 128–40; Franz Thomas, *Die Eichenlaubtraeger, 1940–1945* (1997–98), Vol. 2: 195 (hereafter cited as "Thomas"). Also see Hoffmann: 412–39; 479, 503.

FÜHRER GRENADIER DIVISION

Composition: 101st Panzer Regiment, 99th Panzer Grenadier Regiment, 124th Panzer Artillery Regiment, 101st Panzer Reconnaissance Company, 916th Army Sturm Artillery Brigade, 124th Panzer Engineer Battalion, 124th Panzer Signal Battalion

Home Station: Berlin, Wehrkreis III

Organized as a brigade in East Prussia in July 1944, this unit became division on January 26, 1945. It had about one-quarter of the tank strength remaining to the depleted Army Group Vistula. When Hitler sent it and the 25th Panzer Division south in early April, that Army Group lost half of its panzers on the eve of the Battle of Berlin. The Fuehrer Grenadier Division fought at Lauban and in the Battle of Vienna, and ended the war in Austria, fighting the Russians as part of Dietrich's 6th SS Panzer Army. It surrendered to the Americans in May but was soon handed over to the Russians.

Ostruppen ("Eastern troops") captured by the Americans on D-Day awaiting transport to prisoner-of-war camps in England. These men are from the Georgian area of the Soviet Union. One-sixth of the LXXXIV Corps consisted of these unreliable soldiers, many of whom were returned to Russia after the war and executed. U.S. ARMY PHOTO

It was commanded by Colonel/Major General Hellmuth Maeder.

Notes and Sources: Maeder was promoted to major general on January 30, 1945.

Keilig: 214; *Kriegstagebuch des OKW*, Volume I: 1145; Lucas, *Grossdeutschland*: 128; Tessin, Vol. 14: 77; Thomas, Vol. 2: 56; Ziemke 1966: 455, 469.

INFANTRY DIVISION GENERALGOUVERNEMENT

Composition: two regiments with staffs at Lemberg and Lublin; six battalions in other cities; Engineer Battalion Generalgouvernement; Signal Company Generalgouvernement.

Formed as an Alarm unit on February 13, 1944, this division only existed until February 23, when it was absorbed by the 72nd Infantry Division, which had been smashed at Cherkassy.

Sources: Lexikon; Tessin, Vol. 14: 96.

FORTRESS DIVISION GOTENHAFEN

Composition: Marine Battalion Gotenhafen 1, Marine Battalion Gotenhafen 2, Marine Battalion Gotenhafen 3, Luftwaffe Field Battalion Gotenhafen

Formed as a fortress division in January 1945, this unit was formed at the German naval base of Gotenhafen (now Gdynia, Poland). The base fell on March 28, 1945, and the division ceased to exist. It never exceeded regimental strength.

Sources: Lexikon; Tessin, Vol. 14: 97.

INFANTRY DIVISION GRAFENWÖHR

Composition: Grenadier Regiment Grafenwöhr 1, Grenadier Regiment Grafenwöhr 2

Home Station: Troop Maneuver Area Grafenwöhr

This shadow division was formed on July 4, 1944, and consisted of six grenadier battalions. Eight days later it was disbanded and its men used to build the 544th Grenadier Division, which was also forming in *Truppenübungsplatz Grafenwöhr.*

Its commander was apparently Major General Werner Ehrig.

Sources: Keilig: 79; Lexikon; Tessin, Vol. 14: 96.

INFANTRY DIVISION GROSS-BORN

Composition: 1st Grenadier Regiment Gross-Born, 2nd Grenadier Regiment Gross-Born, Artillery Battalion Gross-Born, Engineer Battalion Gross-Born, Tank Destroyer Company Gross-Born

Home Station: Gross-Born Troop Maneuver Area

This 31st Wave shadow division was formed in Troop Maneuver Area Gross-Born in Pomerania (Wehrkreis II) on August 3, 1944. It was absorbed by the 570th Volksgrenadier Division on August 25.

Sources: Lexikon; Tessin, Vol. 14: 97.

DIVISION GÜMBEL

Composition: Infantry Regiment "A," Infantry Regiment "B," Artillery Regiment Simon

This division was formed in Lorraine on July 10, 1942, as an alarm unit. Its units came from the 182nd Reserve Division. It became Division Karl on August 3, 1942.

It was commanded by Major General Karl Gümbel, who was replaced by Lieutenant General Franz Karl on August 3.

Sources: Keilig: 117; Kursietis: 234; Nafziger 2000: 391; Tessin, Vol. 14: 97.

INFANTRY DIVISION GÜSTROW
(4TH RAD DIVISION)

Composition: 1st Grenadier Regiment Güstrow, 2nd Grenadier Regiment Güstrow, 3rd Grenadier Regiment Güstrow, Artillery Regiment Güstrow, Tank Destroyer Battalion Güstrow (Staff and 1st Company), Engineer Battalion Güstrow, Signal Battalion Güstrow (Staff and 1st Company), Field Replacement Battalion Güstrow

This division was formed on April 29, 1945, from the remnants of the 696th Grenadier Regiment of the 340th Infantry Division, the VI Officer Training School (*Fahnenjunkerschule VI*), and other school units. It was part of Army Group Vistula and surrendered to the British in Mecklenburg in May 1945.

Its commander was Colonel Nobiz.

Sources: Lexikon; Tessin, Vol. 14: 97.

INFANTRY DIVISION "HAMBURG"
(324TH INFANTRY DIVISION)

Composition: 558th Grenadier Regiment, 559th Grenadier Regiment, 324th Artillery Regiment, 324th Fusilier Battalion, 324th Engineer Battalion, 324th Signal Battalion, 324th Divisional Supply Troops

Home Station: Hamburg, Wehrkreis X

This division's formation was authorized as an alarm unit on March 4, 1945, as the British approached Germany's second largest city. By March 8, it was formed. Originally designated 304th Infantry Division, it became Infantry Division "Hamburg" on March 10. Its grenadier regiments and artillery regiment, however, had only two battalions each. Its combat units were sent to the Wesel, where they were attached to other units. The Staff was sent to Essen and was redesignated 618th Special Administrative Division Staff (*Stab Div. z.b.V. 618*). It was destroyed in the Ruhr Pocket, along with Army Detachment Lüttwitz, in

April 1945. The division's commander was Major General/Lieutenant General Walter Steinmüller.

Notes and Sources: Steinmüller was promoted to lieutenant general on April 1, 1945.
Keilig: 331; Lexikon; Tessin, Vol. 9: 154.

INFANTRY DIVISION HANNOVER

Composition: Grenadier Regiment Hannover 1, Grenadier Regiment Hannover 2, Artillery Battalion Hannover, Engineer Company Hannover.

Formed in Stettin, Pomerania on March 7, 1945, this unit was a shadow division. It was incorporated into the East Prussian 547th Volksgrenadier Division on March 10. Its 1st Regiment became the 1091st Grenadier Regiment and the 2nd Hannover Grenadier Regiment became the 1092nd Grenadier Regiment, both of the 547th Volksgrenadier Division. The 547th was sent to the Eastern Front but surrendered to the Americans in May 1945.

Sources: Lexikon; Tessin, Vol. 14: 112.

INFANTRY DIVISION JUTLAND
(325TH INFANTRY DIVISION)

Composition: 590th Grenadier Regiment, 591st Grenadier Regiment, 592nd Grenadier Regiment, 325th Artillery Regiment, 325th Tank Destroyer Company, 325th Engineer Company, 325th Signal Company, 325th Divisional Supply Troops

Home Station: Aalborg, Denmark

Formed on March 9, 1945, near Aalborg on the Jutland peninsula of Denmark, mainly from military hospitals and convalescence troops and units, this division boasted three understrength grenadier regiments of two weak battalions each, as well as a two-battalion artillery regiment. It was officially designated the 325th Shadow Division on April 12. It was nevertheless sent to the 1st Parachute Army on the Western Front and surrendered there in May 1945.

Its commander was Lieutenant General Schaumberg.

Notes and Sources: An early shadow division which was also designated Infantry Division Jutland had been organized in July 1944 and absorbed by the 19th Luftwaffe Field Division in August.

Lexikon; Nafziger 2000: 293; Tessin, Vol. 9: 156; Vol. 14: 125.

DIVISION KARL

Composition: Infantry Regiment A, Infantry Regiment B, Artillery Regiment Simon

Home Station: Lothringen (Lorraine), France

This division was formed on August 3, 1942, from Division Guembel, which controlled the Alarm (emergency) units of the 182nd Replacement Division. It was converted into the 282nd Infantry Division on March 1, 1943. Its units became the 848th Grenadier Regiment, the 849th Grenadier Regiment and the 282nd Artillery Regiment.

Its commander was Lieutenant General Franz Karl.

Sources: Keilig: 163; Tessin, Vol. 14: 133.

DIVISION KÖSLIN

Composition: Regiment Karnkewitz; Regiment Jatzinhen, Artillery Detachment Grützer, 2nd Construction Engineer Replacement and Training Battalion

Home Station: Köslin, Wehrkreis II

This division was formed on January 20, 1945. Its Karnkewitz Regiment consisted of two Alarm battalions and five Volkssturm battalions, while the Jatzinhen Regiment had three emergency and two Volkssturm battalions. The division also had the men of the Waffen-SS NCO School at Lauenburg. In February, the division was reorganized to include 1st and 2nd Regiments Division Koeslin (two battalions each) and the

Artillery Battalion Division Koeslin (formerly Artillery Detachment Gruetzner). Later that month, the division was sent to the front, where it formed part of the Army Group Vistula in Pomerania. Almost as soon as it arrived, however, it was absorbed by Division Pomerania. The following month, on March 12, most of the former soldiers of the Koeslin Division were killed or captured in the Battle of the Dievenow Bridgehead.

Sources: Kursietis: 235; Lexikon; Tessin, Vol. 14: 134.

FIELD TRAINING DIVISION KURLAND

See 388th Field Training Division in the previous chapter.

SPECIAL PURPOSES DIVISION L

This division was formed in Silesia in February 1945, after the Soviets broke out of the Baranov Bridgehead and pushed into southeastern Germany. It consisted of elements of the former 408th Replacement Division. The "L" Division was encircled in Breslau in February and was apparently destroyed by the end of March; in any case, its remnants surrendered to the Red Army when the city fell in May 1945.

Sources: Lexikon; Mehner, Vol. 12: 436; Tessin, Vol. 14: 147.

GRENADIER LEHR DIVISION

Composition: 1147th Grenadier Regiment, 1148th Grenadier Regiment, 1149th Grenadier Regiment, 1563rd Artillery Regiment

This unit was formed in Troop Maneuver Area Doeberitz (Wehrkreis III) on August 3, 1944. The 563rd Grenadier (later Volksgrenadier) Division was ordered to absorb it on August 17. This process was completed by the end of the month. The 563rd was later destroyed on the Eastern Front.

Sources: Lexikon; Tessin, Vol. 14: 270.

SPECIAL PURPOSES DIVISION STAFF M

Formed in Silesia in March 1945, this staff apparently never had units assigned to it. It was absorbed by the 545th Volksgrenadier Division in April.

Sources: Lexikon; Tessin, Vol. 14: 161.

DIVISION MAERKISCH-FRIEDLAND

Composition: 1st Fahnenjunker Regiment, 2nd Fahnenjunker Regiment, 3rd Fahnenjunker Regiment, 4th Fahnenjunker Regiment

Home Station: Gross-Born Troop Maneuver Area, Wehrkreis II

This division was formed from the cadets of the Artillery School Gross-Born in Pomerania on January 20, 1945. It was sent to the Russian Front, where it was destroyed when the Soviets broke out of the Dievenow Bridgehead at the end of March.

Sources: Lexikon; Tessin, Vol. 14: 160.

DIVISION VON MANTEUFFEL

Composition: Parachute Regiment Barenthin, 11th Parachute Battalion, Infantry Battalion T-3, 10th Bersaglieri Regiment (an elite Italian motorized unit), 2nd T-Artillery Regiment, 605th Tank Destroyer Battalion, 190th Signal Platoon

Home Station: Küstrin, Wehrkreis III

This ad hoc division was formed in Tunisia on November 10, 1942, largely from German parachute units available for deployment to Tunisia. It was originally named for its first commander, Colonel/Major General Baron Friedrich von Broich, who was later named commander of the 10th Panzer Division. The Division von Broich (as it was initially called) played a major role in blocking the Allied drive to Tunis in late 1942, following the Operation "Torch" landings, which took the Germans and Italians completely by surprise. The division defended a mountainous sector in eastern Tunisia for the rest of its existence and did an excellent job. Broich was succeeded by Hasso von Manteuffel, for whom the division was renamed, in March 1943. By March 15, the division included the Barenthin Parachute Regiment, the 160th Panzer Grenadier Regiment (three battalions), the IV/2nd "Afrika" Artillery Regiment, the 11th Motorized Parachute Engineer Battalion (Luftwaffe), the Italian 10th Bersaglieri Regiment (three battalions) and assorted divisional troops.

Manteuffel led it until May 8, 1943. He was succeeded by Lieutenant General Karl Bülowius, who surrendered it to the British on May 11, after the Axis supply lines collapsed completely.

Notes and Sources: Broich was promoted to major general on January 1, 1943. Manteuffel was promoted to major general on May 1, 1943. Manteuffel was severely wounded on or about May 8, 1943, and was medically evacuated back to Europe. Bülowius committed suicide in the United States in 1945. Keilig: 52, 55, 216; Lexikon; Nafziger 2000: 397–98; Tessin, Vol. 14, 160. Also see Carell, *Foxes*.

INFANTRY DIVISION MÄHREN

This shadow division began forming in the Milowitz Troop Maneuver Area (Wehrkreis XIII) on August 3, 1944. This process was aborted on August 26; the elements of the division already formed were absorbed by the 565th Volksgrenadier Division.

Sources: Lexikon; Tessin, Vol. 14: 160.

DIVISION MÄRKISCH-FRIEDLAND

Composition: 1st Fahnenjunker (Officer-Cadet) Regiment, 2nd Fahnenjunker Regiment, 3rd Fahnenjunker Regiment, 4th Fahnenjunker Regiment

This division was formed on January 20, 1945, in the Gross-Born Troop Maneuver Area, from officer-cadets in the artillery school. It had 10 infantry battalions. The division was overrun and destroyed by the Red Army on February 11, although remnants of the division were not destroyed or disbanded until March 10, when the Russians broke out of the Dievenow Bridgehead.

Sources: Lexikon; Nafziger 2000: 399; Tessin, Vol. 14: 160.

DIVISION MATTERSTOCK

Composition: Regiment Otwarka, Regiment Teermann, 533rd Grenadier Replacement Regiment

This division was formed on the Oder, in the rear of the 4th Panzer Army, in February 1945. Its Otwarka Regiment consisted of the 122nd and 128th Grenadier Replacement Battalions plus an alarm battalion and a Volkssturm battalion; Regiment Teermann had two Alarm (emergency) battalions; and the 533rd Grenadier Replacement Regiment at a fortress battalion, the 3rd Engineer Replacement Battalion, the 3rd Landeschützen Training Battalion, and Alarm battalion and four Volkssturm battalions. It was given a sector of the Eastern Front almost as soon as it was formed. It was sent to Lausitz in Saxony (now located in the southeastern tip of present-day Germany, near the Czech and Polish borders). Here it was last reported and was apparently absorbed by other divisions of Army Group Center in March and April 1945.

It was commanded throughout its existence by Lieutenant General Otto Matterstock.

Sources: Kursietis: 235; Lexikon; Tessin, Vol. 14: 160.

INFANTRY DIVISION MIELAU

Composition: Grenadier Regiment Mielau 1, Grenadier Regiment Mielau 2, Artillery Battalion Mielau 3, Engineer Battalion Mielau

Home Station: Zegrze, Wehrkreis I

This shadow division was formed on January 27, 1944 in Troop Maneuver Area Mielau, East Prussia. It was created after the 151st Reserve left for White Russia and included parts of that division which were left behind. It was absorbed by the 214th Infantry Division on March 26. The division staff remained intact, however, and was sent to the Gross-Born Troop Maneuver Area, where it became the Staff, 59th Infantry Division on June 26, 1944.

It was commanded by Major General Walter Sauvant.

Sources: Keilig: 292; Kursietis: 235; Lexikon; Tessin, Vol. 14: 159.

INFANTRY DIVISION MILOWITZ

Composition: Grenadier Regiment Milowitz 1, Grenadier Regiment Milowitz 2, Artillery Battalion Milowitz, Engineer Battalion Milowitz

Home Station: Fuerth, Wehrkreis XIII

This unit was formed as a shadow division in Troop Maneuver Area Milowitz in the Protectorate (formerly Czechoslovakia) on January 27, 1944. It included elements of the former north Bavarian 173rd Reserve Division. The division was sent to Russia in February, where it was used to refurbish the 320th Infantry Division. On March 11, 1944, the remainder of the division was absorbed by the 389th Infantry Division, which had been smashed at Cherkassy. The Staff of the Milowitz Division then returned to its original base in the Protectorate, where it was became the Staff, 237th Infantry Division on June 12, 1944.

Sources: Lexikon; Tessin, Vol. 14: 159.

SHADOW DIVISION MÖCKERN

Formed in September 1944 in Pomerania (probably in the Gross-Born Troop Maneuver Area) as the 580th Volksgrenadier Division, this unit was redesignated Shadow Division Möckern on September 28. It was absorbed by the Silesian 320th Volksgrenadier Division on October 10, 1944 and its former soldiers were soon on their way to the Eastern Front.

Sources: Lexikon; Tessin, Vol. 14: 160.

INFANTRY DIVISION MÜNSINGEN

Probable Composition: Grenadier Regiment Münsingen 1, Grenadier Regiment Münsingen 2.

This shadow division was formed at Troop Maneuver Area Münsingen in Württemberg-Baden (Wehrkreis V) on July 4, 1944. It had three battalions and two regimental staffs on July 12, 1944, when the order was issued that it was to be absorbed by the 543rd Grenadier Division. This process was completed by August 1.

Sources: Lexikon; Tessin, Vol. 14: 159.

INFANTRY DIVISION NEUHAMMER

Composition: Infantry Regiment Neuhammer 1, Infantry Regiment Neuhammer 2, Artillery Battalion Neuhammer; Engineer Battalion Neuhammer

Home Station: Cosel, Wehrkreis VIII

Formed in the Neuhammer Troop Maneuver Area on April 17, 1944, this 26th Wave shadow division was incorporated into the 34th Infantry Division three weeks later. Its men were sent to Italy, where most of them ended up in American captivity.

Sources: Lexikon; Tessin, Vol. 14: 174.

SHADOW DIVISION NIEDERGÖRSDORF

Composition: Grenadier Regiment Niedergörsdorf 1, Grenadier Regiment Niedergörsdorf 2, Grenadier Regiment Niedergörsdorf 3, Artillery Regiment Niedergörsdorf

The 585th Volksgrenadier Division (28th Wave) was formed on September 2, 1944, and was redesignated Shadow Division Niedergörsdorf on September 28. In October, the shadow division was sent from Niedergörsdorf to Troop Maneuver Area Döllersheim in Wehrkreis XVII (Austria), where it was absorbed

German grenadiers in the attack, Russia, June 22, 1941. Although they scored some impressive victories, German infantry units suffered an average casualty rate of more than 30 percent in the East in 1941 and, in the end, could not take Moscow. U.S. WAR COLLEGE PHOTO

by the 167th Volksgrenadier Division that same month. The men of the former Niedergörsdorf Division ended up on the Western Front.

Sources: Lexikon; Tessin, Vol. 14: 175.

FIELD TRAINING DIVISION NORTH

See 388th Field Training Division in the previous chapter.

DIVISION POMERANIA

Composition: 1st Pomeranian Regiment; 2nd Pomeranian Regiment, 3rd Pomeranian Regiment

Home Station: Koeslin, Wehrkreis II

This unit was originally formed as the Division Koeslin on January 20, 1945. Its units were from the Commander, Inspector of Replacement Units Koeslin and included the Waffen-SS NCO School Lauenburg and the 2nd Construction Engineer Replacement and Training Battalion. It became the *Division Pommernland* (Division Pomerania) in February 1945. Colonel Seaton described the division as "a motley force of engineers, Luftwaffe ground staff, naval survey units, and Volksturm battalions, without artillery, anti-tank guns, signal equipment, or supply services, in some cases without regimental or battalion commanders." After examining the situation, General Raus, the commander of the 3rd Panzer Army, reported back to Hitler that he doubted if Pomerania could be held. The division was sent to the Dievenow Bridgehead on the Eastern Front, where it was destroyed at the end of March.

Notes and Sources: Koeslin was the largest city in middle Pomerania. Its population dropped from 33,500 in 1939 to 17,000 in late 1945, as most of the German population fled, were expelled, or were murdered. It is now Koszalin, Poland.

Kriegstagebuch des OKW, Vol. IV: 1898; Lexikon; Seaton: 540; Tessin, Vol. 14: 200; *en.wikipedia.org/wiki/Koszalin.*

INFANTRY DIVISION POTSDAM

Composition: Grenadier Regiment Potsdam 1, Grenadier Regiment Potsdam 2, Grenadier Regiment Potsdam 3, Artillery Regiment Potsdam, Fusilier Battalion Potsdam, Tank Destroyer Potsdam, Engineer Battalion Potsdam, Signal Battalion Potsdam

Home Station: Wehrkreis III

This division was formed in Troop Maneuver Area Doebertiz on March 29, 1945, from various replacement and training units in the III Military District, as well as the remnants of the 85th Infantry Division, which it absorbed on April 4. (The 1053rd Grenadier Regiment of the 85th became the 1st Potsdam Grenadier Regiment, the 1054th Grenadier Regiment became the 2nd Potsdam, etc.) The new division joined the 11th Army at Blankenburg in the Harz Mountains on April 11 and served with it until April 18, when it was absorbed by other units in the 11th Army. It men later surrendered to the Americans.

Its commander was Colonel of Reserves Lorenz.

Notes and Sources: Two battalions of the 412th Volks Artillery Corps were attached to this division. Colonel Lorenz was probably Wolfgang Lorenz, the former commander of the III/385th Grenadier Regiment.

Lexikon; Mehner, Vol. 12: 456; Scheibert: 230; Tessin, Vol. 14: 199–200.

DIVISION RÄGENER

Composition: Grenadier Regiment Fischer, Grenadier Regiment Becker, Grenadier Regiment Petersdorf, Fusilier Company Rägener, Tank Destroyer Company Rägener, Engineer Company Rägener, Field Replacement Battalion Rägener

This division was formed on February 2, 1945, from the remnants of the 433rd and 463rd Infantry Divisions, as well as Volkssturm and emergency (Alarm) units. It was sent to the Oder sector and, as part of the 9th Army, was destroyed in the Battle of Berlin.

It was commanded by Major General/Lieutenant General Adolf Rägener.

Notes and Sources: Rägener was promoted to lieutenant general on March 1, 1945.

Keilig: 266; Lexikon; Tessin, Vol. 14: 207.

DIVISION RAESSLER

Composition: Miscellaneous GHQ troops

Home Station: Wehrkreis XII

Formed in the rear of Army Group G on September 11, 1944, this unit lost most of its units to the LXXXIX Corps at the end of December 1944. The Staff withdrew to Landau in the southern Palatinate, where it became a special administrative division staff (*Div Stab z.b.V.*) under Army Group G. It was redesignated Special Administrative Division Staff 616 in April 1945.

Its commander was Major General Rudolf Raessler.

Sources: Keilig: 267; Kursietis. 221; Lexikon; Tessin, Vol. 14: 207.

ASSAULT DIVISION RHODES

Composition: Storm Regiment Rhodes, IV/999th Artillery Regiment, 999th Reconnaissance Battalion, Tank Destroyer Battalion Rhodes, 999th Motorized Engineer Company, Panzer Signal Company Rhodes (formerly the 657th Radio Company), Fla Company Rhodes, Field Replacement Battalion Rhodes, 999th Divisional Supply Troops

Home Station: Zittau, Wehrkreis IV

Sturm-Division Rhodos was formed on May 31, 1943, from elements of the 22nd Air Landing Division, Fortress Division Crete and the remnants of the 999th Light Afrika Division, a penal unit which had been destroyed in Tunisia earlier that month. Its mission was to garrison and, if necessary, defend the island of Rhodes in the Aegean. In September 1944, it was withdrawn to the mainland, where it fought in the Belgrade area. On October 17, 1944, it was absorbed by Panzer Grenadier Division Brandenburg. Its Staff was used to form Headquarters, IV Panzer Corps.

Its commander for most of its existence was Lieutenant General/General of Panzer Troops Ulrich Kleemann. Colonel Ludwig Fricke served as acting division commander in 1944.

Notes and Sources: Kleemann was promoted to general of panzer troops effective October 1, 1944. Keilig: 96, 171; Lexikon; Nafziger 1999: 401-2; Tessin, Vol. 14: 207.

INFANTRY DIVISION RÖHN

Composition: Grenadier Regiment Röhn 1, Grenadier Regiment Röhn 2, Artillery Battalion Röhn, Tank Destroyer Company Röhn, Engineer Battalion Röhn

Home Station: Wekrhreis IX

Formed in the Wildflecken Troop Maneuver Area as a 31st Wave shadow division on August 3, 1944, the Röhn Division existed only until August 26, when it was officially redesignated 566th Volksgrenadier Division. This unit, in turn, was absorbed by the 363rd Volksgrenadier Division the following month. Its soldiers ended up in the Ruhr Pocket on the Western Front.

Sources: Lexikon; Tessin, Vol. 14: 206.

DIVISION SARDINIA

Composition: Panzer Battalion Sardinia, 1st Panzer Grenadier Regiment Sardinia, 2nd Panzer Grenadier Regiment Sardinia, Artillery Regiment Sardinia (later 190th Artillery Regiment), 190th Tank Destroyer Battalion, Engineer Battalion Sardinia (later 190th Engineer Battalion), Signal Company Sardinia (later 190th Signal Battalion)

This unit was formed on May 12, 1943, on the Italian island of Sardinia, from the Staff, *Sturmbrigade XI*. The division was created just as Army Group Afrika surrendered in Tunisia, and the island was exposed to Allied invasion. It was redesignated 90th Panzer Grenadier Division on July 6, 1943, and formed the nucleus for a division which formed a mainstay for the German Army in Italy for the rest of the war.

Its commander was Major General Carl-Hans von Lungers-hausen.

Sources: Keilig: 212; Nafziger 1999: 403; Tessin, Vol. 14: 223.

INFANTRY DIVISION SCHARNHORST

Composition: Grenadier Regiment Scharnhorst 1, Grenadier Regiment Scharnhorst 2, Grenadier Regiment Scharnhorst 3, Artillery Regiment Scharnhorst, Fusilier Battalion Scharnhorst, Tank Destroyer Battalion Scharnhorst, Engineer Battalion Scharnhorst, Signal Battalion Scharnhorst

Home Station: Wehrkreis XI

This division was at 35th Wave unit. It was formed on March 30, 1945, from school and replacement units in Wehrkreis XI (Hanover, Brunswick, and Anhalt). It was a good combat division. Assigned to the 7th and then the 12th Army, it first saw action against the Americans at Barby on April 12, and two weeks later clashed with the Russians at Beelitz. It surrendered to the Americans near Travemünde on May 2, 1945.

Its commander was Major General/Lieutenant General Heinrich Goetz.

Notes and Sources: Goetz was promoted to lieutenant general on April 1, 1945.

Keilig: 110; Lexikon; Mehner, Vol. 12: 456; Tessin, Vol 14: 335.

INFANTRY DIVISION SCHAGETER
(1ST RAD DIVISION)

Composition: Grenadier Regiment Schageter 1, Grenadier Regiment Schageter 2, Grenadier Regiment Schageter 3, Fusilier Battalion Schageter, Tank Destroyer Battalion Schageter, Engineer Battalion Schageter, Signal Battalion Schageter

Home Station: Wehrkreis X

This 35th Wave division was formed in the Munsterland Troop Maneuver Area of East Prussia on March 31, 1945, as

Reicharbeitsdienst-Div z.b.V. 1 (1st Reich Labor Service or RAD Division). It included 7,500 men from the labor service and the elements of the 299th Infantry Division which had not been cut off in the Hela peninsula by the advancing Soviets. It was designated Infantry Division Schageter shortly thereafter and was sent to the 3rd Panzer Army on the Eastern Front. It was very much a composite unit, as demonstrated by its tank destroyer battalion. It included a *Panzer Schreck* company (with shoulder-fired weapons), a Fla (light anti-aircraft company), and an assault gun company. At the end of the war, it disengaged from the Red Army and surrendered to the Americans on May 3, 1945.

Its commander was Lieutenant General Wilhelm Heun.

Sources: Keilig: 139; Lexikon; Mehner, Vol. 12: 456; Tessin, Vol. 14: 224–25.

INFANTRY DIVISION SEELAND (328TH INFANTRY DIVISION SEELAND)

Composition: 593rd Grenadier Regiment, 594th Grenadier Regiment, 595th Grenadier Regiment, 328th Artillery Regiment (all two battalions each), 328th Support Regiment

Home Station: Copenhagen

This formation was made up of convalescence units, composed of men taken from military hospitals in Denmark. Activated on March 9, 1945, it never reached full strength and was not completely formed when Germany surrendered in May 1945.

Sources: Lexikon; Tessin, Vol. 9: 168.

DIVISION SICILY

Composition: Grenadier Regiment Sicily 1, Grenadier Regiment Sicily 2, Grenadier Regiment Sicily 3, Artillery Regiment Sicily, Mobile Battalion Sicily, Anti-Aircraft Battalion Sicily.

Home Station: Landau, Wehrkreis XII

Formed on May 14, 1943, just after the fall of Tunis, this unit became the 15th Panzer Grenadier Division on July 1, 1943.

Its commanders were Colonel Ernst Günther Baade (assumed command May 14, 1943) and Major General Eberhard Rodt (June 9, 1943).

Sources: Tessin, Vol. 14: 223. Also see Samuel W. Mitcham, Jr., and Friedrich von Stauffenberg, *The Battle of Sicily* (1991).

INFANTRY DIVISION SILESIA

Composition: Grenadier Regiment Silesia 1, Grenadier Regiment Silesia 2, Artillery Battalion Silesia, Engineer Battalion Silesia

Home Station: Wadowitz, Wehrkreis VIII

This shadow division was formed in Troop Maneuver Area Neuhammer, Wehrkreis VIII, on July 4, 1944. It was sent to Italy in August and was absorbed by the 94th Infantry Division on August 21. Part of the staff of the 1st Silesia Regiment was used to form the Staff, 281st Grenadier Regiment of the 148th Infantry Division.

Sources: Lexikon; Tessin, Vol. 14: 224.

FORTRESS DIVISION STETTIN

Composition: Fortress Regiment Stettin 1, Fortress Regiment Stettin 2, Fortress Regiment Stettin 3, Fortress Regiment Stettin 4, Fortress Regiment Stettin 5, 3132nd Fortress Artillery Regiment, 85th Fortress Machine Gun Battalion, Fortress Machine Gun Battalion Stettin A, 555th Construction Engineer Regimental Staff (controlling four combat engineer battalions and a construction engineer battalion).

Home Station: Stettin, Wehrkreis II

This division was formed on March 22, 1945, as the Red Army closed in on Stettin, Pomerania (now Szczecin, Poland). It fought at part of 3rd Panzer Army and put up a stout defense.

Stettin did not fall until April 26, 1945. When it did, the fortress division ceased to exist. A good many of its men managed to escape to the west, where they surrendered to the British a week or two later.

Its commanders were Major General Rudolf Höfer (March 22, 1945) and Major General Ferdinand Brühl (April 19, 1945).

Sources: Keilig: 53, 144; Lexikon; Tessin, Vol. 14: 224.

FORTRESS DIVISION SWINEMÜNDE

Composition: 1st Fortress Alarm Regiment, 2nd Fortress Alarm Regiment, 3rd Fortress Alarm Regiment, 4th Fortress Alarm Regiment, 5th Fortress Alarm Regiment, Coastal Artillery Lehr Regiment

Home Station: Swinemünde

As the Red Army closed in on the Third Reich, Hitler and his high commands threw everything they could into the battle. Fortress Division Swinemünde, which was formed in January 1945, is an excellent example. Its headquarters was the former Sea Command Pomerania. The 1st Fortress Alarm Regiment included Luftwaffe school troops, former aviation troops, and personnel from destroyer and torpedo boat crews. The 2nd Regiment came largely from Naval Flak School Misdroy. The 3rd Regiment was the former 128th Naval Rifle Battalion (whose men came from the III Torpedo School in Kolberg). The 4th Regiment was the former Naval Flak School. And the 5th Regiment had five battalions of the Higher Command Naval Flak and Coastal Artillery, including the men of Flak Schools I, IV, VII, and VIII. Swinemuende and the island of Usedom on the Baltic Sea were strategically important naval bases and Swinemuende was the home of the German rocket facilities. On March 12, 1945, when it was full of refugees from the east, it was attacked by 1,000 Allied bombers, who killed approximately 23,000 people. It was then nicknamed "the Dresden of the north" by bitter German civilians. The fortress division formed the northern anchor of Manteuffel's 3rd Panzer

Army and held the fortress until the last week of April 1945. Most of its men then escaped to the west.

Its commander was Colonel/Major General Arthur Kopp (assumed command March 15, 1945).

Notes and Sources: Kopp was promoted to major general on April 1, 1945.

Keilig: 181; Lexikon; Tessin, Vol. 14: 225–26; Ziemke 1968: 484–85.

INFANTRY DIVISION THEODOR KÖRNER

Composition: Grenadier Regiment Theodor Koerner 1, Grenadier Regiment Theodor Koerner 2, Grenadier Regiment Theodor Koerner 3, Artillery Regiment Theodor Koerner, Fusilier Battalion Theodor Koerner, Tank Destroyer Battalion Theodor Koerner, Signal Company Theodor Koerner

Home Station: Wehrkreis III

Also known as the 3rd Special Purposes Division (3rd RAD [Reich Labor Service] Division), this unit was formed in the Doeberitz Troop Maneuver Area from the remnants of the 215th Infantry Division and 7,500 RAD troops on April 4, 1945. Five days later it was redesignated Infantry Division Theodor Koerner. Committed to combat almost immediately, it fought against the U.S. and Red armies south of Berlin. It surrendered to the Americans in May 1945.

Lieutenant General Bruno Frankewitz was the division's commander.

Notes and Sources: This division was named after Carl Theodor Körner (1791–1813), a noted German writer and literary figure killed during the Napoleonic Wars.

Keilig: 94; Lexikon; Tessin, Vol. 14: 239.

INFANTRY DIVISION ULRICH VON HUTTEN
(3RD RAD DIVISION)

Composition: Grenadier Regiment Ulrich von Hutten 1, Grenadier Regiment Ulrich von Hutten 2, Grenadier Regiment Ulrich von Hutten 3, Artillery Regiment Ulrich von Hutten, Fusilier Battalion Ulrich von Hutten, Tank Destroyer Battalion Ulrich von Hutten, Engineer Battalion Ulrich von Hutten (formerly the 845th Engineer Training Battalion), Signal Battalion Ulrich von Hutten

Home Station: Wehrkreis IV

This 35th Wave division was formed in Wittenberg, Saxony on March 30, 1945, mainly from school and replacement troops. It headquarters was the former Staff, 56th Infantry Division. It was assigned to the 11th Army and sent into action against the Americans near Bitterfeld on April 12, where it performed very well. Later it was attached to the 12th Army and fought against the Russians at Beelitz (near Berlin). It surrendered to the U.S. Army near Tangermuende in May 1945.

Its commanders were Lieutenant General Edmund Blaurock (March 1945) and Lieutenant General Gerhard Engel (April 12, 1945).

Notes and Sources: The division was named for Ulrich von Hutten (born 1488), an outspoken critic of the Catholic Church and a supporter of the Lutheran Reformation. He died of syphilis in 1523.

Keilig: 36; Tessin, Vol. 14: 244–45.

INFANTRY DIVISION WAHN

Composition: Grenadier Regiment Wahn 1, Grenadier Regiment Wahn 2, Artillery Battalion Wahn, Engineer Battalion Wahn

Home Station: Troop Maneuver Area Wahn, Wehrkreis VI

This unit was formed on January 27, 1944, as a shadow division under the 182nd Reserve Division at the Troop Maneuver Area Wahn in the Rhineland-Westphalia district. It was sent to Army Group North in late February, where it was used to rebuild the 331st Infantry Division. Infantry Division Wahn ceased to exist on March 16. Its Staff was used to form the 70th Infantry Division. Lieutenant General Heinz Furbach was the division's only commander.

Sources: Bradley et al., Vol. 4: 158; Lexikon; Tessin, Vol. 14: 252.

FORTRESS DIVISION WARSAW

Composition: 8th Fortress Regiment, 88th Fortress Regiment, 183rd Fortress Regiment, 1320th Fortress Artillery Regiment, 22nd Fortress Trench Mortar Battalion, 23rd Fortress Trench Mortar Battalion, 67th Fortress Engineer Battalion, 1320th Signal Troop, 1320th Divisional Supply Troops

This unit was formed in January 1945, and was created to defend Warsaw against the Soviet Army; however, General of Panzer Troops Smilo von Lüttwitz, the commander of the 9th Army, saw no sense in fighting for the city, so he withdrew without authorization, and it fell to the Red Army on January 17. This move cost the general his job. Fortress Division Warsaw was disbanded on January 27.

Its only commander was Lieutenant General Friedrich Weber, who was placed in Fuehrer Reserve and was never re-employed for his part in the unauthorized but highly sensible evacuation of what was left of the Polish capital.

Notes and Sources: The staff of the 88th Fortress Regiment was the former Staff, 88th Security Regiment. The 183rd Fortress Regiment was the former 183rd Security Regiment. Keilig: 363; Kursietis: 238; Lexikon; Tessin, Vol. 14: 253.

INFANTRY DIVISION WILDFLECKEN

Composition: Grenadier Regiment Wildflecken 1, Grenadier Regiment Wildflecken 2, Artillery Battalion Wildflecken, Engineer Battalion Wildflecken

Home Station: Troop Maneuver Area Wildflecken, Wehrkreis IX

Formed as a shadow division on April 17, 1944, this unit was sent to Italy and joined Army Group C on June 19, 1944, just after the fall of Rome. On July 7, it was absorbed by the 715th Infantry Division, which had been smashed at Nettuno (Anzio). Its Staff was sent back to Wildflecken and used to form Headquarters, 232nd Infantry Division.

Sources: Lexikon; Tessin, Vol. 14: 252.

DIVISION VON WITZLEBEN

Composition: Grenadier Battalion Upper Rhine I, Grenadier Battalion Upper Rhine IV, Grenadier Battalion Upper Rhine XIII, Grenadier Battalion Upper Rhine XVI

This division was formed on January 1, 1945, by the XIV SS Corps on the Upper Rhine sector of the Western Front. Its staff came from part of the headquarters of the 553rd Volksgrenadier Division. On January 14, it was absorbed by the 905th Replacement Division.

Sources: Lexikon; Tessin, Vol. 14: 252.

DIVISION WOLDENBERG

Formed as Replacement Division Woldenberg on January 20, 1945, the men of this unit came from the Army Flak School at Greifswald. It was disbanded on January 28 and its men sent to other units in Pomerania.

Its commander was Major General Gerhard Kegler.

Sources: Keilig: 165; Kursietis: 239; Lexikon; Tessin, Vol. 14: 253.

CHAPTER 3

The Jäger and Light Divisions*

1st SKI JÄGER DIVISION

Composition: 1st Ski Jäger Regiment, 2nd Ski Jäger Regiment, 1st Heavy Ski Battalion, 152nd Artillery Regiment, 1st Ski Fusilier Battalion, 152nd Ski Tank Destroyer Battalion, 270th Assault Gun Battalion, 85th Ski Engineer Battalion, 152nd Ski Signal Battalion, 152nd Ski Field Replacement Battalion, 152nd Ski Divisional Supply Troops. The 18th Heavy Rocket Battalion was part of the 152nd Artillery Regiment.

Home Station: Wehrkreis XIII

Formed as the 1st Ski Brigade in September 1943, this unit was converted to a division in Lower Bavaria in the summer of 1944. The 2nd Ski Regiment was created from the former 167th Grenadier Regiment of the old 86th Infantry Division, which had been smashed in Russia. Following the completion of its training (which was conducted in the Pripjet marshes area), the division was sent to the badly mauled Army Group Center in the summer of 1944, and was involved in the retreat to the Vistula. In October it was transferred to the Carpathian Mountains sector and fought in Slovakia and southern Poland. It remained on the Eastern Front until the end of the war. It surrendered to the Russians in middle Silesia (later Czechoslovakia) in May 1945. The 1st Ski Jäger Division never earned any special distinction; as a result, no second ski division was ever created.

The commanders of the 1st Ski Brigade/Division included Colonel Günther von Manteuffel (September 1943), Colonel/

---

* The original German light divisions—the 1st, 2nd, 3rd, and 4th—became the 6th, 7th, 8th, and 9th Panzer Divisions, respectively, in late 1939.

Major General Martin Berg (May 13, 1944), Colonel/Major General/Lieutenant General Gustav Hundt (October 3, 1944), Colonel Emanuel von Kiliani (November 15, 1944), Hundt (December 8, 1944), Major General Hans Streets (January 1945), Hundt (February 1, 1945), and Colonel Bruno Weiler (April 1945).

Notes and Sources: The 1st Heavy Ski Battalion consisted of a tank destroyer company, a self-propelled infantry support gun company (armed with 150mm self-propelled howitzers), a self-propelled flak company (armed with 37mm guns) and an armored car company, outfitted with twenty-two captured Soviet T-34 tanks. Berg was promoted to major general on August 1, 1944. Colonel von Schlebrügge briefly commanded the division in January 1944. Hundt became a major general on August 1, 1944, and a lieutenant general on March 1, 1945. He was reported missing in action near Troppau on April 21, 1945, and was officially declared dead in 1950.

Keilig: 29, 154; *Kriegstagebuch des OKW*, Volume I: 1146; Nafziger 2000: 475; Tessin, Vol. 2: 25; RA: 204; OB 45: 313.

5TH JÄGER DIVISION

Composition (1943): 56th Jäger Regiment, 75th Jäger Regiment, 5th Motorized Artillery Regiment, 5th Bicycle Battalion, 5th Tank Destroyer Battalion, 5th Motorized Engineer Battalion, 5th Motorized Signal Battalion, 5th Field Replacement Battalion, 5th Divisional Supply Troops

Home Station: Ulm, later Colmar, Wehrkreis V

Originally the 5th Infantry Division, this unit was formed at Ulm in October 1934, under the codename "Kommandant of Ulm." (The original 5th Infantry Division, which was formed in 1921, was broken up to provide cadres for a number of divisions.) Its soldiers were recruited from Baden and Wuerttemberg, and were originally divided into the 14th, 56th and 75th Infantry Regiments. The 5th Infantry was posted to the Upper Rhine (and later the Eifel) in 1939, did not take part in the Polish campaign, and was only lightly engaged in the invasion of France the following year. It remained on garrison duty in France until April 1941, when it was transferred to East Prus-

German ski troops move up to the front in Russia, circa 1942 or 1943. Later in the war, the Germans created an entire ski division, the 1st Ski Jäger. NATIONAL ARCHIVES

sia. It crossed into Russia on June 22, 1941, and was involved in bitter fighting in the Vormarsch sector and later at Vyasma. In December, it was sent to France to rest and refit and to be converted into a light division. In this reorganization, it lost its third regiment (the 14th Infantry), which was assigned to the 78th Infantry Division. It was redesignated 5th Jäger Division on June 6, 1942. The 5th was equipped as a pursuit division, with an organizational structure similar to a mountain division, except with more vehicles.

It returned to Russia in February 1942, and was attached to Army Group North, where it remained for some time. In March and April 1942, it was part of Combat Group von Seydlitz and helped break the Russian encirclement of the II Corps at Demyansk. Later, in the second half of 1942 and throughout 1943, it fought in the battles around Staraya Russa. In 1944, as part of Army Group Center, it fought in the Vitebsk battles (January–March) and in the Kovel sector (April–July). After the collapse of Army Group Center, the 5th Jäger was sent west to aid in the defense of Poland and, later, eastern Germany, fighting at Neustettin and Dramburg (now Drawsko, Poland) in Pomerania. It fought its last battle in front of the Nazi capital and was destroyed there in April 1945. The remnants of the division surrendered to the Russians at Wittenberge in May 1945. A few elements of the division did reach Allied lines at Lenzen (north of Wittenberge) and surrendered to the Americans on May 3.

Its commanders included Major General/Lieutenant General Eugen Hahn (October 1, 1934), Major General/Lieutenant General Wilhelm Fahrmbacher (August 1938), Major General/Lieutenant General Karl Allmendinger (October 25, 1940), Colonel Walter Jost (June 1942), Colonel Hans von Rohr (July 1942), Allmendinger (returned August 1942), Colonel/Major General/Lieutenant General Hellmuth Thumm (January 4, 1943), Colonel Johannes Gittner (March 1, 1944), Thumm (returned May 1, 1944), Lieutenant General Friedrich Sixt (November 1, 1944), and Lieutenant General Edmund Blaurock (April 19, 1945–end).

Notes and Sources: Eugen Hahn was promoted to lieutenant general on August 1, 1936. He died on August 10, 1938. The 5th Field Replacement Battalion was transferred to the 163rd Infantry Division and became the III/324th Infantry Regiment in January 1940. Fahrmbacher was promoted to lieutenant general on June 1, 1939. Allmendinger was promoted to lieutenant general on August 1, 1942. Thumm was promoted to major general on March 1, 1943, and to lieutenant general on September 1, 1943. Colonel Hans Wagner briefly served as acting commander of the division in 1943, but the exact dates are not clear.

Bradley et al., Vol. 5: 64–65. Carell 1966: 427–34; Carell 1971: 288; Keilig: 108, 325; Kennedy: 10B; Lexikon; Nafziger 2000: 40; Adolf Reinicke, *Die 5. Jäger Division, 1939–1945* (1962); Tessin, Vol. 2: 288; Helmut Thumm, *Der Weg der 5. Infanterie-und-Jäger-Division, 1921–1945* (1976); RA: 72; OB 42: 68; OB 43: 195; OB 45:313; Ziemke 1966: 477.

8TH JÄGER DIVISION

Composition: 38th Jäger Regiment, 84th Jäger Regiment, 8th Artillery Regiment, 8th Bicycle Battalion, 8th Tank Destroyer Battalion, 8th Engineer Battalion, 8th Signal Battalion, 85th Field Replacement Battalion, 8th Divisional Supply Troops

Home Station: Neisse, Wehrkreis VIII

The 8th Jaeger was formed in December 1934, in Oppeln, under the codename "Artillery Leader III" (*Artillerieführer III*). Its men were from Upper Silesia and later also from the Sudetenland. It was renamed the 8th Infantry Division in March 1935, when conscription was reintroduced in Germany. It initially included the 28th, 38th, and 84th Infantry Regiments. The 8th Infantry fought well in Poland, where it broke through strong enemy frontier fortifications in eastern Upper Silesia. Later it took part in the advance on Krakow. The next year it fought well in Belgium and France, and remained on occupation duty in Rouen until May 1941, when it was sent to East Prussia. It was sent to central Russia in June 1941, and suffered heavy losses in the initial campaign, especially at Bryansk, Vyasma, and the Battle of Moscow. The division was returned to France in late 1941, and was converted into a light division, losing its 28th Infantry Regiment in the process. Returned to

Russia in early 1942, the 8th fought in the Demyansk (Demjansk) relief operations in the northern sector until II Corps was freed in February 1943. The division continued to fight on the northern sector (at Demjansk and Lake Ilmen) until after the retreat from Leningrad began. In March 1944, it was sent to the southern sector and fought in the retreats through the Ukraine, the Carpathians and Slovakia. What remained of the 8th Jäger was surrounded in Czechoslovakia in April 1945, and surrendered to the Russians in May.

Commanders of the 8th Infantry/Jäger Division included Lieutenant General Rudolf Koch-Erpach (May 13, 1935), Major General/Lieutenant General Gustav Höhne (October 25, 1940), Colonel/Major General Count Gerhard von Schwerin (July 23, 1942), Major General/Lieutenant General Friedrich Volckamer von Kirchensittenbach (December 1, 1942), Lieutenant General Christian Philipp (September 1, 1944), and Colonel Joachim Bergener (April 1, 1945–end).

Notes and Sources: The 8th Field Replacement Battalion was abosrbed by the 442nd Infantry Regiment (168th Infantry Division) in January 1940, as its II Battalion. The division was officially redesignated 8th Light on December 1, 1941, and 8th Jäger on June 30, 1942. Höhne was promoted to lieutenant general on August 1, 1942. Gerhard von Schwerin became a major general on October 1, 1942. Volckamer was promoted to lieutenant general on September 1, 1943. Who commanded the 8th Jäger between November 13 and December 2, 1942 is not recorded.

Benoist-Mechin: 133; Carell 1966: 427–34; Carell 1971: 288; Kameradschaftsbund der 8. Jaeger-Division, *Die Geschichte der 8. (oberschlesisch-sudetendeutschen) Infanterie-Jäger-Division* (1979); Keilig: 256, 319; *Kriegstagebuch des OKW*, Volume I: 1146; Volume IV: 1895; Kursietis: 89; Manstein:52; Nafziger 2000: 44–45; Tessin, Vol. 3: 95–96; RA: 130; OB 42: 68; OB 43: 195; OB 45: 272, 314.

28TH JÄGER DIVISION

Composition: 49th Jäger Regiment, 83rd Jäger Regiment, 28th Artillery Regiment, 28th Bicycle Battalion, 28th Anti-Tank Battalion, 28th Engineer Battalion, 28th Signal Battalion, 28th Divisional Supply Troops

Home Station: Breslau, Wehrkreis VIII

Formed in Breslau on October 1, 1936, as part of the peacetime army, this division was initially designated 28th Infantry Division. At this time, it included the 7th, 49th, and 83rd Infantry Regiments. The men were mainly Silesians, with some *Volksdeutsche* from Poland intermixed. The 28th fought well in the invasion of southern Poland, took part in the Western campaign of 1940, and was on occupation duty in northern France and Belgium from June 1940 to May 1941. In June, it struck into Russia with Army Group Center, and fought at Smolensk and in the drive on Moscow, where it suffered heavy casualties. In November, the 28th Division was transferred to France, where it was converted into a Jäger division. Its Staff, 7th Infantry Regiment was reassigned to the 252nd Infantry Division, along with one battalion from each infantry regiment. (It was, however, not officially designated the 28th Jaeger Division until July 1, 1942.)

Early in 1942, the "new" 28th reappeared on the Eastern Front, this time on the southern sector, and fought on the Kerch peninsula and in the final assault on the naval fortress of Sevastopol in the Crimea. Transferred to the northern sector with von Manstein's 11th Army, the Jäger troops were earmarked for attachment to Finland, but they were held up by order of Field Marshal Georg von Küchler, who committed them to action with his Army Group North near Demyansk in late 1942. In January and February 1943, the 28th fought in the Second Battle of Lake Ladoga and remained in the northern zone until mid-1944. Meanwhile, the 28th Jäger absorbed the 1st Luftwaffe Field Division on February 20, 1944. In July, the division was attached to Group von Saucken and tried to prevent the encirclement of the bulk of the 4th Army near Minsk, but failed. Assigned to the tactically bankrupt Army Group Center, the 28th Jäger suffered heavy losses in the retreat into Poland, where it took part in the fighting near the old Brest-Litovsk fortress in the Polish marchland. It was pushed back into East Prussia in September 1944, and fought there for eight months. The remnants of the division, less than a thousand men, ended the war in the Hela (East Prussian) pocket. It surrendered to the Russians on May 8, 1945.

The leaders of the 28th Infantry/Jäger included Major General/Lieutenant General Hans von Obstfelder (October 6, 1936), Major General/Lieutenant General Hans Sinnhuber (May 21, 1940), Major General/Lieutenant General Friedrich Schulz (May 1, 1943), Colonel Hubert Lamey (November 25, 1943), Major General/Lieutenant General Hans Speth (December 1, 1943), Major General/Lieutenant General Gustav Heistermann von Ziehlberg (April 28, 1944), Colonel/Major General Ernst König (November 20, 1944), and Colonel Hans Tempelhof (April 12, 1945).

Notes and Sources: The division absorbed the 1031st and 1032nd March Battalions on October 28, 1944. It also absorbed the 28th Mountain Artillery Regiment (which was at battalion strength) in 1944. Obstfelder was promoted to lieutenant general on February 1, 1938. Sinnhuber received that same rank on April 1, 1941. Schulz and Speth promoted to lieutenant general on July 1, 1943, and January 1, 1944, respectively. Heistermann was promoted to lieutenant general on June 1, 1944. He was relieved of his command and arrested on November 19, after his involvement in the July 20, 1944, assassination attempt against Adolf Hitler was discovered. He was executed in Spandau on February 2, 1945. Koenig was promoted to major general on January 30, 1945.

Carell 1966: 482, 484, 503, 509; Carell 1971: 260, 287, 591–94; Kennedy: 74 and Map 7; Keilig: 134, 196, 328; *Kriegstagebuch des OKW*, Volume IV: 1897; Manstein: 244; Nafziger 2000: 44–45; Salisbury: 538; RA: 130; OB 42: 68; OB 43: 196; OB 45: 314.

42ND JÄGER DIVISION

Composition: 25th Jäger Regiment, 40th Jäger Regiment, 142nd Artillery Regiment, 142nd Fusilier Battalion, 142nd Tank Destroyer Battalion, 142nd Engineer Battalion, 142nd Signal Battalion, 142nd Divisional Supply Troops

Home Station: Krummau, Wehrkreis XVII

This division was set up as the 187th Replacement Division on November 9, 1939. Its troops were mainly Austrian and

Volksdeutsche. It initially controlled the 45th, 130th and 462nd Infantry Replacement Regiments, the 45th Artillery Replacement Regiment, the 17th Tank Destroyer Replacement Battalion, the 86th Engineer Replacement Battalion, and the 17th and 45th Motorized Replacement Battalions. Upon the reorganization of the Replacement Army in the fall of 1942, the 187th was upgraded to reserve division status and transferred to Croatia as a training unit under Home Army control. It was converted into the 187th Jäger Division on November 23, 1943, and was redesignated the 42nd Jäger Division on December 22, 1943.

In March 1944, it took part in the occupation of Hungary but was back in northern Yugoslavia by May. Shortly afterward it was transferred to Genoa, northern Italy, and was in combat in the Gothic Line campaign of September 1944. It fought well there, as it did in the Battle of Bologna (December 1944) and in the final campaign in Italy. By March 1945 it had a strength of less than 2,600 men; nevertheless it fought on until April 24, 1945, when it was crushed by the Anglo-Saxons south of the Po River—the victim of another of Hitler's "hold at all costs" orders. The remnants of the 42nd Jäger surrendered to the British near Belluno at the end of the month.

Commanders of the 187th/42nd Division included Major General Walther Grässner (October 15, 1939), Major General/ Lieutenant General Konrad Stephanus (February 7, 1940), Lieutenant General Josef Brauner von Haydringen (August 15, 1942), and Major General/Lieutenant General Walter Jost (April 26, 1944).

Notes and Sources: Stephanus was promoted to lieutenant general on February 1, 1941. Walter Jost was promoted to lieutenant general on December 1, 1944. He was killed in action at Villadosa, Italy, on April 24, 1945. He was not replaced.

Fisher: 411, 442, 462–66; Keilig: 160; Kursietis: 114–15; Lexikon; Tessin, Vol. 7: 23637; RA: 220–23; OB 45: 315.

90TH LIGHT DIVISION

See 90th Panzer Grenadier Division (Volume Three).

97TH JÄGER DIVISION

Composition (1942): 204th Jäger Regiment, 207th Jäger Regiment, 81st Artillery Regiment, 97th Reconnaissance (later Bicycle) Battalion, 97th Anti-Tank Battalion, 97th Engineer Battalion, 97th Signal Battalion, 97th Field Replacement Battalion, 97th Divisional Supply Troops

Home Station: Bad Reichenhall, Wehrkreis VII

This division was formed on December 10, 1940, in the Bad Toelz area of Bavaria, with cadres provided by the 7th Infantry and 3rd Motorized Divisions. It was initially dubbed the 97th Light Division, but was renamed 97th Jäger Division on July 6, 1942. It was equipped almost entirely with captured French vehicles. Meanwhile, it crossed in to southern Russia in 1941, and fought in the Ukraine and Donets campaigns of that year, including the battles of Lemberg, Vinnitsa, Uman, and Kiev. It was involved in repulsing the Soviet winter offensive of 1941–42, and took part in the Battle of Isjum, the Caucasus campaign of 1942–43, and in the subsequent retreats. It also fought in the Battle of Kursk (July 1943), where it suffered heavy casualties.

Transferred to the lower Dnieper that autumn, it fought very well in the retreats through the Ukraine and in the Nikopol Bridgehead, and was officially cited for bravery. (The men of the division received 10,690 Iron Crosses, 2nd Class, during the war and 1,468 Iron Crosses, 1st Class, as well as 30 German Crosses in Gold, 14 Knight's Crosses, and 4 Knight's Crosses with Oak Leaves. The numbers of Iron Crosses are particularly impressive. Over the course of the war, the division also lost 13,000 men killed in action.) The 97th Jäger—now much reduced by heavy fighting—was routed in March 1944 by the rapidly advancing Russians but continued to resist on the front line for the rest of the war. It was transferred to the Slovakian sector in October 1944, fought in Upper Silesia in early 1945, and ended the war in the huge pocket at Deutsch-Brod (east of Prague) in May 1945, when it surrendered to the Soviets.

Commanders of the division included Major General Walter Weiss (December 10, 1940), Lieutenant General Sigismund von

Förster (January 15, 1941), Major General Maximilian Fretter-Pico (April 15, 1941), Colonel/Major General/Lieutenant General Ernst Rupp (January 1, 1942), Colonel Friedrich-Wilhelm Otte (May 30, 1943), Major General/Lieutenant General Ludwig Müller (June 1, 1943), Major General/Lieutenant General Friedrich Karl Rabe von Pappenheim (December 13, 1943), Colonel Julius Wölfinger (February 1945), Rabe (returned March 1945), and Major General Robert Bader (April 17, 1945).

Notes and Sources: This division's support and supply troops included the 452nd Turkish Battalion and the 97th Pack Mule Company. Ernst Rupp was promoted to major general on February 1, 1942, and to lieutenant general on January 1, 1943. He was killed in action in the Kuban on May 30, 1943. Ludwig Müller (born 1892) was promoted to lieutenant general on July 1, 1943. Bader was a Russian prisoner until 1955.

Carell 1971: 159; Hartmann: 43; Keilig: 233, 366; Lexikon; Nafziger 2000: 536–37; Ernst-Ludwig Ott, *Jaeger und Feind: Geschichte und Opfergang der 97. Jaeger-Division, 1940–1945* (1966); Ernst-Ludwig Ott, *Die Spielhahnjaeger, 1940–1945: Bilddokumentation der 97. Jaeger-Division* (1982); Tessin, Vol. 6: 147-49; RA: 116; OB 42: 69; OB 43: 197; OB 45: 315.

99TH JÄGER DIVISION

See 7th Mountain Division in the next chapter.

100TH JÄGER DIVISION

Composition: 54th Jäger Regiment, 227th Jäger Regiment, 83rd Artillery Regiment, 100th Reconnaissance Battalion, 100th Tank Destroyer Battalion, 100th Engineer Battalion, 100th Signal Battalion, 100th Field Replacement Battalion, 100th Divisional Supply Troops

Home Station: Ried, Wehrkreis XVII

This division was formed in Vienna on December 10, 1940, as the 100th Light Infantry Division. (It was redesignated 100th Jäger on July 6, 1942.) The 54th Jäger Regiment formerly had been an infantry regiment under the 18th Infantry Division. The 369th Reinforced (Croatian) Infantry Regiment was attached to the 100th Jäger in 1941, and remained with it until it was destroyed at Stalingrad. The division itself first saw action in southern Russia with the 17th Army in 1941, where it fought at Uman and Kiev, and was involved in the sweep to Odessa. It opposed the Russian winter offensive of 1941–42, fought in the Battle of Kharkov (May 1942), in the encirclement and Battle of Staryyoskol, in the advance across the Don, in the drive to the Volga, and in the street fighting in Stalingrad (1942). It was with 6th Army when it was encircled in November 1942, and was destroyed when Stalingrad fell in January 1943.

A second 100th Jäger Division was created in the Belgrade area on April 17, 1943. That summer it was transferred to Albania and was rushed to the southern sector of the Eastern Front in March 1944. Here it joined the II SS Panzer Corps and helped rescue the 1st Panzer Army, which was encircled between the Bug and the Dnestr. It also took part in the Battles of Tarnopol and Brody and in the retreat to the Carpathians. Subsequently transferred to Army Group Center, it took part in the withdrawal from Russia and the battles in southern Poland in the fall of 1944. It was fighting the Soviets in Silesia when the war ended and surrendered to the Red Army in May 1945.

Commanders of the 100th Jäger included Major General/Lieutenant General Werner Sanne (December 10, 1940–January 30, 1943), Colonel/Major General/Lieutenant General Willibald Utz (April 25, 1943), Colonel Hans Kreppel (January 1, 1945), and Colonel/Major General Otto Schury (February 9, 1945).

Notes and Sources: Sanne was promoted to lieutenant general on April 1, 1942. He was captured at Stalingrad and died in Soviet captivity in 1952. Utz was promoted to major general on July 1, 1943, and to lieutenant general on February 1, 1944. Schury was promoted to major general on April 1, 1945. He remained in Soviet prisons until 1955.

Carell 1966: 490, 495, 523; Carell 1971: 523; Hartmann: 46–47; Keilig: 291, 317; Kursietis: 133; Hanns Neidhardt, *Mit Tanne und Eichenlaub: Kriegschronik der 100. Jäger-Division, vormals 100. leichte Infanterie-Division* (1981); Tessin, Vol. 6: 161–62; RA: 200; OB 42: 69; OB 43: 197; OB 45: 315–16.

101ST JÄGER DIVISION

Composition: 228th Jäger Regiment, 229th Jäger Regiment, 85th Artillery Regiment, 101st Reconnaissance Battalion, 101st Tank Destroyer Battalion, 101st Engineer Battalion, 101st Signal Battalion, 101st Field Replacement Battalion, 101st Divisional Supply Troops, 101st Pack Mule Battalion

Home Station: Heilbronn and later Karlsruhe, Wehrkreis V

This Baden-Württemberg unit was created near Prague on December 10, 1940. A third of the men were soldiers transferred from the 35th Infantry Division. The 101st fought in the drive across the Ukraine and southern Russia in 1941 (including the battles of Uman, Kiev and Kharkov), and in the winter battles of 1941–42. In 1942–43, it took part in the Second Battle of Kharkov (also called Izyum), in the capture of Rostov, in the Caucasus campaign, and the retreat into the Kuban, during which it suffered heavy casualties, fighting off partisans and regular Soviet troops. Evacuated across the Kerch Straits, it was transported through the Crimea to the lower Dnieper in the latter part of 1943, where it fought at Nikolajew and Vinniza.

In March 1944, it was surrounded with the 1st Panzer Army and formed the rear guard of the XXXXVI Panzer Corps in the subsequent breakout. Cited for its conduct in the retreat across the northern Ukraine, the 101st Jäger fought in the Carpathians and was withdrawn to Slovakia in the fall of 1944. Sent south in early 1945, it fought in the retreats through Hungary and into Austria. It ended the war at battle group strength on the southern sector of the Eastern Front, but managed to surrender to the Americans in the Nesselbach/Rosenberg sector of the Sudetenland. (This area is now called Tschechien and is in the Czech Republic.)

Commanders of the 101st included Major General/Lieutenant General Erich Marcks (December 10, 1940), Lieutenant General Josef Brauner von Haydringen (June 26, 1941), Colonel/Major General Erich Diestel (April 11, 1942), Colonel/Major General/Lieutenant General Emil Vogel (September 1, 1942), and Lieutenant General Dr. Walter Assman (July 12, 1944).

Notes and Sources: By 1945, two of its Jäger battalions were *Ost-truppen* (Eastern troops). Erich Marcks promoted to lieutenant general on March 1, 1941. He was wounded on June 26, 1941, and lost a leg. He later commanded LXXXIV Corps in Normandy and was killed by an Allied fighter-bomber near St. Lo on June 12, 1944. Diestel was promoted to major general on August 1, 1942. Vogel was promoted to major general on October 1, 1942, and to lieutenant general on April 1, 1943. Dr. Assman was a dentist.

Carell 1971: 159, 525; Keilig: 356; *Kriegstagebuch des OKW,* Volume I: 1145; Nafziger 2000: 539–40; Plocher 1941: 295; Tessin, Vol. 6: 168–70; RA: 96; OB 42: 69; OB 43: 197; OB 45: 316.

104TH JÄGER (FORMERLY 704TH INFANTRY) DIVISION

Composition: 724th Jäger Regiment, 734th Jäger Regiment, 654th Artillery Regiment, 104th Bicycle Company, 104th Tank Destroyer Battalion, 104th Engineer Battalion, 104th Signal Battalion, 104th Field Replacement Battalion, 104th Divisional Supply Troops

Home Station: Wehrkreis IV

Formed as the 704th Infantry Division on April 15, 1941, this unit initially included the 724th and 734th Infantry Regiments, the 654th Artillery Regiment, the 704th Reconnaissance and Signal Companies, and the 704th Engineer Battalion. In May 1941, it was sent to Serbia, where it performed occupation duties in the Belgrade area until May 1943. In April 1943, the division was converted into a light division and redesignated 104th Jäger. Its signal and reconnaissance units were expanded, and its tank destroyer battalion added at this time. By June, the new Jäger division was stationed in the Epirus area of western Greece and remained there until the rapidly advancing Soviet armies threatened to take Army Group F and the Balkans in the rear in November 1944. The 104th Jäger withdrew through Yugoslavia and was involved in heavy combat with Tito's partisans. It continued to fight in Croatia on the southern sector of the Eastern Front until the end of the war. It surrendered to the Yugoslavs near Cilli.

Commanders of the 704th Infantry/104th Jäger included Major General Heinrici Borowski (April 1941), Lieutenant General Hans Juppe (August 15, 1942), Colonel/Major General/ Lieutenant General Hartwig von Ludwiger (February 20, 1943), Colonel Ludwig Steyrer (May 1944), Ludwiger (returned May 1944), and Lieutenant General Friedrich Stephan (April 29, 1945–end).

Notes and Sources: Ludwiger was promoted to major general on May 1, 1943, and to lieutenant general on June 1, 1944. Many of the survivors of the 104th Jäger were murdered by the Yugoslavs after they surrendered. General Stephan was apparently among these. He disappeared in 1945, and has not been heard from since.

Keilig: 214, 333; Lexikon; Tessin, Vol. 6: 193; RA: 72; OB 42: 110; OB 43: 186; OB 45: 316.

114TH JÄGER (FORMERLY 714TH INFANTRY) DIVISION

Composition: 721st Jäger Regiment, 741st Jäger Regiment, 661st Artillery Regiment, 14th Bicycle Battalion, 114th Tank Destroyer Battalion, 114th Engineer Battalion, 114th Signal Battalion, 114th Divisional Supply Troops

Home Station: Braunsberg, Wehrkreis I

Originally the 714th Infantry Division—a two-regiment, static unit—the 114th consisted mainly of Poles, Czechs, and Volksdeutsche. It was formed in Prague on May 1, 1941. Initially, it consisted of the 721st and 741st Infantry Regiments, the 661st Artillery Battalion, and the 714th Reconnaissance, Engineer and Signal Companies. It was sent to Yugoslavia in June and took part in numerous anti-partisan operations from then until December 1943. Meanwhile, it was redesignated to a Jaeger division on April 1, 1943, and given the number 114. In January 1944, it was transferred to the Fiume area of Italy, and in February it was thrown into action against the Allied beach-head at Anzio (called Nettuno by the Germans). Later it took part in the Anzio counterattack, the Monte Cassino battles, the retreat from the Gustav Line, the battles of the Gothic Line, and the Battle of Bologna. It fought well but was down to a strength of only 984 effectives by March 1945. The remnants of the division—which now amounted to less than two battalions in terms of real combat strength—were destroyed at Brescia near the Po River, along with the LI Mountain Corps, on April 23, 1945, although remnants of the division continued to resist for the rest of the war.

Commanders of the 714th/114th included Major General/ Lieutenant General Friedrich Stahl (April 15, 1941), Major General Josef Reichert (January 1, 1943), Lieutenant General Karl Eglseer (February 20, 1943), Colonel/Major General Alexander Bourquin (October 11, 1943), Major General Dr. Hans Boelsen (May 19, 1944), Colonel/Major General Hans Ehlert (July 19, 1944), and Major General Martin Strahammer (April 15, 1945).

Notes and Sources: Stahl was promoted to lieutenant general on September 1, 1942. Bourquin was advanced to major general on January 1, 1944. Ehlert was promoted to major general on December 1, 1944, and was captured on April 1, 1945. General Strahammer was killed in action on May 2, 1945.

Blumenson 1969: 313, 361, 419–21; Chant, Volume II: 1511; Fisher: 18, 302, 442, 455–56; Hartmann: 47; RA: 20; Keilig: 48, 78, 336; Lexikon; Tessin, Vol. 6: 254; Vol. 12: 177; OB 42: 112; OB 43: 188; OB 45: 317.

117TH JÄGER (FORMERLY 717TH INFANTRY) DIVISION

Composition: 737th Jaeger Regiment, 749th Jäger Regiment, 670th Artillery Regiment, 116th Reconnaissance Battalion, 117th Tank Destroyer Battalion, 117th Engineer Battalion, 117th Signal Battalion, 117th Field Replacement Battalion, 117th Divisional Supply Troops

Home Station: Vienna-Strebersdorf, later Braunau, Wehrkreis XVII

Formed as the 717th (Static) Infantry Division in Croatia on April 11, 1941, this unit conducted anti-partisan operations in Yugoslavia from the summer of 1941 until the spring of 1943. Up until that time, it included the 737th Infantry Regiment (provided by the 177th Replacement Division), the 749th Infantry Regiment (provided by the 187th Replacement Division), the 670th Artillery Battalion, the 717th Engineer

Company and the 717th Signal Company. On April 1, 1943, it was converted to a Jäger unit and was sent to Greece, where it guarded the Peloponnesus until September 1944. It took part in the withdrawal through the Balkans and suffered heavy losses against Tito's partisans in September and October. It absorbed the 1004th and 1005th Fortress Infantry Battalions in December and the 944th Army Coastal Defense Artillery Regiment in March 1945. In 1945, it fought against the Russians and was in transit to the 6th SS Panzer Army in Austria when Berlin fell. The division then turned west and headed for Steyr, where it surrendered to the Americans in May.

Commanders of the 717th/117th included Major General Paul Hoffmann (May 17, 1941), Lieutenant General Dr. Walter Hinghofer (November 1, 1941), Lieutenant General Benighus Dippold (October 1, 1942), Major General/Lieutenant General Karl von LeSuire (May 1, 1943), Lieutenant General August Wittmann (July 10, 1944), and Colonel/Major General Hans Kreppel (March 10, 1945).

Notes and Sources: Le Suire was promoted to lieutenant general on January 1, 1944. Kreppel was promoted to major general effective May 1, 1945.

Keilig: 202; *Kriegstagebuch des OKW*, Volume I: 1145; Volume III: 261; Volume IV: 1903; Lexikon; Nafziger 2000: 544–45; Tessin, Vol. 12: 186; OB 43: 188; OB 45: 317.

118TH JÄGER (FORMERLY 718TH INFANTRY) DIVISION

Composition: 738th Jäger Regiment, 750th Jäger Regiment, 668th Artillery Battalion (later Regiment), 118th Bicycle Battalion, 118th Tank Destroyer Battalion, 118th Engineer Battalion, 118th Signal Battalion, 118th Jäger Divisional Supply Troops

Home Station: Radkersburg, later Innsbruck, Wehrkreis XVIII

Raised in western Austria in April 1941, this unit was officially activated on April 30. It was originally a static division, as were all German divisions in the 700 series. From 1941 until

1943, when it bore the designation 718th Infantry, it had only an artillery battalion and an engineer and signal company, with no organic tank destroyer or reconnaissance forces. Sent to Serbia in the summer of 1941, it conducted anti-partisan operations and was on occupation duty for two years. Upgraded to Jäger status on April 1, 1943, it was sent to Herzegovina and remained there until the summer of 1944, when it was sent to guard the Dalmatian coast against possible Allied landings from the Adriatic. In early 1945, it was sent to the Eastern Front and fought in Hungary and Austria until the end of the war. It surrendered to the British at Klagenfurt (in the province of Carinthia, Austria) in May 1945.

Its commanders included Colonel/Major General/Lieutenant General Hans Johann Fortner (May 3, 1941), Major General/Lieutenant General Josef Kübler (March 15, 1943), Colonel Rudolf Gertler (July 1944), and Colonel/Major General Hubert Lamey (July 10, 1944).

Notes and Sources: Fortner was promoted to major general on June 1, 1941 and to lieutenant general on November 1, 1942. Kübler was promoted to lieutenant general on January 1, 1944. Lamey was promoted to major general on September 1, 1944.

Keilig: 190; *Kriegstagebuch des OKW*, Volume I: 1134, 1145; Volume II: 1357; Volume III: 261, 735; Volume IV: 1895; Hubert Lamey, *Der Weg der 118. Jäger-Division* (1954); Lexikon; Tessin, Vol. 6: 272; OB 43: 189; OB 45: 318.

164TH LIGHT AFRIKA DIVISION

Composition: 125th Panzer Grenadier Regiment, 382nd Panzer Grenadier Regiment, 433rd Panzer Grenadier Regiment, 220th Artillery Regiment, 220th Reconnaissance Battalion, 220th Tank Destroyer Battalion, 220th Engineer Battalion, 220th Signal Battalion, 220th Field Replacement Battalion, 220th Divisional Supply Troops

Home Station: Dresden, Wehrkreis IV, later Zittau, Wehrkreis XII

This unit was formed on November 27, 1939, at the Königsbrück Maneuver Area, Wehrkreis IV, as the 164th Infantry Demonstration Division. It absorbed the 4th, 14th and 44th Field Replacement Battalions on January 20, 1940, and by the end of the month included the 382nd, 433rd, and 440th Infantry Regiments. It remained in reserve during the French campaign but was sent east in January 1941, and fought in Greece during the Balkan campaign of April 1941. It remained there, on occupation duty at Salonika, for several months. During that period, the 440th Infantry Regiment was detached from the division to form Grenadier Regiment Rhodes. In January 1942, the 164th was transferred to Crete and received the 125th Infantry Regiment, which had previously been a frontier unit stationed at Saarbruecken. It had seen action during the French campaign. The division, meanwhile, was redesignated Fortress Division Crete on January 10, 1942.

In the summer of 1942, the division was transferred to North Africa and was renamed 164th Light Afrika on August 15. Although understrength (each of its regiments had only two battalions, including the artillery regiment), it fought extremely well (mainly against the Australians) in the defensive actions around El Alamein from July through early November 1942. The 382nd Infantry Regiment—without vehicles—arrived at the front on July 10, 1942, just in time to save the Headquarters of Panzer Army Afrika from being captured by the Allies. (It had been threatened because the Italian Sabratha Division collapsed, and Allied infantrymen were within 3,000 yards of the HQ when the 382nd arrived.) Such incidents were fairly common on the North African Front in 1942. Finally crushed, the remnants of the 164th Light retreated a thousand miles across Egypt and Libya into Tunisia, where they were finally destroyed when Army Group Afrika collapsed in May 1943. The 164th was the last German formation to surrender.

Commanders of the 164th Infantry/Light Afrika Division included Colonel/Major General Konrad Haase (December 1, 1939), Major General/Lieutenant General Josef Folttmann (January 10, 1940), Colonel/Major General Karl-Hans Lungershausen (August 10, 1942), Colonel Siegfried Westphal (December 1, 1942), Lungershausen (December 29, 1942)

Colonel/Major General Baron Kurt von Liebenstein (January 15, 1943), Colonel Becker (January 16, 1943), Major General Fritz Krause (February 17, 1943), and Liebenstein (returned to duty, March 13, 1943).

Notes and Sources: Haase was promoted to major general on January 1, 1940. Folttmann was promoted to lieutenant general on February 1, 1941. Lungershausen was advanced to the rank of major general on October 1, 1942. Liebenstein was injured in an automobile accident on January 16, 1943, and was promoted to major general while in the hospital on March 1, 1943. He surrendered the division on May 12, 1943.

Keilig: 212; Lexikon; Samuel W. Mitcham, Jr., *Rommel's Desert Commanders* (2007); Nafziger 2000: 294; I. S. O. Playfair, *The Mediterranean and Middle East*, Volume III, *British Fortunes Reach Their Lowest Ebb* (1960): 246 (hereafter cited as "Playfair"); Erwin Rommel, *The Rommel Papers* (B.H. Liddell Hart, ed.) (1953): 313 (hereafter cited as "Rommel *Papers*"): 313; Tessin, Vol. 7: 138–41; OB 45: 318.

999TH LIGHT AFRIKA DIVISION

Composition: 961st Afrika Rifle Regiment, 962nd Afrika Rifle Regiment, 963rd Afrika Rifle Regiment, 999th Artillery Regiment, 999th Reconnaissance Battalion, 999th Tank Destroyer Company, 999th Engineer Battalion, 999th Signal Battalion, 999th Divisional Supply Troops

Home Station: Heuberg and Baden, Wehrkreis V

This penal unit was formed in Troop Maneuver Area Heuberg on October 6, 1942, as Afrika Brigade 999. It consisted of both political prisoners and real criminals pressed into the military service of the Third Reich, at a ratio of about thirty-five to sixty-five. Upgraded to divisional status on February 2, 1943, it was also known as the 999th Infantry Division (Penal). Its 961st and 962nd Rifle Regiments and many of its divisional support troops were sent to Tunisia in March 1943 and were captured there when Army Group Afrika surrendered in May. The 963rd Infantry Regiment and some of the support units had not yet been sent from staging areas in Italy to Tunisia when the end came, so they were diverted to Greece and either became fortress units or were absorbed into Assault Division Rhodes. The division's replacement headquarters at Heuberg and Baden continued to train criminal and political prisoners for military service, but the division per se was disbanded. In its brief combat career, the 999th fought well against the French, British, and Americans.

Notes and Sources: The telephone exchange at Scotland Yard in London was 999; this is reportedly why the Germans adopted 999 as the number for their penal units. Major General Kurt Thomas, the former commandant of Führer Headquarters, commanded the 999th in Africa. He flew out of the Tunisian pocket as it collapsed on May 5, 1943, but was shot down over the Mediterranean Sea by Allied fighters and was killed. He had been promoted to major general on April 1, 1943, and was posthumously promoted to lieutenant general on September 1, 1943.

Keilig: 345; OB 45: 284. Also see Paul Carell, *Foxes*, for a detailed description of the last battles in North Africa, in which the 999th was involved.

JÄGER DIVISION ALPS (ALPEN)

Composition: 1st Jäger Regiment "Alps," 2nd Jäger Regiment "Alps," 3rd (germ.) Artillery Battalion "Alps," Engineer Company Alps

Home Station: Wehrkreis VII and XVIII

This unit was formed as a thirty-fourth-wave shadow division on March 25, 1945, with men from Bavaria and Austria. Sent to the 1st Army on the Western Front, the division was absorbed by the 2nd Mountain and 212th Infantry Divisions on April 12.

Sources: Lexikon; Nafziger 2000: 382; Tessin, Vol. 12: 15–16.

CHAPTER 4

The Mountain Divisions

1ST MOUNTAIN DIVISION

Composition: 98th Mountain Infantry Regiment, 99th Mountain Infantry Regiment, 79th Mountain Artillery Regiment, 54th Mountain Infantry Battalion, 1st High Mountain Jäger Battalion, 2nd High Mountain Jäger Battalion, 54th Motorcycle Battalion, 54th Bicycle Battalion, 54th Tank Destroyer Battalion, 54th Mountain Engineer Battalion, 54th Mountain Signal Battalion, 54th Mountain Divisional Supply Troops. The 54th Mountain Reconnaissance Battalion was added on April 1, 1943 and the 54th Field Replacement Battalion was added on November 20, 1943.

Home Station: Garmisch-Partenkirchen, Wehrkreis VII

This unit, consisting mainly of Bavarians with some Austrians intermixed, was formed on April 9, 1938. Initially, it was considerably larger than most German divisions in the World War II era. Its third regiment, the 100th Mountain Infantry, was reassigned to the 5th Mountain Division in 1940. Nicknamed "the Edelweiss division" (*Edelweissdivision*), it took part in the Polish campaign as part of the 14th Army and saw action in the Carpathians, where it distinguished itself by capturing the Dukla Pass. It was transferred to the Eifel (the German Ardennes) in October 1939, and played a relatively minor role in the Western campaign of 1940. It fought on the Franco-Belgian border in May 1940, and cross the Maas on May 15. It lost 18 officers and 431 men killed or wounded during these operations. It remained in France (around Arras) and was earmarked for Operation "Sea Lion," the invasion of Britain. Later it was scheduled to capture Gibraltar, but neither operation was ever launched.

259

In the spring of 1941, it took part in the defeat of Yugoslavia, where resistance collapsed so quickly that the 1st Mountain only lost six men killed. In June, it experienced much
heavier fighting in Crete, where it suffered 1,100 casualties but
played a major role in the defeat of the British, New Zealand
and Australian forces. In June 1941, the division crossed into
Russia as part of Army Group South, and on July 15-16 broke
through the Stalin Line. During this battle, the division lost 31
men killed and 74 wounded, but killed several hundred Russians and captured 281 more. It also captured 100 machine
guns, eight guns, a tank and three airplanes. Two days later, it
was fighting on the Bug, where it held a twenty-seven-mile front
with only two infantry regiments. As the Soviet forces tried to
escape from Vinniza, the division was able to take 10,000 prisoners, but was unable to block the escape of 30,000 more.

Later, the 1st Mountain took part in the Battle of the Uman
Pocket (where it suffered 759 casualties), and by the end of the
month, the division's strength had dropped from 17,801 men
to 13,636. It had also lost about 500 of its 6,487 horses. The division nevertheless launched a major assault across the Dnieper
River at Berislav, where it built a bridge 431 meters long. It took
part in the capture of Kiev and the subsequent liquidation of
the Kiev Pocket, then pushed south to help capture Stalino
(now Donetsk, Ukraine) in September, and took part in the
encirclement of Mogila Tokmak (also known as the Cherni-
govka Pocket and the Battle of the Sea of Avoz) from October 5
to 10. During this battle, the Red Army lost 100,000 men captured and 212 tanks and 672 guns captured or destroyed. From
September 6 to October 10, 1941, however, the 1st Mountain
Division had lost 573 men killed and 1,975 wounded. Even
more seriously, 75 percent of its vehicles had broken down or
were in need of major overhauls. The division nevertheless took
part in the drive on and retreat from Rostov and helped defend
the Mius River Line against Stalin's winter offensive of 1941–42.

By May 1942, it was with the III Panzer Corps and fought in
the Battle of Kharkov and in the eastern Donetz. Later, it was
at the spearhead of General von Kleist's Caucasus campaign,

Maj. Gen. Ferdinand Schörner, commander of the 6th Mountain Division, has a snack in Greece, 1941. One of Hitler's most brutal generals, Schörner distinguished himself as a defensive commander on the Eastern Front. He was promoted to field marshal in 1945. NATIONAL ARCHIVES

but was checked in the high mountains. After the disaster of Stalingrad, Kleist's Army Group A was forced to retreat into the Kuban, and the 1st Mountain Division was involved in the first of a long series of withdrawals and rear-guard actions on the road back to Germany. In April 1943, the division was withdrawn from the front and sent to Serbia and northern Greece, where it was rebuilt and engaged in anti-partisan operations. Later it was reported on the Greco-Albanian frontier, and subsequently in western Serbia, Bosnia, Croatia and Montenegro. The division was still fighting south of Belgrade in October 1944. Following the loss of this city, it fought in Hungary (November 1944–March 1945) and in the Austrian Alps. It was redesignated 1st Volks Mountain Division on March 12, 1945, but with no change to its table of organization. The 1st Mountain Division ended the war as part of Army Group South, fighting the Russians in central Styria. It ended up in Soviet captivity in May 1945.

Divisional commanders of the 1st Mountain included Major General/Lieutenant General Ludwig Kübler (March 1, 1938), Colonel/Major General/Lieutenant General Hubert Lang (October 26, 1940), Major General/Lieutenant General Robert Martinek (January 1, 1942), Colonel/Major General/Lieutenant General Ritter Walter Stettner von Grabenhofen (December 17, 1942), Lieutenant General August Wittmann (October 19, 1944), Lieutenant General Josef Kübler (December 27, 1944), and Wittmann (returned March 17, 1945).

Note and Sources: Ludwig Kübler, was promoted to lieutenant general on December 1, 1939. Martinek was promoted to lieutenant general on December 1, 1941. Lanz was promoted to major general on November 1, 1940, and to lieutenant general on December 1, 1942. Stettner was promoted to major general on February 1, 1943, and to lieutenant general on November 1, 1943. He was killed in action near Belgrade on October 18, 1944. Josef Kübler was the brother of Ludwig. Both were executed by the Yugoslavs in February 1947.

Carell 1966: 121, 293, 495, 560; Peter Denniston, "Jaeger Kopold," *www.gebirgsjaeger.4mg.com* (1997), accessed 2006; Keilig: 190, 333; Kennedy: 74 and Map 7; Hubert Lanz, *Gebirgsjäger: Die 1. Gebirgsdivision, 1935–1945* (1954); Manstein: 33; Plocher 1943: 327; Tessin, Vol.

2: 23–24; OB 42: 70; OB 43: 210; OB 44: 292; OB 45: 318, 583; Ziemke 1966: 376. For the story of the German mountain troops in World War II, as well as excellent detailed descriptions of some of their battles, see James Lucas, *Alpine Elite: German Mountain Troops in World War II* (1980) (hereafter cited as "Lucas").

2ND MOUNTAIN DIVISION

Composition: 136th Mountain Infantry Regiment, 137th Mountain Infantry Regiment, 111th Mountain Artillery Regiment, 67th Bicycle Battalion, 11th (later 111th) Reconnaissance Battalion, 47th Mountain Anti-Tank Battalion, 82nd Mountain Engineer Battalion, 67th Mountain Signal Battalion, 67th Mountain Divisional Supply Troops

Home Station: Innsbruck, Wehrkreis XVIII

Consisting primarily of Tyrolean Austrians, the 2nd Mountain Division was the former 6th Division of the Austrian Army. It became the 2nd Mountain Division on April 1, 1938, after the Anschluss made Austria a part of the Third Reich. It was mobilized on August 26, 1939. Initially it was one of the best combat units in the German Army. It fought in Poland in 1939 as part of Army Group South, and the next year it invaded Norway with the XXI Combat Group (later HQ, Army of Norway). From May 5 to June 13, it traveled across a roadless wilderness, from Trondheim to Narvik, to rescue the 3rd Mountain Division, then besieged by a British corps in northern Norway. It remained in Lapland and, in June 1941, advanced on Murmansk with Mountain Corps Norway, but was stopped short by Russian counterattacks and the impossible terrain.

In 1942, the 2nd Mountain campaigned in Lapland, as part of XIX Mountain Corps, and continued to fight on the Arctic sector of the Eastern Front until Finland concluded a separate peace with Russia in autumn 1944. On the retreat back to Norway, the 2nd Mountain was mauled and badly shaken by the Russian winter offensive of 1944–45. After the withdrawal from northern Finland, the division was returned to the European mainland, where its two regiments were rebuilt from personnel taken from supply and other non-combat units. It joined the 1st Army, Army Group G, on the Western Front and, in February 1945, was back in action in the Battle of the Saar-Moselle Triangle; however, the division's best soldiers were dead or captured, and its former elitism gone. The remnants of the 2nd Mountain Division ended the war in Württemberg, southern Germany and in Tyrol, and surrendered to the Western Allies.

The commanders of the 2nd Mountain included Major General/Lieutenant General Valentin Feurstein (March 1, 1938), Major General Ernst Schlemmer (March 4, 1941), Colonel/Major General/Lieutenant General Ritter Georg von Hengl (March 2, 1942), Colonel/Major General/Lieutenant General Hans Degan (November 1, 1943), Colonel Hans Roschmann (February 6, 1945), and Lieutenant General Willibald Utz (February 9, 1945).

Note and Sources: The 111th Field Replacement Battalion was replaced by the 67th Bicycle Battalion (later named the 67th Reconnaissance Battalion) in the fall of 1940. Valentin Feurstein, who had served in the Austro-Hungarian and Austrian armies since 1906, was promoted to lieutenant general on June 1, 1939. Hengl was promoted to major general on April 1, 1942, and to lieutenant general on January 1, 1943. Hans Degen was promoted to major general on January 1, 1944, and to lieutenant general on August 1, 1944. He was severely wounded on February 6, 1945, and did not recover until after the end of the war.

Hartmann: 47, 49; Keilig: 66, 89, 135; Kennedy: 74; Matthias Kräutler and Karl Springenschmid, *Schicksal und Weg der 2. Gebirgs-Division* (n.d.); Lucas: 206, 241–43, 246–47; MacDonald 1973: 153; Nafziger 2000: 476–77; Tessin, Vol. 2: 101–2; Ziemke 1959: 95–97, 326-27; Ziemke 1966: 304, 312; OB 42: 70; OB 43: 210.

3RD MOUNTAIN DIVISION

Composition: 138th Mountain Infantry Regiment, 139th Mountain Infantry Regiment, 112th Mountain Artillery Regiment, 68th Bicycle Battalion, 12th (later 112th) Reconnaissance Battalion, 48th Anti-Tank (later 95th Tank Destroyer) Battalion, 83rd Mountain Engineer Battalion, 68th Mountain Signal Battalion, 68th Mountain Field Replacement Battalion, 68th Mountain Divisional Supply Troops

Home Station: Graz, later Leoben, Wehrkreis XVIII

This unit was formed on April 1, 1938, from the 5th and 7th Divisions of the Austrian Army after that country was annexed by Germany on March 11–12, 1938. It was almost constantly engaged throughout World War II, except for a period of occupation duty in Norway in 1940–41. It first saw action in the invasion of Poland, where it formed part of the 14th Army, Army Group South. The next year, 1940, the division performed its greatest feat of arms when its 138th Mountain Infantry Regiment took Trondheim and the rest of the division seized Narvik, the strategically vital port in northern Norway. A British Expeditionary Force, hoping to deprive Hitler of his strategic iron ore, which had to be shipped to Germany via Narvik, counterattacked the isolated division and at one point succeeded in retaking the city in heavy fighting. The battle lasted from April 9 until mid-June, but was finally won by the mountaineers, but not before the divisional commander seriously discussed marching his troops into internment in Sweden.

From Narvik, the division marched into northern Finland, took part in the invasion of Russia in June 1941, and advanced on Murmansk, the strategic Soviet port on the Arctic Ocean. Finally repulsed by fierce Soviet counterattacks and virtually impassable terrain, the 3rd Mountain was engaged in prolonged skirmishing and patrolling north of the Arctic Circle for more than a year. Sent to Army Group North in August 1942, the division fought at Reval and in the siege of Leningrad. In November 1942, it was sent to the southern sector of the Eastern Front, which was threatening to collapse following the disaster on the Volga. It took part in the effort to relieve Stalingrad but failed. Later, the 3rd Mountain suffered heavy casualties on the southern sector of the Eastern Front in 1943 and 1944, fighting in the Donetz, on the Mius, at Melitopol and in the Nikopol Bridgehead. In August 1944, it was part of the Romanian debacle, where it was attacked by Russians in the front and by Romanians from behind. After suffering heavy casualties, the remnants of the division escaped to the eastern Carpathians. Later the 3rd Mountain Division fought in Hungary and Slovakia, and was still fighting the Soviets in Upper Silesia when the war ended. Along with most of the 1st Panzer Army, it surrendered to the Red Army at Deutsch-Brod, in the present day Czech Republic, in May 1945.

Its commanders included Major General/Lieutenant General Eduard Dietl (April 1938), Major General Julius Ringel (June 14, 1940), Major General/Lieutenant General Hans Kreysing (October 23, 1940), Colonel Hans Mönch (August 8, 1942), Major General Egbert Picker (August 10, 1942), Colonel Siegfried Raps (August 26, 1943), Picker (returned September 10, 1943), Major General/Lieutenant General August Wittmann (October 1, 1943), Colonel Hans Kreppel (May 28, 1944) and Major General/Lieutenant General Paul Klatt (July 3, 1944).

Note and Sources: Dietl, Kreysing, Wittmann and Klatt were promoted to lieutenant general on April 1, 1940, July 1, 1942, April 1, 1944, and December 1, 1944, respectively. Klatt was a Soviet POW until 1955.

Carell 1966: 450-51; Carell 1971: 123; Keilig: 70, 187, 278, 374; Kennedy: 74 and Map 7; Paul Klatt, *Die 3. Gebirgs-Division* (1958); Kursietis: 82-83; Lucas: 207, 242; Manstein: 319, 392; Seaton; 476; Tessin, Vol. 2: 169–70; RA: 234; OB 42: 70; OB 43: 210; Ziemke 1959: 33, 234, 326.

4TH MOUNTAIN DIVISION

Composition: 13th Mountain Infantry Regiment, 91st Mountain Infantry Regiment, 94th Mountain Artillery Regiment, 94th Reconnaissance Battalion, 94th Tank Destroyer Company, 94th Mountain Engineer Company, 94th Mountain Signal Battalion, 94th Divisional Supply Troops

Home Station: Garmisch, Wehrkreis VII

The fourth German mountain division was formed in Austria in June 1940. It included the 142nd and 143rd Mountain Regiments, the 94th Mountain Artillery Battalion, the 94th Tank Destroyer Company, the 94th Mountain Engineer Company and assorted other units. It was dissolved that summer, after the fall of France.

Col. Gen. Eduard Dietl, commander of the 20th Mountain Army, gives orders to General of Mountain Troops Franz Böhme on the Eastern Front. Dietl first distinguished himself as commander of the 3rd Mountain Division at Narvik during the invasion of Norway, prior to which he had commanded the 30th and 32nd Infantry Divisions. NATIONAL ARCHIVES

The second 4th Mountain Division was formed in the Heu-berg Troop Maneuver Area on October 23, 1940. Its 13th Moun-tain Regiment was provided by the 25th Infantry Division, and its 91st Mountain Regiment was supplied by the 27th Infantry Divi-sion. Each of these divisions also provided an artillery battalion. Its headquarters was the former Staff, 412th Special Purposes Division (*Div Stab z.b.V. 412*), which now ceased to exist. The divi-sion was completely formed by the beginning of 1941. The 4th Mountain first saw action in the Balkans campaign of 1941, where it fought in Yugoslavia. Later that year, it invaded Russia as part of Army Group South and suffered heavy casualties in the initial advances toward the Volga, fighting at Vinniza, Uman, the Dnieper crossings and the drive to the Mius. It suffered 1,778 casualties in the Battle of the Uman Pocket alone.

The 4th Mountain spent much of the winter of 1941–42 fighting the Soviets on the Kerch peninsula of the Crimea, east of Sevastopol. That summer, the division took part in the cap-ture of Rostov and in the Caucasus campaign. Following the retreat from the Caucasus, it was engaged in heavy fighting at Novorossiysk, where the Germans contained the Russian am-phibious landings on the Kuban. By early 1944, the 4th Moun-tain had been shifted northward and fought in the battles of the Dnieper Bend, where Field Marshal von Manstein commended it for its part in smashing a Soviet tank army. The 4th Mountain Division continued to fight on the Russian Front as the German forces retreated across southern Russia, Romania, Hungary, Slo-vakia and Upper Silesia. The division ended the war at battle group strength on the central sector of the Eastern Front and surrendered to the Russians at Deutsch-Brod in May 1945.

Its commanders included Colonel/Major General Karl Eglseer (October 23, 1940), Colonel Karl Wintergerst (October 1, 1941), Eglseer (returned November 1941), Colonel/ Major General/Lieutenant General Hermann Kress (October 21, 1942), Major General/Lieutenant General Julius Braun (August 13, 1943), Colonel Karl Jank (June 7, 1944), Lieutenant General Friedrich Breith (July 1, 1944), Colonel Robert Bader (February 23, 1945), and Breith (returned April 6, 1945).

Note and Sources: Karl Eglseer was promoted to major general on April 1, 1941. Hermann Kress was promoted to major general on September 1, 1942, and to lieutenant general on May 1, 1943. He was killed in action at Novorossisk on August 10, 1943. Braun was promoted to lieutenant general on April 1, 1944.

Julius Braun, *Enzian und Edelweiss: Die 4. Gebirgs-Division, 1940–1945* (1955); Carell 1971: 187; Hartmann: 49; Keilig: 78; Kursietis: 84; Lexikon; Tessin, Vol. 2: Lucas: 207, 242; Manstein: 509; Nafziger 2000: 479–81; Schmidt et al., Vol. I: 277; Tessin, Vol. 2: 237–39; OB 42: 71; OB 43: 211.

5TH MOUNTAIN DIVISION

Composition: 85th Mountain Infantry Regiment, 100th Mountain Infantry Regiment, 95th Mountain Artillery Regiment, 95th Mountain Reconnaissance Battalion, 95th Mountain Tank Destroyer Battalion, 95th Mountain Engineer Battalion, 95th Mountain Signal Battalion, 95th Mountain Field Replacement Battalion, 95th Mountain Divisional Supply Troops

Home Station: Salzburg, Wehrkreis XVIII

The 5th Mountain Division was formed in the Salzburg-Tyrol area under Major General Julius "Papa" Ringel in the autumn of 1940, from the 100th Mountain Infantry Regiment of the 1st Mountain Division and elements of the 10th Infantry Division. Its personnel were mainly Bavarians, with some Austrians added. After a training period in the Alps, it first saw action in the Balkans campaign of 1941, where it helped crack the Metaxas Line and took part in the subsequent sweep through Greece. A few weeks later, it was part of General Student's mixed paratrooper mountaineer task force, which defeated the British army on Crete. The 5th Mountain's timely relief of the paratroopers late on the second day of the Battle of Maleme was a turning point of the campaign. The division remained on the island until October, when it was sent back to Bavaria and Austria.

In early 1942, the 5th Mountain was sent to Army Group North and from January to March 1942, it helped check Russian counteroffensives between Lake Ladoga and Novgorod.

Later it took part in the siege of Leningrad and fought in the Volchov sector (near Leningrad) from April 1942 to November 1943. In December, the division was withdrawn from the Eastern Front and sent to Italy, where it relieved the 305th Infantry Division just prior to the First Battle of Cassino in January 1944. Later that month it was fighting against the Allied landing forces in the vicinity of Anzio. The 5th Mountain spent the rest of the war in Italy, and participated in the battles of the Gustav and Gothic Lines (where it distinguished itself), as well as Army Group C's retreat up the peninsula. It surrendered to the Americans near Turin in the western Alps on April 29, 1945.

Commanders of the 5th Mountain Division included Ringel (assumed command October 1940), Colonel/Major General/ Lieutenant General Max Schrank (February 10, 1944), and Colonel/Major General Hans Steets (February 1, 1945).

Note and Sources: Ringel was promoted to lieutenant general on December 1, 1942. Schrank was promoted to major general on May 1, 1944, and to lieutenant general on November 1, 1944. Steets became a major general on April 20, 1945.

Blumenson 1969: 376; Carell 1966: 421; Carell 1971: 242; Fisher: 18, 302; Hartmann: 49, 50; Keilig: 330; Lucas: 208, 245–46; Julius Ringel, *Hurra die Gams: Ein Gedenkbuch für die Soldaten der 5. Gebirgsdivision* (n.d.); Salisbury: 539; Tessin, Vol. 2: 290–91; OB 42: 71; OB 43: 211; Ziemke 1959: 209, 218.

6TH MOUNTAIN DIVISION

Composition: 141st Mountain Infantry Regiment, 143rd Mountain Infantry Regiment, 118th Mountain Artillery Regiment, 1057th (later 112th) Reconnaissance Battalion, 47th Tank Destroyer Battalion, 91st Mountain Engineer Battalion, 96th Mountain Signal Battalion, 91st Field Replacement Battalion, 91st Mountain Divisional Supply Troops

Home Station: Klagenfurt, Wehrkreis XVIII

The 6th Mountain was formed on June 1, 1940, in the Heuberg Troop Maneuver Area, and was sent to France a month

Soldiers of the 1st Mountain Division advance against the British in Crete, May 1941. The 1st Mountain was one of the best divisions to fight in World War II and went on to spend four years on the Eastern Front. NATIONAL ARCHIVES

later. It was earmarked to take part in the invasion of Great Britain in 1940, but this never happened. The 6th Mountain was engaged in occupation duties in France and Poland in 1940 and early 1941, before being transferred to southeastern Europe. During the Balkans campaign, it took part in the drive on Salonika and captured Athens in coordination with the 2nd Panzer Division. It was also lightly engaged in the invasion of Crete. In October 1941, it was transferred to Norway and then to northern Finland, where it formed the northern wing of Mountain Corps Norway on the drive for Murmansk. The 6th Mountain remained in action on the Arctic (Lapland) sector of the Eastern Front until Finland renounced its alliance with Germany in the fall of 1944. It was with the 20th Mountain Army during the retreat across Lapland and was still in Norway when the war ended. It surrendered to the British at Lyngen-fjord in May 1945.

Commanders of the 6th Mountain Division included Colo-nel/Major General Ferdinand Schörner (assumed command May 31, 1940), Major General/Lieutenant General Christian Philipp (January 17, 1942), Major General/Lieutenant General Max Pemsel (August 28, 1944), and Colonel Josef Remold (April 1945).

Note and Sources: The 6th Mountain Division was formed from cadres from the 139th Mountain Infantry Regiment, 3rd Mountain Division. Artillery cadres were provided by the 113th Artillery Regiment, I/752nd Artillery Regiment, and III/112th Artillery Regiment. Ferdinand Schörner was promoted to major general on August 1, 1940. Philipp was promoted to lieutenant general on January 1, 1943. Max Pemsel was promoted to lieutenant general on November 9, 1944.

Brett-Smith: 202–5; Carell 1966: 456–57, 459–60; Keilig: 256; Lucas: 208–9; Mellenthin 1977: 176; Nafziger 2000: 486–87; Karl Ruef, *Gebirgsjaeger zwischen Kreta und Murmansk: Die 6. Gebirgs-Division im Ein-satz* (n.d.); Ryan 1966: 375–76; Tessin, Vol. 3: 15–16; RA: 234; OB 42: 71; OB 43: 211–12; Ziemke 1959: Map 22.

7TH MOUNTAIN DIVISION

Composition: 206th Mountain Infantry Regiment, 218th Mountain Infantry Regiment, 82nd Mountain Artillery Regiment, 99th Reconnaissance Battalion, 99th Tank Destroyer Battalion, 99th Mountain Engineer Battalion, 99th Mountain Signal Battalion, 99th Divisional Supply Troops. The 54th Mountain Field Replacement Battalion and the 54th Ski Battalion were added later.

Home Station: Fuerth, Wehrkreis XIII; later Velder, Wehrkreis XVIII

Originally formed as the 99th Jäger Division on November 15, 1940, this division initially included the 206th and 218th Jäger Regiments. After seeing action at Zhitomir and Kiev on the Russian Front, it was reformed as a mountain division in the Grafenwoehr Troop Maneuver Area on November 15, 1941. In the spring of 1942, it was sent to Finland and remained there until the Finns renounced their military alliance with the Nazis in the fall of 1944. In the subsequent retreat from Lapland the 7th Mountain formed part of the XVIII Mountain Corps, 20th Mountain Army. After arriving in Norway, the High Command ordered the division to return to Europe; however, the war ended before it could embark. The division surrendered to the British at Trondheim in May 1945.

The commanders of the 99th Jäger/7th Mountain Division included Major General/Lieutenant General Kurt von der Chevallerie (December 10, 1940), Lieutenant General Rudolf Konrad (December 1, 1941), Major General Wilhelm Weiss (December 19, 1941), Lieutenant General Robert Martinek (January 1, 1942), Colonel/Major General/Lieutenant General August Krakau (May 1, 1942), Martinek (returned July 22, 1942), and Krakau (September 10, 1942–end).

Note and Sources: The division's replacement battalion was converted into a ski unit in September 1943, and was lost to the division. Chevallerie was promoted to lieutenant general on January 1, 1941. Krakau was promoted to major general on August 1, 1942, and to lieutenant general on June 1, 1943.

Keilig: 184; Lucas: 209; Nafziger 2000: 486–88; Tessin, Vol. 6: 157; RA: 204; OB 42: 71;OB 43: 212; Ziemke 1959: 209, 293, 312; Ziemke 1966: 401.

8TH MOUNTAIN DIVISION

Composition (1945): 296th Mountain Infantry Regiment, 297th Mountain Infantry Regiment, 1057th Mountain Artillery Regiment, 1057th Bicycle Battalion, 1057th Tank Destroyer Battalion, 1057th Engineer Battalion, 1057th Signal Battalion, 1057th Field Replacement Battalion, 1057th Mountain Divisional Supply Troops

Home Station: Mittenwald, Wehrkreis VII

The first 8th Mountain Division was formed around the 139th Mountain Infantry Regiment in Lapland in March 1944. It was soon redesignated Division Group Kräutler (after its commander, Colonel Mathias Kräutler) and then Division z.b.V. 140 on September 7, 1944. It included the 139th Mountain Infantry Regiment, the 3rd Jäger Battalion, the 931st Artillery Regiment Staff z.b.V., plus an engineer company and a signal company. It fought in northern Finland and in the retreat to Norway.

The second 8th Mountain Division began its existence in Munich as the VII Replacement Troop Command (*Kommandeur der Ersatztruppen VII*) upon mobilization on August 26, 1939. It became Division 157 on November 9, 1939, and on December 12 was designated the 157th Replacement Division. By the spring of 1940, it included the 7th and 157th Infantry Replacement Regiments, the 1st Mountain Infantry Replacement Regiment, the 7th Artillery Replacement Regiment, the 7th Forward Observer Replacement Battalion, the 7th Tank Destroyer Replacement Battalion, the 7th Engineer Replacement Battalion, the 7th and 27th Motorized Replacement Battalions, the 7th and 27th Driver Replacement Battalions, and the 7th Construction Engineer Replacement Battalion. The unit became the 157th Reserve Division on October 1, 1942. At that time, it included the 7th and 157th Reserve Grenadier Regiments, the 1st Reserve Mountain Infantry Regiment, the 7th Reserve Artillery Regiment and the 7th Reserve Engineer Battalion.

Reformed in Mittenwald, Bavaria, it was sent to Westphalia and then to Besancon, France, but was sent to Grenoble near the Italian border after Mussolini was overthrown. It was transferred to Army Detachment von Zangen (later the Ligurian Army) to fight partisans in northern Italy in 1944. The division never reached full strength. On September 1, 1944, it was redesignated 157th Reserve Mountain Division. It became the 8th Mountain Division in February 1945. At the same time, it was transferred from the rear area to the front line, fought against the U.S. Army in the Rovereto-Trient sector, and saw action in the Po River Valley in the last campaign in Italy. Although it reported a strength of only 3,000 men in 1945, the 8th Mountain was the largest combat unit in the German 10th Army at that time—an indication of the operational bankruptcy the Germans had reached in Italy by the spring of 1945. The 8th Mountain surrendered to the Americans in northern Italy in late April 1945.

Commanders of the 8th Mountain Division in its various incarnations included Lieutenant General Karl Graf (August 26, 1939), Lieutenant General Hans Schönhärl (December 17, 1941), Graf (second tour began January 20, 1942), Major General/Lieutenant General Karl Pflaum (September 20, 1942), and Major General/Lieutenant General Paul Schricker (September 1, 1944).

Note and Sources: Pflaum was promoted to lieutenant general on October 1, 1943. Schricker became a lieutenant general on March 16, 1945. Fisher: 442; Roland Kaltenegger, *Kampf der Gebirgsjäger um die Westalpen und den Semmering: Die Kriegschroniken der 8. und 9. Gebirgs-Division ("Kampfgruppe Semmering")* (1987); Keilig: 183, 312; Tessin, Vol. 3: 97–98; RA: 234; OB 43: 212; OB 45: 322.

9TH MOUNTAIN DIVISION

Composition (Northern Group): 139th Mountain Infantry Regiment, 3rd Jäger Battalion, 6th Jäger Battalion, 931st Artillery Regiment Staff z.b.V. (controlling I/112th Mountain Artillery Regiment and II/82nd Mountain Artillery Regiment), 124th Mountain Artillery Battalion, 424th Light Assault Gun Battalion, 140th Mountain Engineer Battalion, 140th Mountain Signal Battalion, 140th Divisional Supply Troops

Composition (Eastern Group): See below.

Home Stations: Norway and Dachstein, Wehrkreis XVII

In the last confusing days of the war, the German High Command accidentally gave the number "9" to two different mountain divisions. The northernmost 9th Mountain Division (which was the former 140th Special Purposes Division) consisted of a battle group in Norway that was led by Major General Mathias Kräutler. It was designated 9th Mountain Division on May 6, 1945, and surrendered to the British a few days later.

The other 9th Mountain Division (Ost) was made up of Combat Group Semmering. This unit consisted of forces guarding the Semmering Pass in eastern Austria and included men from the Mountain Artillery School at Dachstein, Mountain Division Steiermark (a shadow division), the SS Mountain Replacement Battalion at Leoben, police and RAD units, and ground crews from the Boelcke fighter wing of the Luftwaffe. It included the Division Staff (the former Mountain Artillery School Staff), the 154th and 155th Mountain Jäger (infantry) Regiments, the 56th Mountain Reconnaissance Battalion (formerly the 13th SS Mountain Jäger Replacement Battalion), the 48th Tank Destroyer Company (formerly the 48th Tank Destroyer Replacement Battalion), the 56th Mountain Artillery Regiment (from the mountain artillery school) and a mountain engineer company. It fought against the Russians from April 12, 1945, but did not receive the designation 9th Mountain Division until May 1945, less a week before the conflict ended. Its was also known as Kampfgruppe Raithel.

The commander of 9th Mountain Division (North) was Major General Mathias Kräutler. The commander of 9th Mountain Division (East) was Colonel Heribert Raithel.

Sources: Keilig: 183; Lucas: 209-10; Lexikon; Tessin, Vol. 3: 133; Schmitz et al., Vol. 2: 156–57.

157TH RESERVE MOUNTAIN DIVISION

See 8th Mountain Division earlier in this chapter.

Soldiers of the 1st Mountain Division on the march in Crete, pursuing the defeated British, Australian, New Zealand, and Greek forces, May 1941. NATIONAL ARCHIVES

188TH RESERVE MOUNTAIN (LATER MOUNTAIN) DIVISION

Composition (1943): 136th Reserve Mountain Regiment, 137th Reserve Mountain Regiment, 138th Reserve Mountain Regiment, 139th Reserve Mountain Regiment, 499th Reserve Grenadier Battalion, 112th Reserve Mountain Artillery Regiment, 48th Tank Destroyer Battalion, 83rd Reserve Mountain Engineer Battalion, 1088th Signal Company, 1088th Divisional Supply Troops

Home Station: Salzburg, Wehrkreis XVIII

As most of the other reserve divisions, the 188th was created as a replacement division on November 5, 1939. It spent the next three years training and supplying replacement personnel for divisions associated with the XVIII Military District in northern Austria. Most of its subordinate elements were mountain units. It became the 188th Reserve Mountain Division on October 8, 1943, and the 188th Mountain Division on March 1, 1944. It now included the 901st, 902nd, 903rd, and 904th Mountain Jäger Regiment (the former 136th, 137th, 138th and 139th Reserve Mountain Regiments, respectively), the 1088th Mountain Artillery Regiment, the 1088th Mountain Engineer Battalion, the 1088th Signal Company and the 1088th Divisional Supply Troops. Meanwhile, in early 1943, the division was stationed at Marburg in Slovenia. In the fall of 1943, it was sent to the Merano area of northern Italy with its mountain training regiments. The 188th was subordinate to Army Group C's Army Detachment von Zangen, a collection of second- and third-rate divisions in northern Italy. In early 1944, it was in the Istrian peninsula area, conducting anti-guerrilla operations in the army group's communications zone. In late 1944, it was sent to the Balkans and took part in the last campaign on the southern sector of the Eastern Front as a regular combat division. It surrendered to the Yugoslavs in May 1945.

Its commander was Major General/Lieutenant General Wilhelm von Hösslin (December 1, 1939–end). It ended the war on the southern sector of the Eastern Front.

Note and Sources: Major General Maximilian Jais served as acting commander of the division from April 1 to 8, 1943. Lieutenant General Ernst Schlemmer commanded it from April 8 to May 15, 1943. Hösslin commanded it for the rest of its existence. He was promoted to Lieutenant General on February 1, 1941. General von Hoesslin was hanged by the Yugoslavian Communists in Belgrade on New Year's Eve, 1947. Most of his men were murdered after they surrendered.

Keilig: 146; *Kriegstagebuch des OKW*, Volume IV: 1903; Kursietis: 154; Tessin, Vol. 7: 240–41; RA: 6; OB 43: 153; OB 45: 197.

MOUNTAIN DIVISION STEIERMARK

Composition: 154th Mountain Jäger Regiment, 155th Mountain Jäger Regiment, 56th Mountain Artillery Regiment, 13th SS Mountain Infantry Training and Replacement Battalion (redesignated 56th Mountain Reconnaissance Battalion), 851st Landesschuetzen Battalion, a Tank Destroyer company from 48th Tank Destroyer Replacement Battalion

This division was formed around Kampfgruppe Raithel. It was activated on April 25, 1945. It included the men from Mountain Infantry NCO School at Admont, the Army NCO School for Mountain Troops at Woergl, Mountain NCO (Unterführer) School Mittenwald, the Mountain Artillery School at Dachstein (from which the 56th Mountain Artillery Regiment was formed), the men of the 27th Bomber Wing Boelcke and other personnel. It fought against the Red Army in Austria as part of the 6th Army. It was redesignated 9th Mountain Division (East) at the end of the war. Most of it surrendered to the Anglo-Americans in May 1945. Its commander was Colonel Heribert Raithel.

Sources: Lexikon; Scheibert: 290; Tessin, Vol. 14: 225.

CHAPTER 5

The Parachute Divisions

1ST PARACHUTE DIVISION

Composition: 1st Parachute Regiment, 3rd Parachute Regiment, 4th Parachute Regiment, 1st Parachute Artillery Regiment, 1st Parachute Anti-Aircraft Artillery Battalion, 1st Parachute Tank Destroyer Battalion, 1st Parachute Engineer Battalion, 1st Parachute Signal Battalion, 1st Parachute Field Replacement Battalion, 1st Parachute Divisional Supply Troops

This unit was formed in Russia in autumn 1942, from the old 7th Air Division, the original German paratroop force. Its first commander was Major General Richard Heidrich, a veteran of France, Crete, and the Siege of Leningrad. In March 1943, the division was withdrawn from the Eastern Front and sent to southern France, where it completed its formation and engaged in training until after the German collapse in Africa. In July, it was sent to Sicily, where it delayed the Allied drive on the Catania Plain and later fought a violent battle at the Primasole Bridge against British paratroopers. After being evacuated to Italy, the 1st Parachute spent the rest of the war in a long retreat up the Italian peninsula. At the time of the Allied landings at Salerno, the division was in action against Montgomery's 8th Army at Foggia, on the heel of the Italian boot. The division fought its most famous battle at Cassino in early 1944, where it held its positions despite massive American ground and air attacks, including aerial bombardments of the heaviest kind. General von Vietinghoff, the commander of the 10th Army, later commented that "No troops but the 1st Parachute Division could have held Cassino." After the fall of Rome

in June 1944, the greatly reduced division was shifted to the
Adriatic sector and later suffered heavy casualties at Rimini and
in the withdrawal to Bologna. It spent November 1944 to April
1945, defending a sector near Imola in north-central Italy, in
the zone of the 10th Army.

It surrendered at the end of April 1945, after the Allies had
pushed across the Po River. Commanders of the 1st Parachute
Division were Major General/Lieutenant General Richard
Heidrich (May 1, 1943), Major General Hans Korte (January 4,
1944), Heidrich (returned February 22, 1944) and Colonel/
Major General Karl-Lothar Schulz (November 18, 1944).

See also 7th Air Division later in this chapter.

Notes and Sources: Heidrich was promoted to lieutenant general
on July 1, 1943. Schulz became a major general on January 17, 1945.

Blumenson 1969: 67, 448; Chant, Volume 17: 2277; Edwards: 135–
37; Fisher: 18; Lexikon.

2ND PARACHUTE DIVISION

Composition (1943): 2nd Parachute Regiment, 6th Parachute Regiment, 7th Parachute Regiment, 2nd Parachute
Artillery Regiment, 2nd Parachute Tank Destroyer Battalion,
2nd Parachute Engineer Battalion, 2nd Parachute Signal Battalion, 2nd Parachute Anti-Aircraft Battalion, 2nd Parachute
Machine Gun Battalion, 2nd Parachute Divisional Supply
Troops

This unit first saw action as the 2nd Parachute Brigade on
the North African Front. In November 1942 it was on the southern flank of Panzer Army Afrika, when Field Marshal Rommel's
famous Afrika Korps was all but destroyed at El Alamein.
Because of a shortage of vehicles and fuel, Rommel was forced
to abandon the brigade (and the Italian X Infantry Corps, which
it was supporting) to its fate. The Italians surrendered but Major
General Hermann Bernard Ramcke, commander of the parachute brigade, carried out a brilliant ambush, captured a British
transport column, and managed to rejoin the remnants of Rommel's army in one of the most daring feats of arms the Germans

German paratroopers bail out of their tri-motor Ju-52 airplanes. Although part of the Luftwaffe, German parachute formations fought as ground combat units in every theater.

executed during World War II. The brigade was evacuated from North Africa before the Axis collapse and formed the nucleus around which the 2nd Parachute Division was created in February 1943. The new division also included the 2nd Parachute Regiment, which had been part of the veteran 7th Air Division before that unit was disbanded in 1943.

Initially stationed in Brittany, the new parachute division was sent south in the summer of 1943, and took part in the occupation of Rome after the Badoglio government tried to defect to the Allies in September of that year. In the latter part of 1943, the 2nd Parachute was transferred to the Russian Front, where its 6th Parachute Regiment was almost wiped out. Down to a strength of 3,200 men by January 1944, the division was still holding thirteen miles of frontage. In January and February 1944 alone, the division fought at Kirovograd, Uman and Cherkassy (Korsum). It was finally withdrawn from combat that May and sent to Cologne-Wahn, Germany, to refit and rebuild, and was then returned to Brittany, minus the 6th Parachute Regiment, which was attached to the 91st Air Landing Division in Normandy. After the collapse of the German front in Normandy, Ramcke (now a lieutenant general) assumed command of the fortress of Brest and forced the U.S. 3rd Army to lay siege to the city. The battle lasted from mid-August until September 19, 1944. Ramcke, Colonel von der Mosel (his chief of staff), and their men put up a fierce resistance and seriously disrupted Patton's timetable. On Hitler's orders Nazi Germany's highest decoration—the Knight's Cross with Oak Leaves, Swords, and Diamonds—was parachuted into the fortress and awarded to Ramcke. Finally, however, the division's supplies ran out, the fortress was overrun, and the 2nd Parachute Division was destroyed. Ramcke and most of his men spent the rest of the war in prison camps.

After the original 2nd Parachute Division was destroyed at Brest, a second division of that name began forming in Germany and Holland in November 1944. It included the 2nd, 7th, and 23rd Parachute Regiments, but its supporting units bore the same numbers as the original. It now included the

2nd Parachute Machine Gun Battalion. Although not as distinguished as its predecessor, the new 2nd Parachute fought well against the British and the Americans in operations around Arnhem in early 1945, in the Reichswald battles, at Cleve, and in the Battles of the Rhine Crossings. As late as March 1945, it was on the northern sector of the Western Front with 1st Parachute Army. In April, however, it was shifted south and was trapped, along with the bulk of Field Marshal Model's Army Group B, in the Ruhr Pocket, and was destroyed there.

The commanders of the elite 2nd Parachute Division were Ramcke (February 13, 1943), Lieutenant Colonel Meder-Eggebert (September 8, 1943), Major General Walter Barenthin (September 13, 1944), Colonel Gustav Wilke (November 1943), Colonel Hans Kroh (November 1943), Major General Wilke (December 11, 1943), Ramcke (returned February 17, 1944), Kroh (March 17, 1944), Ramcke (May 6, 1944), and Colonel/ Major General Kroh (August 11, 1944). Lieutenant General Walter Lackner commanded the second 2nd Parachute Division throughout its existence (November 15, 1944 to April 16, 1945).

Notes and Sources: Ramcke was wounded in action against the Italians on September 8, 1943. Hans Kroh surrendered the division to the Americans at Brest on September 13. He had been promoted to major general five days before.

Blumenson 1960: 639; Chant, Volume 14: 1861; Edwards: 137, 156; Garland and Smyth: 286; Lexikon; Seaton: 415; Vormann: 29.

3RD PARACHUTE DIVISION

Composition: 5th Parachute Regiment, 8th Parachute Regiment, 9th Parachute Regiment, 3rd Parachute Artillery Regiment, 3rd Parachute Tank Destroyer Battalion, 3rd Parachute Engineer Battalion, 3rd Parachute Signal Battalion, 3rd Parachute Heavy Mortar Battalion, 3rd Parachute Anti-Aircraft Battalion, 3rd Parachute Field Replacement Battalion, 3rd Parachute Divisional Supply Troops

Formed in the Reims area of France during September and October 1943, this division had a cadre from the 1st Parachute

Regiment of the 1st Parachute Division. When it completed its training the division was at full strength—more than 17,000 men. Like almost all German parachute units created after 1941, it never saw airborne operations but fought as an infantry division. Initially stationed in Brittany in February 1944, the 3rd Parachute was sent to Rouen in May and was soon committed to the Normandy fighting in June, where it suffered heavy casualties resisting the American advance through the hedgerows to St. Lo. By July 11, 1944, it was down to 35 percent of its former strength. After the front collapsed in late July, the division was surrounded in the Falaise Pocket in August, where most of its survivors were captured. Lieutenant General Schimpf, the division commander, was seriously wounded in the breakout but was carried out of the pocket by his men. General of Paratroops Eugen Meindl, the commander of the II Parachute Corps, assumed personal command of the 3rd Parachute after Schimpf fell and was himself severely wounded in the breakout.

Despite its reduced numbers, the tough division stayed in action, mainly because Army Group B had nothing left but burned-out units with which to fight the Allies. In September 1944, the 3rd Parachute, now "almost insignificant in numbers," was surrounded in the Mons Pocket but again broke out. It was finally sent to the rear and was rebuilt at Oldenzaal, Holland, from personnel released from Luftwaffe ground support units, seven Luftwaffe fortress battalions, and elements of the 22nd, 51st, and 53rd Air Regiments. The resurrected division fought in the Ardennes offensive, where it was part of the I SS Panzer Corps, 6th Panzer Army. It suffered more casualties than it should have; this was because of the inexperience of its soldiers and because it used virtually "human wave" tactics. After the Battle of the Bulge, the 3rd Parachute Division was transferred to the 5th Panzer Army and was engaged in delaying the Allied drive west of the Rhine in early 1945. There the division fell victim to one of Hitler's "hold-at-all-costs" orders and was not allowed to withdraw behind the Rhine when it still had time to do so. Most of the division, including General Schimpf, was captured near Bad Godesberg. The survivors of the disintegrating division fought in the Eifel and the Battle of Remagen, and finally escaped into the Ruhr Pocket, where the 3rd Parachute was encircled for a fourth and final time. Its remnants surrendered to the Americans on April 15, 1945.

The commanders of the division were Major General Walter Barenthin (September 13, 1943), Lieutenant General Richard Schimpf (February 17, 1944), Meindl (August 20, 1944), Lieutenant Colonel Karl-Heinz Becker (August 22, 1944), Major General Walter Wadehn (September 1, 1944), Schimpf (returned from the hospitals, January 6, 1945), Colonel Helmut von Hoffmann (March 8, 1945), Colonel Karl-Heinz Becker (March 8, 1945), and Colonel Hummel (April 9, 1945).

Notes and Sources: Schimpf was captured on March 8, 1945.

Blumenson 1960: 543, 582, 683; Chant, Volume 16: 2133; Edwards: 137–38; Harrison: Map VI; Lexikon; MacDonald 1973: 193, 223; Tessin, Vol. 2: 202–3.

4TH PARACHUTE DIVISION

Composition: 10th Parachute Regiment, 11th Parachute Regiment, 12th Parachute Regiment, 4th Parachute Artillery Regiment, 4th Parachute Tank Destroyer Battalion, 4th Parachute Engineer Battalion, 4th Parachute Signal Battalion, 4th Parachute Anti-Aircraft Battalion, 4th Parachute Heavy Mortar Battalion, 4th Parachute Field Replacement Battalion, 4th Parachute Divisional Supply Troops

The 4th Parachute Division was formed at Perugia, Italy, from cadres furnished by the 2nd Parachute Division and two Italian parachute divisions: Folgore and Nembo. It was commanded by Colonel/Major General/Lieutenant General Heinrich Trettner throughout its existence. The division first saw action in January 1944, against the American beachhead at Anzio, where it formed part of the I Parachute Corps. The 4th Parachute was more or less continuously engaged on the Italian Front for the next sixteen months and fought in the battles for Rome and north of Florence, at Rimini, Bologna, and in the struggle for the Gothic Line, among others. In 1945, while

still part of the I Parachute Corps, it fought its last battle at
Verona, where it was finally surrounded and forced to surrender to the American forces on April 26.

Notes and Sources: Trettner was promoted to major general on
July 1, 1944, and to lieutenant general on April 1, 1945. He was later
a general in the West German Air Force. The last of the German
World War II generals to pass away, he died on September 18, 2006—
one day before his ninety-ninth birthday.

Blumenson 1969: 419–21; Edwards: 138; Fisher: Map III, 302,
501–2; *forum.axishistory.com* Lexikon; Tessin, Vol. 2: 267–68.

5TH PARACHUTE DIVISION

Composition: 13th Parachute Regiment, 14th Parachute
Regiment, 15th Parachute Regiment, 5th Parachute Artillery
Regiment, 5th Parachute Anti-Aircraft Battalion, 5th Parachute Tank Destroyer Battalion, 5th Parachute Engineer Battalion, 5th Parachute Signal Battalion, 5th Parachute Heavy
Mortar Battalion, 5th Parachute Field Replacement Battalion,
5th Parachute Divisional Supply Troops

On March 21, 1943, the 5th Parachute Division was formed
at Reims from the Demonstration (*Lehr*) Battalion of the XI Air
Corps and was posted in Brittany. In June 1944, it was heavily
engaged in the Normandy fighting, including the battles of
Avranches, Mortain and Argentan, and was later trapped in the
Falaise Pocket when the German front collapsed. In late July,
even before it was encircled at Falaise, SS General Paul Hausser,
the commander of the 7th Army, listed the division as practically destroyed. Since the divisional headquarters was lost at
Falaise, the remnants of the 5th Parachute were placed under
the command of the 275th Infantry Division during the retreat
to Belgium. Sometime later the Luftwaffe decided to rebuild
the 5th Parachute from excess ground personnel, thus making
it little more than a Luftwaffe Field division, and an understrength one at that. (It was rebuilt in the The Hague and
Amsterdam areas.) In addition to its poorly trained personnel,
the division was plagued by internal friction, because its staff
officers were appointed by Colonel General Kurt Student and

were very hostile to divisional commander Colonel (later Major General) "King" Ludwig Heilmann, who disliked Student. Friction between the arrogant Heilmann and Hermann Goering did not help matters.

Despite its problems, the 5th Parachute fought in the West Wall battles as part of Army Group G in southern Germany and was later assigned to the 7th Army, Army Group B, for the Ardennes offensive, during which it made a gallant but ultimately unsuccessful attempt to prevent Patton from rescuing the trapped American garrison at Bastogne. It continued to fight in the Ardennes in January 1945, and by February, when it fought at the Battle of Pruem just west of the Rhine, it was down to battle group strength. A month later, as part of the 15th Army, it was trapped with its back to the Rhine and was almost totally destroyed by the U.S. Army. General Heilmann was among those taken prisoner. Some stragglers from the division did manage to escape to the Ruhr Pocket, where they were rounded up a few weeks later.

The commanders of the 5th Parachute were Major General/Lieutenant General Gustav Wilke (April 1, 1944), Heilmann (October 15, 1944), and Colonel Kurt Gröschke (March 12, 1945).

Notes and Sources: Wilke was promoted to lieutenant general on May 1, 1944. Heilmann was promoted to major general on December 22, 1944. He was captured on March 7, 1945.

Blumenson 1960: 422, 442; Cole 1965: 208–13; Edwards: 138, 154; Harrison: 71; Lexikon, MacDonald 1963: Map III; MacDonald 1973: 86; Tessin, Vol. 2: 314.

6TH PARACHUTE DIVISION

Composition: 16th Parachute Regiment, 17th Parachute Regiment, 18th Parachute Regiment, 6th Parachute Artillery Regiment, 6th Parachute Artillery Regiment, 6th Parachute Tank Destroyer Battalion, 6th Parachute Engineer Battalion, 6th Parachute Signal Battalion, 6th Parachute Anti-Aircraft Battalion, 6th Parachute Heavy Mortar Battalion, 6th Parachute Field Replacement Battalion, 6th Parachute Divisional Supply Troops

Formed at Amiens in northern France in June 1944, the 6th Parachute was in action on the Normandy Front within a month. It suffered heavy casualties when the front collapsed and was sent to the rear to reorganize. Meanwhile, it lost the 16th Parachute Regiment, which was transferred to the Hermann Goering Panzer Corps, and other elements of the division formed cadres for the organization of the 7th Parachute Division. As part of the 5th Panzer Army, the remnants of the 6th Parachute Division attempted to halt the Allied drive on Paris, but without success. By September 1944, when the division fought in the Battle of the Mons Pocket, it had a combat strength of only two infantry battalions; nevertheless, it remained on the front line, taking part in the Arnhem operation and in the battles for Holland and the Rhineland. It was withdrawn to Meppel, Holland, to rest and refit in October, and to absorb some Luftwaffe fortress battalions. It was sent back to the front near Arnhem in December. In late March 1945, it was part of the 1st Parachute Army, and was trying to contain the British bridgehead over the Rhine. When the war ended, the survivors of the 6th Parachute surrendered to the Canadians near Zutphen, the Netherlands on May 8, 1945. Although not as distinguished as some of the other German airborne units, the 6th Parachute had been in action almost continuously since its formation and had performed creditably.

Commanders of the 6th included Colonel Walter Lackner (June 1, 1944), Lieutenant General Rudiger von Heyking (June 30, 1944), Lieutenant Colonel Harry Hermann (September 4, 1944), Lieutenant General Hermann Plocher (October 1, 1944), Army Colonel Rudolf Langhaeäuser (November 1944), and Plocher (December 1944–end).

Notes and Sources: General Rudiger von Heyking was captured at Mons on September 4, 1944. Plocher later wrote three books on German Air Force operations in Russia for the United States Air Force Historical Division (see the Bibliography in Volume Three).

Blumenson 1960: 576–77, 683; Edwards: 139; Lexikon; MacDonald 1973: Map XII; and Plocher MS 1941.

7TH AIR DIVISION

Composition: 1st Parachute Regiment, 2nd Parachute Regiment, 3rd Parachute Regiment, 7th Parachute Artillery Battalion, 7th Parachute Anti-Tank Battalion, 7th Parachute Flak Battalion, 7th Air Division Machine Gun Battalion, 7th Air Division Engineer Division

As the original German parachute division, the 7th Air was established in 1938 and was still not completely formed when the war broke out in 1939. Its 3rd Parachute Regiment, for example, was not formed until 1940, after the fall of France. Under the overall command of Major General (later Colonel General) Kurt Student (1938–40), the father of the German parachute forces, the 7th Air was not originally designed to fight as a division. For example, in the Danish and Norwegian campaigns, individual companies parachuted behind enemy lines to seize vital installations and were later relieved by Anny ground units. In the first hours of the campaign in the Low Countries, elements of the division's glider forces took the key Belgian fortress of Eban Emael, while other parachute units seized the vital Albert Canal bridges. To the north, other divisional units were committed behind Dutch lines, preventing the Dutch from blowing up critical bridges before German panzer and motorized units could cross them. They played a key role in the capture of Rotterdam and the elimination of the Dutch Army in only six days.

The paratroopers proved the worth of airborne soldiers in this campaign and in a very real sense were the fathers of modern airborne warfare. As a result of these successes, Hitler decided to expand his parachute arm; this program included enlarging the 7th Air Division by establishing the 3rd Parachute Regiment, as well as divisional engineer, machine-gun, anti-aircraft, and motorcycle units. During this expansion the division was commanded by Major General Richard Putziger, since General Student had been accidently shot in the head by Waffen-SS troops in Rotterdam and critically wounded on May 14. In 1941 the 7th Air was back in action again during the Greek campaign,

Adolf Hitler with members of the 7th Air Division, the first German airborne division. On May 10, 1940, they neutralized the key Belgian fortress of Eben Emael in a gliderborne assault that ranks as one of the most daring operations of the war.

during which the 2nd Parachute Regiment captured the Corinth Canal Bridge by parachute assault. Later, the entire division was employed in the invasion of Crete, where it played the major role in defeating the Allied Expeditionary Force; however, its casualties were so appallingly high that Hitler overreacted, as he frequently did, and declared that he would never again use airborne troops on a massive scale. As a result, after a brilliant beginning, the German parachute arm was relegated to the role of fighting as regular infantry for the rest of the war. All future major airborne operations in World War II were conducted by the Allies. Meanwhile, the survivors of the division were sent to the Russian Front in 1941, where they fought at Rzhev and Mius and in the siege of Leningrad. In February 1943, the division was in southern Russia, defending the Dnepropetrovsk-Stalino rail line as a part of Army Group Don. A month later it was pulled out of the line, sent to southern France, and disbanded. Most of its men were transferred to the newly formed 1st Parachute Division, although some formed cadres for other parachute units.

The commanders of the 7th Air were Major General/ Lieutenant General Student (July 4, 1938), Putziger (May 16, 1940), Major General/Lieutenant General Wilhelm Suessmann (October 1, 1940), Colonel/Major General Alfred Sturm (May 20, 1940), Colonel/Major General/Lieutenant General Erich Petersen (October 1, 1941), and Colonel/Major General Richard Heidrich (August 4, 1942).

Notes and Sources: Kurt Student was promoted to lieutenant general on January 1, 1940. He did not recover from his wounds until 1941. He later commanded the 1st Parachute Army. Suessmann was promoted to lieutenant general on December 1, 1940. He was killed during the Battle of Crete when his glider crashed into the sea. Sturm was promoted to major general on August 1, 1941. Petersen was promoted to major general on October 1, 1941, and to lieutenant general in 1942. Heidrich was promoted to major general on August 4, 1942.
Brett-Smith: 145–47; Edwards: 135, 145–50; Ziemke 1966: 87.

7TH PARACHUTE DIVISION

Composition: 19th Parachute Regiment, 20th Parachute Regiment, 21st Parachute Regiment, 7th Parachute Artillery Regiment, 7th Parachute Tank Destroyer Battalion, 7th Parachute Engineer Battalion, 7th Parachute Signal Battalion, 7th Parachute Anti-Aircraft Battalion, 7th Parachute Heavy Mortar Battalion, 7th Parachute Field Replacement Battalion, 7th Parachute Divisional Supply Troops

Created in the Bitsch area from Alarm units in September 1944, this formation was initially designated Parachute Division Erdmann. It was hastily organized and thrown into battle almost immediately, attacking the British Market-Garden corridor, as their XXX Armored Corps tried to relieve the British 1st Airborne Division at Arnhem. By delaying the relief force, the division rendered significant aid to the II SS Panzer Corps, which annihilated the Allies' first foothold across the Rhine before it could be reinforced. After this distinguished beginning, the emergency unit was upgraded to full parachute division status on October 9, and was augmented with elite personnel from parachute and Waffen-SS schools, as well as combat groups from the 6th Parachute Division. This reorganization took place at Venlo in lower Holland. Lieutenant General Wolfgang Erdmann remained in command of the 7th Parachute throughout its existence.

The new division opposed the British on the northern sector of the Western Front for eight months, fighting at Venlo and Cleve. In February 1945 it again faced the XXX Armored Corps and destroyed a large number of its tanks in the Battle of Kappeln. Later, the 7th Parachute opposed Montgomery's Rhine crossings and subsequent drive across northwest Germany, but with less success. The division retreated to the East Friesland. When the war ended, Erdmann surrendered his veterans to the British near Oldenburg. Despite its hasty creation, the 7th Parachute had shown itself to be an excellent combat unit and proved that Nazi Germany was still capable of putting together solid fighting formations, even in the fifth year of the war.

Notes and Sources: Wolfgang Erdmann died in British captivity at Muenster on September 5, 1946. Edwards: 139; MacDonald 1973: Map XII; Schmitz et al., Vol. 2: 79; Tessin, Vol. III: 76–77.

8TH PARACHUTE DIVISION

Composition: 22nd Parachute Regiment, 23rd Parachute Regiment (never fully formed), 24th Parachute Regiment, 8th Parachute Artillery Regiment, 8th Parachute Tank Destroyer Battalion, 8th Parachute Engineer Battalion, 8th Parachute Signal Battalion, 8th Parachute Heavy Mortar Battalion, 8th Parachute Field Replacement Battalion

The 8th Parachute Division was formed in the Cologne-Wahn area of western Germany in December 1944, after the Allies had already established footholds in German territory. Created too late to fight in the Battle of the Bulge, the 8th Parachute was part of Meindl's II Parachute Corps in the Reichswald battles in northwestern Germany, where it fought well. The division, which apparently never exceeded regimental strength, took part in the defensive battles at Cleve and on the Wesel and Weser, until it was decisively defeated south of Bremen in April 1945. Later that month Lieutenant General Walter Wadehn, the only commander the division ever had, surrendered it to the British on May 5, 1945.

Notes and Sources: This division was officially activated on October 25, 1944, but was not completely formed until December.

Edwards: 139; Lexikon; MacDonald 1973: Map XII; Tessin, Vol. 3: 115.

9TH PARACHUTE DIVISION

Composition: 25th Parachute Regiment, 26th Parachute Regiment, 27th Parachute Regiment (never fully formed), 9th Parachute Artillery Regiment, 9th Parachute Tank Destroyer Battalion, 9th Parachute Engineer Battalion, 9th Parachute Signal Battalion, 9th Parachute Heavy Mortar Battalion, 9th Parachute Anti-Aircraft Battalion, 9th Parachute Field Replacement Battalion, 9th Parachute Divisional Supply Troops

Formed from assorted Luftwaffe ground units in the Stettin area in December 1944, this division was an airborne force in name only, although it did have some paratroopers in it. The 9th was committed to action in two parts: the first battle group of two battalions fought under Major General Niehoff at Breslau, where it was finally destroyed after a bitter siege. Resistance in Breslau, in fact, continued even after Berlin fell. The second group, under divisional commanders Lieutenant General Gustav Wilke and later Major General Bruno Brauer, fought at Stargard, on the Oder, and at Stettin, and in the Kuestrin Bridggehead in Pomerania before being virtually annihilated as the Russians drove on Berlin. The last remnants of the division surrendered in Hitler's capital on May 2, 1945.

Commanders of the 9th Parachute included Wilke (assumed command September 24, 1944), Brauer (March 2, 1945) and Colonel Harry Hermann (April 19, 1945).

Sources: Edwards: 140, 153; Lexikon; Seaton: 575; Tessin, Vol. 3: 152.

10TH PARACHUTE DIVISION

Composition: 28th Parachute Regiment, 29th Parachute Regiment, 30th Parachute Regiment, 10th Parachute Artillery Regiment (never completely formed), 10th Parachute Tank Destroyer Battalion, 10th Parachute Engineer Battalion, 10th Parachute Signal Battalion, 10th Parachute Divisional Supply Troops

This unit was formed in the Krems-Melk area of Austria (near Graz) in March 1945, from detachments of the 1st and 4th Parachute Divisions and miscellaneous troops, including 4,000 men from four air warfare schools. It was, in fact, a division in name only, for it never reached more than battle-group strength. The 10th Parachute fought the Russians in the Danube Valley before being transferred to Moravia (Czechoslovakia) in the last days of the war. It surrendered near Iglau May 1945, and went into Soviet captivity.

Its commanders were Lieutenant General Gustav Wilke (March 10, 1945) and Colonel Karl-Heinz von Hofmann (April 1945).

Sources: Edwards: 140; Lexikon; Tessin, Vol. 3: 185.

11TH PARACHUTE DIVISION

Composition: 37th Parachute Regiment, 38th Parachute Regiment, 39th Parachute Regiment, 11th Parachute Artillery Regiment, 11th Parachute Tank Destroyer Battalion, 11th Parachute Engineer Battalion, 11th Parachute Signal Battalion, 11th Parachute Divisional Supply Troops

Formed on April 5, 1945, from the Parachute Infantry Cadre Brigade, the Parachute Replacement Training Division and Storm Brigade Gericke, the 11th Parachute Division joined the 1st Parachute Army in northwestern Germany in the last days of the war. It was never completely formed and was broken into battle groups. It surrendered to the Western Allies near Linz in May 1945.

Its commander was Colonel Walter Gericke.

Notes and Sources: Apparently the division had no reconnaissance units as such.

Lexikon; Tessin, Vol. 3: 216.

20TH PARACHUTE DIVISION

Composition: 58th Parachute Regiment, 59th Parachute Regiment, 60th Parachute Regiment, 20th Parachute Artillery Battalion, 20th Parachute Motorcycle Battalion, 20th Parachute Tank Destroyer Battalion, 20th Parachute Anti-Aircraft Battalion, 20th Parachute Heavy Mortar Battalion, 20th Parachute Engineer Battalion, 20th Parachute Signal Battalion (?), 20th Parachute Divisional Supply Troops

Activated on March 20, 1945, in the Assens zone of northern Holland from the Parachute Replacement Training Division, the 20th Parachute was not completely organized when the war ended.

Its only commander was Major General Walter Barenthin, a veteran paratrooper who had previously commanded the Parachute Replacement Training Division.

Sources: Lexikon; Tessin, Vol. 4: 147–48.

21st PARACHUTE DIVISION

Composition: 61st Parachute Regiment, 62nd Parachute Regiment, 63rd Parachute Regiment, 21st Parachute Artillery Battalion, 21st Parachute Tank Destroyer Company, 21st Parachute Heavy Mortar Company, 21st Parachute Engineer Battalion, 21st Parachute Signal Company, 21st Parachute Divisional Supply Troops

The 21st Parachute Division was formed on April 5, 1945, from Storm Brigade Gericke and parts of the Parachute Replacement and Training Division. Its commander was Colonel Walter Gericke. Apparently never much more than a regiment in strength, the division never left Holland but apparently did see action against the British in the last days of the war.

Sources: Lexikon; Mehner, Vol. 12: 442; Tessin, Vol. 4: 169.

PARACHUTE REPLACEMENT AND TRAINING DIVISION

Composition: 1st Parachute Jäger Training Regiment, 2nd Parachute Jäger Training Regiment, 3rd Parachute Jäger Training Regiment, 4th Parachute Jäger Training Regiment, 1st Parachute Jäger Replacement Battalion, Parachute Artillery Replacement and Training Battalion, Parachute Engineer Replacement and Training Battalion, Parachute Tank Destroyer Training Battalion, Parachute Tank Destroyer Replacement and Training Battalion, Parachute Heavy Mortar Lehr Battalion, Parachute Signal Replacement and Training Battalion

Formed on January 13, 1945, this unit was reorganized on April 5, 1945, when it became the 20th Parachute Division. Its commander was Major General Walter Barenthin.

Sources: Lexikon; Tessin, Vol. 14: 284.

PARACHUTE DIVISION ERDMANN

See 7th Parachute Division earlier in this chapter.

CHAPTER 6

The Luftwaffe Field Divisions

1ST LUFTWAFFE FIELD DIVISION

Composition: I–IV Field Jäger Battalions, 1st Luftwaffe Field Division (without regimental staff), 1st Luftwaffe Field Artillery Battalion, 1st Luftwaffe Field Bicycle Company, 1st Luftwaffe Field Tank Destroyer Battalion, 1st Luftwaffe Field Engineer Battalion, 1st Luftwaffe Field Signal Company, 1st Luftwaffe Field Flak Battalion, 1st Luftwaffe Field Divisional Supply Troops

In 1942, Hitler authorized the formation of the Luftwaffe Field divisions from excess air force ground personnel, because Reichsmarschall Hermann Goering personally appealed to him not to release his men to the Army where their "fine National Socialist attitudes" would be contaminated. This was a horrible mistake on Hitler's part, for it led to the commitment of well over a dozen inadequately trained Luftwaffe ground divisions to combat, mainly on the Eastern Front, and cost thousands of men their lives. The 1st Luftwaffe Field Division was formed at Koenigsberg, East Prussia, in the summer of 1942, from the 10th Air Regiment. It initially consisted of four infantry battalions (numbered I through IV) but without a regimental staff; an anti-tank battalion; an artillery battalion; a flak battalion; and a bicycle and an engineer company.

The division completed its training in late 1942, and was sent to Army Group North on the Eastern Front. It initially fought in the Lake Ilmen area, but spent the period from December 1942 to October 1943 defending a sector near Novgorod. Its performance fell far short of Hitler's expectations and, on November 1, 1943, it was transferred to the army as *1.*

Feld-Division (L). It was reorganized and given the 1st and 2nd Jäger Regimental Staffs (L). In 1943, the 1st Field saw its first major fighting at Novgorod, and in January 1944, it suffered heavy losses in the withdrawal from Leningrad that it had to be disbanded. Like most of the other Luftwaffe ground divisions, it proved itself utterly inadequate to face the enemy in infantry-style combat. Its survivors were absorbed by the 28th Jäger Division.

The 1st Luftwaffe Field Division's commanders were Colonel Gustav Wilke (September 30, 1942), Major General Werner Zech (January 17, 1943), Wilke (April 14, 1943), Colonel Anton Longin (June 15, 1943), Wilke (returned July 23, 1943), and Major General Rudolf Petrauschke (October 1, 1943).

Notes and Sources: The IV/1st Luftwaffe Field Artillery Regiment was redesignated I/40th Motorized Flak Regiment in October 1943. Wilke was promoted to major general on April 20, 1943.

Egon Denzel, *Die Luftwaffen-Felddivisionen, 1942–1945* (3rd ed., 1976): 25 (hereafter cited as "Denzel"); Lexikon; Tessin, Vol. 2: 26–27, 63; OB 45: 326.

2ND LUFTWAFFE FIELD DIVISION

Composition: I–IV Jäger Battalions, 2nd Luftwaffe Field Division (without a regimental headquarters), 2nd Field Artillery Battalion (later Regiment), 2nd Field Fusilier Company, 2nd Field Tank Destroyer Battalion, 2nd Field Engineer Company, 2nd Field Signal Company, 2nd Field Flak Battalion, 2nd Luftwaffe Field Divisional Supply Troops

Formed in the Gross-Born Troop Maneuver Area in September 1942, the 2nd Field Division was sent to Army Group Center in late 1942. It fought in the Smolensk sector (January 1943), as well as Nevel (February through October) and Vitebsk (November 1943–January 1944). It was in remnants after Nevel and apparently it did not please the army group commander, Field Marshal Ernst Busch, for he succeeded in getting the division disbanded in early 1944. Most of its men were transferred to the 6th Luftwaffe Field Division. Its commanders were Colonel Hellmuth Paetzold (September 1942) and Army Colonel/Major

General Carl Becker (January 1, 1943). As was the case in many Luftwaffe Field divisions, the IV Battalion of its artillery regiment (in this case, the IV/2nd Luftwaffe Field Artillery Regiment) was a flak unit. It was redesignated I/50th Motorized Flak Regiment in October 1943, although it remained attached to the division.

Notes and Sources: The Staff, 3rd and 4th Jäger Regiments (L) were added to the division's table of organization in 1944.

Becker was promoted to major general on April 1, 1943. Denzel: 25; Lexikon; OB 45: 326; Tessin, Vol. 2: 134.

3RD LUFTWAFFE FIELD DIVISION

Composition: I–IV Jäger Battalions, 3rd Luftwaffe Field Division (without regimental headquarters), 3rd Luftwaffe Field Artillery Battalion, 3rd Luftwaffe Field Fusilier Company, 3rd Luftwaffe Field Tank Destroyer Battalion, 3rd Luftwaffe Field Engineer Company, 3rd Luftwaffe Field Signal Company, 3rd Luftwaffe Field Flak Battalion, 3rd Luftwaffe Field Divisional Supply Troops. The Headquarters, 5th and 6th Jäger Regiments (L) were added in 1944.

The 3rd Luftwaffe Field Division was formed in the Gross-Born Troop Maneuver Area in the summer of 1942. Like its sister division, the 2nd Luftwaffe Field, it was sent to Army Group Center in late 1942, and fought in the Nevel and Vitebsk sectors (November 1942–October 1943 and November 1943–January 1944, respectively). It was taken over by the army on November 1, 1943, and was resignated *6. Feld-Division (L)*. It was disbanded in 1944, before the Russians began their gigantic summer offensive. Its personnel remained on the Eastern Front and were assigned to the 4th and 6th Luftwaffe Field Divisions. Its commander throughout its existence was Luftwaffe Major General/Lieutenant General Robert Pistorius.

Notes and Sources: The IV/3rd Luftwaffe Field Artillery Regiment became the I/43rd Motorized Flak Regiment in October 1943. Pistorius was promoted to lieutenant general on July 1, 1943.

Denzel: 25; Lexikon; OB 45: 326; Tessin, Vol. 2: 202.

4TH LUFTWAFFE FIELD DIVISION

Composition: I–IV Jäger Battalions, 1st Luftwaffe Field Division (without regimental staff), 4th Luftwaffe Field Artillery Battalion, 4th Luftwaffe Field Bicycle Company, 4th Luftwaffe Field Tank Destroyer Battalion, 4th Luftwaffe Field Engineer Company, 4th Luftwaffe Field Signal Company, 4th Luftwaffe Field Flak Battalion, 4th Luftwaffe Field Divisional Supply Troops (later Division Troop Number 4 [L]).

Home Station: Klagenfurt, Austria

The 4th Luftwaffe Field Division was formed in the Gross Born Troop Maneuver Area in the summer of 1942, and was sent to Army Group Center. It was given a sector near Vitebsk and generally held its positions against several Soviet attacks. It was transferred to the army on November 1, 1943, and was reorganized. It was redesignated *4. Feld-Division (L)*, absorbed part of the 3rd Luftwaffe Field Division, and was given the Staffs, 7th and 8th Jäger Regiments (L). By the beginning of 1944, it consisted of the 49th, 50th, and 51st Jäger Regiments (L), the 4th Artillery Regiment (L), the 4th Fusilier Battalion (L) and assorted divisional troops. Unlike its sister divisions, the 2nd and 3rd Field, it was still in existence in June 1944, when the Soviet summer offensive virtually destroyed Army Group Center. Along with most of the rest of the 3rd Panzer Army's LIII Corps, the 4th Field Division was surrounded and destroyed at Vitebsk. The few survivors of the division were assigned to Corps Detachment H.

Its commanders included Colonel Rainer Stahel (September 25, 1942), Colonel Wilhelm Voelk (November 28, 1942), Colonel Hans-Georg Schreder (April 1, 1943), Army Major General Hans Sauerbrey (November 5, 1943), Major General Dr. Ernst Klepp (November 20, 1943), and Lieutenant General Robert Pistorius (January 25, 1944).

Notes and Sources: General Pistorius was killed in action on June 27, 1944, when the division was destroyed.

Carell 1971: 584–96; Denzel: 26; Keilig: 172, 292; Tessin, Vol. 2: 239; OB 45: 326.

A Luftwaffe gun crew firing a small mortar.

5TH LUFTWAFFE FIELD DIVISION

Composition (1944): I–IV Jäger Battalions, 5th Luftwaffe Field Division (without regimental staff); 5th Luftwaffe Field Artillery Battalion, 5th Luftwaffe Field Bicycle Company, 5th Luftwaffe Assault Gun Company, 5th Luftwaffe Field Engineer Company, 5th Luftwaffe Field Signal Company, 5th Luftwaffe Field Divisional Supply Troops

The 5th Luftwaffe Field Division was formed in the Gross-Born Troop Maneuver Area in October 1942, and was hurriedly sent to the Eastern Front via the Crimea in December. It took part in the withdrawal from the Caucasus in January 1943, and in the Battle of the Kuban Bridgehead in February, March and April. Evacuated across the Strait of Kersch in May, it remained in the Crimea until September, when it was sent north and fought in the Battle of Malitopel on the Black Sea, where it suffered very heavy casualties. The remnants of the 5th Luftwaffe Field were turned over to the army on November 1, 1943, and were redesignated 5. Feld-Division (L). It also added the Staffs, 9th and 10th Jäger Regiments (L).

The High Command of the Army sent the 5th Field back to Bessarabia in Romania and had it rebuilt. At greatly reduced strength, it now had only two infantry battalions instead of its previous four. Its two infantry battalions were placed under the 9th Field Regiment (L), which was also called the 9th Jäger. The *Kampfgruppe*, 9th Field Division, was sent back to the Eastern Front in January 1944, and fought at the Battle of the Nikolav Bridgehead (on the east bank of the Dnieper) as part of the 3rd Romanian Army. It fought in the Odessa sector from March to May 1944, when it was mercifully taken out of the line and disbanded. The men of the former 9th Jäger Regiment (L) were given to the 76th Infantry Division; the rest of the men of the division were assigned to the 320th and 335th Infantry Divisions.

Commanders of the 5th Luftwaffe Field Division included Luftwaffe Major General Hans-Joachim von Armin (October–November 1942), Colonel Hans-Bruno Schulz-Heym (December 1942–November 1, 1943) and Army Major General Count

Both von Huelsen (March 10–June 1, 1944). Who commanded the division from November 1, 1943, to March 10, 1944, is not known.

Sources: Denzel: 26; Keilig: 153; Lexikon; Tessin, Vol. 2: 291, 313; OB 45: 327.

6TH LUFTWAFFE FIELD DIVISION

Composition (1944): 52nd Jäger Regiment (L), 53rd Jäger Regiment (L), 54th Jäger Regiment (L), 6th Artillery Regiment (L), 6th Bicycle Company (L), 6th Signal Company (L), 6th Flak Battalion (L), 6th Field Divisional Supply Troops (L)

The 6th Field Division was created in September 1942, in the Gross-Born Troop Maneuver Area, from cadres supplied by the 21st Air Regiment. It initially consisted of four field infantry ("Jäger") battalions (of four companies each) with no regimental headquarters, an artillery battalion, a flak battalion, a tank destroyer battalion, and bicycle, engineer and signal companies. All were apparently numbered 6th Luftwaffe Field. In 1943, the 6th Luftwaffe Field Artillery Battalion, the 6th Tank Destroyer Battalion and the 6th Luftwaffe Field Flak Battalion were absorbed by the newly-created 6th Luftwaffe Field Artillery Regiment. Meanwhile, along with the 4th Luftwaffe Field Division, the 6th Field was sent to Army Group Center, which attached it to 3rd Panzer Army. The division fought in the Nevel sector from early 1943 until November 1, 1943, when it was absorbed by the army and became 6th Field Division (L). It also added two regimental headquarters: the 11th and 12th Jäger Regiments (L). The IV/6th Luftwaffe Field Artillery Regiment became the I/34th Motorized Flak Regiment in October 1943. In early 1944, the army reinforced it with parts of the recently disbanded 2nd and 3rd Luftwaffe Field Divisions and reorganized it (see Composition). The 6th Field continued to hold a sector east of Vitebsk until it was encircled and destroyed by the massive Soviet summer offensive of 1944.

Commanders of the division included Luftwaffe Colonel/ Major General Ernst Weber (September–November 1942), Luftwaffe Major General/Lieutenant General Ruediger von

Heyking (November 25, 1942), and Army Lieutenant General
Rudolf Peschel (November 5, 1943).

Notes and Sources: Heyking was promoted to lieutenant general
on July 1, 1943. Peschel was killed in action at Vitebsk on June 27,
1944, as the division ceased to exist.

Carell 1971: 584–96; Denzel: 26; Lexikon; Tessin, Vol. 3: 16–17;
OB 45: 327.

7TH LUFTWAFFE FIELD DIVISION

Composition: I, II, and III Jäger Battalions, 7th Luftwaffe
Field Division (without regimental headquarters), 7th Luft-
waffe Field Artillery Battalion, 7th Luftwaffe Field Fusilier
Company, 7th Luftwaffe Field Tank Destroyer Battalion, 7th
Luftwaffe Field Engineer Company, 7th Luftwaffe Field Signal
Company, 7th Luftwaffe Field Flak Battalion, 7th Luftwaffe
Field Divisional Supply Troops

Formed in the fall of 1942, the 7th Field was perhaps the
first of the Luftwaffe ground divisions to see action. It was sent
to Army Group Don, which was then engaged in the Stalingrad
relief campaipn and was trying to fend off massive Russian
attacks at the same time. The army group attached the field division to newly created Army Detachment Hollidt, which was des-
perately trying to hold the Don River–Upper Chir River line,
and the division first engaged in combat on December 12. The
7th Field did not provide General Hollidt much help and was
badly mauled in the fighting; however, unlike some Air Force
infantry units, it did not collapse completely. It was nevertheless
so badly damaged that it was disbanded in March 1943, and its
personnel absorbed by the 15th Luftwaffe Field Division.

Its commanders were Major General Wolf von Biedermann
(September 1942), Colonel August Klessmann (November 28,
1942), Lieutenant General Willibald Spang (January 3, 1943),
and Biedermann again (February 16, 1943).

Sources: Denzel: 26; Lexikon; Manstein: 319; Tessin, Vol. 3: 76;
OB 45: 327.

8TH LUFTWAFFE FIELD DIVISION

Composition: I–IV Jäger Battalions, 8th Luftwaffe Field Division (without regimental staff); 8th Luftwaffe Field Artillery Battalion, 8th Luftwaffe Field Bicycle Company, 8th Luftwaffe Field Tank Destroyer Battalion, 8th Luftwaffe Field Engineer Company, 8th Luftwaffe Field Signal Company, 8th Luftwaffe Field Flak Battalion, 8th Luftwaffe Field Divisional Supply Troops

Formed in Troop Maneuver Area Mielau (Mlawa) in East Prussia on October 29, 1942, from the 42nd Air Regiment, the 8th Luftwaffe Field Division was sent to Army Detachment Hollidt on the Eastern Front, along with the 7th Luftwaffe Field Division, in December 1942. After fighting on the Upper Chir in the winter of 1942–43 and it the Taganrog sector (where it suffered heavy losses), it had to be taken out of the line, and its remnants were incorporated into the 15th Luftwaffe Field Division. It was officially disbanded in May 1943.

Its commanders were Colonel Hans Heidemeyer (October 29, 1942), Army Colonel Kurt Hähling (January 1, 1943), and army Lieutenant General Willibald Spang (February 15, 1943).

Sources: Lexikon; Manstein: 319; Tessin, Vol. 3: 114; OB 45: 327–28.

9TH LUFTWAFFE FIELD DIVISION

Composition (1944): 17th Field Jäger Regiment, 18th Field Jäger Regiment, 9th Field Artillery Regiment, 9th Field Fusilier Company, 9th Tank Destroyer Battalion, 9th Field Engineer Battalion, 9th Field Signal Company, 9th Field Flak Battalion, 9th Field Divisional Supply Troops

This division was formed in the Arys Troop Maneuver Area of East Prussia in October 1942, from the 62nd Air Regiment. It initially consisted of the I–IV Jäger Battalions, 9th Luftwaffe Field Division (without a regimental staff); the 9th Luftwaffe Field Artillery Battalion; the 9th Luftwaffe Field Flak Battalion; and the 9th Luftwaffe Field Bicycle, Engineer and Signal Companies. The 9th Field Division arrived on the northern sector of the Russian Front in December 1942. It held part of the Leningrad siege line near Oranienbaum for more than a year. On November 1, 1943, it was transferred from the Luftwaffe to the army, which reinforced it and reorganized it (see Composition). The 9th Field Division was caught up in the retreat from Leningrad in February 1944 and suffered such heavy casualties that it had to be disbanded. The remnants of the division were absorbed by the 61st, 225th, and 227th Infantry Divisions.

Commanders of the 9th Luftwaffe Field included Luftwaffe Colonel/Major General Hans Erdmann (October 8, 1942), Luftwaffe Colonel/Major General Anton-Carl Longin (September 1943), army Lieutenant General Paul Winter (November 5, 1943), Colonel Ernst Michael (November 25, 1943), and Colonel Heinrich Geerkens (January 22, 1944).

Notes and Sources: The IV/9th Luftwaffe Field Artillery Regiment became the I/2nd Motorized Flak Regiment in October 1943. On November 1, 1943, the division was redesignated 9th Field Division (L). Colonel Michae was killed in action at Tuganitzky on January 22. Colonel Geerkens was killed in action at Valassova two days later.

Denzel: 27; Keilig: 372; Lexikon; Tessin, Vol. 3: 134–35, 151–52; OB 45: 328.

10TH LUFTWAFFE FIELD DIVISION

Composition (1944): 19th Field Jäger Regiment (L), 20th Field Jäger Regiment (L), 10th Field Artillery Regiment (L), 10th Field Fusilier Company (L), 10th Field Tank Destroyer Battalion (L), 10th Field Engineer Company (L), 10th Field Signal Company (L), 10th Field Divisional Supply Troops (L)

Created in October 1942, from the 72nd Air Regiment at Detmold, this Air Force ground division was sent to Army Group North in January 1943, and fought in the Sieges of Leningrad and Oranienbaun. It was taken over by the army on November 1, 1943, and was redesignated *10. Feld-Division (L)*. The massive Soviet assaults that broke the Siege of Leningrad began on January 14, 1944; by January 17, the 10th Luftwaffe

Field Division was smashed. It suffered further losses in the initial retreats from Oranienbaun through the Baltic area of the Soviet Union to the Narva and was disbanded on February 3, 1944. Its artillery regiment became the Staff, 931st Artillery Regiment z.b.V.; I/10th Field Artillery Regiment and II/10th Field Artillery Regiment became the 1004th and 1003rd Army Coastal Artillery Battalions, respectively. (The IV/10th Luftwaffe Field Artillery Regiment became the II/32nd Motorized Flak Regiment in October 1943.) The rest of the division was absorbed by the 170th Infantry Division.

Commanders of the 10th Luftwaffe Field included Luftwaffe Colonel/Major General Walter Wadehn (September 25, 1942) and Army Major General Hermann von Wedel (November 5, 1943).

Notes and Sources: Colonel Wadehn was promoted to major general on September 1, 1943. He gave up command of the division when it was transferred to the army. General von Wedel was wounded on January 29, 1944, and died in the military hospital at Dorpat on February 3.

Denzel: 27; Keilig: 364; Tessin, Vol. 3: 168, 184; OB 45: 328; Ziemke 1966: 234, 253.

11TH LUFTWAFFE FIELD DIVISION

Composition: 21st Luftwaffe Field Jäger Regiment, 22nd Luftwaffe Field Jäger Regiment, 11th Luftwaffe Field Artillery Regiment, 11th Luftwaffe Field Bicycle Company, 11th Luftwaffe Field Tank Destroyer Battalion, 11th Luftwaffe Field Engineer Company, 11th Luftwaffe Field Signal Company, 11th Luftwaffe Field Divisional Supply Troops

The 11th Luftwaffe Field Division was organized at Troop Maneuver Area Munsterlager in October 1942. It finished its training in early 1943, and was sent to the Aegean Islands off of the coast of Greece as an occupation force. In February 1944, it was transferred to the Megara area of Greece, where it remained until August and took part in antipartisan operations. In September 1944, it retreated through Macedonia, Serbia and Croatia as part of the general withdrawal from the Balkans. It fought Tito's guerrillas in the Drava-Sava area in the fall of 1944, and was still on the southern sector of the Eastern Front in early 1945, when it added a third regiment, the 111th Field (L). It was never dissolved and was still in the East when the war ended. It surrendered to the Yugoslavs.

Its commanders were Luftwaffe Major General/Lieutenant General Karl Drum (October 1942), Army Colonel Alexander Bourquin (November 10, 1943), Army Major General/Lieutenant General Wilhelm Kohler (December 1, 1943), and Army Major General Gerhard Henke (November 1, 1944).

Notes and Sources: The IV/11th Luftwaffe Field Artillery Regiment was renamed the I/28th Motorized Flak Regiment in October 1943. Karl Drum was promoted to lieutenant general on January 1, 1943. Kohler was promoted to major general on June 1, 1943, and to lieutenant general on June 1, 1944. Henke was a Yugoslav prisoner until 1952.

Denzel: 27; Keilig: 179; *Kriegstagebuch des OKW*, Volume IV: 1903; Plocher 1942: 416; Tessin, Vol. 3: 200, 216; OB 45: 328.

12TH LUFTWAFFE FIELD DIVISION

Composition: 23rd Luftwaffe Field Jäger Regiment, 24th Luftwaffe Field Jäger Regiment, 12th Luftwaffe Field Artillery Regiment, 12th Luftwaffe Field Bicycle Company, 12th Luftwaffe Field Tank Destroyer Battalion, 12th Luftwaffe Field Engineer Company, 12th Luftwaffe Field Signal Company, 12th Luftwaffe Field Divisional Supply Troops

The 12th Luftwaffe Field Division was created in Troop Maneuver Area Bergen (near Celle) in October 1942, from the 12th Air Regiment. Its home base was Klagenfurt-Tessendorf, Austria. It was posted to Army Group North in March 1943 and was taken over by the army on November 1, 1943. It suffered heavy casualties in the withdrawal from Leningrad. It received significant replacements from the 13th Luftwaffe Field Divisions, which was disbanded in the spring of 1944. The 12th Field was sent back to the front, fought at Pleskau, Riga and in the retreat to western Latvia. It took part in the Battles of the Courland Pocket in the winter of 1944–45, when the Soviets tried unsuccessfully to crush Army Group North (later Courland) six times. One of the better Luftwaffe field divisions, the 12th was withdrawn to East Prussia in 1945 and fought at Danzig and Gotenhafen. It surrendered to the Soviets on May 9, 1945.

Its commanders included Luftwaffe Major General/Lieutenant General Herbert Kettner (October 1, 1942), Army Colonel/Major General/Lieutenant General Gottfried Weber (November 15, 1943) and Army Major General Franz Schlieper (April 10, 1945).

Notes and Sources: The IV/12th Luftwaffe Field Artillery Regiment was redesignated II/6th Motorized Flak Regiment in October 1943. Kettner was promoted to lieutenant general on October 1, 1943. Weber was promoted to major general on February 1, 1944, and to lieutenant general on August 1, 1944.

Denzel: 28; Keilig: 302; *Kriegstagebuch des OKW*, Volume IV: 1897; Lexikon; Tessin, Vol. 3: 237, 251; OB 45: 329.

13TH LUFTWAFFE FIELD DIVISION

Composition: 25th Luftwaffe Jäger Regiment, 26th Luftwaffe Jäger Regiment, 13th Luftwaffe Field Artillery Regiment, 13th Luftwaffe Field Bicycle Company, 13th Luftwaffe Field Tank Destroyer Battalion, 13th Luftwaffe Field Engineer Company, 13th Luftwaffe Field Signal Company, 13th Luftwaffe Divisional Supply Troops

Formed on November 15, 1942, from the 13th Air Regiment, this division was organized at Fallingbostel, and was almost immediately sent to the northern sector of the Russian Front. It was on the front lines in the Volkhov sector by March 1943, and remained there for almost a year. It was transferred to the army on November 1, 1943, and became the *13. Feld-Division (L)*. Meanwhile, its flak battalion (the IV/13th Luftwaffe Field Artillery Regiment) became the I/54th Motorized Flak Artillery Regiment in October 1943. The division was crushed when the Russians broke the siege of Leningrad in January 1944, and it suffered such heavy losses that it was disbanded on April 1, 1944. The divisional staff was used to form the Staff, 300th Special Purposes Division, in Estonia.

Its commanders included Luftwaffe Major General Herbert Olbrich (November 10, 1942), Luftwaffe Colonel/Major General Hans Korte (December 1, 1942) and Lieutenant General (Army) Hellmuth Reymann (October 1, 1943).

Notes and Sources: Korte was promoted to major general on July 1, 1943.
Denzel: 28; Hildebrand, Vol. III: 6–7; Tessin, Vol. 3: 264–65, 279; OB 45: 329.

14TH LUFTWAFFE FIELD DIVISION

Composition: 27th Luftwaffe Jäger Regiment, 28th Luftwaffe Jäger Regiment, 14th Luftwaffe Artillery Regiment, 14th Luftwaffe Bicycle Battalion, 14th Luftwaffe Tank Destroyer Battalion, 14th Luftwaffe Engineer Company, 14th Luftwaffe Signal Company, 14th Luftwaffe Field Divisional Supply Troops

This division was formed in late 1942 and early 1943, from the 61st Air Regiment. It was not finished with its training nor even fully equipped before its first elements were sent to Norway in January 1943, to replace the 196th Infantry Division, which was on its way to the Russian Front. Initially posted in the Mo area (near Bergen), the 14th Field was later transferred to the Jutland peninsula in Denmark, where it underwent an extensive change in personnel in the summer of 1944. (It had been taken away from the Air Force and given to the army on November 1, 1943, and had been redesignated *14. Feld-Division [L].*) Returning to Norway in mid-1944, it was posted in the Nordland area and remained in Norway until the end of the war. The 14th was never involved in ground combat.

Its commanders were Major General/Lieutenant General Gunther Lohmann (November 28, 1942) and Lieutenant General Wilhelm Richter (February 1, 1945).

Sources: The IV Battalion of the 14th Luftwaffe Field Artillery Regiment became the I/15th Motorized Flak Regiment in October 1943. Lohmann was promoted to lieutenant general on September 1, 1943.
Denzel: 28; Tessin, Vol. 3: 295, 310; OB 45: 329; Ziemke 1959: 262.

15TH LUFTWAFFE FIELD DIVISION

Composition: 29th Luftwaffe Jäger Regiment, 30th Luftwaffe Jäger Regiment, 15th Luftwaffe Field Artillery Regiment, 15th Luftwaffe Field Bicycle Company, 15th Luftwaffe Field Tank Destroyer Battalion, 15th Luftwaffe Field Engineer Battalion, 15th Luftwaffe Field Signal Company, 15th Luftwaffe Field Divisional Supply Troops

This division was formed in October 1942, in the Ssalk area of southern Russia. It was sent to Army Group Don, where it fought in the Mius River sector around Taganrog in January 1943. According to Field Marshal von Manstein, it "disintegrated during its first few days in action." Taken out of the line, it absorbed the survivors of the 7th and 8th Luftwaffe Field Divisions in March and was sent back to the fighting, despite its deficiencies. The fact that von Manstein had to rely on Air Force infantry divisions evidences how desperate the situation on the southern sector of the Russian Front had grown by 1943. In autumn 1943, the 15th Field again fought on the Mius and at Taganrog, and again sustained heavy losses. On November 1, 1943, the Luftwaffe field divisions were taken over by the army. The 15th Field was immediately disbanded, and its personnel were assigned to the 336th Infantry Division, except for the tank destroyer battalion, which became a GHQ unit.

Commanders of the 15th Field included Luftwaffe Lieutenant General Alfred Mahnke (October 1, 1942), Luftwaffe Colonel Heinrich Conrady (December 1942–January 1943), Luftwaffe Colonel Eberhard Dewald (January 1943–February 1943), Lieutenant General (Army) Willibald Spang (February 14, 1943), Luftwaffe Colonel Schulz-Hein (March 1943), and Spang (returned March 1943).

Notes and Sources: The IV. (Flak) Artillery Regiment 15 (L) became the I/46th Motorized Flak Regiment in October 1943. Denzel: 29; Keilig: 327; Manstein: 318–19; Tessin, Vol. 4: 18; OB 45: 330.

16TH LUFTWAFFE FIELD DIVISION

Composition: 31st Luftwaffe Jäger Regiment, 32nd Luftwaffe Jäger Regiment, 46th Luftwaffe Jäger Regiment, 16th Luftwaffe Field Artillery Regiment, 16th Luftwaffe Field Reconnaissance Platoon, 16th Luftwaffe Field Tank Destroyer Battalion, 16th Luftwaffe Field Engineer Battalion, 16th Luftwaffe Field Signal Company, 16th Luftwaffe Field Divisional Supply Troops

Originally a two-regiment Field division, the 16th was formed in the Gross-Born Troop Troop Maneuver Area on December 1, 1942, from cadres provided by the XIII Air Corps. It was sent to the Amsterdam area in January 1943, where it replaced the 167th Infantry Division, which was being sent to Bavaria and then to the Eastern Front. The Divisional HQ was transferred to Amstelveen (three miles south of Amsterdam) in April and remained there for more than a year, directing occupation forces in the Ijmuiden-Haarlem-Leiden-Scheveningen area. The 16th Luftwaffe Field Division was taken over by the army on November 1, 1943, and was redesignated 16th Field Division (L). In June 1944, it created the 46th Luftwaffe Jäger Regiment by reducing its other infantry regiments to two battalions each. At that time it was on garrison duty in Amsterdam as part of the Armed Forces Netherlands. In late June, it was sent to Normandy and on July 2 replaced the Panzer Lehr Division on the front line of Army Group B. That very next day the British launched a major offensive on Caen and immediately overran the 16th Field, which lost 75 percent of its men within hours. The survivors were eventually collected and attached to the 21st Panzer Division. Later they were withdrawn from the line and consolidated with the 158th Reserve Division to form the 16th Infantry Division, which continued to serve on the Western Front until the end of the war. The 16th Field Division, meanwhile, was officially dissolved on August 4, 1944.

The commanders of the 16th Luftwaffe Field Division were Luftwaffe Colonel Otto von Lachemair (November 28, 1942) and Major General (Army) Karl Sievers (November 5, 1943).

Notes and Sources: The IV/16th Luftwaffe Field Artillery Regiment became the I/53rd Motorized Flak Regiment in October 1943.

Blumenson 1960: 561; Carell 1973: 238; Denzel: 29; Harrison: Map VI; Keilig: 324; Lexikon; Speidel: 41; Tessin, Vol. 4: 34; OB 45: 330.

17TH LUFTWAFFE FIELD DIVISION

Composition: 33rd Luftwaffe Jäger Regiment, 34th Luftwaffe Jäger Regiment, 17th Luftwaffe Field Artillery Regiment, 17th Luftwaffe Field Fusilier Company, 17th Luftwaffe Field Tank Destroyer Battalion, 17th Luftwaffe Field Engineer Battalion, 17th Luftwaffe Field Signal Company, 17th Luftwaffe Field Divisional Supply Troops

Originally assembled and trained in the Landshut area of Luftgau VII (near Munich), the 17th Field was posted to Le Havre as a static infantry division on the French Atlantic coast. It was taken over by the army on November 1, 1943, as the 17th Field Division (L). The army added the Staff, 47th Jäger Regiment (L) to its table of organization in 1944, but it took a battalion from each of the other infantry regiments in the process, so the addition of the regiment resulted in no real increase in strength. The 34th Jäger Regiment did add a III Battalion in March 1944, however, when it was given the 835th Battalion, North Caucasian Legion. In the spring of 1944, the division was camped near the Seine River east of Le Havre as part of the 15th Army. After the Normandy Front collapsed, it helped defend Paris as a part of the 5th Panzer Army. On August 28, it was attacked by a much superior force from the U.S. 1st Army, and was virtually destroyed. Soon after, on September 28, it was officially dissolved, and its survivors were absorbed by the 167th Volksgrenadier Division in Slovakia.

The 17th Luftwaffe Field was led by Luftwaffe Colonel Hans Korte (December 1942), Luftwaffe Lieutenant General Herbert Olbrich (January 1942), and Army Lieutenant General Hans-Kurt Hocker (November 5, 1943). From October 30 to November 5, 1943, it was directed by its senior regimental commander.

Notes and Sources: The IV/17th Luftwaffe Field Artillery Regiment became the I/20th Motorized Flak Regiment in October 1943.

Blumenson 1960: 575–76, 579; Cole 1965: 623; Denzel: 29; Harrison: Map VI; Keilig: 144; Tessin, Vol. 4: 60, 73; OB 45: 330.

18TH LUFTWAFFE FIELD DIVISION

Composition: 35th Luftwaffe Jäger Regiment, 36th Luftwaffe Jäger Regiment, 48th Luftwaffe Jäger Regiment, 18th Luftwaffe Field Artillery Regiment, 18th Luftwaffe Field Reconnaissance Platoon, 18th Luftwaffe Field Tank Destroyer Battalion, 18th Luftwaffe Field Engineer Battalion, 18th Luftwaffe Field Signal Company, 18th Luftwaffe Field Divisional Supply Troops

This division was created in France, probably in the Rochefort area, from the 52nd Air Regiment, at the end of 1942, and served in northern France and Belgium throughout its existence. In 1943, it was on duty in the Calais and Dunkirk areas of the North Sea, as part of the 15th Army. On November 1 of that year, it was taken over by the army and renamed the 18th Field Division (L). In the spring of 1944, its third regiment, the 47th Jäger, was formed from the third battalions of the 35th and 36th Field Jäger Regiments. The division first saw action in August 1944, when it took part in the defense of Paris as a part of the 5th Panzer Army. A month later, after it took part in the retreat to Belgium, most of the men of the 18th Field were trapped in the Mons Pocket. Badly understrength when the battle began, the division had practically ceased to exist by the time it was over. Only about 300 men succeeded in breaking out of the trap. Later in September it was dissolved, and its few remaining men joined the 18th Volksgenadier Division.

Its divisional commanders were Luftwaffe Colonel Baron Ferdinand von Stein-Liebenstein zu Barchfeld (December 1942), Luftwaffe Major General Wolfgang Erdmann (April 1, 1943), Luftwaffe Major General Fritz Reinshagen (August 26, 1943), Army Lieutenant General Wilhelm Rupprecht (October 27, 1943), and Army Lieutenant General Joachim von Treschow (February 1, 1944).

Notes and Sources: In October 1943, the IV/18th Luftwaffe Field Artillery Regiment became the II/52nd Motorized Flak Regiment. Blumenson 1960: 575–76, 683; Denzel: 29–30; Harrison: Map VI; Lexikon; Speidel: 41; Tessin, Vol. 4: 92, 105; OB 45: 331.

19TH LUFTWAFFE FIELD DIVISION

Composition: 37th Luftwaffe Jäger Regiment, 38th Luftwaffe Jäger Regiment, 45th Luftwaffe Jäger Regiment, 19th Luftwaffe Field Artillery Regiment, 19th Luftwaffe Field Bicycle Company, 19th Luftwaffe Field Tank Destroyer Battalion, 19th Luftwaffe Field Engineer Battalion, 19th Luftwaffe Field Signal Company, 19th Luftwaffe Field Divisional Supply Troops

The 19th Luftwaffe Field Division was formed in Troop Maneuver Area Bergen (near Celle) on March 1, 1943, and arrived in Chartes, France, the following month. From July until it was taken over by the army on November 1, 1943, the division garrisoned Middelburg. From November 1943 through April 1944, it served in Holland, garrisoning the Walcheren. It was subsequently posted to the Ghent-Bruges area of Belgium. While there it reorganized and added the 46th Field Jäger Regiment to its table of organization by reducing its other infantry regiments from three to two battalions each. In June, when the Italian Front threatened to collapse under severe Allied pounding, the division was transferred to Italy, where it first saw combat later in that month. The *19th Luftwaffe Sturm-Division,* as it had been renamed on June 1, proved to be an inadequate infantry division, as evidenced by its heavy casualties. The remnants of the division were sent to Denmark, and its men reassigned to the newly formed 19th Volksgrenadier Division, which fought on the Western Front for the rest of the war. The 19th Luftwaffe Storm Division was officially disbanded on August 15, 1944. Its I/19th Luftwaffe Field Artillery Regiment was assigned to the 20th Field Division (L), as was its fusilier battalion. The III/19th Luftwaffe Field Artillery Regiment became the 1154th Army Artillery Battalion.

The division's commanders included Luftwaffe Colonel/ Major General Gerhard Bassenge (October 1, 1942), Luftwaffe

Colonel/Major General Hermann Plocher (March 1, 1943), Army Lieutenant General Erich Bässler (July 1, 1943), and Colonel Albert Henze (June 1944).

Notes and Sources: The IV/19th Luftwaffe Field Artillery Regiment became the I/52nd Motorized Flak Regiment in October 1943. After it was transferred to the army, the 19th Luftwaffe Field's home base at Fulda, Wehrkreis IX. Bassenge was promoted to major general on January 1, 1943. Hermann Plocher became a major general on March 1, 1943.

Denzel: 30; Harrison: Map VI; Keilig: 18, 136–37; Lexikon; Plocher 1941: xiii–xiv; Tessin, Vol. 4: 116.

20TH LUFTWAFFE FIELD DIVISION

Composition: 39th Luftwaffe Jäger Regiment, 40th Luftwaffe Jäger Regiment, 20th Luftwaffe Field Artillery Regiment, 20th Luftwaffe Field Bicycle Battalion, 20th Luftwaffe Field Tank Destroyer Battalion, 20th Luftwaffe Field Engineer Battalion, 20th Luftwaffe Field Signal Company, 20th Luftwaffe Field Divisional Supply Troops

Formed in the Munsterlager Troop Maneuver Area on March 8, 1943, the 20th Field remained in Germany only two weeks before it was transferred to Aalborg on the Jutland peninsula of Denmark. Here it absorbed the 23rd Air Regiment in July 1943. Its IV artillery battalion became the I/48th Motorized Flak Regiment in October 1943. In June 1944, it was moved again, this time to a combat zone in Italy where it suffered heavy losses at Orvieto and Livorno. (It was renamed the 20th Luftwaffe Storm Division on June 1, 1944.) By October, it was so small that it was tactically subordinated to the 26th Panzer Division. Pulled out of the line in November, the 20th Field was stationed at Treviso, Italy, where it was dissolved on January 3, 1945. Most of its infantry was sent to the 25th Panzer Division. One artillery battalion and the engineer battalion were sent to the 155th Field Training Division; the Staff and III/20th Field Artillery Regiment (L) were absorbed into the 710th Infantry Division; two Jäger battalions went to the 114th Jäger Division; the 20th Fusilier Battalion (L) was absorbed by the 157th Mountain Division; the 148th Infantry Division inherited the 20th Tank Destroyer Battalion (L); two batteries of artillery were incorporated into the 42nd Jäger Division; and the signals unit was transferred to Headquarters, OB West.

The commanders of the 20th Luftwaffe Field Division included Luftwaffe Major General Wolfgang Erdmann (April 1, 1943), Luftwaffe Colonel Hermann Vaue (April 5, 1943), Luftwaffe Colonel/Major General Robert Fuchs (August 1943), Army Colonel/Major General Erich Fronhöfer (September 1, 1943), Colonel/Major General Wilhelm Crisolli (November 25, 1943), Colonel Völcker (September 12, 1944) and Fronhöfer (returned September 1944).

Notes and Sources: Fuchs was promoted to major general on September 1, 1943. Crisolli was promoted to major general on February 1, 1944. He was killed in a partisan ambush near Modera in the Apennines on September 12, 1944. Fronhöfer was promoted to major general on August 1, 1944. Colonel Völcker,was captured in Italy in November 1944.

Bradley et al., Vol. 2: 478; Denzel: 30; Keilig: 62, 98; Lexikon; Tessin, Vol. 4: 136–37, 147; OB 45: 331–32.

21st LUFTWAFFE FIELD DIVISION

Composition: 41st Luftwaffe Jäger Regiment, 42nd Luftwaffe Jäger Regiment, 43rd Luftwaffe Jäger Regiment, 21st Luftwaffe Field Artillery Regiment, 21st Luftwaffe Field Reconnaissance Company, 21st Luftwaffe Field Tank Destroyer Battalion, 21st Luftwaffe Field Engineer Battalion, 21st Luftwaffe Field Signal Company

This division was formed on September 1942, as Luftwaffe Division "Meindl," after its commander, Major General Eugen Meindl. It initially included the 1st through 5th Luftwaffe Field Regiments. On October 11, 1942, the Meindl Division was divided into the 21st and 22nd Luftwaffe Field Divisions. The 21st Field was sent to Russia at the end of the year and was in combat on the northern sector of the Eastern Front in the winter of by January 1943. It defended a sector near Staraja-Russa for more than a year. Meanwhile, it absorbed the 43rd

Luftwaffe Field Jäger Regiment from the 22nd Luftwaffe Field Division in January 1943, and thus became a three regiment division with nine infantry battalions. This made it the largest of the Luftwaffe Field divisions. It was taken over by the army on November 1, 1943, and became the 21. Feld-Division (L). It suffered heavy losses in the retreat from Leningrad in early 1944. It was heavily engaged in the Lake Ilmen area in February 1944, but it held together during the retreat through the Baltic States and was still in action when Army Group North withdrew to the Latvian coast in October. The division was effectively dissolved as a combat force in November 1944. Three of its infantry battalions remained in the line as Luftwaffe Regimental Group 21, which retained the 21st Field Artillery Regiment (L). The new unit was placed under the command of the 329th Infantry Division. The divisional staff, meanwhile, continued to perform special functions for 16th Army until the end of the war, which it finished in the Courland Pocket. It surrendered to the Soviets on May 9, 1945.

Commanders of this division included Meindl (September 1942), Luftwaffe Lieutenant General Job Odebrecht (September 30, 1942), Luftwaffe Colonel/Major General/Lieutenant General Richard Schmipft (November 10, 1942), Army Major General/Lieutenant General Rudolf-Eduard Licht (October 12, 1943), Colonel Rudolf Goltzsch (April 1, 1944), Colonel/Major General Albert Henze (August 30, 1944), and Major General Otto Barth (February 16, 1945).

Notes and Sources: Who commanded the division from January 28 to February 16, 1945, is not revealed by the available records. Schimpf was promoted to major general on March 18, 1943, and to lieutenant general on August 1, 1943. Licht was promoted to lieutenant general on February 1, 1944. Henze became a major general on November 9, 1944. Barth was in Russian prison camps until 1955.

Denzel: 32; Keilig: 204; Lexikon; Tessin, Vol. 4: 158–59, 168–69; OB 45: 332.

22ND LUFTWAFFE FIELD DIVISION

Composition: 43rd Luftwaffe Jäger Regiment, 44th Luftwaffe Jäger Regiment, 22nd Luftwaffe Field Artillery Regiment, 22nd Luftwaffe Field Reconnaissance Company, 22nd Luftwaffe Field Tank Destroyer Battalion, 22nd Luftwaffe Field Engineer Battalion, 22nd Luftwaffe Field Signal Company, 22nd Luftwaffe Field Divisional Supply Troops

Formation of this division from the extant parts of Luftwaffe Division "Meindl" was started in the rear area of Army Group North in 1943, but was never completed. Why it was stillborn is not clear; however, the poor combat record of the earlier Luftwaffe infantry divisions probably had a great deal to do with it. The divisional headquarters became Staff, 23rd Flak Division. Most of the division's combat units were taken over by the 21st Luftwaffe Field Division or became GHQ units.

The division's only commander was Luftwaffe Major General Robert Fuchs.

Notes and Sources: Plocher 1943: 108, 320; Tessin, Vol. 4: 186–87; OB 45: 332.

LUFTWAFFE DIVISION MEINDL

Composition: 1st Luftwaffe Field Regiment, 2nd Luftwaffe Field Regiment, 3rd Luftwaffe Field Regiment, 4th Luftwaffe Field Regiment, 5th Luftwaffe Field Regiment, 14th Luftwaffe Field Regiment, Signal Battalion, Ski Battalion, 1st Air Fleet

This large division was formed in the rear of Army Group North from excess Luftwaffe personnel in early 1942. It was attached to the 18th Army, where it held a sector near Leningrad and did a credible job in combat. Later in 1942, elements of the division were sent to the 16th Army. It was dissolved in December 1942 and its men were transferred to the 21st and 22nd Luftwaffe Field Divisions.

Its commander was Luftwaffe Major General/Lieutenant General Eugen Meindl.

Sources: Plocher 1943: 108, 320; Tessin, Vol. 4: 186–87; Vol. 14: 164–65; OB 45: 332.

CHAPTER 7

The Flak Divisions

1ST FLAK DIVISION

Composition (late 1944): 22nd Flak Regiment, 53rd Flak Regiment, 72nd Flak Regiment, 82nd Flak Regiment, 126th Flak Regiment, 82nd Searchlight Regiment, 23./III Motorized Flak Transport Battalion, 122./IV Motorized Flak Transport Battalion, 126./IV Motorized Flak Transport Battalion, 121st Air Signal Battalion, Divisional Supply Troops

This unit was formed as *Luftverteidigungskommando* (Air Defense Command) Berlin on July 1, 1938, and was redesignated 1st Flak Division on September 1, 1941. It defended the Reich's capital against some very heavy Allied bomber attacks (with varying degrees of success) and, in the last campaign, was under the command of the LVI Panzer Corps in the Battle of Berlin, where it fought its only ground battle. The survivors of the division surrendered to the Red Army on May 2, 1945.

Commanders of the Air Defense Command Berlin/1st Flak Division included Major General Braun (July 1938), Major General Gerhard Hoffmann (August 1938), Colonel Werner Prellberg (February 29, 1940), Colonel/Major General Ludwig Schilffarth (September 1, 1941), Colonel/Major General Max Schaller (January 20, 1943), Lieutenant General Erich Kressmann (February 18, 1944), Major General Kurt von Ludwig (November 5, 1944), and Major General Otto Sydow (November 15, 1944).

Notes and Sources: Major General Braum was killed in an accident in Berlin in 1938. Schilffarth was promoted to major general on February 1, 1942. Schaller was promoted to major general on October 1, 1943. Sydow remained in Soviet prisons until 1955.

Horst-Adalbert Koch, *Flak: Die Geschichte der deutschen Flakartillerie, 1935–1945* (1955) (hereafter referred to as "Koch"; Lexikon; Tessin, Vol. 2: 67.

1ST FLAK SEARCHLIGHT DIVISION

Composition: 1st Flak Searchlight Regiment, 2nd Flak Searchlight Regiment, 3rd Flak Searchlight Regiment, 4th Flak Searchlight Regiment, 202nd Luftwaffe Signal Regiment, Divisional Supply Troops

The 1st Flak Searchlight Division (*1. Flakscheinwerfer-Division*) was formed on August 1, 1941, from the 1st Flak Searchlight Brigade. (The brigade had been formed in Arnhem in July 1940.) The 1st Searchlight Division was part of the Night Fighter Corps (which later became XII Air Corps) and was responsible for illuminating American bombers flying over the Low Countries. When German fighter tactics changed, the 1st Flak Searchlight was disbanded.

It was commanded throughout its existence by Lieutenant General Alfons Luczny.

Sources: Koch; Lexikon; Tessin, Vol. 2: 67.

2ND FLAK DIVISION

Composition (1942): 41st Flak Regiment, 151st Flak Regiment, 164th Flak Regiment, 4th Flak Transport Battalion, 122nd Air Signal Operations Company, Divisional Supply Troops

The 2nd Flak Division was formed on July 1, 1938, as Air Defense Command Leipzig. It became the 2nd Air Defense Command on August 1, 1939, and was renamed the 2nd Flak Division on September 1, 1941. In January 1942, it was made mobile and was sent to northern Russia, to replace the 14th Flak Division in supporting Army Group North. Its 151st Flak Regiment supported 16th Army, the 164th Flak Regiment supported 18th Army, and the 41st Flak Regiment headquartered in Riga and defended the army group's rear area installations. By 1944, however, the division was supporting 18th Army exclusively. (German 88mm flak guns were excellent anti-tank weapons.) The division remained in northern Russia until September 1944, when it was sent to Trier on the Western Front. By now it included the 41st, 43rd, and 182nd Flak Regiments and the 517th Flak Battalion (with the 431st and 720th Flak Battalions attached). It fought in the Ardennes offensive and in the Eifel and, as of January 8, 1945, had a strength of 18 heavy and 17 light and medium flak batteries. It was stationed in Bonn in February 1945, fought in the Battle of Cologne in March, and had the task of supporting the 5th Panzer Army in the Battle of the Ruhr Pocket. It surrendered to the Americans on April 17, 1945.

Commanders of the 2nd Flak included Colonel/Major General/Lieutenant General Walter Feyerabend (July 1938), Major General/Lieutenant General Heinrich Burchard (April 10, 1940), Feyerabend (July 1, 1941), Lieutenant General Oskar Bertram (September 1, 1941), Feyerabend (January 12, 1942), Colonel/Major General/Lieutenant General Heino von Rantzau (February 3, 1942), Major General/Lieutenant General Alfons Luczny (October 1, 1943), and Colonel Fritz Laicher (November 15, 1944).

Notes and Sources: Feyerabend was promoted to major general on April 20, 1939. Burchard was promoted to lieutenant general on June 1, 1941. Heino von Rantzau became a major general on April 1, 1942, and a lieutenant general on February 1, 1944.

Karl-Friedrich Hildebrand, *Die Generale der deutschen Luftwaffe, 1935–1945*, Volumes 1–3 (1990–1992), Koch: 188; Tessin, Vol. 2: 138; Schmitz et al., *Die deutschen Divisionen*: Vol. I: 149.

2ND FLAK SEARCHLIGHT DIVISION

Composition: 5th Flak Searchlight Regiment, 6th Flak Searchlight Regiment, 7th Flak Searchlight Regiment, 8th Flak Searchlight Regiment, 203rd Air Signal Regiment, Divisional Supply Troops

This division was formed as Staff, II Flak Searchlight Brigade, by the Night Fighter Command in northern Germany.

It was moved to Arnhem shortly thereafter and was upgraded to divisional status on August 1, 1941. Its headquarters was disbanded on July 31, 1942, and its units were absorbed by the 2nd Night Fighter Division (*Nachtjagddivision 2*).

For most of its existence, it was commanded by Colonel Heino von Rantzau.

Sources: Mehner, Vol. 5: 338; Schmitz et al., Vol. 1: 151; Tessin, Vol. 2: 138.

3RD FLAK DIVISION

Composition (1944): 16th Flak Regiment, 51st Flak Regiment, 60th Flak Regiment, 66th Flak Regiment, 161st Flak Searchlight Regiment, 610th Searchlight Battalion, 123rd Air Signal Battalion, Divisional Supply Troops

This unit was formed as Air Defense Command Hamburg on July 1, 1938, and later became the 3rd Air Defense Command. It was redesignated 3rd Flak Division on September 1, 1941. It spent the entire war in the Hamburg area, defending Germany's number two city against Allied bombers. The 3rd Flak's defense was overwhelmed by the Anglo-American air attacks of August 1943, during which most of the city was destroyed. When the Allies arrived in May 1945, the division surrendered to the British.

Commanders of the 3rd Flak Division included Major General/Lieutenant General Ottfried Sattler (July 1938), Major General Wolfgang Rüter (January 15, 1940), unknown (March 1–September 1, 1941), Lieutenant General Theodor Spiess (September 1, 1941), Colonel/Major General Walter von Hippel (July 1, 1942), Colonel/Major General Alwin Wolz (May 1, 1944) and Major General/Lieutenant General Otto Stange (April 2, 1945).

Notes and Sources: Sattler was promoted to lieutenant general on January 1, 1940. Hippel was promoted to major general on April 1, 1943. Wolz became a major general on August 1, 1944. Stange was promoted to lieutenant general on April 20, 1945.

Koch: 188, 228; Lexikon; Nafziger 1999: 429; Nafziger 1999: 429; Tessin, Vol. 2: 205.

4TH FLAK DIVISION

Composition (1941): 24th Flak Regiment, 44th Flak Regiment, 46th Flak Regiment, 64th Flak Regiment, 74th Searchlight Regiment, 4th (later 124th) Air Signal Battalion, Divisional Supply Troops

Formed as Air Defense Command Essen on July 1, 1938, this unit was renamed 4th Flak Division on September 1, 1941. It successively headquartered in Essen, Duesseldorf, Duisburg and Muelheim. By June 1942, it had regiments at Duesseldorf, Essen-Dorsten and Duisburg, as well as smaller units in other locations. Its mission throughout the war was to defend parts of the Ruhr from Allied bombing attacks—a task which ultimately proved impossible to successfully carry out. Meanwhile, the 4th Flak Division was reinforced with the 103rd and 133th Flak Regiments, as well as the 74th Searchlight Regiment and four flak transport batteries. It was surrounded in the Ruhr Pocket, along with Army Group B, in April 1945, and surrendered to the Americans on April 18.

Commanders of the air defense command/flak division included Major General Kurt Steudemann (August 1938), Major General/Lieutenant General Otto-Wilhelm von Renz (October 31, 1939), Major General/Lieutenant General Gerhard Hoffmann (September 1, 1941), Colonel/Major General Johannes Hintz (March 5, 1942), Lieutenant General Ludwig Schilffarth (February 20, 1944), and Colonel Max Hecht (November 15, 1944).

Notes and Sources: Who directed the air defense command from March 17 to August 31, 1941, is not known. Hoffmann was promoted to lieutenant general on June 1, 1941. Renz advanced to the same rank on August 1, 1941. Hintz became a major general on April 1, 1943.

Rudolf Absolon, *Rangliste der Generale der deutschen Luftwaffe nach dem Stand vom 20. April 1945* (1984): 27 (hereafter cited as "Absolon"); Koch: 153, 157, 188, 225; Lexikon; Tessin, Vol. 2: 269.

5TH FLAK DIVISION

Composition (late 1944): 155th Flak Regiment (W), 255th Flak Regiment (W), 125th Air Signal Battalion, Divisional Supply Troops

This division was formed as Air Defense Command West in October 1939. Its mission was to provide ground based air defense for western Germany. Initially headquarters in Frankfurt/Main, with elements in Mannheim and Saarbrücken, it was later transferred to Darmstadt and charged with defending the zone Frankfurt-Mannheim-Saarbruecken. Later it was redesignated 5th Air Defense Command (*Luftverteidigungskommando 5*) and, on September 1, 1941, 5th Flak Division. At that time, it controlled the 29th and 49th Flak Regiments, the 109th and 119th Flak Searchlight Regiments, and the 5th Air Signal Battalion.

The 5th Flak Division was sent to Romania to defend the vital Ploesti oilfields in December 1942. It was transferred to Italy in September 1943, after Mussolini was overthrown, and then back to Romania in November 1943. Here it inflicted heavy casualties on U.S. bombers intent upon destroying Germany's main source of oil. At that time, it had a strength of thirty-one heavy flak batteries, sixteen medium and light batteries, five searchlight batteries, and four rocket batteries, as well as seventeen Romanian heavy batteries, fifteen Romanian light and medium batteries, and a Bulgarian light flak battery. When Romania defected to the Allies in August 1944, however, the 5th Flak Division was trapped and forced to surrender to the Red Army on August 31, 1944. The remnants which managed to escape were temporarily absorbed by the 15th Flak Division.

The 5th Flak Division was reformed at Hamburg and Bad Segeberg on November 1, 1944, as the 5th Flak Division (W), to control all V-1 and V-2 units. The division surrendered to the Western Allies near Hamburg on May 8, 1945. Commanders of the 5th Air Defense

Commanders of 5th Flak Division were Major General Karl Kitzinger (June 1, 1938), Major General Job Odebrecht (October 15, 1939), Major General Wilhelm Elder von Stubenrauch (October 5, 1940), Lieutenant General Kurt Menzel (May 5, 1941), Major General Georg Neuffer (April 18, 1942), Colonel/Major General Julius Kuderna (November 13, 1942), Colonel Adolf Wolf (November 27, 1942), Kuderna again (December 1942), Colonel Eugen Walter (September 1, 1944), Lieutenant General Walter Kathmann (November 1, 1944), and Colonel Max Wachtel (February 6, 1945).

Notes and Sources: Julius Kuderna was promoted to major general on September 1, 1943, and surrendered most of the division at Ploesti on August 31, 1944.

Absolom: 54; Lexikon; Tessin, Vol. 2: 317.

6TH FLAK DIVISION

Composition (1944): 41st Flak Regiment, 43rd Flak Regiment, 136th Flak Regiment, 151st Flak Regiment, 164th Flak Regiment, 126th Air Signal Battalion, 11th Flak Transport Battalion, Divisional Supply Troops

This unit was formed in Hanover on August 1, 1939, as the 6th Air Defense Command. It was transferred to Oldenburg and then to the Brussels-Waterloo sector in May 1940. In the middle of 1941, it was shifted to the east to protect Upper Silesia from Soviet bombers. While there, it was motorized. In April 1942, it was assigned to the 1st Air Fleet and was given the mission of supporting and protecting Army Group North. As of September 1942, its 18th Flak Regiment was with the 11th Army, its 164th Flak Regiment supported the 18th Army, and its 151st Flak Regiment supported the 16th Army. The 6th Flak Division remained on the northern sector of the Eastern Front for the rest of the war, fighting in the siege of and retreat from Leningrad, on the Narva, in the retreat through the Baltic States and in the six battles of the Courland Pocket. It surrendered to the Soviets at Libau in May 1945.

The commanders of this division included Major General Alexander Kolb (August 1, 1939), Major General Wolfgang Rueter (February 29, 1940), Major General/Lieutenant General

Job Odebrecht (October 15, 1940), and Major General/Lieutenant General Werner Anton (November 16, 1942–end).

Notes and Sources: Odebrecht was promoted to lieutenant general on June 1, 1941. Anton was promoted to lieutenant general on July 1, 1944. He was wounded late in the war, and he finally died of those wounds on September 12, 1948. Absolom: 42; Lexikon; Tessin, Vol. 3: 40.

7TH FLAK DIVISION

Composition: 14th Flak Regiment, 47th Flak Regiment, 144th Flak Regiment, 84th Flak Searchlight Regiment, 127th Air Signal Battalion, Divisional Supply Troops.

Formed in Cologne as the 7th Air Defense Command in March 1940, this unit was responsible for defending the Cologne-Aachen sector from Allied bombers. Its was redesignated 7th Flak Division on September 1, 1941, and had regimental headquarters at Cologne, Leverkusen, Wuppertal, Bruehl and Aachen, with smaller units elsewhere. In early 1945, it moved its divisional headquarters to Moenchen-Gladbach and later to Herborn. The 7th Flak was surrounded in the Ruhr Pocket and surrendered to the Americans on April 18, 1945.

Its commanders included Major General Kurt Menzel (February 29, 1940), Colonel Max Hesse (May 5, 1941), Major General/Lieutenant General Heinrich Burchard (August 1, 1941), Major General Rudolf Eibenstein (February 21, 1942), Burchard again (March 1, 1943), and Colonel/Major General Alfred Erhard (August 1, 1944).

Notes and Sources: Burchard was promoted to lieutenant general on August 1, 1941. Alfred Erhard was promoted to major general on January 1, 1945. He committed suicide near Düsseldorf on April 17, 1945, at the end of the Battle of the Ruhr Pocket.
Absolom: 67; Koch: 228; Lexikon; Tessin, Vol. 3: 78.

8TH FLAK DIVISION

Composition (1944): 9th Flak Regiment, 13th Flak Regiment, 26th Flak Regiment, 50th Flak Regiment, 61st Flak Regiment, 63rd Flak Regiment and 89th Flak Regiment, 160th Flak Searchlight Regiment, 129th Flak Transport Battalion, 128th Air Signal Battalion, Divisional Supply Troops

This unit was formed in May 1940, as Air Defense Command Denmark and was responsible for defending that occupied country from Allied air attack. In June 1940, it was renamed 8th Air Defense Command, and its territorial responsibility increased to include Hanover and, in 1941, Bremen. It was redesignated 8th Flak Division on September 1, 1941. Its strength was gradually increased from three to seven regiments. It continued to fight until Allied ground forces overran its area of operations in April and May 1945. It surrendered to the Western Allies near Wesermünde on May 2, 1945.

Commanders of the 8th Flak Division and its predecessors included Colonel Hans Juergen Witzendorff (May 1940), Major General Alexander Kolb (June 4, 1940), Colonel/Major General/Lieutenant General Kurt Wagner (June 30, 1941) and Major General Max Scheller (December 4, 1944).

Notes and Sources: Wagner was promoted to major general on November 1, 1940, and to lieutenant general on November 1, 1942.
Lexikon; Tessin, Vol. 3: 116.

9TH FLAK DIVISION

Composition (Stalingrad): 37th Flak Regiment, 91st Flak Regiment, 104th Flak Regiment, 129th Air Signal Battalion, 9th Flak Divisional Supply Regiment (with several motorized transportation columns)

Formed in Caen and Amiens, France in July 1940, this unit was initially designated 9th Air Defense Command and became the 9th Flak Division on September 1, 1941. Initially it was in charge of defending Belgium and northern France from enemy air attack and controlled the 30th Flak Regiment and 59th Flak Regiments. In early 1942, it was designated a motorized flak unit and its headquarters was sent to the southern sector of the Eastern Front, where it supported the 6th Army. It was surrounded in the Stalingrad Pocket on November 23, 1942, and surrendered to the Soviets on February 2, 1943.

A new 9th Flak Division was formed at Sevastopol on the Crimean peninsula on February 7, 1943. It included the 27th, 42nd and 77th Flak Regiments, as well as three searchlight battalions and the 129th Motorized Air Signal Battalion. It had 28 heavy flak batteries, 27 medium and light batteries, and eight searchlight batteries in October 1943. It was largely destroyed when the Red Army overran the Crimea and captured Sevastopol in April and May 1944.

The 9th Flak Division was rebuilt again in the summer of 1944, this time in Breslau, Silesia. It controlled the 27th, 42nd and 169th Flak Regiments, the 200th Flak Machine Gun Regiment, and the 125./IV, 3./VI, 92./VI, and 72./XI Flak Transport Battalions. On September 3, 1944, it arrived in Saarbrücken sector of the Western Front, where it supported the 1st Army in the Siegfried Line battles and in the retreat through southwestern Germany. As of October, it controlled thirty-three heavy flak and fifty-five medium and light batteries. It surrendered to the Americans in Bavaria on May 9, 1945.

Commanders of the first 9th Flak and its predecessors included Major General Gerhard Hoffmann (June 24, 1940), Major General/Lieutenant General Wilhelm von Renz (March 17, 1941), Colonel/Major General/Lieutenant General Wolfgang Pickert (June 25, 1942), Colonel Wilhelm Wolff (January 13, 1943), and Lieutenant Colonel Richard Haizmann (January 1943–end). Commanders of the second 9th Flak included Pickert (February 7, 1943), Colonel Wilhelm von Koolwijk (May 27, 1944), and Major General/Lieutenant General Adolf Pirmann (June 23, 1944).

Notes and Sources: Renz was promoted to lieutenant general on August 1, 1941. Pickert was promoted to major general on October 1, 1942, and to lieutenant general on November 1, 1943. Although he never officially gave up command of the division, Pickert flew out of Stalingrad on January 13, 1943, and left Colonel Wolff as de facto commander of the 9th Flak. Pirmann was promoted to lieutenant general on January 1, 1945.

Koch: 226; Lexikon; Nafziger 1999: 434; Tessin, Vol. 3: 153–54.

10TH FLAK DIVISION

Composition: 7th Flak Regiment, 17th Flak Regiment, 48th Flak Regiment, 153rd Flak Regiment, 40./IV Flak Transport Battalion, 106./IV Flak Transport Battalion, 108./IV Flak Transport Battalion, 96./VIII Flak Transport Battalion, 140./IV Flak Transport Battalion, 91./VI Flak Transport Battalion, 97./VII Flak Transport Battalion, 46./XII Flak Transport Battalion, 136./XI Flak Transport Battalion, Divisional Supply Troops

This unit was formed as the 10th Air Defense Command in Ploesti, Romania, in April 1941. It became the 10th Flak Division on September 1, 1941. Initially it included the 180th and 202nd Flak Regiments. A motorized unit, it was transferred to the Eastern Front, and first saw major combat at Sevastopol in the Crimea in March 1942. In May 1942, it was attached to Army Group South and was initially assigned to the 2nd Army at Kursk. At that time it included the motorized 153rd and 124th Flak Regiments. The division fought in southern Russia, Galacia (including Lemberg and Krakov) and Poland, working at various times for Army Groups B, North Ukraine and A, as well as for the 17th Army at Troppau. As of October 23, 1944, it had twenty-five heavy batteries, twenty-eight medium and light batteries, and four searchlight batteries. It surrendered to the Red Army at Koeniginhof on May 8, 1945.

Commanders of the 10th Flak included Colonel/Major General/Lieutenant General Johann Siefert (April 12, 1940), Colonel/Major General Franz Engel (June 30, 1943), Colonel Oskar Vorbrugg (February 3, 1945), and Engel (returned February 10, 1945).

Notes and Sources: Siefert was promoted to major general on June 1, 1940 and to lieutenant general on June 1, 1942. Engel was promoted to major general on October 1, 1944.

Lexikon; Tessin, Vol. 3: 186.

11TH FLAK DIVISION

Composition (January 1943): 45th Flak Regiment, 69th Flak Regiment, 85th Flak Regiment, 653rd Flak Regiment, 131st Air Signal Battalion

This unit was formed in Bordeaux, western France, on February 1, 1941, as the 11th Air Defense Command, with the responsibility for providing air defense artillery fire from Brittany to the French-Spanish border. It was redesignated 11th Flak Division on September 1, 1941. In January 1943, it was transferred to southern France, where it headquartered at Nimes. The 45th Flak Regiment defended the Bordeaux area with four flak and two searchlight battalions; the 69th Flak Regiment defended Marseilles with four flak battalions and one searchlight battalion; the 85th Flak Regiment defended the Tarascon area with six flak battalions; and the 653rd Flak Regiment guarded Narbonne with three flak battalions. The division headquarters was redesignated III Flak Corps on February 2, 1944. The commanders of the original 11th Flak Division were Major General/Lieutenant General Helmuth Richter (February 1, 1941) and Lieutenant General Erich Kressmann (November 1, 1943).

A second 11th Flak Division was formed in Heydebreck, Upper Silesia, in September 1944, when the 15th Flak Brigade was upgraded. It was responsible for the air defense of Upper Silesia and consisted of immobile flak batteries. It included the 54th Flak Regiment (Flak Group Auschwitz) with three flak battalions; 106th Flak Regiment (Flak Group Upper Silesia-West) with five battalions; 107th Flak Regiment (Flak Group Upper Silesia-East) with four batteries; 150th Flak Regiment (Flak Group Breslau) with five battalions; the 84th Searchlight Regiment (Flak Searchlight Group Upper Silesia) with three battalions; the 131st Air Signal Battalion; and assorted divisional supply and support troops. In early 1945, as the Soviets entered Silesia, the division was attached to the 1st Panzer Army and fought against the Red Army in a ground combat role in the last days of the war. It surrendered to the Russians in Czechoslovakia in May 1945.

The commander of the second 11th Flak Division was Major General Oskar Krämer.

Notes and Sources: Richter was promoted to lieutenant general on August 1, 1941. Krämer was killed on May 11, 1945.

Absolom: 71; Koch: 189; Schmidt et al., Vol. 3: 33; Tessin, Vol. 3: 218.

12TH FLAK DIVISION

Composition (May 1942): 21st Flak Regiment, 34th Flak Regiment, 101st Flak Regiment, 132nd Air Signal Battalion, Divisional Supply Troops

The 12th Flak was formed in central Russia on February 1, 1942, from the Staff, IX Flak Brigade. In May, it was posted to the southern zone of Army Group Center, where it supported the 2nd and 4th Armies. It fought at Spass-Demensk (1942), Bryansk, Orel, Kursk, and the retreat to the Dnieper (1943), and in Operation Bagration and the defense of Bobruisk (1944), among others. By 1944, it included the 21st, 23rd, 31st, and 77th Flak Regiments. In the retreat across East Prussia and Pomerania, the 12th Flak Division was involved in the defense of Danzig and Swinemuende. Most of the division was destroyed in the Battle of Berlin (April 16 to May 2, 1945), although elements of the 12th did escape encirclement and surrendered to the U.S. Army on May 9, 1945.

Commanders of the 12th Flak included Major General Rudolf Eibenstein (September 22, 1941), Major General Gotthard Frantz (December 1, 1941), Major General/Lieutenant General Ernst Joachim Buffa (December 21, 1942), and Major General/Lieutenant General Werner Prellberg (April 15, 1944).

Notes and Sources: Buffa was promoted to lieutenant general on February 1, 1943. Prellberg was promoted to lieutenant general on August 1, 1944.

Koch: 226; Lexikon; Tessin, Vol. 3: 279–80.

13TH FLAK DIVISION

Composition (1943): 15th Flak Regiment, 30th Flak Regiment, 100th Flak Regiment, 117th Flak Regiment, Divisional Supply Troops

The 13th Flak Division was formed on February 1, 1942, at Caen in Luftgau West France, in order to replace the 9th Flak Division, which had been sent to the Russian Front. Initially, it headquartered at Vernon (northwest of Paris) and included the 18th Flak Regiment at Le Creusot, the 59th Flak Regiment at Paris, and the 100th Flak Regiment, which headquartered at Le Havre. In 1943, its Staff moved to Laval, southeast of Rennes, and was attached to the 7th Army. In 1944, it fought in the ground battles at Le Mans, in the Alsace, at Strasbourg and Kolmar. As of January 22, 1945, it controlled thirty-seven heavy flak batteries, twenty-six medium and light batteries, a barrage balloon battery and a smoke company. It supported the 19th Army in the Black Forest (Schwarzwald) in February 1945. The following month, the 13th Flak gave up its remaining units to the 28th Flak Division, and its staff moved to the Protectorate. When Hitler committed suicide on April 30, 1945, the headquarters was at Eger, in the Pilsen area of Czechoslovakia. It quickly moved west and surrendered to the Americans the following week.

Its commanders included Major General Gaston von Chaulin-Egersberg (February 1, 1942), Lieutenant General Theodor Spiess (July 1, 1942), Major General Max Schaller (March 1, 1944), and Major General Adolf Wolf (October 6, 1944).

Sources: Koch: 188; Lexikon; Nafziger 1999: 438; Tessin, Vol. 3: 279–80.

14TH FLAK DIVISION

Composition: 33rd Flak Regiment, 140th Flak Regiment, 300th Flak Regiment, I/42nd Flak Regiment, 7th Flak Searchlight Regiment, 73rd Flak Searchlight Regiment, Flak Group Lower Silesia, 134th Air Signal Battalion, Divisional Supply Troops

In January 1942, the Headquarters, 2nd Flak Division was motorized and sent to the Eastern Front. That same month, the Staff, 14th Flak Division was created at Leipzig-Schoenau to replace it. The new division controlled the mostly static flak guns emplacements in the Leipzig area. It remained there, conducting the anti-aircraft defense of the region, until the Red Army approached. The HQ (with a handful of mobile units) then retreated to the Elbe and surrendered to the Anglo-Americans near Schwerin-Hagenow on May 2, 1945.

Commanders of the division included Lieutenant General Walter Feyerabend (February 3, 1942), Major General/Lieutenant General Rudolf Schulze (December 1, 1942), Major General Adolf Gerlach (May 15, 1944), Colonel Max Hecht (May 1944), Gerlach (returned May 1944), Colonel Müller (1945), and Gerlach (1945).

Notes and Sources: Schulze was promoted to lieutenant general on September 1, 1943.
Absolom: 59; Koch: 188; Lexikon; Tessin, Vol. 3: 311.

15TH FLAK DIVISION

Composition: See below

The 15th Flak Division (motorized) was formed at Ploesti, Romania, on March 1, 1942, from the staff of the III Flak Brigade and detachments from the 5th Flak Division. By May, it was on the southern sector of the Eastern Front. At various times, it supported Army Group South, Army Group A, 17th Army, 1st Panzer Army, Army Group South Ukraine and 6th Army. It fought in southern Russia, on the drive to Rostov, in the Caucasus, the Kuban, in the retreat to the Dnieper, and into Bessarabia and Romania. As of August 22, 1944, it was supporting 6th Army and included the 4th Flak Regiment at Jassy; the 12th Flak Regiment at Konstanza; the 104th Flak Regiment at Romanesti; and the 133rd Flak Regiment at Klausenburg. That day, Romania defected from the Axis and opened its lines to the Red Army, which launched a huge offensive that morning. The 15th Flak Division was largely destroyed by August 31. Mobile remnants of the division escaped to Hungary, where they absorbed the remnants of the 5th Flak Division. It now included the 4th, 7th and 153rd Flak Regiments. The division spent most of the rest of the war in the Stuhlweissenburg, Hungary area and in the defense of Austria. It surrendered to the Americans on May 8, 1945.

Commanders of the 15th Flak Division included Lieutenant General Gerhard Hoffmann (March 1, 1942), Colonel/ Major General Eduard Muhr (November 10, 1942), Colonel/ Major General Hans Simon (April 15, 1944), Colonel Ernst Jansa (August 29, 1944), Major General Theodor Herbert (September 12, 1944), Colonel T. Peters (January 21, 1945), and Colonel/Major General Johann-Wilhelm (Johannes) Döring-Manteuffel (January 26, 1945).

Notes and Sources: Muhr was promoted to major general while commanding the 15th Flak. He was relieved for reasons of health and was promoted to lieutenant general in September 1, 1944, while in Fuehrer Reserve. He was not reemployed and died on December 27, 1944. Hans Simon was captured in Romania on August 29, 1944, and was promoted to major general on October 1, while in captivity. Doering-Manteuffel was promoted to major general on April 20, 1945. Colonel Rittner apparently served as acting commander from January 19 to 26, 1945, but the author has not been able to confirm this fact.

Absolon: 44; Koch: 189; Tessin, Vol. 4: 19; Schmitz et al., Vol. 3: 189.

16TH FLAK DIVISION

Composition (1942): 8th Flak Regiment, 37th Flak Regiment, 95th Flak Regiment, 129th Flak Regiment, 132nd Flak Regiment, 431st Flak Regiment, 656th Flak Regiment, 136th Air Signal Battalion, Divisional Supply Troops

Created on March 1, 1942, this division replaced the 6th Flak Division, which was on its way to the Eastern Front. The 16th Flak responsible for the flak defense in the northern France–Belgium–The Netherlands zone. It headquartered at Lille and had regiments at Rotterdam, Watten, Antwerp, Dunkirk, Boulogne, and Beauvais. Later, after the Allies broke out of the Normandy beachhead in the summer of 1944, the division retreated into the Netherlands. On February 9, 1945, the divisional headquarters was redesignated Staff, VI Flak Corps. At that time, it controlled the 1st, 18th, and 19th, and Special Purposes Flak Regiments.

Its commanders were Lieutenant General Kurt Steudemann (June 15, 1942), Major General/Lieutenant General Rudolf Eibenstein (March 1, 1943) and Colonel/Major General Friedrich-Wilhelm Deutsch (April 30, 1944).

Notes and Sources: Eibenstein became a lieutenant general on August 1, 1943. Deutsch was promoted to major general on July 1, 1944.
Koch: 227; Lexikon; Tessin, Vol. 4: 46.

17TH FLAK DIVISION

Composition (1942): 4th Flak Regiment, 12th Flak Regiment, 42nd Flak Regiment, 137th Air Signal Battalion, Divisional Supply Troops

Formed in Leipzig on April 1, 1942, the 17th Flak was sent to Stalino in southern Russia in May. Assigned to the 1st Panzer Army, it was attached to the 17th Army in the second half of 1942, but supported the 1st Panzer Army again in 1943 and 1944. It suffered heavy losses in the Kamenez-Podolsk Pocket (the "Hube Pocket"), when the 1st Panzer Army was encircled in March 1944, but formed a "floating pocket" and broke out, reaching German lines in April. The 17th Flak later fought in Lublin, Krakow and Breslau and, in April 1945, was at Goerlitz, supporting the 4th Panzer Army. It surrendered to the Red Army on May 8, 1945, having spent all but the first month of its existence on the Eastern Front.

Commanders of the 17th Flak Division included Lieutenant General Gerhard Hoffmann (June 1, 1942), Colonel Hans Simon (March 15, 1944), Major General Karl Veith (April 15, 1944), and Colonel/Major General Wilhelm Köppen (June 7, 1944).

Notes and Sources: Koepper was promoted to major general on August 1, 1944. Who commanded the division from April 14 to June 7, 1944, is not clear.
Koch: 188; Lexikon; Mehner, Vol. 5: 338; Tessin, Vol. 4: 74.

18TH FLAK DIVISION

Composition: 6th Flak Regiment, 10th Flak Regiment, 125th Flak 339Regiment, 133rd Flak Regiment, 138th Air Signal Battalion, Divisional Supply Troops

The Headquarters, 18th Flak Division was formed in Smolensk, Russia, on April 10, 1942, from the Staff, II Flak Corps. Its mission was to support the northern wing of Army Group Center (3rd Panzer and 9th Armies) from Vyasma to Rzhev. It did its job well, but suffered heavy casualties when Stalin's summer offensive of 1944 smashed Army Group Center and virtually destroyed the 9th Army and smashed the 3rd Panzer Army. The 18th Flak managed to withdraw across Lithuania and Poland and into East Prussia. On January 21, 1945, it took control of all flak units in East Prussia and the Heiligenbeil Pocket. It included the 16th Flak Brigade (which was withdrawn to Germany proper in March), the 87th Flak Regiment at Koenigsberg, and the 116th and 125th Flak Regiments in Heiligenbeil (later in Samland and the Hela peninsula). Later, the division took over the regiments of the 12th Flak Division, whose headquarters was transferred from East Prussia to Berlin. The 18th Flak Division was isolated on the Hela peninsula as of May 3, 1945; however, it took some of the last ships out of East Prussia and surrendered to the Western Allies in Schleswig, northwestern Germany, on May 10.

Commanders of the 18th Flak Division were Major General/Lieutenant General Richard Reimann (April 10, 1942), Major General Prince Heinrich XXXVII of Reuss (March 10, 1943), Colonel/Major General Adolf Wolf (February 1, 1944), and Major General Günther Sachs (October 2, 1944).

Notes and Sources: Reimann was promoted to lieutenant general on March 1, 1943. Wolf was promoted to major general on April 1, 1944. According to one source, he assumed command of the division that same day. Koch: 188; Tessin, Vol. 4: 106–7.

19TH FLAK DIVISION

Composition (1943): 102nd Flak Regiment, 114th Flak Regiment, 135th Flak Regiment, Divisional Supply Troops

The original 19th Flak Division was formed in Sicily from the Staff, VII Flak Brigade. Activated on August 15, 1942, it was immediately sent to Libya, to support Field Marshal Rommel's Panzer Army Afrika, which was in the process of invading Egypt. After the Allies landed in French North Africa in November 1942, the 19th Flak was rushed back to Tunisia, where it supported the 5th Panzer Army and the 1st Italian-German Panzer Army. It was forced to surrender on May 13, 1943, after the German supply lines to Africa collapsed. Lieutenant General Heinrich Burchard (August 6, 1942) and Major General/Lieutenant General Gotthard Frantz (December 21, 1942) commanded the first 19th Flak Division.

The 19th Flak was reformed in Athens on June 23, 1943. It took control of all flak units in Greece on November 1, 1943. It now included the 91st, 201st, and 66th Flak Regiments in Greece and the 58th Flak Regiment in Crete, and the 139th Air Signal Battalion. In October 1944, the division was headquartered in Salonika, when the German withdrawal from the Balkans began. By December, it was in Rugusa, directing the withdrawal of the anti-aircraft artillery. By late April 1945, the division was on the Aegean, and it surrendered to the Americans on May 8, 1945.

Colonel/Major General Paul Pavel commanded the second 19th Flak Division throughout its existence.

Notes and Sources: Frantz was promoted to lieutenant general on April 1, 1943. He was captured when Tunisia fell. Pavel was promoted to major general on February 1, 1944.

Koch: 189; Lexikon; Hildebrand; Tessin, Vol. 4: 126.

20TH FLAK DIVISION

Composition (Africa): 78th Flak Regiment, Flak Group Bizerta, Flak Group Soussa

The 20th Flak Division was formed in Leipzig on November 13, 1942, and was immediately rushed to the Tunisian Bridgehead, where it provided air defense and ground support for the 5th Panzer Army and Army Group Afrika. It surrendered after the German Mediterranean supply lines were severed by the U.S. and British navies and air forces. The division's only commander, Major General Georg Neuffer, surrendered on May 9, 1943.

A second 20th Flak Division was formed in Belgrade, Yugoslavia, on October 1, 1943. In 1944, it controlled the 37th, 38th and 40th Flak Regiments. It began withdrawing from the Balkans (along with OB Southeast) in October 1944, and was at Steinamanger (now Szombathely) in northwest Hungary when the war ended. It fell into Soviet captivity.

Commanders of the second 20th Flak were Colonel/Major General Otto Sydow (October 1, 1943), Colonel Dr. Hermann Rudhart (October 1944), Colonel Johann-Wilhelm (Johannes) Doering-Manteuffel (October 30, 1944), Major General Theodor Herbert (January 19, 1945), and Colonel Ernst Schluchtmann (April 12, 1945).

Notes and Sources: Sydow was promoted to major general on April 1, 1944.

Koch: 227; Lexikon; Tessin, Vol. 4: 149.

21st FLAK DIVISION

Composition (November 1943): 29th Flak Regiment, 49th Flak Regiment, 169th Flak Regiment, 189th Flak Regiment, 70th Flak Searchlight Regiment, 109th Flak Searchlight Regiment, 119th Flak Searchlight Regiment, 139th Flak Searchlight Regiment, 141st Air Signal Battalion, Divisional Supply Troops

This division was formed in Darmstadt from the Staff, VI Flak Brigade, in March 1943. It was responsible for the anti-aircraft artillery defense of the Rhine-Main area and included flak groups at Frankfurt/Main, Mannheim, Saarbrücken, Mainz, and Koblenz. It continued in this mission until its cities were overrun by the Allied armies. The divisional headquarters, meanwhile, moved to Weisbaden in February 1945. The remnants of the 21st Flak Division surrendered in the Tegernsee (Lake Tegern) sector on May 8, 1945.

Its commanders were Lieutenant General Kurt Steudemann (March 1, 1943), Lieutenant General Ernst Buffa (June 6, 1944) and Colonel Erich Groepler (December 1, 1944).

Sources: Koch: 226; Lexikon; Tessin, Vol. 4: 170–71.

22ND FLAK DIVISION

Composition (1943): 54th Flak Regiment, 67th Flak Regiment, 103rd Flak Regiment, 112th Flak Regiment, 124th Flak Regiment, 183rd Flak Regiment, 146th Flak Searchlight Regiment, 142nd Air Signal Battalion, Divisional Supply Troops

This division was formed in Dortmund, around cadres provided by the 10th Flak Brigade, which was serving on the Eastern Front, and by Luftgau VI. Its regiments were stationed at Dortmund, Münster, Bochum, Kassel, and Hagan. It continued to provide air defense for the Ruhr Industrial Area and nearby sectors until it was surrounded by the U.S. Army. It surrendered to the Americans at Iserlohn on April 16, 1945.

Commanders of the division were Colonel Johann Elder von Krziwanek (April 1943) and Colonel/Major General Friedrich Roemer (May 1, 1943–end).

Notes and Sources: After the division was formed, Krziwanek returned to the X Flak Brigade. Roemer was promoted to major general on October 1, 1943.

Lexikon; Mehner, Vol. 6: 551; Nafziger 1999: 445–46; Tessin, Vol. 4: 187.

23RD FLAK DIVISION

Composition (April 1945): 7th Flak Regiment, 23rd Flak Regiment, 34th Flak Regiment, 35th Flak Regiment, 53rd Flak Regiment, 182nd Flak Regiment, Flak Regiment Wegener, Divisional Supply Troops

This division was formed in Bobruisk on October 10, 1943. Its staff was the former Staff, 22nd Luftwaffe Field Division. Charged with the task of supporting and providing air defense for Army Group Center, it initially concentrated at Baranowitschi and Minsk. In March 1944, it controlled the 22nd, 31st, 101st, and 125th Flak Regiments, and the 143rd Air Signal Battalion. Later in 1944, after Army Group Center had been smashed by Stalin's summer offensive, the 23rd Flak was supporting 9th Army in the Warsaw-Radom-Posen zone. By February 1945, it was on the Oder and was supporting 9th Army with five flak regiments—twenty battalions in all. On April 26, it was still fighting in eastern Germany with seven flak regiments, two of which were in the Frankfurt/Oder sector, which had been surrounded by the Red Army. After suffering heavy losses in the last campaign, the division surrendered to the Soviets at Doeberitz on May 1945.

Its commanders were Colonel Hans-Wilhelm Fichter (October 10, 1943), Lieutenant General Walter Kathmann (August 21, 1944), Colonel Oskar Vorbrugg (October 24, 1944), and Colonel/Major General Kurt Andersen (January 30, 1945).

Notes and Sources: Andersen was promoted to major general on February 17, 1945.

Koch: 186; Lexikon; Nafziger 1999: 446–47; Tessin, Vol. 4: 203.

24TH FLAK DIVISION

Composition (1943): 28th Flak Regiment, 76th Flak Regiment, 88th Flak Regiment, 98th Flak Regiment, 184th Flak Regiment, 1st Flak Searchlight Regiment, 6th Flak Searchlight Regiment, 144th Air Signal Battalion, Divisional Supply Troops

The 24th Flak Division was formed in Vienna-Kobenzl from the Staff, XVI Flak Brigade. Its mission was to provide anti-aircraft artillery defense for Luftgau XVII (the Greater Vienna area), and it spent virtually the entire war in the former Austrian capital. On April 1, 1944, parts of the division were used to form the VII Flak Brigade in Linz. In the fall of 1944, the division controlled only three flak regiments (the 28th, 98th, and 102nd) plus the 6th Searchlight Regiment. It was caught up in ground combat in April 1945, as the Red Army attacked Vienna, and suffered heavy casualties. The remnants of the division surrendered in May 1945.

Colonel/Major General Fritz Grieshammer commanded the 24th Flak throughout its existence.

Notes and Sources: Grieshammer was promoted to major general on April 1, 1944.
Koch: 227; Lexikon; Tessin, Vol. 4: 219.

25TH FLAK DIVISION

Composition: 5th Flak Regiment, 131st Flak Regiment, 137th Flak Regiment, 149th Flak Regiment, 145th Air Signal Battalion, Divisional Supply Troops

This division was formed in Italy on April 1, 1944, from the XVII Flak Brigade, under the supervision of the General of Flak Artillery South. It was charged with the task of providing air defense for northern Italy, especially the Mailand and Brescia zones. In December 1944, it moved its headquarters from Mailand to Brescia, and was made responsible for the air defense in the Brescia-Bergamo-Trient area. After OB Southwest collapsed, the 25th Flak Division surrendered to the British on May 2, 1945.

Commanders of the division were Major General/Lieutenant General Walter von Hippel (April 1, 1944) and Colonel/Major General Oskar Vorbrugg (February 10, 1945–end). Colonel Alfred Thomas briefly served as acting commander in March 1945.

Notes and Sources: Hippel was promoted to lieutenant general on August 1, 1944. Vorbrugg was promoted to major general on April 1, 1945.
Koch: 226, 228; Lexikon; Tessin, Vol. 4: 223.

26TH FLAK DIVISION

Composition (December 1944): 19th Flak Regiment, 55th Flak Regiment, 93rd Flak Regiment, 114th Flak Regiment, 115th Flak Regiment, 8th Flak Searchlight Regiment, 146th Air Signal Battalion, Divisional Supply Troops

The 26th Flak Division was officially formed in Munich on May 1, 1944, from the Staff, IV Flak Brigade, for the air defense of Munich, Upper Bavaria and Swabia. It initially included the Flakgruppen North Munich and South Munich (which became the 19th and 55th Flak Regiments, respectively), the 130th Flak Regiment, and the 2nd and 8th Searchlight Regiments. On September 6, 1944, it took over the 93rd Flak Regiment in Nuremberg and Franconia. The division continued to oppose the Allied air offensive until the Americans captured Munich on April 30, 1945. For most practical purposes, the 26th Flak Division ceased to exist at that time, and had been ordered to disband on April 28. The last remnants of the division, however, did not surrender to the Americans until May 3, 1945.

The division's commanders were Colonel Ernst Uhl (April 26 to July 1, 1944) and Lieutenant General Rudolf Eibenstein (July 1, 1944–end).

Sources: Koch: 189, 226; Lexikon; Tessin, Vol. 4: 247.

27TH FLAK DIVISION

Composition (November 1944): 62nd Flak Regiment, 81st Flak Regiment, 97th Flak Regiment, 121st Flak Regiment, 171st Flak Searchlight Regiment, 5./III Home Flak Battalion, 6./III Home Flak Battalion, 7./III Home Flak Battalion, 27./I Home Flak Battalion, Divisional Supply Troops

This division was formed in Königsberg, East Prussia, from the Staff, XI Flak Brigade, which had served in Belgium and northern France (1941–42), southwestern France (1942–43) and the Channel coast (1943–44). It was returned to East Prussia in September 1944, and was upgraded to become the 27th Flak Division. In December, it was attached to the 3rd Panzer Army and fought on the Oder. It left East Prussia on January 21, 1945, five days before it was cut off from the rest of the Reich, and moved to central Germany, where it was attached to the 11th Army. In April 1945, it was in Pasewalk, controlling the 171st Flak Regiment at Greifenhagen and the 21st Motorized Flak Regiment south of Stettin. After suffering heavy losses in the East, the division finally surrendered to the British at Plate (near Schwerin) at the end of the war (May 8, 1945).

Commanders of the 27th Flak Division included Colonel Alexander Nieper (September 1944), Lieutenant General Walter Kathmann (October 21, 1944), Lieutenant General Walter von Hippel (February 1, 1945), Lieutenant General Walter Feyerabend (April 1945), and Major General Oskar Vorbrugg (May 2, 1945).

Notes and Sources: Colonel Nieper had assumed command of the XI Flak Brigade in June 1944.

Absolom: 43; Koch: 189; Lexikon; Tessin, Vol. 4: 258.

28TH FLAK DIVISION

Composition: 68th Flak Regiment, 69th Flak Regiment, 130th Flak Regiment, 139th Flak Regiment, 148th Air Signal Battalion, Divisional Supply Troops

This division was formed in Stuttgart in October 1944, from the Staff, IX Flak Brigade, which had served in western France since the spring of 1941. It was given the task of providing air defense for the Baden–Württemberg–Upper Rhine regions. It fought in the defense of Alsace and southwestern Germany and, in March 1945, absorbed the combat units of the 13th (Motorized) Flak Division. The 28th Flak Division surrendered to the Western Allies on May 5, 1945.

Commanders of the 28th Flak were Colonel Hans-Juergen Heckmanns (October 24, 1944) and Major General Kurt von Ludwig (November 24, 1944–end).

Sources: Koch: 189; Lexikon; Tessin, Vol. 4: 269.

29TH FLAK DIVISION

Composition: See below

The 29th Flak Division was formed in Oslo, Norway, on February 26, 1945, from the Staff, XIV Flak Brigade. Responsible for the air defense of occupied Norway, it included the 83rd Flak Regiment at Narvik, the 92nd Flak Regiment at Stavanger, the 152nd Flak Regiment at Drontheim, and the 162nd Flak Regiment at Oslo. It also controlled the 148th Air Signal Battalion and had a total strength of 513 officers and 14,822 men. The division surrendered to the British on May 8, 1945.

Colonel Alexander Nieper commanded the division throughout its brief existence.

Sources: Lexikon; Nafziger 1999: 449; Tessin, Vol. 4: 280.

30TH FLAK DIVISION

Composition: 50th Flak Regiment (E), 71st Flak Regiment (E), 97th Flak Regiment (E), 112th Flak Regiment (E), 122nd Flak Regiment (E), Flak Regiment (E) 159th Flak Regiment (E)

This division was created in Berlin in February 1945, from the V Flak Brigade (E). Its mission was to control all of the railroad flak units in Germany. All of its regiments ended with the designation "(E)," which stood for *Eisenbahn* or railway. It was commanded throughout its existence by Colonel Egon Baur, who surrendered the Staff and elements of the division to the Americans in Upper Bavaria (Oberbayern) on May 8, 1945.

Sources: Lexikon; Tessin, Vol. 4: 290.

31ST FLAK DIVISION

Composition: 52nd Flak Regiment, 143rd Flak Regiment, 108th Flak Searchlight Regiment, 162nd Air Signal Battalion

The 31st Flak was formed in northern Germany from the Staff, II Flak Brigade on January 1, 1945. Its mission was to provide air defense for the Magdeburg-Bielefeld zone. It was greatly understrength.

It was commanded by Colonel/Major General Herbert Giese (January 1, 1945) and Colonel Herbert Roehler (April 20, 1945).

Notes and Sources: Giese was promoted to major general on April 20, 1945, the day he gave up command of the 31st Flak. Absolom: 71; Lexikon.

CHAPTER 8

Miscellaneous Divisions

1ST CAVALRY DIVISION*

Composition (1939): 1st Cavalry Brigade (1st and 2nd Cavalry Regiments), 2nd Cavalry Brigade (21st and 22nd Cavalry Regiments), 1st Mounted Artillery Regiment (two battalions), 1st Bicycle Battalion, 40th Tank Destroyer Company, 40th Engineer Battalion, 86th Signal Battalion, 40th Divisional Supply Troops

Home Station: Insterburg, Wehrkreis I

The 1st Cavalry Division was formed as the 1st Cavalry Brigade on October 1, 1934. It should not be confused with the earlier 1st Cavalry Division, which was formed in 1921 and disbanded in April 1936. The brigade fought well in Poland in 1939, attacking from East Prussia and driving south on Warsaw. It was expanded into the 1st Cavalry Division on October 25, 1939. The new division overran most of the eastern Netherlands in May 1940, and fought in the Somme and Loire areas of France the following month. Stationed on the Atlantic coast in July and August, it was sent back to Poland in September and remained there until the invasion of the Soviet Union. It fought in the battles of Minsk, Gomel, and Kiev (1941), and was used in anti-partisan operations in the Pripjet marshes. It took part in the huge battle of encirclement at Bryansk in October 1941, as part of the 2nd Panzer Army. The 1st Cavalry was sent back to East Prussia the following month and was reorganized as the 24th Panzer Division. The 1st Cavalry Division officially ceased to exist on November 28, 1941.

---

*Miscellaneous divisions are arranged by number.

Its commander throughout its existence was Colonel/
Major General/Lieutenant General Kurt Feldt, although Colo-
nel Otto Mengers briefly served as acting commander in
November 1940.

See 24th Panzer Division (Volume Three).

Notes and Sources: Feldt was also the first commander of the
24th Panzer Division. He was promoted to major general on February 1, 1940, and to lieutenant general on February 1, 1942.

Keilig: 88; Kursietis: 107; Tessin, Vol. 2: 35-36; Lexikon; Frido von
Senger und Etterlin, *Neither Fear Nor Hope* (1964). Also see Dr. F. M.
von Senger und Etterlin, *Die 24. Panzer-Division, vormals 1. Kavallerie-
Division, 1939–1945* (1962).

1ST COSSACK CAVALRY DIVISION

Composition (1944): 1st Cossack Cavalry Brigade Don (1st
[Don] Cossack Cavalry Regiment, 2nd [Ural] Cossack Cavalry
Regiment, 3rd [Sswodno] Cossack Cavalry Regiment, Cossack
Horse Artillery Battalion Don), 2nd Cossack Cavalry Brigade
(4th [Kuban] Cossack Cavalry Regiment, 5th [Don] Cossack
Cavalry Regiment, 6th [Terek] Cossack Cavalry Regiment, Cos-
sack Cavalry Artillery Battalion Kuban), 55th (Kuban) Cossack
Horse Artillery Regiment, 55th Reconnaissance Battalion, 1st
Cossack Engineer Battalion, 55th Cossack Engineer Battalion,
1st Signal Battalion

Home Station: Praschnitz, Wehrkreis I

Formed in Poland in the late summer of 1943, this unit
included Don, Kuban, Terek, and Siberian Cossacks, who had
been operating in separate cavalry squadrons against Russian
guerillas. (A great many of the Cossacks volunteered to fight
the Communist regime.) At that time the division was composed of two brigades, each of three sabre regiments and an
artillery battalion. Subsequently sent to Yugoslavia in the fall of
1943, it was used in anti-partisan operations along the middle
stretch of the Zagreb-Belgrade Railroad. It was transferred to
the control of the Waffen-SS in December 1944, and was

placed under the direction of the XV SS Cossack Cavalry Corps in 1945. It was sent into action on the Eastern Front in early 1945, and by February was fighting on the Yugoslav-Hungarian border. It surrendered to the British 8th Army on the Italian-Yugoslav frontier in May 1945, but its men were subsequently turned over to the Soviets, who killed them.

The division's commanders were Colonel/Major General/ Lieutenant General Helmuth von Pannwitz (May 1, 1943), Colonel Constantin Wagner (November 30, 1944), Colonel Hans-Gert von Baath (January 1945), Colonel Körner (February 1945), and Wagner (March 1945–end). Colonel Alexander von Bosse briefly commanded the division in 1945, but the exact dates of his tenure are not cited in the appropriate documents.

Notes and Sources: General von Pannwitz took over the XV Cossack Cavalry Corps in February 1945. He was executed in Moscow on January 16, 1947, for leading White Russian troops.

Lexikon; James Lucas, *War on the Eastern Front, 1941–1945* (1979): 115; Mellenthin 1977: 49–52; Scheibert: 25; Tessin, Vol. 2: 37; OB 45: 285.

2ND COSSACK CAVALRY DIVISION

Composition: 3rd (Kuban) Cossack Cavalry Regiment, 5th (Don) Cossack Cavalry Regiment, 6th (Terek) Cossack Cavalry Regiment

Formed in France in November 1944, from the 2nd Cossack Cavalry Brigade of the 1st Cossack Cavalry Division, this unit consisted of Cossacks volunteers, many of whom were released from POW camps to fight against their former masters. Some of the regimental headquarters of the 1st Cossack Cavalry were transferred to the 2nd also (see Composition, 1st Cossack Cavalry Division). The division was transferred to the SS in December. The 2nd Cossack Cavalry fought partisans in Yugoslavia and on the southern sector of the Eastern Front in Yugoslavia and Hungary but surrendered to the British 8th Army on the Italian border in May 1945. In accordance with the Yalta agreements, however, its personnel were turned over to the Russians, who executed them. The division's commander was Colonel Hans-Joachim von Schultz.

Notes and Sources: It is not clear which of the 1st Cossack Cavalry Division's support units were transferred to the 2nd Cossack Cavalry Division.

Mellenthin 1977: 49–52; Tessin, Vol. 2: 149.

3RD CAVALRY DIVISION

Composition (September 1944): 31st Cavalry Regiment, 32nd Cavalry Regiment, 869th Artillery Regiment, 69th Panzer Reconnaissance Battalion, 69th Tank Destroyer Battalion, 69th Motorized Engineer Battalion, 238th Signal Battalion, 69th Field Replacement Battalion, 69th Divisional Supply Troops

Home Station: Lüneburg, Wehrkreis X

The 3rd Cavalry Brigade was built around Cavalry Regiment Center (of Army Group Center) in March 1944. At that time, it included Cavalry Regiment Center, the 105th Light Artillery Battalion, the 177th Assault Gun Battalion, and the 3rd Heavy Cavalry Battalion, which included two engineer companies and an anti-aircraft company. The 3rd Brigade fought on the central sector of the Eastern Front, including the Battle of Pinsk, the retreats across the Bug and the Narev, and in the early stages of the fighting in East Prussia (October–December 1944). At the end of 1944, it was sent to Hungary, where it joined the I Cavalry Corps of the 6th Army in February 1945. It now had a strength of 11,333 men; as a result, OKH upgraded it to the 3rd Cavalry Division, effective March 1. The new division fought in the retreat through eastern Hungary and into Austria. It was in Steiermark when Adolf Hitler committed suicide. The 3rd Cavalry then disengaged from the Red Army and headed west. Part of the division surrendered to the British at Mauterndorf, south of Tauern Pass, on May 8; the rest surrendered to the Americans at Graz that same day.

Commanders of the 3rd Cavalry Brigade/Division included Colonel Baron Hans von Wolff (March 1944), Lieutenant Colo-

nel Baron von Eckardstein (June 28, 1944), Colonel Baron
Georg von Böselager (June 29, 1944), Lieutenant Colonel
Baron Friedrich Wilhelm von Holtey (August 27, 1944), and
Colonel/Major General Peter von der Groeben (December 1,
1944–end).

Notes and Sources: The 177th Assault Gun Brigade became the
69th Tank Destroyer Battalion on August 9, 1944. Colonel von Wolff
was killed in action on June 28, 1944. Eckardstein was an acting commander only. Colonel von Boeselager was killed in action at Lomza
am Bug on August 27, 1944. Groeben was promoted to major general on March 1, 1945.

Keilig: 115; Mehner, Vol. 12: 460; Nafziger 1999: 334; Tessin, Vol.
2: 179; Hans Joachim Witte and Peter Offermann, *Die Boeselagerschen
Reiter: Das Kavallerie-Regiment Mitte und die aus ihm hervorgegangene 3.
Kavallerie-Brigade/Division* (1998).

4TH CAVALRY DIVISION

Composition: See below

Home Station: Lüneburg, Wehrkreis X

The 4th Cavalry Brigade was formed under Headquarters,
Army Group Center on May 29, 1944, from Cavalry Regiments
South and North. Cavalry Regiment North became the 5th Cavalry Regiment "Feldmarschall von Mackensen" and Cavalry
Regiment South became the 41st Cavalry Regiment. Each had
two battalions. Each of the two regiments lost its artillery battalion, which was assigned to the 870th Horse Artillery Regiment,
along with the 70th Cavalry Heavy Mortar Battalion. The new
unit also included the 70th Panzer Reconnaissance Battalion,
the 70th Engineer Battalion, the 70th Field Replacement Battalion, the 70th Divisional Supply Troops and the 238th Signal
Battalion. The 189th Assault Gun Battalion was added in August
and was redesignated the 70th Tank Destroyer Battalion.

The new brigade was sent to the 2nd Army on the southern flank of Army Group Center and thus escaped the destruction which befell most of the units of the army group's 3rd
Panzer, 4th and 9th Armies when they were struck by Stalin's

summer offensive on June 22. The 4th Cavalry nevertheless saw plenty of action, fighting at Pinsk, the retreat to the Bug, and on the Narev. It was in East Prussia by October. Assigned to the I Cavalry Corps in November, the 4th Cavalry was soon in combat as part of the 6th Army in Hungary. Here, on February 28, 1945, it was upgraded to divisional status, but without any change in its table of organization. Its theoretical strength was 11,333 men (including 953 "Hiwis" or Russian volunteers). It continued to fight in Hungary and in the retreat into Austria. It was in Steiermark when Hitler committed suicide. The 4th Cavalry then turned west and surrendered to the British at Mauterndorf (near Tauern Pass in the Austrian Alps) on or about May 8, 1945.

Commanders of the 4th Cavalry Brigade/Division were Colonel Lothar von Bischoffshausen (May 29, 1944), Colonel Alex von Nordenskjoeld (June 29, 1944), Colonel/Major General Rudolf Holste (July 15, 1944), Colonel von Woedtke (September 13, 1944), Nordenskjoeld (February 18, 1945), Lieutenant General Rudolf Holste (February 28, 1945) and Lieutenant General Helmuth von Grolman (March 20, 1945).

Notes and Sources: Rudolf Holste was promoted to major general on October 1, 1944.

Keilig: 149; Nafziger 1999: 336–37; Stoves, *Gepanzerten*: 283–84; Tessin, Vol. 2: 247–48.

18TH ARTILLERY DIVISION

Composition: 88th Motorized Artillery Regiment, 288th Motorized Artillery Regiment, 338th Motorized Artillery Regiment, 741st Assault Gun Battery, 88th Rifle Battaion, 40th Forward Observation Battalion, 88th Signal Battalion, 88th Field Replacement Battalion, 88th Divisional Supply Troops

Home Station: Leisnig, Wehrkreis IV

This division was the brainchild of Field Marshal Erich von Manstein and was created in the rear area of Army Group

South on October 1, 1943, under what was formerly the Staff, 18th Panzer Division. By the end of the month, it included the 88th Artillery Regiment (formerly the 88th Panzer Artillery Regiment of the 18th Panzer Division); the 288th and 388th Artillery Regiments, which had been created from a variety of sources; the 741st Assault Gun Battery (with ten assault guns); the 280th Army Flak Artillery Battalion; the 4th Forward Observer Battalion; the 18th Fire Control Battery from Artillery School II at Gross-Born; the 88th Rifle Battalion, 88th Signal Battalion of the 18th Panzer Division; the 88th Artillery Field Replacement Battalion; and the 88th Divisional Supply units, also from the 18th Panzer Division. Modeled on the mobile Russian artillery divisions that were responsible for heavy German losses from late 1942, the 18th Artillery included nine tracked or motorized artillery battalions. It had a total strength of nine 210mm howitzers, thirty 150mm guns, 48 105mm guns, and a dozen 100mm guns.

The division joined the 4th Panzer Army in January 1944, and first fought at Vinniza. Shortly thereafter it was at the Battle of Zhitomir as a part of XXXXVIII Panzer Corps and later played a major role in the destruction of the Russian 1st Tank Army south of Cherkassy in early 1944. In March 1944, it was defending near Tarnopol as part of the 4th Panzer Army, when Hitler finally worked up the resolve to rid himself of the brilliant but independent-minded von Manstein, whom he finally sacked on March 31, 1944. Meanwhile, the Russians encircled the 18th Artillery Division—along with the rest of the 1st Panzer Army—in the Hube Pocket. The panzer army broke out the following month. The 18th Artillery was almost immediately sent to the rear and was dissolved a few weeks later, apparently on the orders of Field Marshal Model. Of the 18th Artillery, Peter Young wrote: ". . . much was expected of it. But it proved a disappointment and was disbanded after a few months." The divisional staff was used to form Headquarters, Grossdeutschland Panzer Corps. The artillery units were used to form self-standing artillery brigades.

Major General/Lieutenant General Karl Thoholte commanded the 18th Artillery Division throughout its existence.

Notes and Sources: The Staff, 18th Panzer Division, was used to form Headquarters, 18th Artillery Division. The 18th Artillery officially ceased to exist on July 20, 1944. Thoholte was promoted to lieutenant general on March 1, 1944.

Manstein: 497, 509; Tessin, Vol. 4: 97; Peter Young (ed.), *The Marshall Cavendish Illustrated Encyclopedia of World War Two* (1981) Volume 5: 1325.

309TH ARTILLERY DIVISION z.b.V.

Composition (1944): 621st Artillery Regiment (456th and 457th Artillery Battalions, 660th Battery), 761st Artillery Regiment (460th, 985th, 1151st Artillery Battalions, 659th Battery), 101st Rocket Launcher Regiment, 33rd Light Forward Observer Battalion

Home Station: Brunswick, Wehrkreis XI

This unit was formed as Harko 309 (*Höherer-Artillerie-Kdr. 309*) or the 309th Higher Artillery Command on January 15, 1942. It was initially assigned to the 16th Army on the northern sector of the Eastern Front. In late 1943, it was transported to Paris and, on January 16, 1944, was redesignated 309th Artillery Division z.b.V. ("for special purposes"). Initially subordinate to OB West, it provided heavy GHQ artillery support as assigned by the Supreme Commander, Western Front, or by his chief of artillery. In 1945, this command was attached to the 5th Panzer Army. It was destroyed in the Ruhr Pocket in April 1945.

Its commanders were Major General/Lieutenant General Karl Prager (January 13, 1942), Major General Paul Riedel (April 6, 1943), Major General Gerhard Grassmann (January 16, 1944), Lieutenant General Richard Metz (November 15, 1944), and Lieutenant General Karl Burdach (April 8, 1945).

Notes and Sources: Prager was promoted to lieutenant general on February 1, 1943.

Keilig: 113; Lexikon; Tessin, Vol. 9: 106.

310TH ARTILLERY DIVISION z.b.V.

Composition: 310th Artillery Brigade Staff, GHQ artillery units, 310th Signal Battalion, 44th Forward Observer Battalion, 310th Transportation Battalion, 310th Motorized Maintenance Battalion

This unit was formed in April 1943, under the newly reformed 6th Army, to control General Headquarters artillery units on the Eastern Front. Initially designated Harko 310 (the 310th Higher Artillery Command), it was upgraded to division status on November 23, 1943, and was attached to Army Group South. Like other units on the southern sector, it suffered heavy casualties. In August 1944, part of its remnants (including the 310th Signal Battalion) were sent to Silesia, where they were absorbed by the XII SS Corps. The rest became part of a new 310th Higher Artillery Command, and fought on the Eastern Front for the rest of the war. The division's only commander, Colonel/Major General Werner Haack, assumed command of the new Harko 310.

Notes and Sources: Haack was promoted to major general on April 1, 1943. As commander of Harko 310, he was wounded on September 15, 1944, and died in Schweidnitz on October 28.

Keilig: 120; Lexikon; Nafziger 1999: 364; Tessin, Vol. 9: 110.

311TH ARTILLERY DIVISION

Composition: 311th Artillery Brigade Staff, GHQ artillery units, 311th Signal Battalion, 311th Transportation Battalion, 311th Motorized Maintenance Battalion

This headquarters began its existence as Arko 106 (the 106th Artillery Command) on October 1, 1939. It was upgraded to Harko 311 in February 1942 and to the 311th Artillery Division on November 23, 1943. It provided GHQ artillery support for the units of Army Group South from then until July 20, 1944, when it was dissolved. Part of its staff was used to form another Harko 311 under Army Group North Ukraine and 1st Panzer Army; the rest was sent to Silesia and used to help form the Staffs, XI SS, XII SS and XIII SS Corps. Harko 311 served on the Eastern Front until the end of the war.

Major General/Lieutenant General Joseph Prinner was the commander of the 311th Artillery Division/Harko 311.

Notes and Sources: Prinner was promoted to lieutenant general on November 1, 1943.

Keilig: 263; Lexikon; Nafziger 1999: 364; Tessin, Vol. 9: 113.

312TH ARTILLERY DIVISION z.b.V.

Composition: 312th Artillery Brigade Staff, GHQ artillery units, 312th Signal Battalion, 312th Transportation Battalion, 312th Motorized Maintenance Battalion

Originally created as the Staff, 801st Special Purposes Artillery Regiment and in February 1942, this unit became the 312th Artillery Division on November 20, 1943. Its mission was to control GHQ units under Army Group South. (Field Marshal Erich von Manstein, the commander-in-chief of Army Group South, liked the concept of artillery divisions, so he had the 18th, 310th, 311th and 312th Artillery Divisions created.) On July 20, 1944—after Hitler had relieved Manstein of his command—the 312th Artillery Division was disbanded. Part was sent to Silesia to form the XI SS, XII SS and XIII SS Corps Headquarters. The rest was used to form a new Harko 312, which was assigned to the 4th Panzer Army. It spent the rest of the war on the Eastern Front.

The division's commanders were Lieutenant General Wihelm Raithel (November 20, 1943), Major General Johannes Krause (April 1, 1944), and Lieutenant General Rudolf Friedrich (May 5, 1944).

Sources: Keilig: 185; Lexikon; Nafziger 1999: 364; Tessin, Vol. 9: 116–17.

BRANDENBURG DIVISION

See Panzer Grenadier Division "Brandenburg" (Volume Three).

VOLUNTEER CADRE DIVISION
(FREIWILLIGEN-STAMMS-DIVISION)

Composition: 1st Volunteer Cadre Regiment, 2nd Volunteer Cadre Regiment, 3rd Volunteer Cadre Regiment, 4th Volunteer Cadre Regiment, 5th Volunteer Cadre Regiment

Home Station: Lyons, France

This division—which was also known as the Volunteer Depot Division—was formed in southwestern France on February 1, 1944, from Eastern (Ost) and Turkish peoples from the Soviet Union. The divisional headquarters was in Lyons, France. The division administered five cadre (depot) regiments occupying areas of western Europe, particulary France. During the retreat from France in September 1944, it was temporarily designated 19th Army Security Division and controlled miscellaneous troops during the retreat from the French Mediterranean to Alsace. That fall it was reestablished as the Volunteer Depot Division and headquartered in the Ohrdruf Troop Maneuver Area of Wehrkreis XIII. It was disbanded shortly thereafter.

Its commanders included Colonel Wilhelm von Henning (March 10, 1944) and Major General Bodo von Wartenberg (September 9, 1944).

Sources: Keilig: 362; Lexikon; Tessin, Vol. 14: 270; OB 45: 285.

Index

Stackpole Military History Series

Real battles. Real soldiers. Real stories.

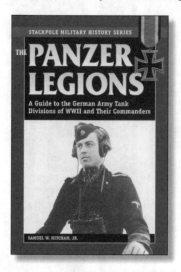

Stackpole Military History Series

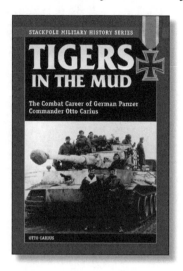

TIGERS IN THE MUD
THE COMBAT CAREER OF GERMAN PANZER COMMANDER OTTO CARIUS

Otto Carius,
translated by Robert J. Edwards

World War II began with a metallic roar as the German Blitzkrieg raced across Europe, spearheaded by the most dreadful weapon of the twentieth century: the Panzer. Tank commander Otto Carius thrusts the reader into the thick of battle, replete with the blood, smoke, mud, and gunpowder so common to the elite German fighting units.

$19.95 • Paperback • 6 x 9 • 368 pages
51 photos • 48 illustrations • 3 maps

WWW.STACKPOLEBOOKS.COM
1-800-732-3669

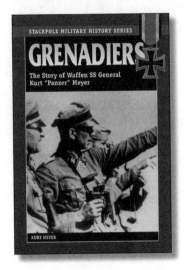

Stackpole Military History Series

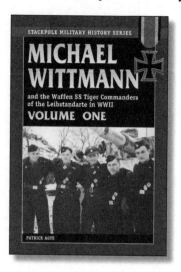

MICHAEL WITTMANN AND THE WAFFEN SS TIGER COMMANDERS OF THE LEIBSTANDARTE IN WORLD WAR II

VOLUME ONE

Patrick Agte

By far the most famous tank commander on any side in
World War II, German Tiger ace Michael Wittmann destroyed 138
enemy tanks and 132 anti-tank guns in a career that embodies the
panzer legend: meticulous in planning, lethal in execution, and
always cool under fire. Most of those kills came in the snow and mud
of the Eastern Front, where Wittmann and the Leibstandarte's
armored company spent more than a year in 1943–44 battling the
Soviets at places like Kharkov, Kursk, and the Cherkassy Pocket.

$19.95 • Paperback • 6 x 9 • 432 pages • 383 photos • 19 maps • 10 charts

Stackpole Military History Series

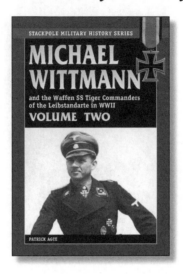

MICHAEL WITTMANN AND THE WAFFEN SS TIGER COMMANDERS OF THE LEIBSTANDARTE IN WORLD WAR II

VOLUME TWO

Patrick Agte

Barely two months after leaving the Eastern Front,
Michael Wittmann and the Leibstandarte found themselves in
Normandy facing the Allied invasion in June 1944. A week after D-Day,
Wittmann achieved his greatest success, single-handedly destroying
more than a dozen British tanks and preventing an enemy
breakthrough near Villers Bocage. He was killed several months later
while leading a Tiger battalion against an Allied assault. The
Leibstandarte went on to fight at the Battle of the Bulge and in
Hungary and Austria before surrendering in May 1945.

$19.95 • Paperback • 6 x 9 • 400 pages • 287 photos • 15 maps • 7 charts

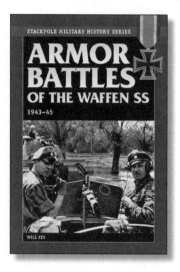

Stackpole Military History Series

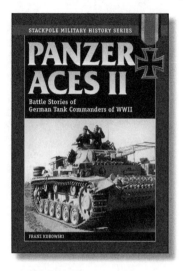

PANZER ACES II
BATTLE STORIES OF
GERMAN TANK COMMANDERS OF WORLD WAR II

Franz Kurowski,
translated by David Johnston

With the same drama and excitement of the first book,
Franz Kurowski relates the combat careers of six more
tank officers. These gripping accounts follow Panzer
crews into some of World War II's bloodiest engagements—with Rommel in North Africa, up and down
the Eastern Front, and in the hedgerows of the West.
Master tacticians and gutsy leaders, these soldiers
changed the face of war forever.

$19.95 • Paperback • 6 x 9 • 496 pages • 71 b/w photos

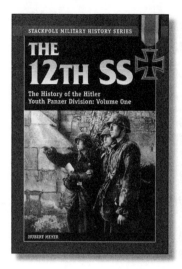

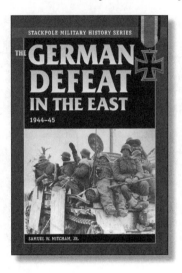

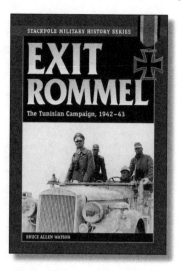

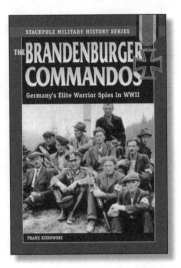